e-Business

Strategic Thinking and Practice

Brahm Canzer

John Abbott College
and McGill University

Houghton Mifflin Company
Boston   New York

This book is lovingly dedicated to my late brother, Saul Canzer.

Editor-in-Chief: George T. Hoffman
Associate Editor: Damaris R. Curran
Senior Project Editor: Nancy Blodget
Editorial Assistant: Kristin Penta
Senior Production/Design Coordinator: Sarah Ambrose
Senior Manufacturing Coordinator: Jane Spelman
Marketing Manager: Steven W. Mikels
Marketing Associate: Lisa Boden

Cover photo by Gary S. and Vivian Chapman/The Image Bank

Printed in the U.S.A.

Library of Congress Control Number: 2001133236

ISBN: 0-618-15236-6

123456789-QF-06 05 04 03 02

Brief Contents

Contents

Chapter 3	The Internet and Related Technologies 62

Chapter 4	Ethical, Legal, and Social Concerns 89

Module II Strategic Business Planning for the Internet 113

The Internet has clearly emerged as a powerful global force that is influencing, and sometimes significantly changing, strategic behavior in many organizations. A number of observers, including Harvard Business School professor Michael Porter, suggest that the Internet simply provides a new communications tool that can be used to improve conventional business practices by, for instance, building closer relationships with customers, suppliers, and employees. Others, however, believe that the Internet has precipitated a radical change in the traditional business paradigm, opening up new opportunities to those willing to venture forth. Regardless of where the truth lies, it is clear that the early years of commercial Internet activity have been dramatic, resulting in many e-business successes as well as many failures. This early body of experiential knowledge, the focus of this book, can provide important lessons to those concerned with strategic planning in the future.

Purpose of the Book

e-Business: Strategic Thinking and Practice presents a wide variety of topics important to understanding e-business strategy, including: the Internet and related technologies, environmental factors that can influence e-business and online behaviors, research methodologies in e-business planning, and important marketing, management, and financial issues related to the preparation of an e-business plan. Furthermore, the text takes a strategic planning approach in order to help structure this information so that it can be readily applied to actual business situations.

The use of web sites to market products and organizations, web-enabled Customer Relationship Management and Supply Chain Management software solutions that improve operations and increase efficiencies, and e-commerce ventures that can reach global customers 24/7 are only a few of the popular e-business strategies available to decision makers. However, for many strategists, e-business is a field characterized by complexity, requiring a map to help sort and simplify this growing body of new vocabulary, concepts, and thinking. Furthermore, an ideal map would also help lead the intrepid travelers to an understanding of how opportunities might be converted into concrete business actions in their own organizations. This text is an attempt to create such a map.

e-Business: Strategic Thinking and Practice presents a comprehensive overview of the fundamental concepts, vocabulary, and strategic thinking taking place in e-business practice today. Furthermore, the text explores these at all three primary organizational levels of the firm—corporate, SBU, and operational—and within small as well as larger enterprises. By providing a learning environment that illustrates how strategic e-business plans can be developed at any level of the firm, learners are guided toward the objective of preparing their own plan. This might be an independent start-up plan or one that involves the introduction of e-business strategies into an existing business operation.

Strategists are assisted in this effort by appendices to the text that provide a sample e-business plan that also serves as a comprehensive case study and a step-by-step structure of the tasks involved in researching and writing an e-business plan.

In addition, an *Online Journal and Information Gateway* to regularly updated resources is provided on the student web site. The resources will be tagged and categorized according to the chapters and topics within each chapter. This value-added benefit provides both students and instructors with a highly versatile and up-to-date database of information with which to conduct research.

Intended Audience

This text is written primarily for learners at the college and undergraduate university levels, where e-business is finding its way into the curriculum as a single-semester management course, as a stream of several courses comprising a major in e-business, and as a full certificate, diploma, or degree program focusing on e-business decision making and strategic thinking.

The integration of theoretical content and strategic thinking makes the text ideal for an introductory e-business course and makes it a logical complementary second text if a general (principles) business textbook has been used earlier in a program of study. It will also be of great interest to instructors seeking an alternative small-business management text for e-business entrepreneurs.

Programs at the college and university levels are typically found in these academic areas: business (management and marketing), computer technology, and web site development. Business programs tend to focus on strategic thinking about e-business opportunities for established firms, and especially entrepreneurial dot-com start-ups that receive much public attention. Computer technology programs are generally concerned with hardware, networks, and engineering issues. Web development programs (diplomas) are more often found at the college level and as shorter programs (certificates) at both universities and colleges where the focus is on teaching students how to use web-authoring tools for designing and maintaining web sites. These programs often produce entrepreneurs who launch independent small businesses providing services to clients as well as employees of firms responsible for web site activity.

An additional target audience for this textbook is businesspeople interested in an academic overview of e-business and strategic approaches to planning for their organizations. The book and appendices provide an excellent foundation and resources for corporate training seminars and online learning programs. Business learners can use the text to develop their organizational e-business plan.

Features of the Book

e-Business: Strategic Thinking and Practice is designed to help learners understand and organize e-business developments to date and to provide a structure that can facilitate the assimilation of new e-business information that appears each day. Most importantly, the text emphasizes an analytical and critical approach to understanding strategic decision making so that learners emerge from their course better prepared to create real plans for their own organizations.

Text Content and Organization

Module I: A Framework for Understanding e-Business   Module I presents a map for exploring e-business and understanding how business activity on the Internet has evolved into what it is today. This framework focuses attention on several important subject areas that help lay the groundwork for strategic business planning, which we examine later in Modules II and III. In Chapter 1 we define and explore the world of e-business and fundamental models and industry participants. We also focus on several examples of e-business strategies in managerial, marketing, and financial situations in order to illustrate how e-business is applied across primary functional areas. In Chapter 2 we take a closer look at the major environmental forces, such as globalization, that affect e-business planning and practices. In Chapter 3 the technology of the Internet and devices communicating over the Internet is explained. Finally, in Chapter 4 we look at the complex and controversial ethical, legal, and social concerns that have emerged as use of Internet technology and e-business continues to impact societies around the world.

Module II: Strategic Business Planning for the Internet   Module II introduces the strategic business planning process in greater detail. We focus attention on the three key components of strategic planning: research, analysis, and the formulation of an e-business plan. In Chapter 5 we present a structure for organizing and understanding the variety of e-business models and how each model serves to direct the entire organization in its search to generate revenues and create competitive advantage online. In Chapter 6 we examine these activities from the point of view of strategists working at each of the three primary organizational levels of the firm: corporate, division/strategic business unit, and operating/functional levels. In Chapter 7 we detail the research- and information-gathering process, and then in Chapter 8 we explore online communication and user behaviors. The module presents a broad base of understanding about what e-business models and their strategies can help the firm achieve and how they can be incorporated within the existing organization and business plan. Managerial details and implications inherent in any e-business plan are addressed in the third module.

Module III: Implementing the e-Business Plan   In Module III we link the strategic-thinking concepts generated thus far in the e-business planning process with the specific marketing, management, and financial plans of action. These three functional components are universally recognized as the core foundations for any strategic business plan. Therefore, we incorporate them into our study of the design and creation of the complete e-business plan while also examining related issues that affect e-business strategy. Each chapter helps e-business planners answer questions related to each of these core subject areas. The final chapter in this unit brings closure to the entire planning process by looking at how the e-business plan can be integrated into an organization's current structure, and then controlled, measured, and evaluated for future decision making.

Chapter Pedagogy

The text chapters are written in a clear style, making use of a variety of pedagogical techniques that facilitate both academic knowledge and a student's ability to apply what they have learned. Case study reports, exercises, and especially the research and preparation of an e-business plan as a group or individual course assignment tie theory and practice together for students.

Learning Objectives Each chapter is organized around a set of Learning Objectives that introduce and structure the content students are about to study.

Key Glossary Terms Important terms in each chapter are identified in boldface, and definitions are highlighted in the margin for easy reference.

Inside e-Business Each chapter begins with an opening vignette called *Inside e-Business* that focuses on a theme asociated with that chapter. Examples of featured companies include AOL Time Warner, IBM, Research In Motion, Microsoft, Jupiter Media Metrix, and Forrester.

Case Study: Return to Inside e-Business A related feature at the end of each chapter, *Case Study: Return to Inside e-Business,* provides additional information related to the opening vignette and builds on the content of the chapter. Questions for discussion help generate class debate and offer direction for preparing a case study report.

e-Business Insight To help highlight and explore important issues, each chapter contains two *e-Business Insight* boxes that focus on relevant topics. For example, "Can Socially Undesirable Online Behaviors Be Stopped?" and "Using the Internet to Help Nonprofit Organizations" are featured in Chapter 4, Ethical, Legal, and Social Concerns.

Chapter Review Near the end of each chapter a *Summary* presents the main ideas contained in the chapter in a format that follows the Learning Objectives. To further reinforce what was learned, the Chapter Review includes a set of *Review Questions* that focus on chapter definitions and concepts and a set of *Discussion Questions* designed to encourage critical thinking and writing about chapter topics.

Building Skills for Career Success Near the end of every chapter is a feature called *Building Skills for Career Success.* All exercises in this section provide detailed introductory material along with a student assignment. The five exercises include *Exploring the Internet, Developing Critical Thinking Skills, Building Team Skills, Researching Different Careers,* and *Improving Communication Skills.*

Exploring Useful Web Sites Every chapter ends with a feature called *Exploring Useful Web Sites.* This feature is a comprehensive list of web sites that provide information related to the topics discussed in the chapter.

A Fully Integrated Package

The *e-Business: Strategic Thinking and Practice* text is the centerpiece of a package of ancillary materials created to assist instructors and learners. An instructor web site and the *Instructor's Resource Manual with Test Bank* contain a variety of tools tied to the text and designed to facilitate instructor-led classes as well as online learning environments. The student web site is integrated with the text structure and content, thereby creating an expanded, richer learning environment for students to explore.

Instructor Web Site

The instructor web site contains a variety of content designed to enhance the learning and teaching experience. Instructors will find PowerPoint slides, class lecture outlines, quizzes, and a variety of other resources related to the *Instructor's Resource Manual with Test Bank* content. All content is written and frequently updated by the main text author.

Student Web Site

The student web site is an extension of the text and is updated on a regular basis. Like the instructor web site, all content is written by the main text author. Students will find the hyperlinks from the *Exploring Useful Web Sites* feature along with additional study and research aids.

Instructor's Resource Manual with Test Bank

The *Instructor's Resource Manual with Test Bank*, written by the text's author, features the following items for each chapter: Notes from the Author; Learning Objectives; Brief Chapter Outline; Comprehensive Lecture Outline; Answers to Text Review Questions, Discussion Questions, and Case Study Questions; suggested answers to assigned questions; and ideas about using *Building Skills for Career Success* exercises. The Test Bank contains a variety of essay, true/false, and multiple-choice questions. Each question is tied to a learning objective and a text page reference. Answers are provided.

Acknowledgments

This text would not have been possible without the considerable contributions of many talented people. I would first like to thank the following reviewers whose suggestions and comments helped shape the final product.

Maryam Alavi
Emory University

David Ambrosini
Cabrillo College

Lloyd W. Bartholome
Utah State University

Brent Beal
Louisiana State University

Joseph Bell
University of Northern Colorado

Tom Bryant
Rutgers University

John R. Bugado
National University

John W. Clarry
College of New Jersey

Wilfred T. DeMoranville
Kishwaukee Community College

Wolfgang Grassl
Hillsdale College

Chris Grevesen
DeVry College of Technology

John Hafer
University of Nebraska at Omaha

Kathy Harris
Northwestern Oklahoma State University

John Heinemann
Keller Graduate School

Keith C. Jones
Lynchburg College

F. Scott Key
Pensacola Junior College

Robert Mills
Utah State University

Jim Newtown
Baker College

Carolyn Predmore
Manhattan College

Sandra S. Reid
Dallas Baptist University

Linda Salchenberger
Loyola University

Srivatsa Seshadri
University of Nebraska

Nagaraj Sivasubramaniam
Binghamton University

Kenton B. Walker
University of Wyoming

Dennis Williams
Penn College

In addition, I would like to express my gratitude to the Houghton Mifflin team, beginning with Editor-in-Chief George Hoffman, Development Editor/Technology Manager Damaris Curran, Senior Production Editor Nancy Blodget, and copyeditor Alice Manning.

Finally, I would like to express my love and gratitude to my wife Carole, son Matthew, and daughter Sarah, whose encouragement and presence made this project possible.

Brahm Canzer

About the Author

Brahm Canzer currently teaches business management courses to John Abbott College and McGill University MBA students in Montreal. During his 27-year teaching career he has also taught undergraduate-level marketing courses at Concordia University and corporate learning programs under the auspices of the University of Toronto. With a strong interest in the use of Internet technology in education, he was among the early pioneers to design and teach MBA courses online for Simon Fraser University. Professor Canzer is a contributing author to several business textbooks and editor of the Canadian edition of the Houghton Mifflin textbook *Business* (Pride, Hughes, Kapoor, Canzer). He has helped create a variety of web-based supplemental learning materials in academic and corporate learning settings. Professor Canzer also provides consulting services to businesses seeking assistance as they explore web-based opportunities and solutions for improving their operations.

Module I

A FRAMEWORK FOR UNDERSTANDING e-BUSINESS

Module I presents a map for exploring e-business and understanding how business activity on the Internet has evolved into what it is today. This framework focuses attention on several important subject areas that help lay the groundwork for the strategic business planning that we examine in Modules II and III. First, in Chapter 1, we define and explore the world of e-business and its fundamental models and industry participants. We also focus on several examples of e-business strategies in managerial, marketing, and financial situations to illustrate how these strategies are applied across primary functional areas. In Chapter 2 we take a closer look at the major environmental forces, such as globalization, that affect e-business planning and practices. In Chapter 3 the technology of the Internet and of devices communicating over the Internet is explained. Finally, in Chapter 4 we look at the complex ethical, legal, and social concerns that have emerged as Internet technology and e-business continue to have an impact on societies around the world.

Exploring the World of e-Business

Chapter 1

INSIDE
e-BUSINESS
AOL and Time Warner
Team-Up

Difficult as this may be to comprehend today, America Online (AOL) started out in 1985 as simply one of many service firms providing customers with a way to connect to the Internet. Remarkably, only fifteen years later, AOL entered the new millennium as the world's leading online service firm, with more than 20 million paying subscribers and a phenomenal growth in revenue. By merging with the world's leading media company, Time Warner, AOL has transformed itself into an Internet colossus. With combined revenues of $36 billion, the new firm, AOL Time Warner, is being touted as "the world's first media and communications company of the Internet age."

The union of AOL and Time Warner illustrates how partnerships and mergers between firms can benefit Internet-related businesses. Partnerships and mergers can be quicker and less expensive ways for firms to grow. By merging with Time Warner, AOL has enhanced its delivery of Internet content, since it can now offer its customers some of Time Warner's rich variety of entertaining and informative products, such as CNN online news services and journals. By the same token, Time Warner has found a partner that can deliver its internationally appealing content to a large existing audience— the audience that AOL has built up through earlier mergers and acquisitions, as well as through the introduction of its internally developed products and services. For instance, in 1998 AOL acquired ICQ from Israel-based Mirabilis, the world's largest communications community, comprising more than 50 million registered users. ICQ's free access service allows users to locate and chat with individuals and groups online regardless of which Internet service provider they use. More than two-thirds of ICQ registrants live outside the United States, and so AOL's acquisition of ICQ has helped the company open the door to the customers worldwide. Given that people living in North America are still the dominant users of the Internet, this strategic merger continues to make sense in the race to enlist customers globally and build brand recognition on the Internet.

According to AOL's research, 70 percent of all online consumers regularly or occasionally receive their news through the Internet. The synergy of the fit between AOL and Time Warner (**www.aoltimewarner .com**) thus becomes even more obvious. With the merger, both parties have made considerable progress in their efforts to grow their e-businesses. AOL's exclusive access to Time Warner content, which may attract new customers, gives the company a major competitive advantage over other Internet service providers that lack access to this content. The merger may also increase the number of consumers of Time Warner's magazines (*Business 2.0, InStyle, Time, Sports Illustrated, People, Teen People, Entertainment Weekly*) and other products, including music (Atlantic Records, Rhino Records, Warner Brothers Records), cable television (WB, TNT, Cartoon Network, Turner Classic Movies, CNN, HBO), films (Warner Brothers, New Line Cinema), and the accompanying web sites. Furthermore, the variety of communication products AOL Time Warner offers—such as telephone service through cable, e-commerce products, and cross-promotion of a variety of consumer products—will generate many more new opportunities for growth.[1]

AOL is an example of a firm that can trace its history only as far back as the start of commercial activity on the Internet. Like other well-known e-business firms such as Yahoo! (**www.yahoo.com**), eBay (**www.ebay.com**), and MP3 (**www.mp3.com**), AOL owes its very existence to the Internet. Quite simply, without the Internet, there would be no AOL, Yahoo!, or MP3.

Most firms, on the other hand, have developed or will develop an Internet presence by gradually transferring some of their business activities to the Internet. This was the route taken by Time Warner, which had placed some of its entertainment and information content online well before its merger with AOL. Providing services on the Internet delivers added value to a firm's customers, an important goal for any business. For reasons that we will examine more closely throughout this textbook, many businesses will eventually find themselves seeking opportunities to conduct more of their affairs on the Internet.

There is a fundamental division between businesses that invented themselves on the Internet, such as AOL, and previously established firms that have transferred only some of their activities to the Internet, such as the Gap. Firms with no history other than the one defined on the Internet make their business decisions with a clear focus on the online world. They are not concerned about interfering with other, established business activities. At the other extreme, firms like the Gap are very much concerned about how developing their presence on the Internet will affect their current retail store sales, costs, customer relations, and so forth.

This chapter examines the development of both types of businesses and provides a structure for understanding how and why business activities finding their way onto the Internet will change the way businesses function in the future. We also take a closer look at how firms conduct business on the Internet and what growth opportunities may be available to both new and existing firms. But before we explore this new and exciting arena for business competition, let's begin by building a framework that can help us understand how all of this came about.

Defining e-Business

e-business (electronic business)
The organized effort of individuals to produce and sell, for a profit, products and services that satisfy society's needs through the facilities available on the Internet.

Business can be defined as the organized effort of individuals to produce and sell, for a profit, products and services that satisfy society's needs. In a simple sense, then, **e-business (electronic-business)** can be defined as the organized effort of individuals to produce and sell, for a profit, products and services that satisfy society's needs *through the facilities available on the Internet.* And just as we distinguish between any *individual* business and the general term *business*, which refers to all such efforts within a society, we similarly recognize the *individual* e-business, such as AOL, as well as the general concept of *e-business*. IBM's e-business web site, **www.ibm.com/ebusiness/**, defines this concept as the transformation of key business activities through the use of Internet technologies.[2] It is this transformation of key business activities, such as buying and selling products and services, building better supplier and customer relationships, and improving general business operations, that has stimulated so much excitement about this new and rapidly evolving business environment.

e-commerce

A part of e-business; the term refers only to the activities involved in buying and selling online, which may include identifying suppliers, selecting products or services, making purchase commitments, completing financial transactions, and obtaining service.

Sometimes people use the term *e-commerce* instead of *e-business*. In a strict sense, *e-business* refers to all business activities conducted on the Internet by an individual firm or industry. In contrast, **e-commerce** is a part of e-business; the term refers only to the activities involved in buying and selling online. These activities may include identifying suppliers, selecting products or services, making purchase commitments, completing financial transactions, and obtaining service.[3] We generally use the term *e-business* because of its broader definition and scope.

Organizing e-Business Resources

Every business must properly organize a variety of *human, material, informational,* and *financial resources* in order to conduct business successfully. Many highly specialized forms of these resources are required if the firm is to succeed on the Internet. For example, in the area of human resources, people who can design, create, and maintain web sites are only a small part of the specialists required by businesses that are considering an Internet presence. The material resources required include specialized computers, equipment, software, and high-speed Internet connection lines. Computer programs that track the efficiency of the firm's web site operations and that offer insight into customers' interactions with the web site are generally among the specialized informational resources required. For firms whose primary emphasis is online, financial resources, the money required to start the firm and allow it to grow, usually reflect greater participation by individual entrepreneurs and venture capitalists, instead of conventional financial sources like banks.

The difficulties and even failure of so many early Internet-based start-up firms during the industrywide downturn in 2000 can best be understood in terms of the reasons why most new businesses fail: management and financial problems. In general, the managements of these companies failed to build sufficient continuous revenue flows to keep the company going before their start-up financing was consumed. In some cases, customers failed to materialize in sufficient numbers once the web site and the necessary infrastructure to run the e-business were created. Building a web identity was more complicated than many might have thought at first.

Of course, the more complicated question is why the management of any particular firm failed to organize the necessary resources and then use them properly to assure the long-term viability of the business. The answer to this question is specific to each organization; however, it is probably safe to say that many of the early enthusiastic entrepreneurs and investors were simply unprepared for what would be required. Information changed quickly and was often unknown. While learning through practical experience, managers made mistakes—and these mistakes were often fatal if the company's financial backers were unwilling to continue funding the business development process. Those firms that have survived the first industry shakeout and others that are now entering the field for the first time can benefit from the knowledge we all have gained by studying past successes and failures.

Satisfying Needs Online

The customer needs that are satisfied by Internet firms may be unique to the Internet environment, or this environment may be an improvement over conventional business practice. For example, AOL provides Internet access, browser services, chat rooms, databases, and exclusive Time Warner entertainment content, among other services, to its customers. Amazon.com gives customers anywhere in the world access to the same virtual store of books, videos, and CDs. And at eBay's global auction site, customers can, for a fee, buy and sell almost anything. Even your college's web site satisfies informational needs for people in the area who are interested in courses and educational programs. In each of these examples, customers receive a value-added service through the Internet.

Internet users can now access print media, such as newspapers and magazines, and radio and television programming at a time and place that is convenient to them. In addition to offering such a wide selection of content, the Internet provides the opportunity for *interaction*. In other words, communication between the online program and the viewer is an active two-way street. In contrast to the passive position customers occupy vis-à-vis traditional media, Internet customers can respond to Internet programming by requesting more information about a product or by posing specific questions, which may lead to a purchase decision. In any case, the ability to engage the viewer in two-way communication means that e-businesses can have a more involved, and therefore more valuable, viewer. For example, CNN.com and other news-content sites encourage dialogue among viewers in chat rooms and exchanges with the writers of articles posted to the site. Live televised programming such as talk shows includes viewers' questions, which can be sent by email.

The Internet allows customers to specify the content they receive. For example, they can custom-design daily online newspapers and magazines that contain only articles that are of interest to them. Knowing what is of interest to an individual customer allows an Internet firm to direct appropriate advertising to that customer. For example, someone who wants to read articles on the New York Yankees might be a potential customer for products and services related to baseball. Advertising that is likely to be of interest to the viewer has a greater chance of resulting in a sale. For the advertiser, knowing that its advertisements are being intelligently directed to the most likely customers represents a value-added service.

Creating e-Business Profit

Generating profit is both a fundamental goal of business and a measurement of business success. Profits are instrumental in rewarding employees and investors for their skills and efforts. Profits also help pay for the development of the new products that will eventually be needed to replace older and outdated items whose sales are declining. Strategically, firms can increase their profits by either increasing sales revenue or reducing expenses. Internet-based technology provides a wide variety of ways to accomplish both objectives. Although much of this textbook is about developing e-business strategies, let's just examine a few examples in the following sections.

Revenue Growth

Online merchants have the advantage of being able to reach a global customer base twenty-four hours a day, seven days a week. The opportunity to shop on the Internet is virtually unrestricted, as the Internet removes such barriers to retail shopping as limited store operating hours and the inability of some customers to get to a conveniently located outlet. The removal of barriers that might keep some customers from shopping at conventional retail stores explains the ever-increasing hopes and expectations for the sales revenue of e-businesses like Amazon (**www.amazon.com**), Barnes & Noble (**www.barnesandnoble.com**), and The Walt Disney Company (**www.disney.com**).

Intelligent informational resource systems are another major factor in generating sales revenue for Internet firms. Such systems store information about each customer's purchases, along with a variety of other information about the buyer's preferences. Using this information, the system can assist the customer in making a purchase decision the next time he or she visits the web site. For example, if the customer has bought a Shania Twain or Garth Brooks CD in the past, the system might suggest CDs by similar artists.

Interestingly, customers may use a web site simply to browse and delay making an actual purchase until they are in the firm's physical store. For instance, when buying clothing, customers often consider it critical to try on a garment before they purchase it. A site like **Gap.com** thus serves not only online customers but also those who eventually come to Gap stores to finalize their selection. Similarly, **Toyota.com** can provide basic comparative information for shoppers so that they are better prepared for their visit to an automobile showroom. Thus, while in certain situations customers may not make a purchase online, the existence of the firm's web site and the services it provides may lead to increased sales in the firm's physical store.

A fundamental concern for online firms is how to select, develop, and nurture sources of revenue. Each source of revenue flowing into the firm is referred to as a **revenue stream**. Since revenue streams provide the dollars needed to operate the firm, developing them is a primary strategic issue for any business. Furthermore, the simple redirection of existing revenue to an online stream is not desirable. For example, shifting revenues received from customers inside a real store to revenues received from those same customers online does not create any real new revenue for the firm. A Web-based business may not generate sufficient new revenues to offset the high start-up costs of going online for a long time. Investors examine the probability of the company's reaching the targeted revenue projections in the e-business plan and assess the firm's current and long-term value on the basis of these numbers. This orientation helps to explain why an e-business such as Amazon.com could command high investor confidence in the absence of any real profit during its start-up phase. Investors take a longer-term view of the level of profit that they hope will materialize when a firm like Amazon reaches its full potential and settles down to stable revenue streams and expenses.

Typically, e-business revenue streams come from the sale of products and services, from advertising placed on the businesses' web pages, and from subscription fees charged for access to online services and content. For example, AOL's principal revenue streams include subscription fees paid by members who connect to

revenue stream
A source of revenue flowing into the firm, such as revenues earned from selling online or selling advertising.

portals

Web sites that serve as entry points to the Internet, providing users with a gateway to other web sites.

the Internet through local dial-in connections and adverting revenues earned on AOL web sites. AOL competes with Sprint, Microsoft, Yahoo!, and dozens of other online portals. **Portals** are web sites that serve as entry points to the Internet, providing users with a gateway to other web sites. Portals may focus on providing news, entertainment, a search engine service for the Internet, and so forth. Portals such as Microsoft's **www.msn.com** generally allow users to select and customize their view of news, local weather, topics of interest, and other content.

Many Internet firms that distribute content, such as news or magazine and newspaper articles, generate revenue primarily from advertising and from commissions from the sellers of products linked to the site. Online shopping malls now provide communities of related vendors of electronic, computer hardware and software, health foods, fashion items, and other products. Sites like Petco.com (**www.petco.com**) and Petsmart.com (**www.petsmart.com**) compete in the large market for pet supplies. WebMD (**www.webmd.com**) and other health information sites provide information about remedies, disease, and a variety of health-related topics and issues. In many cases, the vendors share online sales revenues with the site owners.

Expense Reduction

Expense reduction is the other major way in which e-business can help increase a firm's profitability. Providing online access to information that customers want can reduce the cost of dealing with customers. For example, most airlines routinely provide updated scheduling and pricing information, as well as promotional material, on their web sites. This can reduce the costs of dealing with customers through a call center operated by employees and of mailing brochures, which may be outdated within weeks or easily misplaced by customers. Sprint PCS (**www.sprintpcs.com**) maintains an extensive web site where potential customers can learn more about cell phone products and services. Current customers can access personal account information, send email questions to customer service, and purchase additional products or services. With such extensive online services, Sprint PCS probably does not have to maintain as many physical store locations as it would without these services.

A Framework for Understanding e-Business

The Internet was originally conceived as an elaborate military communications network that would allow vital messages to be transmitted in the event of war. Should one element of the network be destroyed, the system was designed to ensure that an alternative route could be found in the remaining network, thus allowing messages to be communicated to decision centers.

Prior to 1994, the National Science Foundation, the agency that funded and regulated the use of the Internet, restricted its use to noncommercial activities, such as email communication among university researchers and the sharing of data. However, as the potential commercial benefits of the Internet became increasingly obvious, a growing number of commercially interested groups demanded that the doors be opened to business activity. At about the same time, new technology emerged that simplified the use of the Internet and allowed the addition of multi-media content. This multimedia environment of audio, visual, and text data came to be known as the **World Wide Web** (or, more simply, **the Web**).

The Internet can be envisioned as a large network of computers, connected by cables and satellites, which pass small, standardized packets of electronic data from one station to another until they are delivered to their final destination. In a sense, the Internet is the equivalent of the telephone network, which was first created almost one hundred years ago. However, instead of just voice communication, the Internet can transfer many types of multimedia data around the world at speeds far faster than those of the telephone network. In order to be transferred over the Internet, data need to be **digitized**, which means that they are converted into the type of digital signal that the computers and telecommunications equipment that make up the Internet can understand.

Most firms involved in e-business fall more or less into one of three primary groups that are defined by their e-business activities: those that create the telecommunications infrastructure, Internet software producers, and online sellers and content providers. In this section we examine a framework for understanding e-business by looking at these three groups, and then considering global and small e-business perspectives.

Telecommunications Infrastructure

Telecommunications hardware and equipment producers, computer hardware manufacturers, and Internet service providers supply the telecommunications infrastructure of the Internet. Lucent Technologies (**www.lucent.com**), Cisco Systems (**www.cisco.com**), and Nortel Networks (**www.nortelnetworks.com**) produce most of the telecommunications equipment and hardware that allows the Internet to work. Companies such as IBM (**www.ibm.com**), Hewlett-Packard (**www.hp.com**), Dell Computer (**www.dell.com**), Sun Microsystems (**www.sun.com**), Apple Computer (**www.apple.com**), and Gateway (**www.gateway.com**) produce many of the computers used by consumers and businesses. Internet service providers (ISPs), which buy their technological capability from the makers of telecommunications hardware, provide customers with the necessary technology to connect to the Internet through various phone plugs and cables. The last link to the Internet, provided by local telephone and cable television companies, is the shortest, but typically the slowest, in the global electronic network. However, as home users' lines are replaced by faster cable and fiber-optic connections, they will come to enjoy the same speed as businesses in city centers where the telecommunications infrastructure has already been upgraded. AOL is the largest and best-known ISP, but hundreds of smaller ISPs in both urban and rural areas also provide access to the Internet.

Internet Software Producers

Producers of software that provides the functional capability to do things on the Internet are the second primary group of e-business firms that have emerged since the start of online commercial activity. Searching the Internet, browsing

---

World Wide Web (the Web)
The multimedia Internet environment; it may present a blend of audio, visual, and text data to viewers.

digitized
For data, converted into the type of digital signal that the computers and telecommunications equipment that make up the Internet can understand and transfer.

web sites, sending email messages, shopping online, viewing multimedia content, and other online activities require specialized computer software programs. Browser software is the single most basic product for user interaction on the Internet. Currently, the dominant browser is Microsoft's Internet Explorer, followed well back by AOL's Netscape Communicator. Not many years ago in the short history of the Internet, the rankings for these two browsers were just the opposite, with Netscape the dominant leader. Microsoft's rapid expansion into Internet software and services illustrates the dynamic nature of e-business. However, Microsoft's dominance in the software market also makes it a target of criticism and government legal action. Other software producers claim that Microsoft has an unfair competitive advantage because of the strength of its Windows software and should be broken up into two or more separate companies. Although this scenario seems unlikely, pressure by the U.S. Congress and the states is likely to open the market to greater competition and lead to a greater variety of products, to the benefit of customers. Competition in other online areas is more obvious, as there is a wide variety of software products in such areas as web management, e-commerce, and conferencing available from Oracle (**www.oracle.com**), IBM (**www.ibm.com**), Lotus Development (**www.lotus.com**), and Sun Microsystems (**www.sun.com**).

Online Sellers and Content Providers

The third primary group of e-business firms consists of all the firms that customers actually interact with on web sites. The Internet would still be limited to communication between individuals and among groups of special-interest researchers were it not for the activity of online sellers and content providers. In this area of e-business, we have just begun to see the development of online strategies for reaching out to existing and new customers.

As noted earlier, some e-businesses, such as AOL and eBay, owe their existence to the Internet. They offer products and services that can be found only online. In contrast, other firms—among them the Gap, Nike, Martha Stewart, and Gear—carry out only some of their business activities on the Internet. They use the Internet simply to provide information and supplement their regular business activities.

Although it is uncertain what content and activities will eventually make their way to the Internet, it is clear that what we are experiencing today is dominated by the movement of existing business activities to the Internet. Time Warner's decision to merge with AOL is a case in point. By arranging for online distribution of content that was formerly distributed through the technologies of magazines, radio, and television, Time Warner has found new opportunities for revenue growth. Similarly, traditional ways of shopping have been transferred to a virtual environment, where cyberspace retailers can provide more information to customers and exert a greater degree of influence on the customer's decision. The Internet is jammed with shopping, as anyone who has entered the keyword *shop* on a search engine like Yahoo! has discovered.

Businesses that operate exclusively online, such as eBay and Amazon, are at one extreme of the e-business spectrum; conventional businesses that have only begun the process of developing an Internet presence are at the other. The pace at which firms adapt their business activities to a business environment that includes the Internet generally depends on the value they perceive to be gained by going online. If the case presented to management is that expenses can be reduced dramatically, that revenues can be increased, or that new customers in new markets can be reached in a more cost-effective way, then online strategies will appear more attractive. If, on the other hand, the impact of an online program is less predictable and the benefits are less certain, then decision-makers would be expected to be more cautious, and slower to charge ahead into the unknown.

The greatest area for entrepreneurial adventure on the Internet is in the production of some service or content. Anyone with a good idea that might appeal to a globally distributed audience stands a chance of successfully launching an e-business. As the short history of the Internet indicates, we are only at the beginning of developing new and exciting applications that can be delivered online. According to Timothy Draper, an insider in the world of e-business and managing director of Draper Fisher Jurvetson, a West Coast venture capital firm, "The Internet has opened the world up and that means everyone's now going to be part of the world economy."[4]

Global e-Business

All three primary groups of e-business firms are in a race to capture global business revenues that are only just now emerging. Telecommunications firms are competing to build the infrastructure in countries all over the world; in many cases, they are skipping technological stepping-stones. For example, in areas of poor countries where telephone poles have never existed, ground-based wireless systems are now providing instant state-of-the-art communications. In many places, ISPs and software producers like AOL are competing against better-known local firms. And online sellers and content providers see no limits to their ability to penetrate markets anywhere in the world where customers want their products.

The ability to customize content for individual customer needs makes the Internet an adaptable tool for global enterprise. Consider Berlitz's web site **www.berlitz.com**, which allows anyone in the world to jump quickly to a web site designed in the viewer's preferred language. By clicking on the appropriate icon, viewers can move forward to a web site created to meet their needs in one of a wide variety of languages presented. Once there, the viewer can examine a wide range of products and services, including multimedia language-learning material, online translation services, and referrals to local Berlitz classroom-based instruction. This global strategy, which reaches out to the world and yet allows for individual viewer customization, is at the heart of e-business strategic thinking.

Despite the enormous potential for growth, generating global success is demanding and complex. Markets are substantially different around the world, reflecting different economic conditions and consumption patterns. Understandably, firms with an established global presence and global experience, like Berlitz, are likely to venture ahead of others that lack such a history.

Small e-Business

If early experience is any indication of the future, the Internet will continue to be an attractive and powerful strategic tool for small business. According to a report by Access Markets International (AMI) Partners (**www.ami-partners.com**) and *Inc.* magazine, small-business online activity got off to a very quick start. Research showed that an estimated 400,000 U.S. small businesses sold their products and services on e-business sites in 1998, and that number jumped 50 percent to 600,000 in 1999. During the same period, online transactions and purchases grew more than 1,000 percent, rising from $2 billion to $25 billion, and the actual number of small businesses transacting online increased 55 percent, from 1.8 million to 2.8 million. Interestingly, a significant number of small firms—six out of ten—were reluctant to sell their products online at the time because of security concerns, technology challenges, or the belief that their products were unsuited for online selling.[5]

However, despite these early concerns, online activity continues to grow, as suggested by a recent AMI survey of small-business spending on human resources management. This 2002 report found that small businesses were expected to spend more than $50 billion on human resource–related services alone, including such services as temporary staffing, employee training, and other outsourced services. Furthermore a 2002 American Express survey reported that 66 percent of small businesses had already integrated the Internet as a tool to help them run their businesses, using it for making travel plans and purchasing office supplies, equipment, or other business services (tied at 36 percent), conducting industry or market research (34 percent), marketing or advertising (29 percent), networking with other entrepreneurs (24 percent), purchasing goods from wholesalers (22 percent), and managing accounts and making payments (16 percent).[6]

Although the global-scale firms that dominate e-business are well known to many people, the remarkable thing about the Internet is how accessible it is to small businesses. The relatively low cost of going online means that the Internet is open to thousands of small businesses seeking opportunities to grow internationally. In some cases, small firms have found a *niche* service or product to sell online. Special online shopping malls bring shoppers a wider selection of unique crafts or artistic creations. And many small online magazines, or **e-zines**, as they are often called, have found their special audience through the virtual world of online publishing. In fact, many small publications that began online have gone on to create print versions of their e-zines. In each case, audiences were attracted to a specialized product that could take advantage of lower online delivery costs.

Writers like Stephen King and recording artists like Sarah McLachlan have discovered that they can earn higher profits by dealing directly with customers online rather than going through conventional intermediaries such as wholesalers and retail distributors. Interestingly, Sarah McLachlan was an early financial supporter of MP3 and earned substantial capital gains as an investor. The Internet has given even unknown artists a new venue for finding an audience; after reading or listening to a sample of these artists' work, newfound fans can order their books or CDs directly or download and create their own copies. MP3

e-zines
Online magazines.

(**www.mp3.com**) and Napster (**www.napster.com**) were two early challengers to the traditional methods of entertainment distribution, and both firms have been at the center of legal conflicts over the ownership of distribution rights to content on the Internet. In the summer of 2001, Napster capitulated to industry demands and concluded a deal to become the third distribution partner with MusicNet in **www.musicnet.com**, a music subscription service set up jointly by RealNetworks Inc., AOL Time Warner, EMI Group PLC, and Bertelsmann AG's BMG. By the summer of 2002, Napster was declared legally bankrupt and was folded into the operations of Bertelsmann AG's BMG. At that time, the future of Napster was unclear; however, given its strong brand name recognition, it seems unlikely that Bertelsmann will allow the name to fade away any time soon or will shelve it.

In general, the music industry feels threatened by the loss of control over the distribution of its products online, and large companies are being forced to adapt to the Internet. MusicNet was created to act as an intermediary that would license the member firms' music to online services using RealNetworks' secure technology, which would control distribution.[7] Similarly, Sony and Vivendi Universal Music formed a second main competitor called PressPlay (**www.pressplay.com**) to deal with the threat posed by the unauthorized free distribution of content. According to research conducted by Jupiter Media Metrix, the online music industry will be worth over $6 billion by 2006, suggesting that there is a huge market opportunity for both large and small competitors.[8]

Fundamental Models of e-Business

business model
A group of shared or common characteristics, behaviors, and methods of doing business in order to generate profits by increasing revenues and reducing costs.

One way to get a better sense of how businesses can adapt to the opportunities made available to them through the Internet is to identify and understand the fundamental nature of e-business models. A **business model** is a group of shared or common characteristics, behaviors, and methods of doing business that enables a firm to generate profits through increasing revenues and reducing costs. For example, large food stores share a basically similar business model when it comes to their selection of merchandise, their organizational structure, their employee job requirements, and often, their financing needs. The models discussed in this section focus attention on the identity of the firm's customers, the users of the Internet activities, the uniqueness of the online product or service, and the firm's degree of online presence.

Business-to-Business Model

**business-to-business
(B2B) model**
A business model in which firms use the Internet mainly to conduct business with other businesses.

Many e-businesses can be distinguished from others simply by their customer focus. For instance, some firms use the Internet mainly to conduct business with other businesses. These firms are generally referred to as having a **business-to-business (B2B) model**. Currently, the vast majority of e-business is B2B in nature. When firms with a B2B model are examined, two clear types emerge. In the first type, the focus is simply on facilitating sales transactions between businesses. For example, Dell manufactures computers to specifications that customers enter on

Dell's web site. The vast majority of Dell's online orders are from corporate clients who are well informed about the computer products they need and are looking for fairly priced, high-quality products that will be delivered quickly. Basically, by building only what is ordered, Dell reduces storage and carrying costs and rarely is stuck with unsold older technology. By dealing directly with Dell, customers eliminate the costs associated with wholesalers and retailers, thereby helping to reduce the price they pay for equipment.

A second, more complex type of B2B model involves the relationships between companies and their suppliers, which often are numerous, geographically dispersed, and difficult to manage. Suppliers today commonly use the Web to make bids on the products and services that they wish to offer, learn about the conditions under which business will be conducted, find out which rules and procedures to follow and so forth. Likewise, firms that are seeking specific items can now ask for bids on their web sites and choose suppliers from those that make offers in response through the online system. For example, the online leader in the auto industry, Ford Motor Company, links 30,000 auto-parts suppliers and 6,900 dealers in its network, resulting in an estimated $8.9 billion savings each year from reduced transaction costs, materials, and inventory. This $8.9 billion savings represents about a quarter of the retail selling price for an average new car, providing Ford with a considerable competitive advantage in the marketplace through its ability to either reduce selling prices or earn higher profits. In addition, Ford expects to earn approximately $3 billion a year from the exchange fees it charges for use of its supplier network.[9] Similarly, the supplier system at General Motors is expected to eliminate the costs of processing more than 100,000 annual purchase orders, which average $125 each.[10]

Given the magnitude of Ford's cost savings, it is all the more surprising to learn that these savings are derived primarily from the elimination of transaction costs related to manual labor and errors created by the repetitive entry of data. For example, under the old system, Ford might fax an order for parts to a supplier. The supplier would fill out its own order form and send a copy to Ford for confirmation. The data would have to be entered into each company's computer system at each step of the way. However, under the new system, the supplier has access to Ford's inventory of parts and can place bids for parts online. Ford eliminates the labor costs of data entry and much of the order-processing costs by connecting suppliers to the system. Ford's system is an illustrative example of an advanced **electronic data interchange (EDI)**, which uses the Internet to exchange information and thereby avoids the use of printed forms. Before the Internet, EDI systems were much more expensive to set up, since connections between users had to be made directly between exchange members. Furthermore, Internet-based EDI has been a welcome addition to **enterprise resource planning (ERP)**, the back-office accounting software systems that handle order entry, purchasing, invoicing, and inventory control. Today, the Internet facilitates the data exchange process and is a primary reason for the strong growth in B2B activity.

Given the substantial savings from such networks, it is little wonder that many other manufacturers and their suppliers are beginning to use the same kind of system. These systems reduce costs and create a structure that makes it simpler

electronic data interchange (EDI)
An electronic system that allows for the exchange of formatted information typically found in such documents as purchase orders and invoices without the use of printed forms.

enterprise resource planning (ERP)
The back-office accounting software systems that handle order entry, purchasing, invoicing, and inventory control.

for suppliers to deal with each of the automakers. The suppliers are also able to use the system to bid on work and monitor their participation with the manufacturers. Their activities are integrated with those of their customers. There is less separation between the buyer and the seller, as suppliers become part of the production strategy designed by the companies they serve.

Although managing the dealings between a firm and its suppliers is an established business activity that existed before the Internet came along, it is a focal point of e-business activity for many firms. This is due mostly to the savings and improvements that can be found through changing a firm's existing business processes and practices to better ones that are structured around a web site. The result is not only the financial improvement gained by cost savings but also the establishment and control of standard procedures of operation that are clearly visible through the firm's web site. However, firms that are considering the implementation of e-business strategies often face resistance—both internally from employees and externally from customers and suppliers—to changing what might be long-established and familiar practices.

Business-to-Consumer Model

business-to-consumer (B2C) model

A business model in which firms use the Internet mainly to conduct business with consumers.

In contrast to those firms using a B2B model, firms like Amazon and eBay are clearly focused on individual buyers and so are referred to as having a **business-to-consumer (B2C) model.** In a B2C situation, understanding how consumers behave online is critical to the firm's success. Will consumers simply use web sites to simplify and speed up comparison shopping and end up buying at a traditional store? What sorts of products and services are well suited for online consumer shopping, and which ones simply are not good choices at this stage of online development? (The question of whether stock trading is improved by moving online is examined in the e-business insight "Online Trading Changes Everything.") Although an enormous amount of research has been done to answer these and other questions about consumer shopping behavior in traditional stores, relatively little research on online consumer behavior has been done to date. No doubt as more and more consumers make use of online environments, an increasing amount of research will help explain how best to meet their needs.

In addition to giving customers round-the-clock global access to their products and services, online B2C firms often make a special effort to build long-term relationships with those customers. The thinking behind this is that customers should be valued not only for the sale at hand but also for their long-term contribution to the firm's profitability. The cost incurred in earning a customer's trust is high, but if a firm gains a loyal customer for life, that customer's repeated purchases will repay the investment many times over. Many financial models that attempt to evaluate the real value of a dot-com business make use of estimates of the long-term value of the current customer base.

The Internet has enhanced firms' ability to build good customer relationships. One factor contributing to this enhanced ability is specialized software that allows sellers to track the decisions customers make as they navigate a web site. Using the resulting data on buying preferences and customer profiles, management

e-Business Insight
Online Stock Trading Changes Everything

Online stock trading is provided by many brokerage firms, including Charles Schwab, TD Waterhouse Group, and E-Trade Group. With this model, individuals are able to open a trading account by depositing a sum of money and providing a short personal profile of their financial position. They are able to execute their trades directly through the user-friendly web pages that these firms provide. As customers buy and sell stocks, the brokerage firms earn revenue through commissions. They also earn revenue by lending the online customer money to buy more stocks; the stocks held in the customer's account secure the loans.

On the surface, this arrangement appears to be a good one both for customers who are seeking personal control over their stock trading and for brokerage firms that are looking for ways to further satisfy a niche of investors. However, what is not clear is just how different any individual investor's behavior would be in the isolation of cyberspace from what it would be when dealing with a real financial adviser. As traditional methods of conducting business change in the online environment, it is important to question whether change is necessarily best for all parties. On reflection, one might find that the old method is preferable for some clients and the new one for others. The result most likely will not be the elimination of the traditional method, but rather the addition of a new one, thus allowing greater choice for all.

---

can make well-informed decisions about how best to serve its customers. This approach can also enhance inventory decisions, buying selections, and decisions in many other managerial areas. In essence, this is Amazon's selling approach. By tracking and analyzing customer data, Amazon can provide individualized guided service to its customers.

Consumer-to-Consumer Model

consumer-to-consumer (C2C) model
A business model in which firms facilitate the exchange of data directly between individuals over the Internet using peer-to-peer software

peer-to-peer (P2P) software
Software that allows individuals to exchange data directly with one another over the Internet without the use of an intermediary central computer.

server
A central computer that distributes requested files to individual users.

Unlike the B2B and B2C models, which focus on business transactions and communications, the **consumer-to-consumer (C2C) model** involves the growing popular use of **peer-to-peer (P2P) software** that facilitates the exchange of data directly between individuals over the Internet. The traditional method of distribution of files on the Internet requires an individual to request a copy of a file from a central computer, called a **server** and then receive it. P2P software like MP3 (**www.mp3.com**) and Napster (**www.napster.com**), however, allows individuals to directly access files—including music and digital images—stored on one another's computers. As we have already discussed, the opportunity for users to violate copyright law is a concern associated with the use of P2P software. However, P2P software is also a legitimate collaborative tool for employees who need to be able to share data that are distributed among many geographically dispersed individuals. For example, software from NextPage Inc. (**www.nextpage.com**) of Salt Lake City allows clients like the legal firm Baker and McKenzie to share documents that are stored on computers around the world. Attorneys can work together on a project without having to be concerned about the physical location of important files. According to project director Mark Swords, NextPage's software helps the firm move 25 percent faster and improves client relationships.[11]

A broader definition of a C2C model can also include hybrid web sites such as eBay that facilitate exchanges between consumers but also have a commercial dimension. Another example, SnapFish (**www.snapfish.com**), allows customers to display their photographic images online free of charge. Individuals can be granted access to as many images as the customer wants to permit them to see—in effect, the customer can create customized photo albums for friends and relatives online. SnapFish earns revenue by processing film and prints for customers, and also generates additional revenue by selling copies of prints to those who are granted access to online views of the images. Customers can also upload digital photographic images for display and then order prints as well.

Applying e-Business Strategies to Managerial, Marketing, and Financial Situations

Another way to approach the study of e-business is to focus attention on how operations within each of the three primary functional areas of business—management, marketing, and finance—can be improved through the adoption of online software and solutions. We'll examine several strategies within each area to illustrate this approach.

Management Activities and Practices

Management activities and practices focus on how best to organize and coordinate the work carried out by employees so that basic business objectives like building profitability and maintaining good customer and supplier relationships can be achieved. Moving management activities to the Internet can often improve a firm's internal practices and procedures. For example, allowing a company sales representative to enter a customer's order while at the customer's place of business can be facilitated through a web-based order-entry system. The sales representative can verify quantities of available inventory and set a delivery date. Internet-based systems can provide information, improve performance, and generally assist employees in both selling and nonselling situations. However, any change in procedure will normally require employees to invest some time and effort in learning how to use the new system. The question that management must consider, then, is whether the investment is warranted given the benefits that would be derived. Just as managers once weighed the cost of exchanging typewriters for computers and word–processing against the benefits that would be derived from the switch, today they must evaluate the benefits that might follow from adoption of any of the Internet-based solutions that are available relative to the costs that would be incurred.

Communications

The first such Internet-based solution offered, and perhaps the reason that the Internet grew so quickly in popularity right from the beginning, was email. After the installation of the software and a little employee training, email can quickly facilitate and improve communication between users both inside and outside of the organization—twenty-four hours a day, seven days a week. Today, the cost of the software, training, and Internet connection services for a firm is relatively small and insignificant when compared to the time and money saved by switching from a communication system based on regular mail, couriers, and the telephone. The increase in employee productivity adds to a firm's profitability through a reduction in costs for such things as long-distance telephone calls and travel. Email also provides an efficient means for people in various locations who are working on a common project to have access to the same documents and to modify them and circulate them within the working group. A variety of Internet-based communication software solutions are available to firms, such as Microsoft's NetMeeting and MSN Messenger Service and AOL's ICQ and Instant Messenger. Many products incorporate visual imaging using cameras and file sharing so that users can see each other as well as the documents they need to refer to during their exchanges online.

Sales Force Automation

sales force automation
Programs that support sales representatives by providing organized databases of information such as names of clients, status of orders, and sales leads and opportunities, as well as any related advice or recommendations from other personnel.

In addition to all-purpose communication tools that can be deployed in many situations, there are also specialized Internet-based software application programs that focus on the informational needs of particular classes of personnel. For example, **sales force automation** programs support sales representatives by providing organized databases of information such as names of clients, status of orders, and sales leads and opportunities, as well as any related advice or recommendations from other personnel. Sales force automation systems can provide sales representatives with information that they need before they visit clients. A sales representative for a pharmaceutical company who is planning to visit doctors, health providers, hospitals, and institutions in the Chicago area might use a sales force automation system to help map out who should be visited and when. The system would indicate how long it had been since a client was last contacted, how that client was last contacted, by whom, and the results. The databases should also list who else in the pharmaceutical firm has had contact with any individual client, as well as any history of earlier work that the sales representative should know about before the actual visit.

Large organizations like pharmaceutical firms that deal with other large organizations like hospitals generally need several sales representatives to serve the different client departments and individual decision-makers. Sales force automation systems can prevent embarrassment for representatives who are working in their own specialized areas and may not be aware of their firm's overall dealings with the client. Ideally, as each representative completes a visit, any information learned would be input into the sales force automation system as soon as possible so that everyone can be sure of having up-to-date information and can take actions that are consistent with current conditions. For example, while visiting a client, a sales representative might learn that another department is seeking information about a product that could provide a sales opportunity for the firm. Although the sales representative may not be directly involved in that field, the representative can enter a note into the system that will automatically notify the sales management team in the office that a new opportunity has been identified. This lead would in turn be transferred to the personnel responsible for that product and trigger an action. A good sales force automation system will be programmed to automatically transfer information to those who need to know it. The communication system of a sales force automation program has the capability to automatically record document notes and transfer data to appropriate personnel. In this way, decisions about who should actually be notified of a sales opportunity do not necessarily have to be made by the sales representative in the field who uncovered the opportunity. Instead, the system can intelligently notify the people who are likely to be interested in the information. The industry-leading sales force automation software program is distributed by Siebel Systems (**www.siebel.com**). Many other systems, such as OverQuota from Relavis Corporation (**www.relavis.com**), also compete in this growing sector of the B2B field.

Educational and Training Solutions

According to recent data gathered for the industry trade journal *Training*, U.S. companies with more than one hundred employees and with formal training programs in place spend more than $62.5 billion annually on education and training programs for employees. More than 14 percent of this instruction is currently delivered online via computers.[12]

By distributing information about the firm and its people, organization, products, methods, and philosophy to employees through the Internet for viewing at convenient times and places, firms can reduce their education costs enormously. For example, new recruits are generally put through an orientation or training program that includes the presentation of a wide variety of information about the firm. Online training, alone or in conjunction with in-class learning, can help to reduce the costs of training and provide a learner-controlled environment that is more suitable to the needs of the individual.

Online training sessions on ethical and socially positive behavior and on how to properly handle difficult situations such as a perceived harassment problem or discrimination can sometimes be better distributed through web site information centers. In many cases, these sites will rarely be needed. However, it is important that employees know of them and that they be made readily available to employees, if for no other reason than to publicly display the official corporate attitude on such matters. Furthermore, updating and distribution problems involving changes in policies and procedures are solved, as important announcements about these changes are emailed to employees and linked to the appropriate document, which is maintained on the web site. This sort of Internet-based management solution is provided by web-enabled software like Lotus Notes (**www.lotus .com**), which includes a variety of educational software solutions for courseware design and presentation in its LearningSpace product.

Recruiting Employees

A common menu selection item on web sites belonging to major organizations is an employment link to the human resources management department. Firms that are looking for people with specialized skills can post their hiring needs on their web sites and reach a global marketplace of potential candidates. This is particularly an issue in the global information technology job market, where labor shortages are common and individuals with skills that are in high demand can easily find new opportunities online. Furthermore, large firms like IBM and Microsoft receive untold numbers of unsolicited employment applications from people all over the world. The cost of organizing and processing this information using a paper-based system is clearly high, and an Internet based input system can help. An organization may initially want to know only certain critical data, such as the applicant's level of knowledge concerning the management of an IBM AS400 computer. By structuring the input screens so that this important information is entered, the firm can be sure of finding the candidates they want to contact. In addition, by making applicants rather than the firm's employees input data, the firm saves more time and money.

Besides applying for employment directly through an organization's web site, job seekers can make use of a host of online recruiting firms. Perhaps the best known of these sites, with more than half the market share, is Monster.com (**www.monster.com**). Like other online recruiting firms, Monster.com recognized the advantages of creating an Internet-based alternative to the existing, but dated procedures followed by job seekers and their potential employers. Online systems are particularly beneficial to geographically dispersed employees and organizations.

Marketing Applications and Solutions

Marketing involves a variety of activities that, when done well, add value to the product or service purchased by the customer. The Internet can help provide strategic marketing solutions that reduce customer service and order-entry costs, minimize inventory levels, and provide a variety of valuable information to customers. Let's examine a few specific examples in greater detail.

Promotion on the Web

A firm's web site can provide a wide assortment of opportunities for communicating with customers, investors, suppliers, and other interested public groups. Archived press releases and public relations statements posted online by the firm can serve to inform both internal and external parties. The most important promotional tool that is readily available online is advertising, which can motivate customers to either enter their order online immediately or delay their actual purchase until a later time at the firm's retail store.

For most purchase decisions, customers must weigh certain information before making their selection. As a marketing medium, the Internet has advantages over television and radio, since customers are able to interact with the multimedia information they receive over the Internet. Advertisements can be linked to other information, allowing customers to control their research. For instance, consider a web page that presents a home entertainment electronics system, complete with home theater and stereo sound systems. By clicking on different areas of the screen, the customer could explore the information found in those highlighted areas.

A successfully designed web site can provide a high level of personalized communication between the web site sales presentation and the customer. The informed customer should come away empowered and confident of having the necessary information for making the best selection of merchandise. And a satisfied customer will share that experience and sense of control with friends and family and thereby create a ripple effect that will influence other potential customers. Many web sites offer their customers a bonus of some sort for referring the site to a friend. Furthermore, customers who have confidence in their purchase are more likely to be loyal and to return for other purchases in the future. This sort of strategy, whereby knowledge of the site is voluntarily spread from individual to individual, is referred to as **viral marketing** and lends itself well to the online environment. Anytime a web site message describes how the user can forward a link and message about the site to a friend, the organization is using viral marketing.

viral marketing
A strategy whereby marketing information is voluntarily spread from one individual to another.

Well-designed web sites attract targeted customers, create interest in the products presented, and stimulate the desire to explore the purchase decision further. The job of the web site designer is to anticipate the customer's behavior and thinking processes. The online experience should simulate the real experience that the customer would actually have in the store. Where possible, however, aspects of the real experience that might be counterproductive should be improved upon. For instance, being able to pause, ask questions, and find information at any time and then return to the same point in the presentation is a powerful capability of online marketing design. Offering the customer intelligent and helpful suggestions based on knowledge inferred from the choices that he or she made on the site is another smart marketing feature of good web site design. Information about what the customer has bought previously, selected online, or volunteered in profile data can be intelligently used to better the online buying experience for customers. This sort of intelligent online marketing and customer relationship management capability is the primary reason for the success of firms like Amazon.com. In fact, this approach to online customer relationship management and web design is often referred to as the Amazon business model.

Enabling Trial Use

A major marketing advantage offered by the Internet is the ability to inexpensively provide potential customers with a trial or sample of the product or service. This is particularly important when the cost of providing samples is high and reaching potential customers with a trial offer is difficult. For example, we are all familiar with the free sample packages of hair shampoo or conditioner that are periodically delivered to our home mailboxes. These are expensive marketing efforts designed to reach people at a place where they are likely to respond in a positive way. Trial-sized sample containers are also sold in drug stores at very low prices to reach those potential customers who might not have been part of the mail delivery effort. Marketers know from experience that it is necessary to incur these costs if the company is to create a sufficient number of trial users to allow the product to find enough long-term customers.

Home delivery of a sample may still work best, even when the firm is attempting to encourage the trial of an online product. For example, AOL routinely delivers to selected households CDs that provide a free promotional period of access time. Although AOL could attempt to reach these households only through online promotion, which it also uses, traditional mailbox insertions have evidently proved their worth by persuading some people to actually use the CD and try the AOL service.

For many firms, the ability to offer trials of their products and services online has opened up potential marketing opportunities at very low costs. For example, publishers of magazines and newspapers, recording artists and their distribution firms, and software producers can all make trial access to their content easy for interested customers. These efforts are often preceded by requests for customer profile information and the use of a password key that allows the user temporary access to certain layers of the software or literature. Demonstration software versions are often designed to allow the users to create files, enter their own data, and generate reports that realistically illustrate the product's capabilities.

If designed well, the site should provide information at various points that will help sell the potential customer on the merits of purchasing and address any concerns the customer might have. Online support staff that can be reached by email and telephone should make it easier for the potential customer to evaluate the product or service being sold. Besides providing a free online edition of the magazine, a sample song from a CD, or the first chapter from a book, marketers can also solicit feedback about the product to help with future improvements. Once again, the interactive capability inherent in the Internet allows marketers to gather information about their customers' preferences for use in developing future content.

Some firms have discovered that the Internet provides them with the ability to offer their regular business customers additional products and services. *Business Week* (**www.businessweek.com**), for instance, provides exclusive access to online articles and other content to subscribers to the journal. Regardless of whether this remains the strategy or whether the online content eventually becomes a new spin-off product that is sold separately, *Business Week* has been able to provide a valuable promotional benefit to its subscribers while exploring a new publishing opportunity.

Developing Niche Markets

niche markets
Smaller, more specialized markets.

The Internet provides opportunities for firms to develop products and services for smaller, more specialized **niche markets**. Because the costs of conventional marketing and distribution efforts are high, niche markets are often charged higher prices to cover costs or do not receive the same quality of service that would traditionally be found with mass-market items. The catalog mail-order business has found the Internet to be a very welcoming environment for conducting e-commerce globally. What is more interesting though, is the growing number of niche markets that continue to spring up on the Internet all over the world. Anyone can start an online business with very limited financial resources. The operation may remain small, but the ability to at least enter the marketplace and distribute music, literature, games, or other such products through the Internet has opened the floodgate for online entrepreneurs.

Internet-based Advertising

Not only does the Internet permit self-promoting advertising on a firm's own web site, but it also can be viewed as an entirely new medium for general advertising. The conventional television and radio business model, in which sponsor-supported content is distributed to an audience free of charge, is just beginning to take hold on the Internet. The first firms to migrate onto the Web with this business model were the existing radio and television broadcasters and magazine and newspaper publishers. Currently, there are only a small number of distributors of sponsor-supported content—relative to the potential, given the low barriers to market entry for talented content creators. Real5.com (**www.real5.com**) is just one example of the many new web sites that have emerged to fill the demand for niche content. These sites, which encourage entrepreneurial artists to exert their independent creative effort to produce *webcast* programming, would never generate the large audiences required in order to be viable in regular media like television or magazines. The term **webcast** refers to the distribution through the Internet of multimedia content that typically used to be limited to television and radio broadcasting.

webcast
The distribution through the Internet of multimedia content that typically used to be limited to television and radio broadcasting to viewers.

smart advertising
The display of advertising that is intelligently selected on the basis of the viewing customer's profile and behavior data.

The Internet advertising industry infrastructure is already well developed and poised to connect with the new webcasters. Using **smart advertising**, which refers to the display of advertising that is intelligently selected on the basis of the viewing customer's profile and behavior data, Internet advertising firms such as 24/7 Media (**www.247media.com**) and DoubleClick (**www.doubleclick.com**) create, store, and distribute advertisements for clients, who can be either advertisers or web site content providers.

Here's how the arrangement typically works. The web site content provider, such as Yahoo!, the number one search-engine firm, identifies several areas of its web pages that it wishes to have filled with advertising. An Internet advertising firm like DoubleClick will then link an appropriate advertisement for each viewer to the advertising spaces on Yahoo!'s web pages. As the system learns more about the viewer, more intelligent advertising will be distributed to the current or new web pages as the viewer moves from page to page. For instance, a viewer who has just made a request for tourist sites in New York City may be shown advertisements for Broadway plays, local hotels, local restaurants, and so forth. These advertisements would be displayed in addition to whatever was revealed in the list generated by the Yahoo! search engine.

Because DoubleClick stores all of the advertisements on its computers, Yahoo! and the advertiser do not have to do so. Nor does the advertiser have to answer any calls about its advertisements from Yahoo! or any of the thousands of other web pages that might be asked to display the advertisements. In this way, the advertiser is saved from both the task of storing the ads and the unwanted traffic on its computer systems. Furthermore, the advertiser relies on DoubleClick to find the most effective outlets for displaying its advertisements, relieving the firm of the burden of determining where and when to advertise on the Internet. This service from firms like DoubleClick will add even more value as the Internet becomes more and more crowded with web sites and the solicitation of advertising from major firms or traditional advertising agencies becomes unmanageable. In exchange for these services, firms like DoubleClick receive payment from the advertisers and then in turn pay the web site that displays the advertisement a portion of the revenue received.

The more valuable the web page, the more revenues are earned by both parties. As with traditional media, advertising rates are based on the number of viewers that see the advertisement. However, the Internet can also provide intelligent selection of advertising. This value-added benefit tends to command a premium rate, since advertisers can be more confident of who is actually viewing their advertisements. Furthermore, Internet advertising is interactive, providing the viewer with the opportunity to respond to the displayed advertising. Therefore, special bonus rates generally apply when advertisements generate a response by the viewer. The click response is interpreted to mean that the viewer is more aware, interested, and motivated. Clicking on the advertisements delivers a valuable piece of information to the advertiser. The result is a premium rate, which can be double or triple the basic display rate for banner-style advertisements that are simply seen, but not clicked on.

The basic rate for banner-style advertising is a function of the popularity of the web site and competitive market forces. Currently, a web site might expect to earn two or three cents for each viewer that receives the advertisement. This rate is competitive with the rates for traditional print media, and if the web site can attract a few thousand viewers each day for just a few minutes, the revenue potential is huge. Just as one would expect to pay higher advertising rates for *Business Week* than for an unknown publication, popular web sites like Yahoo.com can generate millions of dollars of advertising display revenue because of the volume of traffic that they attract. With advertising placement services supplied by firms like DoubleClick, webcasting and content providers can concentrate on the design and development of their site, their core business, and need not be concerned with finding and nurturing advertising revenues. It should be apparent that the fundamental strategy being followed by all content-focused web sites is to build up a loyal following of regular visitors in order to cash in on the advertising that this traffic can generate. This also helps to explain the motivation of AOL Time Warner. Along with e-commerce, the ability to generate smart advertising revenue is the clear breakthrough opportunity for Internet content distribution businesses.

Financial Services and Solutions

Financial applications include all matters involving money, such as online banking services, the collection of payments for e-commerce transactions, and tracking employee expenses. In most applications, online forms facilitate the secure entry and search of financial data from any location connected to the Internet, reducing much of the associated overhead and service costs. Let's explore a few examples to help illustrate how the Internet is being used to facilitate financial activities.

Online Banking Services

The banking and financial services industries were quick to recognize the inherent advantages of using the Internet. Today, online banking and financial services are available to both businesses and the consumer market. Financial institutions can provide customers with direct access to their accounts, allowing them to make payments, transfer funds between accounts, secure loans, apply for credit, and generate reports. The enthusiasm for the use of online services and the motivation for using them are shared by both clients and the financial institutions because of the increased efficiencies provided by the electronic processing of large numbers of standardized transactions. These systems also provide an added measure of security, since transactions can be handled without human intermediaries and paper documents. Savings in processing charges to the banking industry are huge and contribute directly to the banks' profitability.

Collecting e-Commerce Payments

secure electronic transaction (SET)
An encryption process that prevents merchants from ever actually seeing any transaction data, including the customer's credit card number, that are sent through the Internet.

A well-designed web site should provide easy-to-understand instructions for completing a transaction and protect the confidential information provided by customers online. Credit card information theft is a common concern for online shoppers and is generally a deterrent to online transactions. The **secure electronic transaction (SET)** (**www.setco.org**) encryption process prevents merchants from ever actually seeing any transaction data, including the customer's credit card number. To handle the concern over security, online shoppers may be offered the choice of calling in their orders to a customer service representative over the phone, using a special online-use bank credit card, such as Visa's NextCard, or opting to be billed through a third party like the phone company, which, like bank credit cards, assumes the responsibility for collection. Electronic billing and payment collection will remain a growth opportunity as more and more B2B and B2C transactions find their way onto the Internet. However, the problem with security is accentuated when international sales take place over the Internet, as collections on international sales have traditionally been a concern for North America–based businesses.

Employee Expense Tracking and Approval Systems

The introduction of expense tracking and approval systems provides an opportunity for firms to improve the tracking and approval of employee expenses. For example, Boomerang is a web-enabled software program from Acceleron Inc. (**www.acceleron.com**) that allows employees to report their business-related expenses to the firm's accounting system through the Internet. Boomerang makes use of the Lotus Notes platform and forwards the data that sales representatives input to the appropriate individuals for approval. Expenses are then charged to the appropriate accounts and employees are issued reimbursements if they paid for the expenses themselves. Sales representatives can input data whenever they wish and wherever in the world they happen to be, as long as they can access the Internet. The information they input will be securely transferred to the appropriate cost centers of their firm, and reimbursements are issued automatically and quickly. Companies such as Procter & Gamble are simplifying expense recording and reducing their internal financial management costs by using products like Boomerang.

The Future of e-Business: Growth, Opportunities, and Challenges

Since the advent of commercial activity on the Internet, developments in e-business have been rapid and formidable. Forrester Research, Inc. (**www.forrester.com**), a research firm located in Cambridge, Massachusetts, predicts that global Internet commerce will soar to $6.8 trillion by the year 2004, up substantially from earlier growth estimates. Although most of this activity will continue to be centered on North America, growth is also expected to explode in some Asian-Pacific and Western European countries.[13]

The slowdown in e-business activity that began in 2000 continues to undermine confidence in such predictions. However, we can safely say that the long-term view held by the vast majority of analysts is that the Internet is now part of a new global communications technology that will continue to expand along with related technologies. The only point that is debated is whether growth rates will return to the levels seen during the early years of commercial activity on the Internet. Although many analysts believe that the first rush of enthusiasm to create an online presence has been exhausted, only a small percentage of the potential global users have yet gone online. Current estimates suggest that perhaps between 400 to 500 million people use the Web on a daily basis. However, according to research by Ipsos-Reid Inc. (**www.ipsos-reid.com**), even among the most developed Internet markets in the world, such as the United States, Canada, Sweden, and the Netherlands, about one-third of the people who could use the Internet choose not to do so. In fact, Ipsos-Reid found that only 6 percent of the world's 6 billion people are online, suggesting great opportunities for growth if more people can be persuaded that the benefits are worthwhile. About 40 percent of those surveyed expressed no need for or interest in going online, while 33 percent lacked a computer. As barriers to Internet access are removed and nonusers are persuaded of the utility of the Web, it is clear that greater usage is likely.[14]

Measurements of Growth

Measurements of e-business growth not only illustrate the magnitude and scope of what has happened in just a few short years but also help to indicate future trends.

According to research by Jupiter Media Metrix (**www.mediametrix.com**), by 2006 there will be about 210 million online users in the United States, or about 71 percent of the population, up from the current level of about 157 million, or 55 percent percent of the population. Furthermore, online retail shopping will grow from the current $40 billion to $130 billion by 2006.[15]

Research suggests that global Internet users spend an average of 7.6 hours online each month. Users from the United States and Canada spend the most time, with a combined average of nearly 13 hours per visitor per month, while users in Europe spend on average just over 5 hours a month on the Internet.[16] More indicative of Internet usage, however, are the data from Nielsen/NetRatings surveys showing that monthly average use was 10 hours online at home and 25 hours at work—suggesting the importance of the Internet as a work-related tool.[17]

Ratings of the popularity of web sites vary depending on the country and the research firm's methodology. Because users' preferences change over time, these ratings, like those of television and radio shows, are meaningful only if they are current. Up-to-date usage statistics, ratings, and rankings are available through links to sources displayed on the web site for this textbook. One of those sources, Jupiter Media Metrix (**www.mediametrix.com**), reported that AOL was the most popular site in 2002, with about 93 million "unique visitors." (A unique visitor is a single person who visited at least once during the month; repeat visits by the same person are not counted.) Microsoft sites followed AOL, with 84 million unique visitors, and Yahoo! ranked third, with 80 million. These ratings reflect continuous year-over-year growth and ranking stability among the top three sites.[18]

The Internet will continue to provide great growth opportunities for existing bricks-and-mortar firms as well as for firms that exist exclusively online. Firms that simply adapt their existing business models to an online environment will continue to dominate development. Books, CDs, clothing, hotel accommodations, car rentals, and travel reservations are products and services that are well suited to online buying and selling and are likely to remain popular online, according to research by Jupiter Media Metrix (**www.mediametrix.com**). These near-commodities will continue to be sold in the traditional way, as well as in a more cost-effective and efficient fashion over the Internet. To date, only a fraction of businesses have ventured into the e-business arena. Certainly, the development of e-business has just begun.

The most exciting prospect for businesses and customers, however, is not the conversion of existing processes to e-business processes, but the creation of altogether new and unique products and services. As noted earlier, MP3 and Napster are only two of the firms providing software for the distribution of music directly to customers. Also now emerging are independent online music webcasters, which are presented to users as online radio stations. So in addition to enabling existing radio stations to find a global audience for their product, the technology exists for independent producers to set up their own unique radio webcasting stations. And given the rapidly developing technologies for wireless communications, webcast radio will very shortly become as commonplace as any local radio station received in the customer's physical broadcast area. Netscape's webcast radio services, located at **http://radio.netscape.com**, provide more information about how private and public webcasts can be created.

Convergence of Technologies

convergence of technologies
The merging of the overlapping communications capabilities of such technologies as television, wireless devices, and the Internet into one fully integrated interactive system.

As webcast radio illustrates, the borders of telecommunication technologies for the electronic distribution of sound, images, and text have become less clear. Today, we can send and receive email from pagers, interact with the Internet from a small screen on a cell phone, and even have visually active telephone conversations. This phenomenon of overlapping capabilities and the merging of products and services into one fully integrated interactive system is referred to as the **convergence of technologies**. This convergence may well lead to interactive television programs, which will allow viewers to select the way a program is presented. Viewers of a cooking show, for example, might be able to select instructions for either regular or nonfat cooking. The profile of the viewer's personal tastes and preferences could be maintained, so that the next time the viewer watched the cooking show, that profile would be entered automatically and the appropriate data provided on a hybrid television–web site screen.

Online Communities

online communities
Groups of individuals or firms with a shared interest who generally use a web site to exchange information, products, or services over the Internet.

Online communities, which are groups of individuals or firms who want to exchange information, products, or services over the Internet, are a phenomenon that is likely to grow. One example of a thriving online community is iVillage (**www.ivillage.com**), a commercial community for women (see the e-business insight "iVillage—A Global Community for Women"). Other communities include buyers' groups such as OnVia (**www.onvia.com**), a site that caters to the small-business market. Small businesses can use this site to search out other businesses that might provide a needed product or service, and they can also make use of automated bidding agents that will locate the best deals. Online learning communities continue to evolve, as sites in a wide variety of fields allow people who share an interest or concern to communicate with one another. Geocities (**www.geocities.com**) is only one portal to a huge selection of online communities.

Partnering Online

While opportunities for independent e-business effort will continue, online partnerships, which can be of benefit to both large and small firms, are likely to become increasingly common. By playing a role within a larger entity, smaller firms can enjoy competitive advantage and access to marketable items, thereby increasing their rate of market penetration. A review of the major e-business sites, including those of IBM, Microsoft, and Oracle, indicates that the e-business approach taken by these firms involves local geographic partnerships.

e-Business Insight
iVillage—A Global Community for Women

Creating a web site that focuses on the lifestyles and interests of one group of viewers is a popular e-business strategy. In many ways, iVillage.com, a site that caters to women who are mostly college-educated and between twenty and fifty years old, is a logical extension of a print-based magazine strategy. Here, women can find information and advice on such topics as health, family, education, business, and career. Chat rooms and links to related sites make iVillage a portal for women on the Internet. Like similar online communities such as Martha Stewart's **www.marthastewart.com**, iVillage earns revenues through advertising placed on the site by other firms and through its own online shopping service, which offers daily special promotions. Its relationship with its audience is a long-term one; gift-giving ideas and online learning about everything from gardening to nutrition provide a reason for viewers to visit the site regularly. Maintaining a reason to return to iVillage is the challenge for site managers. Future possibilities for iVillage include spin-off web sites focusing on more narrowly defined target audiences, like single lifestyle interests such as fashion.

Many Internet firms have been able to realize rapid growth though partnerships with smaller firms. For example, Amazon.com pays its web site partners a commission on items bought by users that the partners send to Amazon. Suppose an online learning community made up of students of Spanish and small vendors of related products and services had a link on its web page that took viewers to Amazon.com. By connecting with Amazon.com, the site can earn revenue and satisfy those users who cannot find what they are looking for within the learning community's limited selection. The learning community's range of products is thus automatically extended to include the wide selection carried by Amazon, and both Amazon and the learning community benefit.

Conclusions

This chapter has presented an overview of the fast-paced emerging world of e-business. Several structured approaches have been discussed, including an organizational overview of the firms in the industry that supply products and services, strategic models (B2B, B2C, and C2C) that focus on targeted audiences and activities to achieve specific goals, and a functional focus on the managerial, marketing, and financial situations faced by businesses. Throughout the text you will find more e-business references and examples as they apply to different aspects of business. Chapter 2 will take a closer look at the primary environmental forces affecting e-business strategic thinking. The structure presented here will help explain what areas decision-makers need to research and monitor on a continuous basis in order to develop and manage e-business plans properly.

RETURN TO
INSIDE e-BUSINESS

Because customers can change Internet service providers with relative ease, they have begun to see little difference between firms except with respect to price. Being able to offer its customers Time Warner content allows AOL to avoid competing with other Internet service providers on a price basis alone. This major competitive advantage changes the way the battle for customers will be fought. Internet services providers will begin to focus their attention not on price, but on the value-added services they can offer their customers. Whether these services take the form of entertainment content or access to specialized communications and software, customers will find a growing selection of services being offered by Internet service providers as each seeks to attract and keep customers.

AOL Time Warner will continue to make news regularly as it brings new products onto the Internet.

ASSIGNMENT

1. What content would you put online to attract customers to AOL?
2. Besides lowering prices, what else would you do to help AOL retain customers?

Chapter Review

SUMMARY

1. Define and explain the meaning of e-business.

e-Business, or electronic business, can be defined as the organized effort of individuals to produce and sell, for a profit, products and services that satisfy society's needs through the facilities available on the Internet. The term *e-business* refers to all business activities conducted on the Internet by an individual firm or industry. In contrast, *e-commerce* is a part of e-business; the term refers only to the activities involved in buying and selling online; these include identifying suppliers, selecting products or services, making purchase commitments, completing financial transactions, and obtaining service. e-Business needs highly specialized forms of the human, material, informational, and financial resources that any business requires. New customer needs created by the Internet as well as traditional ones can be satisfied in unique ways by e-business. By using a variety of e-business activities, firms can increase their sales revenues and reduce their expenses in order to increase profits.

2. Explore a framework for understanding e-business.

Most firms involved in e-business fall more or less into one of three primary groups as defined by their e-business activities: those that create the telecommunications infrastructure; Internet software producers, which provide the ability to do things on the Internet; and online sellers and content providers. The Internet would still be limited to communication between individuals and among groups of special-interest researchers were it not for the activity of online sellers and content providers. In this area of e-business, we have just begun to see the development of online strategies for reaching out to existing and new customers. The special characteristics of e-business provide increased opportunity for firms to reach global markets and for small businesses to start up and grow.

3. Identify and explain fundamental models of e-business.

e-Business models focus attention on the identity of the firm's customers, the users of the Internet activities, the uniqueness of the online product or service, and the firm's degree of online presence. Many e-businesses can be distinguished from others simply by their customer focus. Firms that use the Internet mainly to conduct business with other firms are generally referred to as having a business-to-business, or B2B, model. Currently, the vast majority of e-business is B2B in nature. In contrast to the focus of the B2B model, firms like Amazon.com and eBay are clearly focused on individual buyers and so are referred to as having a business-to-consumer, or B2C, model. Unlike the B2B and B2C models, which focus on business transactions and communications, the consumer-to-consumer, or C2C, model involves the growing popular use of peer-to-peer, or P2P, software to facilitate the exchange of data directly between individuals over the Internet.

4. Examine the application of e-business strategies to managerial, marketing, and financial situations.

The three primary functional areas of business—management, marketing, and finance—can all make good use of e-business solutions. For example, using email and other software for communication between managers saves time and reduces travel costs. Marketers can inexpensively provide existing and potential customers with a trial of their products and services, and financial transactions can be expedited and facilitated in a secure environment using the Internet as a communications tool with customers and employees alike.

5. Explore the growth, future opportunities, and challenges of e-business.

Since the advent of commercial activity on the Internet, developments in e-business have been rapid and formidable. Although most of this activity will remain centered on North America, growth is expected to explode in some Asian-Pacific and Western European countries. Online activity, the creation of new products and services, the convergence of technologies, and the development of more online communities are expected to increase. While opportunities for independent e-business effort will continue to grow, online partnerships, which can be of benefit to both large and small firms, are also likely to increase. By playing a role within a larger entity, small firms can enjoy competitive advantage and access to marketable items, and thereby increase their rate of market penetration. Larger firms like Amazon.com have already realized the benefits of partnering with small businesses.

REVIEW QUESTIONS

1. What are the major characteristics that define e-business?
2. How does e-business differ from e-commerce?
3. How do e-businesses generate revenue streams?
4. What roles do telecommunications firms and Internet service providers play in e-business?

5. How do software producers contribute to e-business?
6. What does the term *content providers* mean?
7. Why does e-business represent a global opportunity to reach customers?
8. What are the three fundamental e-business models?
9. What does *smart advertising* mean?
10. What does *convergence of technologies* mean?
11. What are online communities?
12. How can partnering with other e-businesses help firms compete on the Internet?

DISCUSSION QUESTIONS

1. Can advertising provide enough revenue to enable an e-business to succeed in the long run?
2. How can small businesses compete against large-scale e-businesses?
3. What distinguishes the B2B, B2C, and C2C e-business models?
4. Explain why it is worth paying more for *smart advertising*.
5. Describe how to create a viral marketing campaign using the Internet.
6. Describe the growth of e-business since the start of commercial activities on the Internet.

Building Skills for Career Success

EXPLORING THE INTERNET

In order to thrive, all web sites need visitors. Without the revenue that comes from firms that buy banner advertising on web sites or the subscription fees paid by viewers, firms simply would not have the cash needed to create and maintain a web site and to expand their activities. What attracts viewers varies according to their lifestyle, age, gender, and information requirements. Many online communities focus on the interests of a selected target audience. MarthaStewart.com and iVillage.com are two well-known sites catering mostly to college-educated women who are interested in leisure, parenting, business, nutrition, and the like. However, these are only two sites in a sea of choice.

ASSIGNMENT

1. Identify and describe two or more web sites whose content attracts you and keeps you returning on a regular basis.
2. How would you describe the target audience for these sites?
3. What advertisements are typically displayed?

DEVELOPING CRITICAL THINKING SKILLS

Although the variety of products available to online shoppers is growing rapidly, many people are reluctant to make purchases over the Internet. For a variety of reasons, some individuals are uncomfortable with using the Internet for this purpose, while others do so easily and often. The considerations involved in making a business-to-business purchase decision differ from those involved in making a personal purchase. However, the experience of buying office supplies from Staples.com for a business might influence an individual to visit other online sites to shop for personal items.

ASSIGNMENT

1. Which sorts of products or services do you think would be easy to sell on-line? What kinds of things do you think would be difficult to purchase on-line? Explain your thinking.
2. Have you ever purchased anything over the Internet? Explain why you have or have not.
3. Explain how the considerations involved in buying office supplies from Staples.com for a business might differ from those involved in making a personal purchase.

BUILDING TEAM SKILLS

An interesting approach taken by Yahoo.com and several other web sites is to provide viewers with the tools needed to create a personal web page or community. Yahoo.com's GeoCities site (**http://geocities.yahoo.com/home/**) provides simple instructions for creating a site and posting your own content, such as articles and photographs. Yahoo! earns money by selling banner advertising, which is visible to viewers of all the different communities that Yahoo! hosts free of charge.

ASSIGNMENT

1. Working in a group, examine some of the GeoCities communities and personal web pages. Discuss which sites you think work well and which do not. Explain your reasoning.
2. Develop an idea for your own site and sketch out how you would like to see the site appear on the Internet. You may use ideas that look good on other personal pages.
3. Who is your target audience, and why do you think they will want to visit the site?

RESEARCHING DIFFERENT CAREERS

The Internet offers a wide assortment of career opportunities in business as well as in Internet-related technologies. As firms seek opportunities online, new e-businesses are springing up every day. In many cases, these firms want people with a fresh outlook on how e-businesses can succeed, and they prefer individuals without preconceived notions of how to proceed. Web site managers, designers, creative artists, and content specialists are a few of the positions available. Many large online job sites, such as Monster.com, can help you find out about employment and the special skills required for jobs.

ASSIGNMENT

1. Summarize the positions that appear to be in high demand in e-business.
2. What are some of the special skills required to fill these jobs?
3. What salaries and benefits are typically associated with these positions?
4. Which job seems most appealing to you personally? Why?

(continued)

IMPROVING COMMUNICATION SKILLS

Describing web sites in summary form can be difficult because of the mix of information involved. A useful exercise is to create a table, which can serve not only as an organizational tool for the information but also as a means of quick comparison.

ASSIGNMENT

1. Create a table that will compare ten web sites that you have visited. Place the title of one type of information at the head of each column. For example, you might start with the firm's name in the first column, the type of product it sells online in the second column, and so forth.
2. Enter short descriptive data in each column.
3. Write a descriptive summary of the table you have prepared, identifying a few of the outstanding characteristics listed in the data.

Exploring Useful Web Sites

These web sites provide information related to the topics discussed in the chapter. You can lean more by visiting them online and examining their current data.

1. AOL Time Warner (**www.aoltimewarner.com**) is the world's largest online service and media company.
2. IBM's e-business web site, **www.ibm.com/ebusiness/**, contains strategic e-business information, case studies, white papers on emerging issues, and information on software and hardware.
3. Amazon.com (**www.amazon.com**) is considered the largest retailer selling exclusively online and is responsible for developing many of the strategies that are now considered standard for all online vendors.
4. Barnes & Noble (**www.barnesandnoble.com**) is a major competitor of Amazon.com that has transferred some of its business to the Internet to complement its bricks-and-mortar stores.
5. The Walt Disney Company (**www.disney.com**), which also owns the ABC television network, is a major media corporation that uses the Internet to develop new products and to help promote well-established ones like the Disney characters and Disneyland.
6. Petco.com (**www.petco.com**) and Petsmart.com (**www.petsmart.com**) sell pet supplies exclusively online.
7. WebMD (**www.webmd.com**) provides information about remedies, disease, and a variety of health-related topics and issues.
8. Sprint PCS (**www.sprintpcs.com**) is a telecommunications service firm that maintains an extensive web site where customers can learn about

products, access personal account information, send email questions to customer service, and purchase additional products or services.

9. Lucent Technologies (**www.lucent.com**), Cisco Systems (**www.cisco.com**), and Nortel Networks (**www.nortelnetworks.com**) produce most of the telecommunications hardware that allows the Internet to work. Companies such as IBM (**www.ibm.com**), Hewlett-Packard (**www.hp.com**), Dell Computer (**www.dell.com**), Sun Microsystems (**www.sun.com**), Apple Computer (**www.apple.com**), and Gateway (**www.gateway.com**) produce many of the computers used by consumers and businesses. Microsoft (**www.microsoft.com**) and Oracle (**www.oracle.com**) provide software.

10. Berlitz's web site, **www.berlitz.com**, allows anyone in the world to jump quickly to a web site designed in the viewer's preferred language.

11. MP3 (**www.mp3.com**) and Napster (**www.napster.com**) are only two of the P2P software firms that are challenging the traditional method of distributing content on the Internet.

12. MusicNet (**www.musicnet.com**) and PressPlay (**www.pressplay.com**) are two large music subscription services.

13. NextPage (**www.nextpage.com**) P2P software allows collaboration and sharing of documents anywhere in the world.

14. SnapFish (**www.snapfish.com**) allows customers to display their photographic images online free of charge and earns revenues by selling film processing and print copies of photos to those allowed to view them.

15. The industry-leading sales force automation software program is distributed by Siebel Systems (**www.siebel.com**). Many other programs, such as OverQuota from Relavis Corporation (**www.relavis.com**), also compete in this growing sector of the B2B field.

16. Lotus Notes (**www.lotus.com**) software allows databases to be shared over the Internet.

17. Monster.com (**www.monster.com**) is the largest online recruiting firm.

18. *Business Week* (**www.businessweek.com**) provides exclusive access to online content to its print subscribers.

19. Real5.com (**www.real5.com**) encourages entrepreneurial artists to exert their independent creative effort to produce *webcast* programming.

20. Internet advertising firms such as 24/7 Media (**www.247media.com**) and DoubleClick (**www.doubleclick.com**) create, store, and distribute advertisements for clients, who can be either advertisers or web site content producers.

21. The secure electronic transaction, or SET (**www.setco.org**), encryption process prevents merchants from ever actually seeing any transaction data, including the customer's credit card number.

(continued)

22. Acceleron Inc. (**www.acceleron.com**) provides a demo version of its Lotus Notes employee expense-reporting software program called Boomerang.

23. Forrester Research, Inc. (**www.forrester.com**), Ipsos-Reid Inc. (**www.ipsos-reid.com**), Nielsen/NetRatings (**www.nielsen-netratings.com**), Jupiter Media Metrix (**www.mediametrix.com**), and Cyberatlas (**http://cyberatlas.internet.com**) are good sources of online statistics and usage behavior.

24. The toy retailer e-Toys.com was later acquired by KB Kids of Denver, Colorado (**www.kbkids.com/etoys**).

25. Netscape's webcast radio services (**http://radio.netscape.com**) provide more information about how private and public webcasts can be created.

26. iVillage (**www.ivillage.com**) is an online community for women, while OnVia (**www.onvia.com**) is a site that caters to the small-business market. Geocities (**www.geocities.com**) is a portal to a huge selection of online communities and allows users to create web sites free of charge.

Environmental Forces Affecting Planning and Practice

Chapter 2

**INSIDE
e-BUSINESS**

IBM—Selling Customer Relationship Management Solutions

According to IBM's (**www.ibm.com/ebusiness/**) own published reports, the more than 41 million annual technical self-service inquiries handled over its web site result in more than $750 million in cost avoidance and productivity gains for the global computer hardware and consulting services giant. By showing how it uses the Internet to improve its own customer services and save money, IBM is illustrating practical applications to clients and others who are seeking e-business solution case studies. But this is only one illustration of the three primary customer relationship management (CRM) strategies that IBM promotes by example to potential clients seeking advice and consulting services.

To begin with, IBM has established an *online community* for users of IBM products; for example, where a dedicated chat room allows users of IBM's ThinkPad portable computer to discuss technical and operational issues related to the product. Besides facilitating the exchange of opinions, ideas, and other useful information among users, IBM technicians are able to survey the comments entered and use this customer feedback to improve the development of future ThinkPad enhancements and new product designs.

Second, IBM's strategy is to maintain an *ongoing dialogue* with its customers and to continuously analyze its communications with them. This may mean monitoring what customers view while they are on the IBM web site or what they say in chat rooms, responding to email requests for information, or using registration forms that offer customers a long list of topics and ask them to select those that interest them for free email informative messaging. The objective is to better understand customer needs and to project when customers will be most likely to be open to buying a product or service that the firm can sell.

A third customer relationship management strategy demonstrated by IBM is improving *personalized* *value* by gathering and packaging resources to meet the needs of each individual customer. For instance the firm tries to use information about a customer that it has gathered and analyzed to help it guide that customer toward a satisfactory purchase. Consider the following example: A customer dialogue may have been initiated by a television or newspaper advertisement that promotes the sale of several models of the ThinkPad computer line. The potential customer may then be motivated to continue the dialogue by connecting to IBM's web site, where more information is provided and the purchase order can be entered into a form. At various moments, pop-up windows might make intelligent suggestions for the customer to consider. For example, if the customer is unable to decide how much memory to order, a short quiz that calculates input data might appear, allowing IBM to better understand the needs of the customer.

Should this computer-generated information be insufficient to close the sale, a customer service representative can be reached at the telephone number provided on the screen. The customer service representative is able to join the buying process and facilitate the customer's decision making by offering recommendations based on the customer information that has been entered online, along with any data about this customer that IBM may have previously recorded. In this way, IBM spends time and financial resources only with customers that want assistance and call for it, improving the efficiency and productivity of operations even further.[1]

Reproduced by permission from www.ibm.com. Copyright © 2002 by International Business Machines Corporation.

IBM closely monitors the continuous changes that are taking place in the e-business environment in order to be able to respond properly with new strategies in a timely fashion. Improving customer relationships through communication strategies facilitated by the Internet is but one example of strategic thinking in response to technological, economic, and other forces that are at work. Developing new plans to better serve customers and compete in the marketplace begins with an understanding of the changes that are taking place both outside and within the business organization.

Chapter 2 will take a closer look at the primary environmental forces that can influence e-business strategic planning. We will present a simplified but comprehensive model of these forces to facilitate your efforts in research and development of e-business plans, case study analysis, and other activities presented later in the text. Although a variety of forces are always at work at any moment, we will examine those that can be considered more critical to managers involved in the strategic planning process. We will start with an overview of the model and then examine each force individually.

The Environmental Forces Affecting Planning and Practice

external environmental forces
Those factors affecting e-business strategic planning that originate from outside the organization proper and are unlikely to be controllable by business decision-makers; they include globalization, sociocultural, demographic, economic, competitive, intermediary and supplier, technological, and political and legal forces.

Although the environmental forces that are at work are complex, often overlapping, and interrelated, it is useful to think of them as falling into two broadly defined categories. **External environmental forces** are those factors affecting e-business strategic planning that originate from outside the organization proper. External environmental forces are unlikely to be controllable by business decision-makers. Instead, planners and strategists will generally react to these forces, attempting to shield the organization from any undue negative effects and seeking ways to exploit positive ones. For example, a large firm's decision to reduce its selling prices is generally recognized as a strategic action that a competing firm's business manager must respond to in some manner but that is outside of his or her direct control. Thus, when Intel decides to reduce the prices of its latest Pentium computer chips, AMD and other semiconductor manufacturers must respond in some way to offset that decision and protect their market share. However, Intel's decision to cut its prices is beyond the direct control of its competitors; they can only respond to it.

The primary external environmental forces that we will explore include globalization, sociocultural, demographic, economic, competitive, intermediary and supplier, technological, and political and legal forces. As a group, these forces present management with a list of areas to regularly survey and monitor for changes and developing trends. As we will see later in the text, research and intelligence-gathering efforts must begin with an understanding based on information that is continuously gathered from the external environment.

In contrast, **internal environmental forces** are those factors that are closely associated with the organizational functions and activities taking place within the

internal environmental forces

Those factors that are closely associated with the organizational functions and activities taking place within the firm, including the firm's management and organization structure, human resources, information and knowledge, and finance.

firm. These forces emerge from a variety of internal interacting forces, including the firm's management and organization structure, human resources, information and knowledge, and finance. Internal environmental forces can have a significant impact on e-business strategic planning and should be continuously monitored so that managers can incorporate into their planning any changes that are taking place, along with the influences from external environmental forces. For example, existing job market shortages of skilled employees needed for specialized project work can undermine the firm's ability to sell its services to clients. However, management might consider a particular project or client worthy of the effort required to recruit the needed staff from another country or pay premium salaries. Unlike the external environmental forces affecting the firm, internal forces such as this one are more likely to be under the direct control of management. In this case, management can either go out and hire the needed staff or choose to pass over a prospective project.

Understanding this multidisciplinary framework and the forces that are at work can help decision-makers develop a better appreciation of both the opportunities and the many challenges facing the firm. As we will see later in the text, developing new e-business plans and revising existing plans begin with intelligence gathering that focuses on these forces in the e-business environment.

External Environmental Forces

Among the external environmental forces that influence e-business decision making and predictions for future development, perhaps none is more complex or sensitive than globalization. Globalization is interrelated with many of the other external forces as well as with internal environmental forces. As such, it is appropriate that we begin our examination of the primary sources of influence and their connection to e-business thinking here (see Figure 2-1).

Globalization Forces

globalization forces

The forces drawing the people of the world together to live under universally shared standards of culture, communication, technologies, and economics.

Globalization is currently the focus of a great deal of discussion and debate, and with good reason. From many people's point of view, **globalization forces** are inevitably drawing the people of the world together to live under universally shared standards of culture, communication, technologies, and economics, and they see this as positive. To others, globalization represent a threat to individual national cultures, identities, languages, and sovereignty that have managed to survive until today but that may not be able to survive the growing pressures created by the process of globalization in the future.

To those who see globalization as a positive force for change, the most important factor is their belief that globalization provides the best foundation for the global creation and distribution of wealth. They believe it to be the best system for creating the greatest amount of wealth because of the efficiencies inherent in standardizing global business practices. They consider it to be the best system for creating products quickly and efficiently and then distributing that newly created wealth to those who contributed to its creation.

FIGURE 2.1 External Environmental Forces

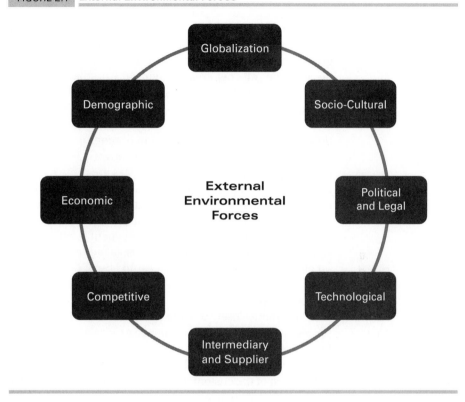

Globalization obviously did not originate with the Internet. Historians trace the patterns of globalization back two thousand years to the days of the Roman Empire, when trade routes, common currency, and political control by Rome spread the Roman way of life across much of Europe and Asia. Today, however, globalization is highly associated with the growth of the Internet, which helped speed the delivery of new ideas, information, and communications technologies, thus changing the geopolitical boundaries of the world the way the Roman military did in its day. The Internet exemplifies globalization—for whether a person or a machine is in North America, Europe, Africa, or Asia, the Internet demands conformity to its standards and protocols. Computers, fax machines, and wireless devices like cellular telephones that wish to connect to and play a part in the global communications network must comply, or they simply will not function.

As a result of the Internet, workers in third-world economic zones are able to join forces with the first world on a more equal footing. Today, it is not uncommon to find software engineers in India doing programming for American-based firms that are selling products to German customers. Along with this collaboration by workers on the production of globally distributed products comes the transfer of common business practices and the necessary capital investments to provide the infrastructure for communications equipment. Jobs that previously would not have been available to engineers in India because of geography, trade barriers, and other restrictive factors are now made accessible because the Internet creates a virtual workplace, allowing individuals anywhere to be part of a global network of production and marketing efforts.

Among the economic spin-offs that benefit the local economy is an accelerated leap forward as the knowledge and skills gained from multinational corporations are applied to the production of other products that also can be channeled to markets through the same global network. For example, local Indian firms that provide software programming services are more likely to channel their products and services to global markets because of their association with firms that are already doing business through the Internet. Furthermore, the risk of losing skilled knowledge workers such as software engineers, who in the past might have left third-world countries to seek advancement for their careers and personal financial success in first-world economies, is reduced now that these workers are better able to find opportunities closer to home.

Success Stories

Let's look more closely at some examples of what would be considered globalization success stories and the trends toward expansion of e-business activities by individual firms. Call centers that provide telephone- and computer-based customer information and services are now a booming business in India, thousands of miles away from where most of the customers they serve live—in North America and Europe. General Electric and British Airways are only two of the many firms that have invested heavily in Indian information technology centers, located in cities like Bangalore and Hyderabad. The reasons are India's recently installed reliable high-capacity telephone lines in most major centers, which make calls to India sound as clear as local calls, and its large base of low-cost English-speaking employees. Call center employees are even trained to assume American identities and speaking styles in order to artificially create the perception that the customer is in fact dealing with a local customer service representative who may just live nearby in, say, Chicago.

In addition to customer service representatives in low-cost call centers, who earn about $1,600 to $2,100 annually, higher-paid Indian professionals such as accountants, software engineers, developers, web site designers, and animators are increasingly joining the global information technology industry back office. According to a report by Boston-based McKinsey & Company, by 2008 India's involvement in the global information technology industry will generate 800,000 new jobs and contribute $17 billion to the economy. Today more than 2.8 million people work in India's information technology sector, and firms like Infosys Technologies—the first Indian software firm to be listed on NASDAQ—Wipro, Customer Asset, and Bangalore Labs have already established or have made plans to establish offices in the United States so as to be closer to their clients. A senior India-based technology executive accurately described the effect of globalization when he said, "We see ourselves as a next-generation company that is neither Indian nor American."

A New World Order?

According to proponents of globalization like author and *New York Times* columnist Thomas L. Friedman, the global free marketplace demands minimal interference by governments in the form of taxation and regulations, American-style capitalism and free movement of capital investments, and the establishment of democratically elected governments, courts, and institutions. Friedman's thesis is that globalization represents the emergence of something of a new world order that will eventually find its way to all corners of the globe. He argues that globalization is a self-directed movement guided by principles of democracy, technology, and free-market capitalism. Friedman warns that no one and no country controls globalization and that even the United States is subject to its rules. He believes that individuals and nations will have no choice but to dismantle the barriers between them if they are going to be players in this new emerging global business club. In short, either nations and individuals will conform to internationally accepted standards of business and political behavior or the other club members will exclude them from membership. If there is a club that favors globalization, it might be the World Trade Organization (WTO; **www.wto.org**). See the Developing Critical Thinking Skills exercise at the end of this chapter for more information.

According to Friedman, as globalization expands, the political, legal, and cultural barriers that tend to divide people are going to become less clear. Eventually, the only differences that will remain will be some degree of local language and culture. This is one of the reasons there is so much antiglobalization protest around the world. The acceptance by supporters of globalization of the loss of individual sovereignty, culture, and, most importantly, the ability of governments to control activities of all sorts within their borders is incomprehensible to opponents to globalization. Opponents argue that they are not against free trade, but rather against the terms of free trade, which they believe give the majority of benefits to multinational corporations with little regard for the local culture, the natural environment, and the poor. They believe that individuals will lose whatever ability they may have to handle local concerns through labor laws, unions, and contracts, as these might be overruled by global trade tribunals. Instead of their own national courts and elected governments, they argue, cases will be decided by unelected trade bureaucrats who, they believe, will be motivated to promote the expansion of globalization and favor its proponents rather than local interests.

Critics of the globalization movement, such as MIT economist Paul R. Krugman and the English philosopher John Gray, view globalization with much concern. Both of these critics question the very premise that globalization is in fact the political and economic panacea that its supporters see it to be. Regardless of which position you take with regard to globalization, it will remain a force to contend with for the foreseeable future and one that will play an important role as e-business strategies and the influence of the Internet spread around the world.[2]

Sociocultural Forces

Perhaps the broadest and most complex component of the external environment is the relevant social and cultural influences on the individual Internet user. The more

e-Business Insight
Changing the Way We Learn About Health-Care

According to a recent study by AOL and the journal *American Demographics*, the Internet dominates traditional media as a source of information for shoppers before they make any online or traditional bricks-and-mortar purchase. And according to a Harris Interactive study, approximately 100 million Americans now seek medical and health-care advice, treatments, and the latest research information through web sites. Whereas in the past people might have consulted their family and friends and sought literature in their local public library or bookstore in addition to their doctor, today the Internet is regarded as a vault of supplementary information, resources, and referrals. These web users tend to be older than the general population, and to have a medical condition or have a family member who does. In response to these developments, pharmaceutical firms like Pfizer and Johnson & Johnson are using their web sites to market their prescription drugs directly to potential patients, who they hope will visit their doctors armed with knowledge about their condition and brand-named treatments available. Customization of web sites in support of a firm's marketing activities is likely to expand to other industries as buyers find the information sites that can increase their ability to make informed decisions about important choices.[3]

---

sociocultural forces
The forces that can influence the socially and culturally defined characteristics of a firm's customers, suppliers, and employees.

managers know about the **sociocultural forces** that can influence their customers, suppliers, and employees, the more accurately they will be able to design appropriate e-business strategies. But what scope should be used to limit and set boundaries for such a broad study? Providing sociocultural descriptions of all groups of people around the world would not be practical for this textbook. Instead, e-business strategists are advised to research and study the local sociocultural factors that are important to their firms' specific e-business planning requirements. Since the majority of the users of this book are likely to be interested in North American e-business plans and, as we have already suggested, globalization effectively transmits shared American values, we will discuss a short list of some basic North American cultural values that are likely to be among the forces at work.

Achievement and Success

People are motivated to achieve socially and culturally honored goals. Our culture celebrates the achievements of those who overcome obstacles and adversities. We admire the drive, discipline, and talent associated with achieving excellence in life. Winning may not be the only thing, but it counts for a lot in our view of life as a competition among products, firms, and people. We willingly trade up from one computer or software version to another because trading up reflects our view that the newer version is a better product and will succeed in some area where earlier versions had poorer performance. Customers will be drawn to firms that present images of success and especially to those that promise to make the customer successful by way of the use of their products and services. In short, firms that look like winners in the race will attract customers.

The culture of achievement and success is often an integral component of the marketing of Internet technology. Advertisements portray successful firms that are using the Internet and outperforming their competitors, who are slow to realize the value of initiating online strategies for success. Virtually every web site vendor of Internet solutions, such as IBM or Microsoft, provides corporate and individual profiles of successful adoptions of their Internet strategic solutions, such as CRM or e-commerce. The message communicated is that the Internet represents success: If you want to be successful like these people, get the same solutions they have adopted for their firms.

Besides selling the idea of success and achievement by businesses, these vendors also portray individuals as being more successful in their personal lives when they adopt Internet-provided solutions. Financial planning, investing online, home decorating, and even cooking nutritious meals for your family are only a few common Internet lifestyle activities that focus on providing information for successful personal behaviors. The popular image portrayed of the Internet user is that of a successful high achiever who became successful because of what she learned through the Internet and can do with the Internet as a technological tool.

Freedom and Individualism

Our culture embraces the concept of individual liberty and concurrently suggests that others should not attempt to interfere with that right. This makes it difficult for governments, corporations, or other people to impose restrictions or behavioral demands in areas that are basically viewed as belonging in the realm of individual choice and freedom. Hence, passing legislation to ban the distribution or sale of certain content on the Internet might be viewed as a challenge to personal liberty. For instance, peer-to-peer (P2P) software programs like Napster are designed to bypass the centralized controlled distribution of material over the Internet. The belief of those who share content over the Internet is that once an item has been produced and released, it is fair game for distribution by whoever wishes to pass it along to others who, in turn, have chosen to receive it. Even the unauthorized distribution of copyrighted material is considered a part of the free-exchange culture of the Internet, not to be regulated by governments.

The argument that is often heard from people who wish to see the Internet left alone by governments and corporate interests is that the Internet is sort of a freedom frontier where no one should attempt to control the exchange processes among users. The proponents of this view argue that there is a fair trade-off between the benefits and costs associated with providing a high degree of unregulated Internet use. Although there are some negative aspects, such as the illegal distribution of copyrighted material, the Internet also has done more than anyone can imagine to spread ideas about freedom, democracy, and individual rights to parts of the world that would have not known about these cultural gifts in any other way.

Finally, the Internet is built around the idea of individualism. Individuals can often choose to select only the sort of information that they want to view when visiting a web site rather than accepting the default generic version for all viewers. So, for example, a viewer of MSN from upstate New York and another from southern California can select different weather and news displays that match their local geography and interests.

Efficiency, Progress, and Technology

Our culture embraces the idea that when a better way to do something is found, then a change to that behavior is natural and represents human progress. We tend to believe that technological discoveries and inventions will solve current problems. Nowhere is this more evident than in the rapid acceptance of Internet-based solutions to both work and personal problems. For example, the widespread use of email and other personal messaging systems was a clear improvement over the regular postal service or courier delivery firms for facilitating communication. Internet messaging is instant and virtually free after the initial costs of connection to a service provider. Both factors have helped make Internet messaging a huge success, with rapid adoption by even the most technologically challenged users.

The continuously evolving nature of social behaviors—especially behaviors that are related to the virtual worlds created on the Internet—is among the key environmental forces influencing e-business strategic planning and decision making. Knowing about how people in general behave in social situations and their cultural characteristics provides the foundation for understanding how they are likely to behave on the Internet. Any business strategy will require an understanding of the target group of customers, and any management strategy will require an understanding of the firm's employees.

Demographic Forces

demographic forces
Descriptive population characteristics such as age, gender, race, ethnicity, marital status, parental status, income, and educational level

Demographic forces involve descriptive population characteristics such as age, gender, race, ethnicity, marital status, parental status, income, and educational level. In addition to its use in describing groups in the general population, demographic categorization is also a tool that provides a high degree of predictability of current and future behavior. For instance, if research shows that large numbers of married women with young children in preschool are users of iVillage.com's (**www.ivillage.com**) informational services about child care, then iVillage will be better able to predict the potential size of the total iVillage.com market if it researches the demographic characteristics of this group. These data might come from government or private sources, but the result will be a better sense of the scale of the site user base, the sorts of products that users might buy online, and so forth.

In order to begin any e-business strategic plan, it is critical to define and then continuously monitor the changing patterns of behavior of the demographic group that has been identified. Let's look at some current information about different demographic groups and their online behaviors.

According to Forrester Research Inc. (**www.forrester.com**), up until the late 1990s, the fundamental demographic characteristics of people online were pretty simple: Internet use was limited to technologically knowledgeable and career-oriented middle-aged white males—not surprisingly, the same group that started

e-Business Insight
Online and Offline Lives Are Similar After All

According to a Media Metrix study, there is a strong synergy between online and offline adult age-appropriate lifestyle activities. For example, women in their twenties and thirties generally look to relationship and parenting web sites for information, those in their forties are likely to be found perusing hobby and gardening sites for ideas, and those in their fifties tend to be found seeking advice at financial and health sites—and men are not much different. In general, the research suggests that online and offline behavior are more alike than what used to be predicted, given the anonymous virtual world of the Internet. For instance, it was the conventional wisdom that the Internet would lead to a breakdown of social behaviors like contact and communication with real friends and relatives as cyberfriendships and cybercommunities drew people away. However, research by the Pew Internet & American Life Project suggests quite the opposite—that the Internet has simply strengthened real social relationships with friends and family by facilitating communication, mostly through email. This was confirmed by a Harris Interactive study, which found that 48 percent of people reported greater frequency of communication with friends and family because of the Internet.[4]

up the Internet. As a result, the online activities and products and services provided by e-business to serve the online marketplace were pretty much limited to the interests of this group of users. There was little in the way of commercial activity as we know it today until the demographics of the Internet changed. Regardless of which came first, the products and services or the entry of new demographic groups, research today clearly shows a changing pattern of demographics emerging online that is beginning to reflect the same demographic portrait as the overall population of North America.

A recent Nielsen/NetRatings (**www.nielsen-netratings.com**) survey reported that the average users of the Internet were changing from younger to older, richer to poorer, and white to those of color. The survey indicated that the fastest-growing group of Internet users was over 55 years old, with working-class incomes and matching tastes. Those who were cruising online were as likely to be found cruising the aisles at their local Wal-Mart. As cheaper, more widely available, and easy-to-use connection services to the Internet like AOL continue to penetrate, the market continues to grow. According to research by Jupiter Media Metrix (**www.mediametrix.com**), by 2006 there will be about 210 million online users in the United States, or about 71 percent of the population, up from the current level of about 157 million, or 55 percent of the population.[5]

A survey by Harris Interactive Inc. shows that Internet usage by women has caught up to and surpassed that of men, growing 900 percent in six years, and whereas technology news used to be the most popular subject for information online, now it's the weather. Research also shows that the group that spends the most time surfing from home is urban, working-class, African Americans, who use the Internet mostly to chat online, send email, and visit entertainment and sweepstakes sites. Single African

Americans residing in the South spend 12.6 hours online each month, 26 percent more than the overall American average. Other groups of heavy Internet at-home users mostly have lower incomes, modest educations, and blue-collar jobs, and live in the South. An interesting consistency emerges from the research: It suggests that a user's income is strongly associated with the length of time he or she spends online—the lower the income, the more time spent online.

The Nielsen/NetRatings survey also found that experience and efficiency are beginning to have an effect on online usage and behavior. For instance, the average number of web sites that a user visited each month dropped in a year from fifteen to ten, but users are now examining more pages at these ten sites, spending an average of 50 seconds on a page. This suggests that familiarity and loyalty are forming; users are shifting from surfing to checking in at their favorite sites. And although the Internet is clearly breaking down the barriers between socioeconomic groups, the research suggests that the online behaviors of different socioeconomic groups are quite different, with those on the upper end of the scale using the Internet as a convenient tool for gathering information for big-ticket purchases and those on the lower end using it as an alternative to television where they can chat, play games, and enter sweepstakes.

According to research by the Pew Internet & American Life Project, men and women equally use the Internet to do banking, send instant messages, and download music. However, men tend to use the Internet more to buy stocks, get news, compare products, buy products, bid at auctions, and visit government web sites and women are more likely to send email, play games, score coupons, and get information on health, jobs, and religion reflecting their lifestyles offline. Furthermore, a Media Metrix Inc. (**www.mediametrix.com**) study of teenagers found that boys are much more likely to download software and play games online, whereas girls are more interested in reading online magazines, doing homework, and staying in touch with their friends online.

The continuing research into the demographics of those people who use the Internet and what they actually do while they are connected is helping to build a clearer understanding of the basic social and cultural nature of the Internet. This in turn contributes to the development of e-business strategies for serving markets.[6]

Economic Forces

The forces at play in the economy can have major impact on individual and industrywide decision making. Employment and income levels, interest rates and inflation, foreign exchange values of currencies, individual corporate growth as measured by annual percentage increases in earnings, and overall general economic growth as measured by gross domestic product (GDP) are only a few of the economic forces that should be of interest to strategic e-business planners. We will briefly examine the basic concepts associated with each of these potential sources of influence on planning.

Employment and Income Levels

The percentage of the workforce that is gainfully employed and how much money people earn is a strong indicator of their ability to spend on all sorts of products and services. When employment and incomes are rising, it is likely that more spending will find its way to the cash drawers of both firms in the local economy and global firms that are involved with the Internet. To put it simply, people without money cannot be customers. The ability of any individual or firm to spend money on Internet products and services is tied to the ability of that individual or firm to generate income. For example, as employment levels and incomes rise for the technology workers in India that are paid more than the average, their spending would be expected to increase. Some of this economic growth will eventually result in additional spending by the firms they work for in India that bought the original necessary infrastructure of computers, fiber-optic cables, and satellite dishes.

Interest Rates and Inflation

The interest rates charged to borrowers for short- or long-term bank loans, bonds, and other lending instruments are a cost to a business for the temporary use of someone else's money. If the cost of borrowing money increases, it follows that some projects that might have been worthwhile and profitable when interest rates were lower may no longer be so. As a result, small increases in interest rates can precipitate a slowdown in economic activity as a variety of projects are shelved. For example, the telecommunications industry slowdown that began in 2000 and affected the drive to install Internet solutions around the world by firms like Cisco Systems, Lucent, and Nortel Networks was largely caused by several consecutive rounds of interest-rate increases by the U.S. Federal Reserve, the central banking authority responsible for setting monetary policy for the United States. As a result of the reduction in sales growth, thousands of employees around the world were laid off, further slowing global economic activity.

inflation
A general rise in prices or fall in the buying power of a currency.

Interest rates are directly related to the level of inflation in an economy. **Inflation** can be defined as a general rise in prices or a fall in the buying power of a currency. Interest rates are generally 2 to 3 percent above whatever the inflation rate happens to be. So if the central bank borrowing rate—rate at which the Federal Reserve lends to its member banks—is 5 percent, then inflation is probably running at about 2 to 3 percentage points below that. The rates for all other forms of lending, from credit cards to leases on computers by consumers, are set taking into consideration the anticipated rate of inflation for the duration of the loan. In this way, lenders are compensated for the loss of buying power that they experience while their money is temporarily being used by a borrower who will be paying back the loan in a currency that will have less buying power than when it was borrowed.

Explanations for the causes of inflation, why it is a bad thing for an economy, and how central banks attempt to deal with it are beyond the scope of this textbook. However, it can be said that inflation forces people and businesses to change their spending priorities and thereby generally causes a loss of business activity for some firms and less growth for most others. For example, if inflation has caused rent and employees expenses to rise, a business may have to cut back on plans to install a web site and e-business solutions because of its lack of internal sources of funds to pay for the effort. An individual who was planning to buy a powerful laptop computer may, if the price of the computer or of other goods and services that the individual buys rises too much, choose instead to buy a less powerful machine, which generally means an older model. As a result sales of newer models slow down, and the logical negative effects on the manufacturers and distributors follows. The slowdown in sales partly explains the merger of Compaq Computer with Hewlett-Packard in 2002.

Foreign Exchange Values

Like inflation and interest rates within a country, the foreign exchange value of one country's currency in terms of another country's currency is an important economic factor, especially for e-business. In general terms, a rise in a currency's foreign exchange value means that the holders of that currency have gained buying power for purchasing foreign-made products and services. Since e-businesses buy many of these from North American–based suppliers like IBM, Microsoft, Nortel Networks, and Sun Microsystems, the purchasing ability of these firms' foreign customers is directly related to the buying power of their currency. In short, a strong U.S. dollar may make imports inexpensive for Americans, but it simultaneously means potentially fewer sales in foreign markets, where customers must trade their currencies for dollars to pay for purchases from U.S. firms. Part of the drop in telecommunications business activity that began in 2000 was also attributed to the strong U.S. dollar, especially against the weaker currencies in Europe and Asia.

Individual Corporate and Overall Economic Growth

It is important for e-business strategic planners to monitor the growth of individual corporations as well as overall general economic growth, as both can have an impact on important areas of decision making. For example, firms like Yahoo! that earn a major portion of their revenues from advertisements placed on their web sites can often be harbingers of things to come—both good and bad. By looking at these firms, decision makers can gain some idea of what is happening in the industry and the implications of that for their planning. The large drop in online advertising revenues at Yahoo! and other firms that began in 2000 was an early indication that the so-called dot-com firms were running out of cash for advertising campaigns on the Internet. All of the web sites that wanted to build a customer base of users were looking to online advertising (along with traditional print and television advertising for those that could afford to) as a logical way to reach Internet users. When sales revenues at many of these web sites failed to provide satisfactory returns on the total investments that had been made, the dot-com bubble burst and corporate stock market values collapsed. Many, like Yahoo!, fell dramatically by 70 to 80 percent in value, while others went bankrupt. The message for planners is that by watching the reported developments at other industry players, like Yahoo!, they can better understand what is likely to be happening to their firm now or what might happen in the near future if a trend is developing. Most observers look at the trend in percentage growth of earnings (or the lack of it), which in turn is based on changes to both revenues and expenses.

Similarly, it is worthwhile to pay close attention to the overall growth in economic activity as measured by changes in GDP. A healthy, noninflationary expanding economy grows at a rate of about 3 to 4 percent annually. Growth that occurs faster than this is generally associated with potential inflation and subsequent interest-rate increases. A slowdown in the overall economy will generally lead to an eventual slowdown in e-business earnings—if not concurrently, then shortly thereafter.

Competitive Forces

The competitive forces that are at work in the external environment relate mostly to the direct competition between firms that offer similar or substitute products and services. In terms of e-business, there are giants in all three primary industry sectors, but there are also many smaller firms that seek niche markets in the globally expanding marketplace for products and services. Generally speaking, the barriers to entry in many areas of e-business are relatively low and partnering opportunities, as discussed in Chapter 1, are increasingly being used to leverage the advantages offered when smaller and larger firms find ways to work together.

Competition also exists between the providers of e-business solutions and the providers of alternative solutions from competing industries. For example, an e-business provider of access to email communication services is not just in competition with other email providers. Email service providers are also in competition with alternative services available from the Postal Service, couriers, telephone voice communication services, and even personal travel service firms that provide face-to-face communication between participants. The convenience, cost, and time-saving advantages of email over alternative choices generally mean that it will be used unless there are mitigating issues. For example, suppose either the sender or the receiver does not have access to email services. In this case, the next logical competitive choice will likely be selected. It is important for e-business strategic thinkers to recognize the range of alternative competitors they are facing and the particular issues, such as access to technology, that relate to the user's decision set.

Intermediary and Supplier Forces

Intermediary and supplier forces refer to the behaviors of wholesalers, online brokerages, and auctions where buyers and sellers are able to efficiently conduct exchanges and secure a supply of needed materials. A firm like Dell Computer relies on a supplier network in order to locate, purchase, and deliver the components that Dell uses to manufacture high-quality computer hardware at competitive prices.

Along with the broader network of suppliers that provide needed materials, the firm must closely watch for changes that might affect the prices it pays for parts and how its competitors are responding to the same environmental circumstances. For example, is there a new supplier that is attracting attention because of its better service or lower prices? New intermediaries are emerging every day as large vendors and financial institutions look for ways to participate in the huge volume of transactions conducted through the Internet. All decision makers need to monitor their continuously changing supply chain in order to know when circumstances suggest that it might be advantageous to switch to alternative sources of supply.

Technological Forces

Technological forces refer to the influence on planning of the complex hardware and software used in e-business. Since technology is such a large and critical part of understanding e-business strategic thinking, we dedicate Chapter 3 to covering the Internet and related technologies. However, examples of the influence of technological change on e-business thinking are presented throughout the text. As well as decisions about what technology to buy, whether it is better to lease or to own, and what new technological breakthroughs will affect current planning, e-business managers must weigh countless decisions that relate in some manner to technological forces. For example, the following illustrates the influence that technology can have on e-business strategic planning for both buyers and sellers of products and services.

hosting
Providing hardware and software services to clients who connect to their files over the Internet

Consider the decision to use hosting services provided by a firm like IBM as a means of dealing with the rapidly changing forces of technology. **Hosting** refers to providing hardware and software services to clients who connect to their files over the Internet. For example, rather than trying to keep up with quickly outdated e-commerce computer servers, software, and security systems, many businesses prefer to have their e-commerce activities hosted by a firm that specializes in this field. This eliminates the need to hire experts to manage the site and keep them trained and informed of constantly changing technology. Hosting also generally means less chance of downtime, since the host usually provides multiple back-up operations should one part of its network experience technical problems. A firm that opts for hosting also will not have to be concerned with customers overloading its Internet connection or its computer servers. This is particularly important to firms that expect large volumes of traffic on their site.

Technology also provides a bridge that can simplify transacting with customers in a global economy. For example, Internet software technology can provide customer-selected web pages and menus in a preferred language, links to international online credit card services that allow anyone with a card to make a purchase and assure payments to vendors, and search agents that can be used to assist buyers looking for suppliers.

Political and Legal Forces

Political and legal forces refer to activities related to governments and government agencies. In general, governments and the courts treat e-business activity as an extension of the regular activities carried out by the non-e-business part of a firm. Therefore, in a general sense, a firm located in California is expected to function according to the laws of that state, regardless of the fact that its activities may be partly or entirely carried out over the Internet. In short, if it illegal to do something in the state of California, then it is illegal for a firm located in California to do it anywhere.

In our discussion of globalization earlier in this chapter, we discussed the forces tending toward the emergence of global standards for government and courts as a condition for firms investing in any country. As globalization expands, it was argued, these standards will also migrate to places that wish to participate in the global economy. In the meantime, however, standards are far from the rule. There are places in the world where businesspeople need to watch out, where the rule of law means something quite different from the conventional North American and European model. In our economy, disputes are generally settled through negotiation between parties who have signed contractual agreements stipulating their positions and outlining their rights in a business arrangement. If negotiations fail, one or both parties can take the matter to the courts, where judgment is rendered according to interpretation of business laws. Clearly, this is not universally true throughout the world today, and businesses need to be concerned with whom they are in business with as the Internet opens possibilities for both large and small firms around the world.

Internal Environmental Forces

Although managers may tend to focus their attention on researching the external environmental sources of influence on the firm, thereby seeking opportunities and threats to current planning and operations, they must also recognize the internal environment of the organization itself as a force to be reckoned with. Some managers may incorrectly assume that the internal environmental forces are already known to planners and therefore do not require any study. However, without careful attention to the forces originating from within the internal environment as well, it is highly unlikely that whatever planning does emerge will be optimal for the firm (see Figure 2-2).

Management and Organization Structure Forces

The firm's management and organization structure forces include those related to theories about leadership and motivation of employees, the organization culture, communications styles, and operations of the business. Together, these forces form a descriptive definition of the nature and character of the organization; that is to say, they define just who and what the firm is. For example, the more liberal-thinking and flexible of the information technology firms, the dot-coms, have been celebrated in countless journal articles as places where work environments are radically different from the traditional North American model. Executive leaders often attempt to motivate staff by using a coaching and team style approach in the workspace and may be indistinguishable from the lower-level employees they work alongside. Offices without walls or conventional barriers to emphasize a culture of equality among all staff members are commonplace, and a dress code that generally allows staff to dress in whatever way they feel most comfortable and policies that allow people to work whatever hours they want from whatever

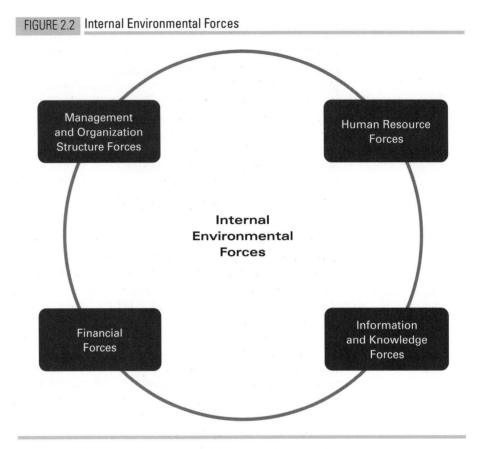

FIGURE 2.2   Internal Environmental Forces

location (office or home) works best for them are hallmarks of the new management and organization structure of today's information technology firm.

If there is a new managerial culture emerging in business, it is more likely to emerge from the countercultural organizational environments of the information technology industry. This is particularly true in areas such as web site design, where work production requires creative energy and is often spontaneous rather than metered out as it would be in producing automobiles on an assembly line. This is not to suggest that all managerial structures encourage or even permit radically loose organizational environments. The assembly line that puts together Dell Computer's products does not operate very differently from the assembly lines at Ford Motor Company. However, even in these positions the atmosphere is generally reported to be more relaxed, team-oriented, and sociable.

Because the information technology industry is relatively new and enjoys low barriers to entry, many firms were started and are still led by the same principal personalities. Examples of some better known industry leaders in this category include Bill Gates of Microsoft, Larry Ellison of Oracle, Michael Dell of Dell Computer, Thomas Siebel of Siebel Systems, and Steve Case of AOL. In each case, a managerial style was established that reflected the personal vision of the founders of these firms. How they conceptualized their company and their relationships with people inside and outside the organization is still very much reflected in the leadership and managerial structures that are currently in place. Although industry giants like IBM are not led by the same people who started the firm, each of them has a unique corporate culture that has an equivalent influential effect on its strategic planning.

Human Resource Forces

Closely related to the internal forces associated with management and organization structure are the forces connected to the firm's human resources. Human resource forces include issues related to employees: the work they are assigned to do, how new employees are recruited, development and advancement strategies within the organization, and even how the firm maintains employee expertise through training and promotions. When competitive job markets make it difficult to find, hire, and keep skilled and knowledgeable employees, planning strategies need to reflect these conditions and the effect they may have on the workplace. Besides offering hiring bonuses, stock options, and very relaxed working conditions, firms may also seek additional means of attracting desirable personnel. For example, providing day care and health club facilities on the company work site are not unusual today at many firms.

Planners need to recognize the impact that human resources can have on operations. For example, a belief among employees that their personal career is stalled if they are not promoted every two years can be problematic in terms of the individual's performance and overall corporate operations. If corporate growth has not provided for a level of internal mobility and advancement that meets employee expectations, then the firm may lose valuable people who might be difficult to replace. Furthermore, replacing these people will certainly require time and money and reduce current levels of operating efficiency. The problem faced by most information technology firms is how to provide their employees with fair opportunities for career growth that are competitive with those offered by other technology firms in e-business. A firm's success or failure in responding to this challenge will determine not only the human resources available to operate the business but also the overall long-term performance of the entire organization.

Information and Knowledge Forces

Information and knowledge forces include employee skills, availability of information, and the general level of employee knowledge. These can have considerable influence on the ability of the firm's human resources to perform the work they are expected to do. Information and knowledge should be thought of as the tools that employees need in order to do their job. Providing poor information services or information that is difficult to understand or locate obviously weakens the potential performance of the employee.

Besides training employees so that they have specialized knowledge about the firm, its customers, its suppliers, its products and other important things, the information technology industry faces more rapid obsolescence of information than most industries do. The firm's human resources effort must incorporate regular training of employees so that they can maintain their expertise in a variety of areas. To answer this need, an entire training industry specializing only in software and hardware for the information technology worker provides regularly scheduled seminars for employees. For example, Siebel Systems provides dozens of courses globally through Siebel University on the use of its products and services. Courses are available through Siebel's web site, **www.siebel.com**, as well as through instructor-led classroom sessions. Clients can receive certification after completing prescribed courses for specific Siebel knowledge areas. This training model is fundamentally the same for Microsoft, IBM, Lotus Development, and many other information technology firms.

legacy software

Older and sometimes very dated programs that a firm is still using, sometimes in conjunction with recent software additions.

Access to training is especially important once a firm has decided to acquire a particular software or hardware product solution. It is certain that the current version of the software will be revised and eventually replaced. When that day arrives, the firm must also be ready with employees who have been trained to move with the changeover to newer technologies. This issue is such a problem for many firms that they decide to continue using older software rather than scrap it for a more up-to-date technology. **Legacy software** is a term that refers to the older and very dated programs that a firm is still using, sometimes in conjunction with recent software additions. Legacy programs may simply be so familiar to so many employees that the task of training everyone who would need to be trained to work with a new program is considered too costly. Furthermore, the chance of failing to successfully switch over to the newer software may be considered too great a risk to take. Sometimes, adoption of a new software solution is considered only when the old solution can no longer satisfy the firm's needs or support is unavailable from its creators.

Financial Forces

Financial forces include any money-related influences on e-business planning. A firm's financial conditions, structure, and other related issues play an important role in determining the available range of strategic planning possibilities. For example, just as managerial and human resources conditions set limits, so too does the amount of funding available, whether it is in the form of a loan or equity, and whether it is from external sources or from investors who are also playing a managerial or planning role in the firm. We will examine financial topics in greater detail throughout the text but particularly in Chapter 11, where we will explore investing and financial topics.

Conclusions

In this chapter, we explored a model that helps organize both the external and internal forces that can influence e-business strategic planning. By remaining current on changing conditions of factors external to the firm and those within the organization as well, managers are better able to develop and control the planning process. In the next chapter, we will examine the technology of the Internet and the various products, services, and related technologies that make e-business possible.

CASE STUDY

RETURN TO
INSIDE e-BUSINESS

IBM is perhaps the quintessential corporate example of globalization. Its products and services are readily marketable in any country and can be easily adapted to suit the linguistic requirements of local users simply by changing the input and output user screens to the appropriate language. Firms like IBM will play important roles in expanding usage of the Internet both through partnerships with local information technology firms around the world and independently where they can succeed independently.

ASSIGNMENT

1. What are some of the current external environmental forces influencing IBM's strategic planning? What are some of the current internal environmental forces?
2. How would sociocultural and intermediary and supplier forces influence IBM's e-business strategic planning decisions to seek a local partner or operate independently in any country?

Chapter Review

SUMMARY

1. **Explore the major environmental forces that can affect e-business planning and practice.**

   Although the environmental forces that are at work are complex, often overlapping, and interrelated, it is useful to think of them as belonging to two broadly defined categories. External environmental forces are those factors affecting e-business strategic planning that originate from outside the organization. External environmental forces are unlikely to be controllable by business decision-makers. Instead, planners and strategists must generally react to these forces and attempt to shield the organization from any undue negative effects and seek ways to exploit positive ones. The primary external environmental forces include globalization, sociocultural, demographic, economic, competitive, intermediary and supplier, technological, and political and legal forces. In contrast, internal environmental forces are those that are closely associated with the organizational functions and activities taking place within the firm. These forces emerge from a variety of internal interacting forces, including the firm's management and organization structure, human resources, information and knowledge, and finance.

2. **Examine the primary external environmental forces that can affect e-business planning and practice.**

   From many people's point of view, *globalization* is an inevitable force drawing the people of the world together to live under universally shared standards of culture, communication, technologies, and economics. To others, it represents a threat to individual national cultures, identities, languages, and sovereignty that have managed to survive until today but that may not be able to survive the growing pressures created by the process of globalization in the future. Principal North American *sociocultural* values include achievement and success, freedom and individualism, efficiency, progress, and technology. The more managers know about the socially and culturally defined characteristics of their customers, suppliers, and employees, the more accurately they will be able to design appropriate e-business strategies. *Demographic* characteristics refer to population descriptors such as age, gender, race, ethnicity, marital status, parental status, income, and educational level. Besides describing groups in the general population, demographic categorization is also a tool that provides a high degree of predictability of current and future behavior. *Economic forces* include employment and income levels, interest rates and inflation, foreign exchange values, and individual corporate and overall economic growth. The *competitive forces* at work in the external environment relate mostly to the direct competition between firms that offer similar or substitute products and services. Businesses will increasingly develop strategies that include working with *intermediaries and suppliers* such as wholesalers, online brokerages, and auctions where buyers and sellers are able to efficiently conduct exchanges and secure a supply of needed materials. *Technology* is a large and critical part of e-business strategic thinking. Finally, *governments* and the courts treat e-business activity as an extension of the regular activities carried out by the non-e-business part of the firm.

3. Examine the primary internal environmental forces that can affect e-business planning and practice.

Internal environmental forces can have a significant impact on e-business strategic planning. A variety of issues and concerns emerge from the firm's *management and organization structure*, including those related to leadership and motivation, the organization culture, communications, and operations. Closely related to the internal forces associated with management and organization structure are those connected to the firm's *human resources*. These include the employees who have been hired, the work they are assigned to do, how new employees are recruited, development and advancement strategies within the organization, and even how the firm maintains employee expertise through training and promotions. The sort of *information and knowledge* available to employees operating within the organization will substantially influence their ability to perform the work they are expected to do. Information and knowledge should be thought of as the tools that employees need in order to do their job. And finally, *financial* conditions, structure, and other related issues play an important role in determining the range of strategic planning possibilities available.

REVIEW QUESTIONS

1. What is globalization?
2. How is the Internet related to globalization?
3. What are the primary sociocultural characteristics that describe the North American population?
4. What are the primary demographic characteristics that describe the North American population?
5. Describe the current North American Internet user in demographic terms.
6. Name one economic factor that affects strategic planning. Describe how it does this.

7. Describe how intermediaries and suppliers affect strategic planning.
8. How do governments influence Internet use? How might they?

1. Discuss the advantages and disadvantages of globalization.
2. Are the benefits that accompany globalization worth the risks?
3. Why do you suppose the demographic characteristics of Internet users appear to reflect those of the population as a whole?
4. How can management and organization structure forces influence strategic e-business planning?

**Building
Skills
for Career
Success**

EXPLORING THE INTERNET

IBM's three-pronged CRM strategy of serving customers better through on-line communities, maintaining an open dialogue, and producing personalized value for customers serves as a model for other firms. IBM's web site (**www.ibm.com**) provides a variety of research articles and case studies of customer decisions that serve to inform current and potential customers as they consider complex installations in a technological environment that is difficult to understand. Of particular value are the resources made available through IBM's e-business web site, located at **www.ibm.com/ebusiness**.

ASSIGNMENT

1. What content on IBM's web site do you consider most useful to customers? Why?
2. What additions would you make to IBM's e-business web site that could help serve the interests of customers?

DEVELOPING CRITICAL THINKING SKILLS

The WTO is perhaps the most widely recognized and visible representative voice of the growing movement favoring greater global trade. Established in 1995 after the Uruguay round of trade negations, the WTO replaced the General Agreement on Trade and Tariffs (GATT), which was born out of the need to reconstruct trading relations among countries in the chaotic aftermath of World War II in 1945. The WTO's 140 members include most of the world's industrialized nations. Its mandate is to facilitate expanding trade relations among member countries and settle any trade disputes that might develop. As such, the WTO is the primary target of protest by the movement against greater globalization, especially at its regular meetings, which are held in various cities around the world. The WTO web site, located at **www.wto.org**, is an excellent source of information about many of the issues and arguments favoring and opposing globalization and expanding trade.

(continued)

ASSIGNMENT

1. Describe the information found at the WTO web site that is related to technology and the Internet.
2. After viewing the information presented on the web site, what is your opinion about the benefits of growth in information technology trade?

BUILDING TEAM SKILLS

Learning how to build an understanding on some topic among group members is an important skill, especially in the information technology field. Productive business meetings typically have clear objectives; such as establishing what the members of a strategic planning team believe is true about the external and internal forces at play that affect the firm and its customers.

ASSIGNMENT

Working in a group, select a business or industry that all of you are somewhat familiar with, such as a sports team. Using the structure established in this chapter for exploring forces that may influence the e-business strategic planning for your selection, establish a description of those forces that is acceptable to all, or at least most of, your team members. Start by determining how one team member views the degree to which the current forces of globalization are acting on your selection. Build on your group understanding by allowing each member to add his or her opinion. Have someone take notes and then prepare a final summation of the team's position. Then move on to the next environmental force until the list has been completed.

RESEARCHING DIFFERENT CAREERS

Although many people think that careers involving e-business require advanced technological knowledge of hardware and software, in fact these requirements are limited to specific areas of the organization, such as the installation of software systems and the writing of customized software applications. Interestingly, much e-business activity demands the same skill set needed in any business setting—such as the ability to understand customer needs, communicate with customers and fellow staff, and report on changes and trends in the external and internal environments. For example, a firm like IBM needs to understand the forces of globalization that are at work in different parts of the world in order to build a better e-business plan. Individuals with this expertise are as important a part of the team that is designing IBM's e-business strategic plan as are the software engineers.

ASSIGNMENT

1. Write a brief job description for a nontechnology position that would involve helping the organization build a better e-business plan through understanding the external and internal environmental forces at play.
2. Explain what skills this individual should have and for what reason.

IMPROVING COMMUNICATION SKILLS

The web site set up by your academic institution is primarily designed to serve the current student body, potential students, and the community at large. The images and information displayed reflect the understanding that the designers of the school's e-business plan have of the groups the school is trying to communicate with online and their informational needs. In many ways, the presentation is very similar to messages and designs used at other institutions because students are similar, regardless of where they attend school. And most academic institutions try to communicate similar messages concerning their scholarly staff, hard-working students, and pleasant surroundings conducive to higher learning.

ASSIGNMENT

1. Describe the sociocultural environmental forces at work at the institution you attend. In other words, describe the student body in sociocultural terms.
2. Explore your institution's web site and summarize the key messages communicated online.
3. Explain why, in your opinion, the messages are either successful or not in light of the sociocultural forces at play at your institution.
4. What message would you add to the web site? Explain your reasoning.

Exploring Useful Web Sites

These web sites provide information related to the topics discussed in the chapter. You can lean more by visiting them online and examining their current data.

1. IBM's e-business web site, **www.ibm.com/ebusiness/**, contains strategic e-business information, case studies, white papers on emerging issues, and information on software and hardware.
2. The World Trade Organization's web site, **www.wto.org**, is a primary source of information favoring the globalization movement.
3. The online community iVillage.com (**www.iVillage.com**) provides information on a variety of topics designed to appeal mostly to women.
4. Forrester Research, Inc. (**www.forrester.com**), Nielsen/NetRatings (**www.nielsen-netratings.com**), and Jupiter Media Metrix (**www.mediametrix.com**) are good sources of online statistics and usage behavior.
5. Siebel Systems Inc. provides informational technology courses through its web site at Siebel University, **www.siebel.com**, as well as through instructor-led classroom sessions.

The Internet and Related Technologies

Chapter 3

INSIDE
e-BUSINESS
Research In Motion—
Toward the Wireless Internet

When most people think about the Internet, they picture a desktop computer screen displaying web sites that have been retrieved using a browser software program like Microsoft's Internet Explorer or AOL's Netscape Navigator. However, this is only one part of the Internet technology story. Another is the fast-growing segment of new wireless (mobile) technologies that are attracting significant customer attention by bringing Internet solutions such as email, instant messaging, and web pages to people wherever they may be at any time of the day or night. Companies like Palm (**www.palm.com**), Motorola (**www.motorola.com**), Sony, Microsoft, IBM, Hewlett-Packard, Nokia Oyj, Ericsson AB, and others are developing hand-held devices that are technologically superior to simple cellular phones and pagers but less complicated and smaller than laptop or notebook-style portable computers. These manufacturers of products ranging from cellular phones to pocket organizers are expanding their product design and technology features to compete in this field against the industry's current leading product—the Blackberry from Waterloo, Ontario–based Research In Motion (RIM; **www.rim.com**).

For about $500, depending on the particular Blackberry model, and a monthly service fee that is typically under $100, users can interact with the hand-sized screen and keyboard to send and receive email—the primary application for these devices. Unlike cellular phones and some competing hand-held devices, the Blackberry is constantly on and therefore is monitoring the user's office email system and alerting him or her to email as it arrives. There is no need to dial up a separate number to check email, nor is a separate email address necessary when the user is mobile.

When the Blackberry was first introduced in 1999, it was an instant hit with mobile executives who needed to be in constant touch with their email systems. The Blackberry was ideal for people whose work involved sending and receiving time-sensitive information, like financial brokers and analysts. The early models included a memo pad, calculator, and alarm clock and consumed very little power relative to competing devices. According to a survey of Blackberry users by New York brokerage firm Goldman Sachs, these users spent 45 percent less time on their laptop computer and preferred the compact portability of the unit to their laptop when they were on the go around town. The always-on connection to their office email and annual costs that averaged only 20 percent of the cost of using a laptop made the Blackberry a hit with managers as well.

Today's Blackberry models compete directly with notebook-sized computers that can cost several times as much, and in many work environments the Blackberry provides communication benefits that are superior to those built into a notebook. Furthermore, many mobile executives have no need for the computing technology that they are paying for in a notebook, and the compact size of a Blackberry is making it a hit in many industries where continuous communication and the distribution of timely information are important. For instance, although financial services firms still account for about a third of sales, employees in the oil, insurance, and pharmaceutical industries and

BlackBerry Wireless Handhelds™

Courtesy © 2002 Research in Motion Limited. (*Source:* www.rim.com.)

in government are beginning to use Blackberries as a less expensive means of maintaining continuous contact with their offices.

However, this is only the tip of the wireless technology iceberg, as RIM is beginning to introduce models that incorporate voice technology. The betting is that an alternative to cellular phones and pagers that is always on and that ties in with a firm's computer network will be a big hit with business users. This is expected to be the next wave of devices that will help build revenues for U.S. wireless carriers like Pacific Bell Telephone, VoiceStream Wireless, and AT&T, which have invested heavily in wireless networks, and many eyes are watching the adoption rate of mobile users. Currently, only 2 percent of North Americans use mobile devices for accessing data, but this figure is expected to grow to 6 percent by 2007, and although RIM's 164,000 subscribers from 7,800 corporate customers make it the current market leader, we have only begun to see the beginning of serious competition for wireless Internet applications and devices.[1]

Part of the challenge facing anyone who is trying to understand e-business strategic planning is to understand the technologies that are associated with the Internet. This is especially important because e-business strategic planning is inherently interrelated with these fast-changing technologies and the opportunities for new products and services that they bring to the marketplace. For a full appreciation of how and why e-business has become the global economic force that it has, some degree of familiarity with telecommunications systems, computer hardware and software, and devices used to communicate through the Internet is needed.

This chapter is dedicated to helping e-business students achieve a functional level of understanding of that technology. In other words, we will examine Internet technologies to a sufficient degree to allow readers to understand how email, web pages, browsers, e-commerce software, and other e-business activities actually work. In addition, we will explore several developments in related technologies, such as wireless communications. We will begin by looking at how the current set of technologies came together to form the Internet we have today.

The Early History of the Internet and the World Wide Web

In the opening chapter of this textbook, we briefly described the origins of the Internet as an American military communications system designed to assure the flow of information among many strategic locations. Should part of the network be destroyed in wartime, the remainder of the system would still be able to function, providing a path for the flow of vital information between decision centers. The fundamental concepts and major design thinking that made this possible are credited to many individuals and, true to the tradition of science and engineering, have continued to evolve organically through the inventions and contributions of individuals and corporations around the world to this day.

Among the early contributors, Paul Baran, an engineer employed by the Rand Corporation (**www.rand.org**), stands out. During the early 1960s, when the Rand Corporations was conducting research for the U.S. Air Force, Baran discovered that the key to maintaining open channels in the event of partial destruction of a communication system was *decentralization of control*, so that local computers that were still functioning did not need to receive instructions from a central computer in order to know what to do with the data they were handling.

mainframe computers
Large-scale computers designed to handle multiple users simultaneously.

At about the same time, Donald Davies, a researcher in London, England, was seeking ways to improve efficiencies in the way existing large-scale or **mainframe computers** functioned. He found that computers could be designed to handle many tasks from multiple users more efficiently if these tasks were broken into smaller units. When this was done, while one user was entering the next computer instruction through a keyboard, the computer could be processing the work of other users and then return to the first user once that user had completed the entry. Like a chess master who is simultaneously playing several matches with different opponents by circulating around the room from chessboard to chessboard, the computer could be designed to circulate among multiple users. The wait time for users would not be noticeable because the computer could be back for the next interaction with the individual almost instantaneously.

Advanced Research Projects Agency (ARPA)
An agency of the U.S. Department of Defense that was responsible for the forerunner of the Internet.

ARPAnet
The forerunner of today's Internet.

Along with the work of many other researchers, these ideas about ways to exploit the thinking power of the computer to improve communications efficiencies and reliability began to find their way into popular use. By the end of the 1960s, about a dozen mainframe computers located at universities across the United States were linked together in a network to facilitate the sharing of data and computing power. This project was funded by the **Advanced Research Projects Agency (ARPA)** of the Department of Defense, and what developed became known as the **ARPAnet**—the forerunner of today's Internet. (The ISOC [Internet SOCiety] web site, located at **www.isoc.org/internet-history/#Introduction**, provides several historical overviews of the Internet.)

Packet Switching—The Technological Basis of the Internet

packet switching
A technology for sending data on the Internet in which messages are broken into packets or parts and reassembled into the correct order at the destination point.

During most of the 1970s and 1980s, the Internet was used primarily by academics in institutions of higher education to share data using early software versions of *electronic mail*, or *email*. Instead of using a dedicated communication line between a single sender and receiver, as the telephone system did, the network made use of a technology called **packet switching**. Messages were broken into packets or parts, with various identification tags carrying data such as the computer addresses of the senders and receivers, error-control information, and sequencing information attached to each part of the actual message data. As the packets moved along the network, their destination address tags would tell computers and other routing devices where each packet was headed. The packets that made up a complete message did not all necessarily travel the same route to the final destination address. If traffic along one possible route was slow, some packets could be channeled along another path. As long as they all arrived and could be reassembled in their correct sequence, it did not matter which route the parts traveled.

To better understand how this process works, let's look at how a packet system for printed documents might work. Suppose someone in New York wanted to send a five-page document to the firm's San Francisco office through the postal system, but had to work within one technological limitation: Each envelope could contain only one sheet of paper. In order to successfully send the five-page document, the sender in New York would label each sheet with a page number and the same unique document title so that it could not be confused with any other document. If each page (packet) was labeled and numbered correctly, the document could easily be reassembled at its destination point.

This revolutionary technology allowed multiple users to send messages at the same time using the same lines, such as telephone wires, and thereby greatly reduced the cost of sending messages. But in order to be organized into packets and receive identification tags, the message had to be in a **digital form** (coded in on and off signals represented by 0s and 1s or **bits**) so that the computers handling the message data could understand them. Every letter in the alphabet and any other character transmitted through the Internet is still represented by a string of 0s and 1s while it is en route through the computerized electronic world of the Internet. For example, the capital letter A is digitally represented by the code 01000001.

Of course, encoding information into strings of 0s and 1s would make it more difficult, if not impossible, for a person to read. However, this conversion process makes it easier for computers to read data. Complying with these technological requirements greatly increases transmission efficiencies, and therefore transmission is less expensive for everyone. Also, the speed of data transmission has increased steadily and continues to improve. Communication lines between the original ARPAnet computers of the 1960s would allow data transfers at a rate of 56 kilobits (56,000 bits) per second—about the slowest rate currently in use by home personal computers hooked up to the Internet over telephone lines through a modem today, but considered incredibly fast at that time.

Once at their proper destination, the packets, which would probably arrive out of their correct sequence, would be reassembled in the correct order based on their tag attachments. In order for the system to work properly, every packet had to use a standard set of identification tags, codes, and steps for assembling data; these are referred to as **protocols.** The ARPAnet protocols became known as **Transmission Control Protocol (TCP).** At the same time, corporations and governments were developing their own internal set of protocols so that their computers could transfer data within their own organizational networks. In order to allow these independent networks to connect to one another and to be able to transfer data within this larger network, a *network of networks*, ARPA established a set of protocols called **Internetworking Protocol (IP).** The combined set of protocols that allows today's Internet to work properly is called **TCP/IP.** TCP is responsible for creating the connection, and IP is concerned with sending packets of data. Together they are responsible for assuring communication between devices connected to the Internet.

---

digital form
The series of on or off signals, or code, represented by 0s and 1s, that computers handling data can understand.

bits
The individual digits (either 0 or 1) in a string of digital code.

protocols
A standard set of identification tags, codes, and steps for assembling data that are transferred by connected computers.

Transmission Control Protocol (TCP)
The ARPAnet protocols used to transfer data over the early version of the Internet.

Internetworking Protocol (IP)
A set of ARPAnet protocols that allowed independent networks of computers to transfer data.

TCP/IP
The combined set of protocols that allows today's Internet to work properly; TCP protocols are used to create the connection between computers, and IP protocols are used for sending data packets.

As new products come onto the scene, new protocols are added to enable these products to communicate with the existing infrastructure. You probably have come across many such protocols while installing software, checking configuration settings, or troubleshooting problems. For example, most users connect to the Internet by borrowing their Internet service provider's (ISP's) connection through a telephone service called **PPP** or **SLIP,** and one of the popular protocols for delivering email to users is **POP3,** while **SMTP** is another protocol for sending email. As new technologies and their components, such as the Blackberry and Palm Pilot, join the Internet, their manufacturers will introduce additional protocols that will allow these devices to be compatible with the existing and expected future technological infrastructure.

The combined **open standards** of TCP/IP have allowed the Internet to grow rapidly while preventing any one firm from creating its own *proprietary* standards. Open standards are not owned by any individual organization, whereas proprietary standards are. Any individual or organization that is willing to do the work may contribute additions and modifications to the current standards. Generally, a governing body or committee evaluates these changes, and eventually new standards emerge. This is an important point to acknowledge, as it has resulted in no single company creating a communication system that it can control and prevent others from using. Students of history may recall that when the railroads of Europe were first built, different countries used tracks with different widths in order to prevent unwanted foreign use. In essence, anyone who wished to travel the rails within a country or territory with a common rail standard was obliged to use the trains that fit that country or territory's tracks. The parallel exists with recent thinking about control and access to markets, particularly as Microsoft Corporation deals with competitors' accusations and U.S. Department of Justice legal action over its business approach to open access and control of its Internet browser, Internet Explorer, and its computer operating system, Windows.

IP Addresses and the Universal Resource Locator Code

Every computer that is connected to the Internet must have an IP address that designates its location. An **IP address** is a structured number that is separated into a series of segments. For example, 164.109.49.250 is the IP address of the computer located at Houghton Mifflin Company in Boston that provides information about this and other textbooks to students and instructors anywhere in the world who choose to connect to it through their computers. However, instead of remembering this number, it is much easier to remember a name that can be looked up in a directory just as you would look up a company's telephone number in a telephone directory. The comparison is an accurate one. The registered name that is equivalent to an IP address is referred to as the **Universal Resource Locator Code (URL).** For example, the URL for the IP address 164.109.49.250 is **www.hmco.com.** You can connect to the Houghton Mifflin computer in Boston by entering either the IP address or the URL in your web browser software.

PPP

A popular protocol that connects users to the Internet through a telephone service by borrowing their Internet service provider's connection.

SLIP

A popular protocol that connects users to the Internet through a telephone service by borrowing their Internet service provider's connection.

POP3

A popular protocol for delivering email to users.

SMTP

A popular protocol for sending email.

open standards

A term used to refer to the fact that a protocol or other coded information is not owned by any individual organization, whereas proprietary standards refers to those that are.

IP address

A structured number separated into a series of segments that identifies the location of a computer connected to the Internet.

Universal Resource Locator Code (URL)

The registered name that is equivalent to an IP address; it tells the browser where the web page is located on the Internet so that it can be found when requested.

Domain Name System (DNS)
The software that translates a computer's URL into its IP address and vice versa.

DNS root servers
Special computers on the Internet that provide IP addresses to a computer that does not know where to send a particular packet next.

The software that translates a computer's URL into its IP address number and vice versa is the **Domain Name System (DNS).** The TCP/IP software on routing computers needs to be able to read the IP address tags in order to direct data packets along the Internet to their proper destination. If a computer does not know where to send a particular packet next, it asks special computers on the Internet called **DNS root servers** for the IP address and directions.

Let's suppose that you want to open a web page located on the Houghton Mifflin web site. When you enter the URL or IP address in your browser, a request to send back information (the web page) is encoded and tagged and sent on its way through the Internet from your computer to Houghton Mifflin's main computer. Once your message is delivered to Houghton Mifflin's root computer, whose address would be listed on a DNS root server, it is very likely that the actual information requested for, say, a textbook will be located on another computer within the company's network. That computer is connected to Houghton Mifflin's root computer, and just as the DNS root servers direct packets along the Internet to Houghton Mifflin's root computer, this same root computer takes responsibility for assuring the delivery of the packet to its correct final destination.

Early Internet Software Applications

group or **list email software**
Software that facilitates mailing a single message to members whose email addresses are recorded on a mailing list.

File Transfer Protocol (FTP)
A popular early Internet application that allowed users to send a file to or retrieve it from a remote location at a faster speed than through other methods, such as copying or using email.

Telnet
An early Internet software application that allowed a remote user to log on to a mainframe computer from a remote site and interact as though the connection were on site.

Although email was by far the most common activity on the Internet in the early days, there were also other popular software applications. **Group** or **list email software** facilitated mailing a single message to members, whose email addresses were recorded on a mailing list. Members could subscribe to the mailing list by sending an email message with the proper coding to an administrative email address. Authorized members of the list could send email messages to a second distribution email address, which would automatically trigger the software to relay the message to all members on the list. The software administrators could control who could relay messages to the list members and who could not.

Transferring files using **File Transfer Protocol (FTP)** was another popular early application; it allowed users to send a file to or retrieve it from a remote location at a faster speed than through other methods, such as copying or using email. The early Internet also allowed a user to log on to a mainframe computer from a remote site using **Telnet** software and interact as though the connection were on site.

Today all of these applications are transparent to users, who may launch them unknowingly through their web browser's menu of commands. For example, free updates to owners of popular software such as Windows and Norton AntiVirus are typically transferred from FTP computer servers to customers.

The Beginning of the World Wide Web

In 1990, Tim Berners-Lee, a physicist at the European Laboratory for Particle Physics (CERN) in Switzerland, developed several communication protocols that established the World Wide Web. The World Wide Web, or simply the Web, is a part of the Internet that allows users to locate and view multimedia content, such as audio, visual, text, and animation material, using a web browser. The most recognized part of the Internet, the World Wide Web has its own set of protocols that allows easy-to-use graphics browsers to link users to multimedia files at remote locations. **Web browsers** are software programs that obey TCP/IP protocols for the transmission of multimedia content. The breakthrough in browser development meant that users no longer needed to understand the far more complicated open-standards operating language of the Internet, called **Unix,** but only needed to understand the meaning of the graphical symbols, or **icons,** that represent actions on the Internet.

Tim Berners-Lee also created the **hypertext transfer protocol (HTTP)** and the Universal Resource Locator Code, or URL. HTTP provides the formatting codes that tell a browser how to display web page content. The URL tells the browser where on the Internet the web page is located so that it can be found when requested. The result is that by clicking on a **hypertext link,** or "hot spot" in an HTTP-formatted document displayed on a screen, the user can automatically open the linked web page or document. The browser software is programmed to read the instructions connected to the hypertext link and to carry out the tasks of searching the Internet and displaying the requested content.

These additional technologies were the breakthroughs that began the phenomenal growth in Internet use that has yet to peak. By making it a simple matter to add new multimedia web page content to the existing Internet and to locate any page from anywhere in the world, these technologies made the Internet a truly global communications tool of a sort never known before.

One of the first browsers, called **Mosaic,** was developed by a group of researchers at the National Center for Supercomputer Application at the University of Illinois and distributed to the public without charge. Among its principal developers was Marc Andreesen, now with AOL's Netscape division. The idea of free public distribution of software to build public awareness and use is a strategy that is often successful, as witness the success of the Netscape Navigator browser, ICQ messaging software, and the Linux operating system.

By the early 1990s, the National Science Foundation (NSF), the last U.S. governmental agency to effectively control the Internet, decided to end direct governmental control. With the entry of businesses seeking more efficient means of communication, the scale of Internet operations exploded, and it continues to grow as new users join the system.

web browsers
Software programs that obey TCP/IP protocols allowing the transmission of multimedia content.

Unix
The open-standards operating language of the Internet.

icons
Graphical symbols on the computer screen that represent actions.

Hypertext Transfer Protocol (HTTP)
A protocol that provides the formatting codes that tell a browser how to display web page content.

hypertext link
A "hot spot" in an HTTP-formatted document displayed on a screen that triggers an action when activated by the user's cursor.

Mosaic
One of the first Internet browsers; it was distributed to the public without charge.

The Internet Infrastructure and Related Technologies

The Internet is just the latest advance in new telecommunication technologies that businesses are finding increasingly useful for acquiring information and distributing it to global users. According to Jupiter Communications research, the amount spent to upgrade and expand the infrastructure on which the Internet depends is estimated to grow from $150 billion in 1999 to $350 billion in 2003.[2] The Gartner consulting firm predicts that nearly 30 percent of U.S. households will have high-speed access to the Internet by 2004 and that Internet traffic will continue to grow at a 200 percent annual rate.[3] Clearly, the task of building the Internet infrastructure is far from complete. Nevertheless, the industry can experience dramatic changes in sales, as illustrated in 2000 and 2001. According to the Semiconductor Industry Association, after a boom year, monthly sales fell in 2001 to about half of what they were in September 2000, when they peaked at $21 billion. The drop was attributed mostly to falling demand for computers, wireless telephones, and other devices.[4]

The Internet infrastructure comprises many different types of computers and other components, as illustrated in Figure 3.1. The system is able to function be-

FIGURE 3.1 The Internet Infrastructure

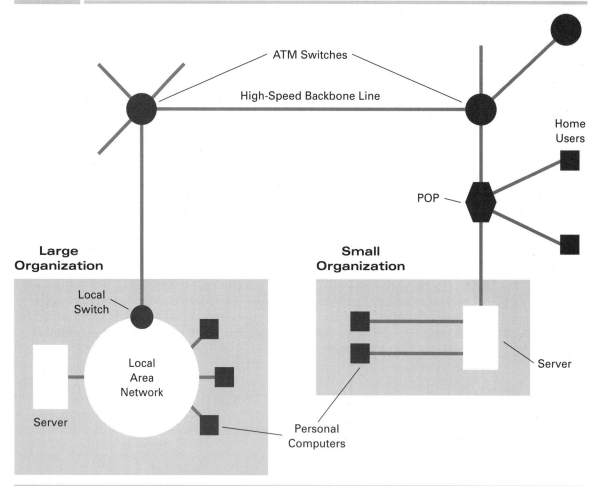

computer workstation
A computer designed to function as part of a network, unlike a fully independent microcomputer.

Windows NT
The version of the Windows operating software that has, built in, all the protocols required to allow a workstation to function properly as a part of the network environment.

Windows
The Microsoft operating software that allows a stand-alone computer to handle routine functions.

Windows 2000
The Internet version of Windows for computers and networks that wish to connect to the Internet.

Linux
A popular Unix-like open-standards operating system that was developed voluntarily by programmers and is distributed free around the world.

kernel
The core software program code.

backbones
The mainline telecommunications channels of the Internet, built with high-capacity fiber-optic cables that move data at the speed of light.

bandwidth
The capacity of Internet lines to carry data.

digital switches
Specialized computers that move data from one high-speed intersecting backbone line to another.

cause of the many established protocols that are built into both software and hardware. Hardware manufacturers and software developers choose to produce products that support (understand) some kinds of data using certain protocols and not others. This is why you can't run Microsoft's Internet Explorer or Windows software on every computer. There must be compliance between the hardware and the software that you intend to use. For example, a **computer workstation** is designed to function as part of a network, unlike a fully independent operating microcomputer. Microsoft's **Windows NT** is the version of the **Windows** operating software that has, built in, all the protocols required to allow the workstation to function properly as a part of the network environment. A stand-alone microcomputer, on the other hand, requires a different version of Windows software in order to function.

Organizations like Microsoft, Sun Microsystems, Linux, and Oracle produce *operating software* that is used to run many of the computers that currently provide services to Internet users. For example, Microsoft's **Windows 2000** is the version of Windows for computers and networks that wish to connect to the Internet. Sun's Solaris and IBM's AIX operating systems are direct competitors of Windows, and Oracle's 8i database is an industry leader in providing software that focuses on processing e-commerce transactions. **Linux** (**www.linux.org**) is a popular Unix-like open-standards operating system that was developed voluntarily by programmers and is distributed free around the world. Initiated in 1991 by Linus Torvalds, a student at Helsinki University, to provide an alternative web server software program, Linux has become a worldwide movement of individuals and corporations. IBM, Sun Microsystems, and Hewlett-Packard are some of the better-known backers who make their contributions to the *open source code* freely known through web sites like the Gnome Foundation (**www.gnome.org**). Firms like Red Hat (**www.redhat.com**) and VA Linux Systems (**www.valinux.com**) sell their clients customized solutions that use the Linux **kernel,** or core software program code.

The Five Primary Internet Infrastructure Components

The Internet infrastructure is currently made up of five primary components: backbones, digital switches (routers), servers, point of presents (POPs), and finally individual (client) users' devices, generally connected to the Internet through telephone modems, DSL and ISDN lines, and cable television modems.

The **backbones** are the mainline telecommunications channels of the Internet, built with high-capacity fiber-optic cables that move data at the speed of light. The backbones are owned by companies like MCI WorldCom, AT&T, and Sprint. MCI WorldCom is the largest in terms of **bandwidth,** or the capacity of the lines to carry data. These firms run parallel backbone lines between major city centers and compete in markets as wholesale suppliers to local telephone companies, just as major power utilities sell supply to local electric companies.

Specialized high-speed fiber-optic **digital switches** connect intersecting backbone lines belonging to the major carriers. Digital switches are really specially

routers
Digital switches that are connected to more than one Internet backbone and are able to decide the direction in which to pass traffic.

nodes
Connecting points of Internet backbones.

T1 and **T3 connections**
Types of connections used to connect large-scale users such as universities and corporations to the Internet backbones.

gateway (local area network [LAN] server)
A switch that brings large-scale T1 and T3 Internet lines to individual user connections.

firewall
A security feature to prevent undesirable access to the LAN by outsiders.

point of present (POP)
The name of a special switch that connects smaller-scale users, such as individuals and small businesses, to their ISP using a dial-up modem, ISDN, and DSL telephone lines.

Integrated Services Digital Network (ISDN)
A high-speed connection to the Internet that is faster than regular telephone lines.

Digital Subscriber Line (DSL)
A high-speed connection to the Internet that is faster than ISDN.

analog signal
The type of signal that is used on conventional twisted-pair telephone wires.

designed computers that move data from one line to another. Digital switches that are connected to more than one backbone and are able to decide the direction in which to pass traffic are called **routers.** Tens of thousands of other switches connect users to the **nodes** (connecting points) of the backbones. Fiber-optic cables connect each switch to large-scale users such as universities and corporations through **T1** and **T3 connections,** which in turn are connected to another type of switch called a **gateway (local area network [LAN] server).** The LAN, in turn, uses a wide variety of software and hardware to connect individual users to the server.

LANs are local networks of computers that connect an organization's users and allow them to exchange information. Not all LANs are connected to the Internet. Organizations may be reluctant to connect their LANs to the Internet because of security concerns. LANs generally have a software security feature called a **firewall** to prevent undesirable access to the LAN by outsiders. Firewalls are part of the effort to prevent unauthorized use of the LAN. Besides gaining access to the information that is stored on the network, outsiders could create a wide range of problems if they managed to gain access to pass codes and take control of the LAN. For instance, a computer running e-commerce software could have prices in the online catalog changed and customer accounts altered. Because of automated screening features that are designed to recognize certain software codes, legitimate LAN users may sometimes have difficulty bringing some Internet data into the LAN.

Finally, smaller-scale users, such as individuals and small businesses, who connect through an ISP like AOL do so through another special switch called a **point of present (POP).** POPs are similar to LAN servers and make the connection through dial-up modems or the faster **Integrated Services Digital Network (ISDN)** and the even faster **Digital Subscriber Line (DSL)** telephone lines. The ISDN uses digital signals, whereas modems work with the slower **analog signals** over the telephone's twisted-pair wires. There are three types of DSL connections with data transfer rates that vary depending on the direction in which the data are traveling—**downstream** toward the user (faster) or **upstream** back to the Internet backbones (slower).

Most individuals connect to the Internet using a web browser and a dial-up connection to an ISP like AOL. Browser software like Microsoft's Internet Explorer and AOL's Netscape Navigator is referred to as the **client.** Clients make requests for data such as web pages and email from another computer, known as the **server,** which acts as a holding or storage place. As companies add more information to their web sites for the world to retrieve, they need to buy more servers. A company's ability to add more content and increase the volume of activity on its system is termed **scalability.** Some systems are limited in their ability to expand in order to meet greater needs and serve growing demands for their resources. Scalability is thus a major selling point for vendors of both computer hardware and software, who need to be able to deliver what is today considered a basic design requirement.

As we have mentioned before, the specialized computers that transfer data along the Internet are called digital switches or routers. Anyone who wants to have a connection to the Internet does so through a router. Routers are designed and programmed to read the identification tags on packets quickly and move the packets along the network correctly so that each packet eventually reaches its ultimate

downstream
The direction in which data are traveling on the Internet when they are going from the server toward the user.

upstream
The direction in which data are traveling on the Internet when they are going from the user toward the server.

client
The computer running browser software that makes requests for data such as web pages and email.

server
A computer that stores files that are requested by client computers.

scalability
The ability to add more content and increase the volume of activity on a computer system.

kilobits per second (kb/s)
A measure of the speed at which data are moving through the Internet.

broadband service
A term referring collectively to higher-speed cable television and telephone connections.

last mile
The last leg connecting the Internet to the user's computer; usually provided by the telephone or cable company.

destination. Routers are also needed to move data within a firm's LAN. Once again, as a business increases its use of information technology, it will need more routers to move information around. The highly visible manufacturers of computer hardware, such as IBM and Dell Computer, have brought their routers and servers to everyone's attention through daily newspaper advertising. Information technicians who are responsible for maintaining a firm's system regard the addition of more servers and routers or memory chips to existing units that are currently in operation as a routine responsibility, not much more complicated than you or I plugging in a new higher-capacity printer to our own computers.

Speed on the Internet is measured in **kilobits per second (kb/s).** Table 3.1 lists the speeds of the major Internet connection choices available. Currently, most users connected use 56-kb/s telephone connections through ISPs such as AOL. This is important to know, since a document that may take only a second or two to transfer through a firm's LAN may require several minutes for an outsider to download if that outsider is connected to the Internet at a slower speed.

Higher-speed cable television and telephone connections are collectively called **broadband service.** Although recent developments have improved data transfer speeds, transmission in this last leg of the Internet—referred to as the **last mile**—is slow. This last mile is generally dominated by local telephone and cable television companies, who understandably fight encroachment by outside competition through regulatory efforts.

The Internet is also accessible without any wired connections. Satellite technology can provide a wireless bridge to a mainline backbone for individual users. Although slower than fiber-optic connections, satellite technology allows users the freedom to connect to the Internet from anywhere. As wireless technology in combination with satellite bridging to the Internet increases in popularity, more applications, such as video-telephone communications, will gradually find their way into popular use. However, given the cost advantage of wired technology, it will be some time before satellite systems are greatly appealing to the masses of Internet users. And until fiber-optic cable connections make their way throughout the network right through to individual users, bandwidth and delivery speed limits will slow the development of Internet content delivery and the convergence of technologies. However, once a fully developed fiber-optic Internet is in place, it will mean clear, high-quality video-telephone communications and unlimited distribution of interactive audiovisual entertainment with a signal quality

TABLE 3.1   Delivery Speeds of Major Internet Connections

Types of Internet Connections	Speed (kb/s)
Popular analog modem for PCs	56
ISDN	128
Cable Modem	128 to 1,500
T1	Up to 1,500
T3	Up to 43,000
DSL	384 to 55,000

superior to that delivered through satellite and cable television services today. When high-speed technology like this is available in more places, a new era of Internet activity will be unleashed.

Computer Technology and the Internet

The device that is most often associated with connection to and interaction on the Internet today is the personal computer. The reason for this lies somewhere in the history of how computer science contributed to the development of the Internet in the first place.

mathematical algorithms
Sequences of mathematical steps that lead to a final numerical result.

Up until the early 1980s, computers were for the most part simply calculating devices designed to carry out **mathematical algorithms**—sequences of mathematical steps that lead to a final numerical result. Large quantities of data were generally entered by a computer operator using a keyboard or scanner of some sort, and the results were then displayed on a computer screen or printed on paper. Software programming became popular because it was a more efficient and productive way to process large quantities of repetitive data, such as telephone bills, credit card and bank statements, and business bookkeeping entries for customer accounts, inventories, purchases, payrolls, and so forth.

code
Instructions in a language understood by the computer.

When decision-makers needed a report, such as a list of the most delinquent customer accounts ranked by date, a programmer would write the necessary **code**—a set of instructions written in a language understood by the computer that told it to retrieve the right data, make the appropriate calculations, and then print out the results. Until the advent of the microcomputer (desktop size) around 1980, few individuals interacted directly with the data that were stored in the firm's centralized computers. Instead, they would have to make a request, detailing what was needed, to the computing services staff, who, because of their specialized knowledge of the programming code that the computer could understand, were able to carry out the task.

computer chip or **semiconductor**
A device that contains the logic circuits that allow the computer to make calculations and other decisions.

The rate of advancement in **computer chip** or **semiconductor** development resulted in the number of logic circuits on a computer chip doubling with some regularity every 18 to 24 months, leading to faster microcomputers and lower prices. This pattern is referred to as Moore's Law of Semiconductors, after the scientist who first noticed it. Customers became used to this technology life cycle pattern and regularly replaced the old technology with newer devices. As the power of microcomputers increased, new software was developed that enabled microcomputer users to carry out a variety of tasks without going to specialists within the firm. As interaction was gradually transferred to an individual's desktop, these desktop computers in large organizations were connected to the firm's main computer, forming LANs. This allowed individuals to interact directly with the accounting, financial, and other data stored on the company's main computer without going through the firm's computing services center. Gradually, software was introduced that focused on the tasks that one individual might be expected to perform, without giving that person access to other areas of the firm's complete computer system. For example, accounting software programs were set up in modules for different parts of the accounting system. A member of the clerical staff might simply be responsible for entering data into a form on the computer screen, which would then be automatically processed by the system at the end of the day. Word processing, spreadsheet, and database software designed to run on microcomputers brought new technology to employees' desktops that allowed them to do things independently and quickly as never before.

The boost to productivity was quickly realized, and the rush to bring computer technology to employees who could use these new software tools to improve their productivity was on. As software and technology improved, most of these activities became **web-enabled,** meaning that the software residing on the firm's server could be accessed from anywhere in the world using a browser. Sales representatives could access the firm's inventory record system while visiting a customer, place their orders directly, and tell customers when they could expect delivery. Because each order would have an identification number, the customers would be able to track their own orders until they were completed and delivered in their entirety. As illustrated by this simple example, the Internet and related technologies have radically changed what used to be a highly centralized and controlled work environment with limited access to information. Today, many individuals, including suppliers and customers, who wish to know certain information can have access to limited areas of the firm's knowledge system through the use of passwords and account numbers. In this way, the Internet has increased productivity by reducing the number of people needed to deal with the input and distribution of information and has increased customer satisfaction by expanding customers' access to information that concerns them.

At the same time, it quickly became apparent that a LAN of computers was ideal for facilitating communication and data exchanges among employees. At first, the orientation was to share a centrally located data center with a multitude of users, who could be given the data they needed in order to make more informed and better decisions in their job. But it soon became clear that technological changes in communications also changed the way in which work could be done.

What followed next was the development of more software that would facilitate communication among users over the Internet. The level of software knowledge and expertise required fell to such a low level that using a computer to communicate with someone in the same office or around the world became as easy as using a typewriter. What had once been a reserved and specialized staff function of the firm became democratized for use by everyone.

web-enabled
Software that can function on the Web using a browser and so can be accessed from anywhere in the world.

Hand-Held Devices and Other Telecommunication Devices

According to the Tower-Group, a Needham, Massachusetts–based research firm, North American wireless subscriptions are expected to grow to 35 million by 2005, and financial institutions will spend about $700 million developing wireless services.[5] Although computers are still the most common technology for interacting with the Internet, they are likely to lose their dominance in the near future, as smaller, less expensive, and more versatile wireless devices make their pervasive

e-Business Insight
Microsoft's .NET—Software for the Internet

According to Bill Gates, .NET is simply Microsoft's platform for XML, a standard for categorizing data that will allow communication across Internet devices and software and enable them to work together seamlessly. For example, suppose that after someone books airline tickets, car rental, and hotel accommodations on various web sites, the person's plans change and he has to take a flight on the following day. .NET will allow software to automatically send messages to the affected web sites as well as to various wireless PDA and cellular phone devices. The basic idea behind Microsoft's .NET (**www.microsoft.com/net**) project is the development of an Internet-based solution that integrates the accessibility of Microsoft applications by all sorts of devices. Whether one uses a computer, a cellular telephone, a PDA, or some other device, access to centrally stored applications and data will be available anytime from anywhere. Microsoft's .NET package of development tools is used to help build what are referred to as distributed computing systems—where the combination of access to greater bandwidth and the availability of distributed content is facilitated on the Internet. For example, rather than distributing application software to individual devices, users can access the current version of the software, which is kept resident on computers connected to the Internet. Users might also select to store the files they create on the Internet so that others can access them at any time, rather than storing them on their own computers.[6]

---

personal digital assistants (PDAs)
Small electronic communication devices, such as Palm Pilots, cell phones, notebook-sized computers, e-book readers, and personal organizers, that generally take advantage of Internet technology.

way into the marketplace. Today, the power and sophistication of microcomputers is built into a range of hand-held devices like Palm Pilots and cell phones, which are smaller and weigh less than even laptop computers and are much more portable. Collectively, these devices are called **personal digital assistants (PDAs);** this category includes very small notebook-sized computers, e-book readers, personal organizers, and so forth.

Interaction through the Internet is now gradually shifting to alternative devices, which, in turn, are opening up more e-business strategies. For example, wireless technologies such as cell phones are now used for making micropayments at vending machines as an alternative to cash or debit cards. A screen that is built into the vending machine provides the purchaser with information and instructions. The purchaser calls in a code on her or his phone, and a charge is applied to the cell phone monthly statement. The vending machine receives instructions that payment has been approved, and the item is dispensed without the exchange of cash. The vending machine operator need not be concerned with loss or theft of cash from the machine or coins jamming the mechanism. And consumers need not carry small change for small purchases.

Another fast-developing application area to watch is the increasing distribution of web content, such as books, newspapers, and music, to individual PDAs. Although models for generating revenues are still being explored, it appears that a subscriber-payment system will be used, possibly with a "bit meter" that will make a variety of data available and charge users for the quantity of bits they download within some time frame, much the way cellular telephone packages are priced today.

However, according to Andrew Odlyzko, an influential telecommunications engineer at AT&T, Internet growth never has been and never will be dependent on the availability of multimedia content. Contrary to popular belief, the Internet will remain a medium dominated by individual and business communication and exchange. Although content will be a substantial part of the Internet, it will not gain much more attention because people are unwilling to pay very much for it. On the other hand, Odlyzko argues, people do value communication and are willing to pay well for fast and high-quality services. Pointing to the fact that U.S. theater box office receipts for the entire year 2000 totaled $7.5 billion, while North American telephone companies earned the same amount in only ten days, he argues that the Internet and the telecommunications industry are thriving and can continue to thrive by concentrating on providing channels rather than worrying about how to fill the communications capacity with content.[7]

Building a Web Site

Hypertext Markup Language (HTML)
The principal programming language used to instruct computers how to display web page content such as images, colors, and the size and position of letters.

Java
A programming language that produces rotation and movement of graphic images on users' computer screens, is understood by any computer, and is promoted by some advocates as a possible universal computer programming language for the Internet.

Extensible Markup Language (XML)
A programming language that allows for the customization of web documents by creating forms for describing and structuring data.

From a cost-benefit analysis point of view, there is little argument that creating a web site for the dissemination of information to customers, investors, potential employees, and other interested internal or external groups is generally a wise business decision. Just how far the firm should go in developing its web presence and how decisions should be weighed by management is a complex topic; it is the focus of the strategic planning chapters presented in Module 2 of this textbook. Furthermore, the artistic and creative work involved in designing an esthetically pleasing web site is a specialized area of study. The web site for this textbook can direct you to other learning resources that focus more closely on web design. Also, entering a key term like *web design* in a search engine on the Internet will produce a long list of links to a variety of resources. Many of these links will lead to sites like **http://geocities.yahoo.com/home/**, which will give you free access to simple tools for producing your own web pages. In the following section, we will examine the basic technology of web page design and maintenance in order to provide an overview of some of the fundamental points that are involved in the process.

Computer Programming Languages for Creating Web Page Content

Hypertext Markup Language (HTML) is the principal programming language used to instruct computers how to display web page content such as images, colors, the size and position of letters, and so forth. Sun Microsystems' **Java** programming language produces rotation and movement of graphic images on users' computer screens, and **Extensible Markup Language (XML)** allows for the customization of web documents by creating forms for describing and structuring data. Both Java and XML code can be embedded within an HTML document and read by browsers. Java can be used to instruct computers to perform a variety of actions and is understood by any computer. Because of this, some advocates are promoting it as a possible universal computer programming language for the Internet.

The first figure shown here is a screen shot of a web page as your browser would interpret and display the HTML-coded instructions it receives over the Internet. Figure 3-2 shows some of the HTML code for this screen shot. Much of HTML involves tagging the starting and finishing points for some data that are to be displayed, such as a title or a paragraph of text. You can ask your browser to display the code for any page by selecting the command from the menu bar. Microsoft's Internet Explorer will display the HTML code for a page if you select *Source* from the *View* selection of commands in the menu, although the code will be easier to understand if it is displayed in a web page editing or authoring software program like Microsoft's FrontPage.

RealNetworks' RealPlayer, Macromedia's Shockwave, and Microsoft's Windows Media Player are software programs that allow the streaming of audio and visual media, so that viewers on the Internet can see them. **Streaming software** creates

streaming software
Software that creates data from audio and video content and sends them along to the receiver in small packets.

Web Page

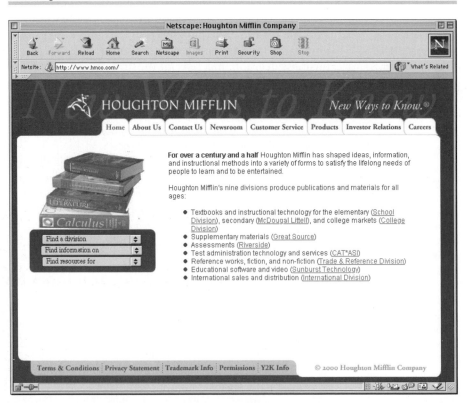

Reprinted by permission of Houghton Mifflin Company. (*Source:* www.hmco.com.)

FIGURE 3.2   HTML code

```
<BASE HREF="http://www.hmco.com/">
<HTML>
<HEAD>
<TITLE>Houghton Mifflin Company</TITLE>
<script language="JavaScript">
<!--
function MM_swapImgRestore(){//v3.0
var i,x,a=document.MM_sr;for(i=0;a&&i<a.length&&(x=a[i])&&x.oSrc;i++)
x.src=x.oSrc;
}
```

The first ten lines of HTML coding for www.hmco.com. Reprinted by permission of Houghton Mifflin Company. (*Source:* www.hmco.com.)

streaming

The encoding process that converts video content into a digital form for distribution over the Internet.

data from audio and video content and sends them along to the receiver in small packets. As the packets are received, they can be viewed even as more packets continue to be sent. Many webcasting efforts can be seen on the web sites of CNN, ABC, NBC, and other sources. Broadcast.com (**www.broadcast.com**) is a good source for connection to this programming content, as are the producers of the software that is used to generate the digitized content for transmission on the Web. RealNetworks, with more than an 85 percent share of the streaming media market, is clearly the dominant player in this sector.[8]

Streaming, the encoding process that converts video content into a digital form for distribution over the Internet, can cost about $7 a minute. However, because there are many platforms, speed formats, and players, an hour of video can easily cost more than $3,000 to prepare. Recognizing an opportunity to help firms reduce their conversion costs by as much as 85 percent and simplify their operations, Generic Media Inc. (**www.genericmedia.com**) of Palo Alto, California, can convert any video into ten formats and any downloading speed. According to the firm, customers can reduce their overall media costs by 45 percent by using the firm's software and updating services, which keep all video content ready for downloading to users of the latest player software.[9]

Web Page Authoring/Editing Software

template

The structure of a web page.

Although programming code can be written to create web pages using HTML and other languages, many easier-to-use program editors have been developed to allow users to generate the necessary coded instructions that are understood by computers. For example, Microsoft's FrontPage (**www.microsoft.com/frontpage/**), the leading web site creation and management tool, requires a minimal amount of user programming knowledge. Generally, once a **template,** or structure of the

The Houghton Mifflin Company Home Page Displayed in FrontPage Editing Software

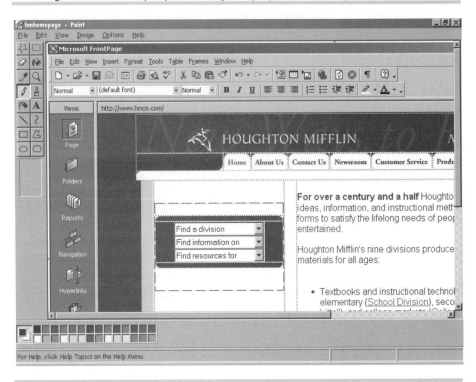

This is how the Houghton Mifflin home page would appear in Microsoft's FrontPage. The editing software allows quick and easy modifications to a web page by translating the image on the page into the correct HTML code. Reprinted by permission of Houghton Mifflin Company.

web page, has been created, content such as text or images can be readily changed, allowing the site to remain current—an important factor if the web site is intended to attract viewers and keep them coming back often. The screen shot shown here illustrates Houghton Mifflin's home web page as it would appear ready for editing in FrontPage.

The design of the firm's web site should be carefully thought out. After all, the web page is the global image that is distributed to customers, suppliers, and other parties who are interested in knowing more about the firm and possibly doing business with it. What the web site says is as important as anything else the firm does publicly. Therefore, it is understandable that most firms that do not have the internal human resources to design, launch, and manage a web site turn to creative experts available through web consulting firms. Once the web site is established, a firm may choose to manage its own site with its own personnel or to continue to use the services of firms that specialize in web page design, updating, e-commerce, and so forth.

Although, generally speaking, most companies manage their web sites on their own computers, many have opted to contract for hosting services provided by other firms; these services can provide guaranteed user accessibility, e-commerce shopping software, site updating services, and other specialized operational products and services for fees starting at about $100 monthly. A firm can often benefit by outsourcing these activities, as the specialized companies that provide hosting services have the expertise to help it maintain uninterrupted and usually faster access service to users as well as lower operational costs. And given the separation of the host computer system from the firm's computer, there may be greater protection from unauthorized access by outsiders to the firm's other computer data and activities.

Related to this notion of outsourcing and minimizing expenses, a new source for software is beginning to find its way to market through the Internet. Known as **application service providers (ASPs),** these software producers sell access to their software to customers for a monthly fee rather than a one-time purchase price. Given the number of other services that businesses outsource, this approach is expected to grow in popularity.[10]

application service providers (ASPs)
Firms that sell software access over the Internet to customers for a monthly fee rather than for a one-time purchase price.

According to Louis Gerstner, chairman of IBM, the next big wave in information technology is going to be the delivery of computer services online. Using the Internet, IBM has transformed itself into a firm that focuses far more on selling services to its customers than it did not that many years ago. Originally, IBM viewed itself as an engineering firm that manufactured mainframe computers for a limited number of big corporate and government clients around the world. The current strategy of generating large amounts of revenue from services was not a major part of management's focus in the past. Today, IBM's e-business web site provides a wide range of products and services for large and small firms that are interested in using the Internet to improve their business operations. For example, a recently developed revenue stream called **e-sourcing** provides software and various technological services to customers on a pay-as-you-go basis, even hosting and maintaining their software on IBM's computers. This arrangement eliminates the need for customers to acquire and support their own systems, allowing them instead to focus their resources on improving their business operations. Gerstner predicted that e-sourcing would grow into a $55 billion market by 2003 and that IBM expected to own a large share of that market.[11]

e-sourcing
Providing software and various technological services to customers on a pay-as-you-go basis over the Internet.

Convergence of Technologies

We will conclude our brief examination of Internet-related technologies by focusing attention on the important idea of convergence and the opportunities presented by this development. In Chapter 1, we briefly defined convergence as the merging of the overlapping capabilities of various technologies into one fully integrated interactive communications system. Convergence of technologies refers to the idea that a variety of technologies such as telecommunications, computers, television, and radio will eventually merge in such a way that access to them and their content will be available through a range of devices in a multitude of environments. For example, we discussed earlier the success of RIM's Blackberry, which will soon incorporate voice technology to complement constant two-way

e-Business Insight

IBM's Project Eliza—Building Internet Computers That Run Themselves

The goal of IBM's Project Eliza is to create a new kind of computer server that can do the work that is now done by highly skilled and knowledgeable human technicians—things like fixing software problems when something goes wrong, protecting the system from hackers and unauthorized access, reconfiguring the system to use new operating systems and data, and so forth. The idea is to automate the management and maintenance of computer servers as much as possible and make the computers that run the Internet and corporate LANs as easy to use as a kitchen appliance. This is becoming more and more important as the variety of systems that connect to the

Internet increases through the convergence of technologies. Devices such as wireless PDAs, cellular telephones, and so forth are a growing challenge for technical staff to handle. Add to the equation the shortage of skilled technicians to do the work, and the economic imperative to develop an automated solution for firms using large numbers of servers, like IBM and AOL Time Warner, becomes clear.

The project will incorporate developments in open-source software like Linux and Apache Web, in recognition of the importance that IBM places on the open-source approach to development. Project Eliza is expected to involve hundreds of researchers around the world and receive 25 percent of the firm's annual budget for research into computer servers—estimated to be several hundreds of millions of dollars, part of the more than $6 billion the computer industry leader spends on all research.[12]

---

wireless email connection for mobile users. Eventually, e-books, journals, television programs, movies, games, and other forms of entertainment will be delivered to hand-held devices, home entertainment centers, or any other device connected to the Internet on a demand basis.

The opportunities to explore business strategies that utilize the advantages of convergence are still in the early stages of development, and businesses are generally taking a slow, experimental approach. For example, perhaps in an effort to test the reaction of audiences to a blended strategy of product placement and e-commerce, as well as to raise funds for a nonprofit organization, NBC television concluded a broadcast of an episode of the popular television program *Will and Grace* with a 10-second message that said, "If you'd like to buy a Ralph Lauren pink pony T-shirt like the one Grace is wearing in tonight's episode and help the fight against cancer, log on to Polo.com." The shirt's purchase price of $52 included a $15 donation to organizations dedicated to raising awareness about the disease. The response was considered a huge success: More than twice the normal volume of web site traffic was recorded in the days after the message was delivered on television, and more than 3,000 T-shirts were sold, raising about $45,000 for a nonprofit organization.[13]

Whether this effort at motivating immediate commercial activity on the part of a viewing audience will be repeated outside of the not-for-profit context is difficult to say. However, as Internet technology that allows an immediate response to televised information gradually makes its way to more and more of our television screens, efforts to interact with potential customers are likely to become more prevalent. Furthermore, firms will have the opportunity to determine the value of advertising on specific television programs and at certain times and to learn more about how well they are selecting media to deliver their advertising messages and the level of audience interest in their products. We will expand on this and other marketing opportunities in Chapter 9.

Conclusions

In this chapter we explored some of the principal technologies that permit the Internet to function. Following a timeline that began in the early 1960s, we examined the progressive developments and contributions made by individuals and organizations to new hardware devices and software. We concluded by focusing attention on the future developments that are expected to emerge from the convergence of technologies and the business opportunities that are likely to arise from the greater convergence of communication capabilities.

CASE STUDY
RETURN TO
INSIDE e-BUSINESS

As the industry leader in this technology, RIM is already preparing for what it considers a breakthrough in the way people will use the Internet. RIM and others believe that mobile devices will lead the way toward greater reliance on centralized databases and remote access to records stored there. Because of Blackberries' advanced encryption and security features, RIM believes that these devices will eventually be used as "wireless wallets" and portable automated teller machines, providing users with password-coded access to their bank accounts wherever they are. The user's funds will remain in the bank until the device is used to pay for a transaction. There would be no loss of funds should the device be lost or stolen. Developers of mobile technologies like the Blackberry believe that eventually sensitive information such as an individual's medical history will be retrievable on demand through portable devices whenever and wherever it is needed.

According to eTForecasts, about 40 million subscribers used wireless services in 2000, and sales are expected to continue expanding tremendously in the coming years.[14] To be successful, small hand-held wireless devices like the Blackberry and the Palm Pilot will have to deliver content in a format that is suitable for the size of the display screen. Currently these devices are ideally designed for short voice and data messages. Traditional web pages are not likely to be of much value to mobile users of these devices, and firms are likely to face the task of developing content for small-screen displays in addition to their web site.

ASSIGNMENT

1. What PDA content design ideas would you suggest to an online brokerage firm?
2. How could a content provider overcome the deficiencies of the small display screen in its effort to alert customers to an important breaking news story?
3. What other wireless applications do you think would be successful, in addition to the ones we have mentioned? Explain your reasoning.

Chapter Review

1. Explore the early history of the Internet and the World Wide Web.

The Internet was born out of an American military communications system designed to assure the flow of information among many strategic locations. Should part of the network be destroyed in wartime, the remainder of the system would still be able to function, providing a path for the flow of vital information between decision centers. During most of the 1970s and 1980s, the Internet was used primarily by academics in institutions of higher education to exchange and share data using early software versions of email. Instead of using a dedicated communication line between a single sender and receiver, as the telephone system did, the network made use of a technology called packet switching. Messages were broken into packets or parts, with various identification tags carrying data such as the computer addresses of the senders and receivers, error control information, and sequencing information attached to each part of the actual message. In order for the system to work properly, every packet had to use a standard set of identification tags and codes, which were known as protocols. The protocols that allow today's Internet to work properly are called TCP/IP. The World Wide Web, or simply the Web, is a part of the Internet that allows users to locate and view multimedia content such as audio, visual, text, and animation material using a web browser. The most recognized part of the Internet, the World Wide Web has its own set of protocols that allows easy-to-use graphics browsers to link users to multimedia files at remote locations. Web browsers are software programs that obey TCP/IP protocols, allowing the transmission of multimedia content.

2. Examine the primary components of the Internet infrastructure: computers, devices, and related technologies.

The Internet infrastructure comprises many different types of computers and other components. The system is able to function because of the many established protocols that are built into both software and hardware. Hardware manufacturers and software developers choose to produce products that support (understand) some kinds of data using certain protocols and not others. The Internet infrastructure is currently made up of five primary components: backbones, digital switches (routers), servers, point of presents (POPs), and finally individual (client) users' devices, which are generally connected to the Internet through telephone modems, DSL and ISDN lines, and cable television modems. The backbones are the mainline telecommunications channels of the Internet, built with high-capacity fiber-optic cables that move data at the speed of light. Digital switches are really specially designed computers that move data from one line to another. Digital switches that are connected to more than one backbone and are able to decide the direction in which to pass traffic are called routers. Smaller-scale users such as individuals and small businesses who connect through an ISP like AOL do so through another special switch called a POP, or point of present. Although recent developments have improved data transfer speeds, transmission in this last leg of the Internet—referred to as the last mile—is slow.

3. Understand how web sites are built and electronic information is distributed using specialized software.

Hypertext Markup Language, or HTML, is the principal programming language used to instruct computers how to display web page content such as images, colors, the size and position of letters, and so forth. Sun Microsystems' Java programming language produces rotation and movement of graphic images on users' computer screens, and Extensible Markup Language, or XML, allows for the customization of web documents by creating forms for describing and structuring data. Both Java and XML code can be embedded within an HTML document. Although programming code can be written to create web pages using HTML and other languages, many easier-to-use program editors have been developed to allow users to generate the necessary coded instructions that are understood by computers.

4. Describe the business opportunities that are emerging as a result of the convergence of technologies.

Convergence of technologies refers to the idea that a variety of technologies such as telecommunications, computers, television, and radio, will eventually merge in such a way that access to them and their content will be available through a range of devices in a multitude of environments. Eventually, e-books, journals, television programs, movies, games, and other forms of entertainment will be delivered to hand-held devices, home entertainment centers, or any other device connected to the Internet on a demand basis.

REVIEW QUESTIONS

1. Explain the idea behind packet switching.
2. What are protocols?
3. Define TCP/IP and explain how these protocols control the movement of data on the Internet.
4. What is a browser, and what does it do?
5. What are clients and servers?
6. What are routers and switches?
7. What are PDAs?
8. What is meant by convergence of technologies?

DISCUSSION QUESTIONS

1. Describe the key historical developments that contributed to creating the Internet.
2. Discuss the importance of speed and bandwidth for developments in the Internet.
3. What are the important concepts to keep in mind when designing a web site for PDAs?
4. How do you think the convergence of technologies will change television?

Building Skills for Career Success

EXPLORING THE INTERNET

The Internet has many good sites that provide information about developing technologies and the Internet. For example, the ISOC (Internet SOCiety) web site, located at **www.isoc.org/internet-history/#Introduction**, provides several historical overviews of the Internet. The ISOC is a professional membership society with more than 150 organizational and 6,000 individual members in over 100 countries. In addition, the W3C (World Wide Web Consortium) web site, located at **www.w3.org**, provides, among other things, descriptions of the technologies that are currently in popular use and information about emerging Internet technologies.

ASSIGNMENT

1. Explore the ISOC web site at **www.isoc.org/internet-history/#Introduction** and summarize the highlights of one historical overview that is made available there.
2. Explore the W3C web site at **www.w3.org** and describe one of the topic areas listed there.

DEVELOPING CRITICAL THINKING SKILLS

The convergence of technologies opens the door to greater opportunities to develop new products and services for current and new customers. For example, *Business Week* magazine has a special online edition, **www.businessweek.com**, that is accessible only to its print subscribers. Consider some of the possible ways in which the publishers of *Business Week* can reach customers through wireless devices and in tandem with interactive television programming.

ASSIGNMENT

1. What product or service would you suggest that *Business Week* develop for delivery through hand-held devices?
2. How should this product or service be sold? Explain why this method would work best.

BUILDING TEAM SKILLS

Many college students were quick to recognize the value of owning their own laptop computer and have also rapidly adopted cell phones with text messaging and other hand-held wireless devices. Using your team as a focus group, explore the appeal of owning wireless devices.

ASSIGNMENT

1. Report which device is most popular among the group members and the reasons given.
2. Report how your team would approach selling this device to those group members who have not yet acquired it. For instance, would some sort of free-service promotional period help get subscribers to sign on?

RESEARCHING DIFFERENT CAREERS

Many careers in e-business involve selling products and services. Often sales representatives need to be able to explain how the products they are selling would solve a customer's problems, reduce costs, or increase productivity. Representatives need not have very advanced technical knowledge in order to be successful; however, they should be capable of understanding and explaining to customers how a product functions and of relating its value to the customer's needs. Select an e-business product or service that you have some experience with, such as a Blackberry or Palm Pilot. Research the key product characteristics that would interest a potential buyer by exploring web sites that promote the product or those that simply provide information for buyers.

ASSIGNMENT

1. Describe a buyer who you think would be interested in the product and explain why you believe this to be true.
2. Which buyer needs would the product help to satisfy?
3. What would you say to a potential buyer to persuade him or her to buy the product?

IMPROVING COMMUNICATION SKILLS

Research some of the electronic products and services that we have discussed in this chapter by visiting the web sites of their manufacturers and competitors. Suppose you were asked to present a summary of the key characteristics of each group of products by listing the advantages and disadvantages of adopting this type of product, alternative competing products, and costs.

ASSIGNMENT

1. Create a grid with the various categories, such as laptop computer, cell phone, wireless text messaging, and interactive television, in the first column.
2. Then create column titles that highlight the principal characteristics of each product and fill in the grid with descriptive details.
3. Now present an oral report to your class, using the grid as your guide.

Exploring Useful Web Sites

These web sites provide information related to the topics discussed in the chapter. You can learn more by visiting them online and examining their current data.

1. The hand-held wireless industry's current leading messaging product, the Blackberry, is produced by Research In Motion (RIM) (**www.rim.com**). Palm (**www.palm.com**), Motorola (**www.motorola.com**), and other firms produce a variety of competing wireless products.

2. Paul Baran, an engineer employed by the Rand Corporation (**www.rand.org**), stands out among early contributors to the development of the Internet. Linux (**www.linux.org**) is a popular Unix-like operating system that was developed voluntarily by programmers and is distributed free around the world. IBM, Sun Microsystems, and Hewlett-Packard are some of the better-known backers that make their contributions to the open source code freely known through web sites like the Gnome Foundation (**www.gnome.org**). Firms like Red Hat (**www.redhat.com**) and VA Linux Systems (**www.valinux.com**) sell their clients customized solutions that use the Linux kernel, or core software program code.

3. Sites like **http://geocities.yahoo.com/home/** provide free access to simple tools for producing your own web pages.

4. Broadcast.com (**www.broadcast.com**) is a good source for connection to webcasting content. Generic Media Inc. (**www.genericmedia.com**) can convert any video into ten formats and any downloading speed.

5. Microsoft's FrontPage (**www.microsoft.com/frontpage/**), the leading web site creation and management tool, requires a minimal amount of user programming knowledge.

6. The ISOC (Internet SOCiety) web site, located at **www.isoc.org/internet-history/#Introduction**, provides several historical overviews of the Internet. The W3C (World Wide Web Consortium) web site, located at **www.w3.org**, provides, among other things, descriptions of the technologies that are currently in popular use and information about emerging Internet technologies.

7. Microsoft's .NET (**www.microsoft.com/net**) project is the development of an Internet-based solution that integrates the accessibility of Microsoft applications by all sorts of devices.

Ethical, Legal, and Social Concerns

Chapter 4

INSIDE e-BUSINESS
Zero-Knowledge Systems Inc.—Providing Privacy and Security Online

Zero-Knowledge Systems Inc. (**www.zeroknowledge .com**), of Montreal, Canada, is the leading provider of Internet privacy technologies and services for consumers and businesses. Its current version of its Freedom software, available as a free download over the Internet (**www.freedom.net**), provides users with the ability to create their own personal firewall to protect their computer from unwelcome intrusion while they are connected to the Internet; a form filler that saves them the trouble of entering common information like passwords and identification each time they register at a new site or buy something; a cookie manager that controls unauthorized surveillance of their Internet activities, such as sites visited and information entered; an ad manager that filters out unwanted advertisements as they browse and therefore speeds up screen generation of web pages; and finally a keyword alert feature that prevents any data, such as names, passwords, credit card numbers, or any other item that is recorded by the user, from being sent out unintentionally.

In addition, Zero-Knowledge provides consulting services for the development, implementation, and audit of privacy-enhancing solutions for businesses that enable these businesses to comply with privacy legislation, maximize customer relationships, and build consumer trust while respecting their customers' privacy. Zero-Knowledge believes that companies should simply attempt to create honest, open, and meaningful relationships with clients over the Internet rather than attempting to gather data in a clandestine manner through the unauthorized use of cookies and other privacy-violating tools.

In order to build a large customer base and achieve market dominance quickly, Zero-Knowledge distributes its basic product without charge over the Inter-

net and then supplements its free software with a modest fee-based package. For about $50 annually, users can take advantage of Zero-Knowledge's encryption and distribution service, which allows them to establish *nyms,* or substitute anonymous identities that are known only to them. In effect, an online user can visit any web site, shop online, or exchange email under several different names. Advocates argue that this feature enhances free speech and the exchange of ideas, particularly in chat rooms, because the identity of the speaker is shielded and so he or she need not be concerned with retribution or with the consequences of expressing ideas and opinions in a public forum.

What makes this service controversial, though, is the facility this same software affords to unethical and even illegal actions by motivated individuals who take advantage of the identity protection. The irony is that a product that was created to protect Internet users from unscrupulous individuals online or to allow users to avoid unwanted participation in online data collection and corporate consumer profiling strategies can also assist criminals, terrorists, hatemongers, and other undesirables to function anonymously online. Furthermore, this sort of software can help them evade law enforcement agencies' and Internet service providers' efforts to control their use of the Internet and thus can abet their undesirable behaviors. The efforts of law enforcement agencies to prevent crime will clearly be handicapped if they are unable to trace online exchanges. However, this ability to shield one's identity is a vital communications tool for political dissidents in undemocratic countries, informants who wish to remain anonymous in order to protect themselves from retaliation, and possibly even victims of abuse. Privacy and encryption software like that developed by Zero-Knowledge is likely to continue to receive more government study and popular debate as we attempt to balance the needs of societies and the legitimate rights of individuals to protect their freedom and privacy.[1]

self-regulated behavior
The idea that individuals and firms generally police themselves by choosing to do things that, in their view, are ethically correct and to avoid doing things that are not.

In addition to the complex mix of environmental forces (presented in Chapter 2) that can influence e-business planning and practice, managers must also deal with the special circumstances of operating in a new frontier—a world without geographic borders or much in the way of governmental or other organizational control or regulation. For better or worse, the cyberworld of e-business is an emerging industry, presenting great beneficial opportunities for businesses and customers, but with equally great concerns about social behaviors. Those are for the most part **self-regulated behaviors,** meaning that individuals and firms generally police themselves by choosing to do things that, in their view, are ethically correct and to avoid doing things that are not.

Gradually, global standards are emerging. For instance, the U.S.–based Better Business Bureau web site, located at **www.bbbonline.org/intl/code.asp**, provides an international code of ethical behaviors that was developed jointly with the Federation of European Direct Marketing (FEDMA) and the Association of European Chambers of Commerce. The site promotes a trademark that identifies member businesses that adhere to the organization's rules of conduct. By organizing and creating an international symbol, the group hopes to establish an instantly recognizable sign that can reassure buyers who are dealing with firms online. The BBBonLine web site provides a variety of information related to ethical online behavior and how users can file complaints if they believe that they have been mistreated.

This chapter will explore the ethical, legal, and social concerns related to e-business and the unique and artificial social environment created by the Internet. In addition, the role of governments and the ideas of control and regulation of Internet activity will be examined, as well as privacy, security, copyright, trademark, crime, and taxation issues.

A Framework for Understanding Ethical, Legal, and Social Behavior

ethics
The study and evaluation of what constitutes proper or correct behavior as defined by a community of people.

The ethical, legal, and social environmental forces that are at work in e-business can be explored using the same basic models that apply to all businesses, regardless of whether or not they have any connection to the Internet. The general framework for approaching these subjects and making judgments about individual and organizational behaviors begins with an examination of ethics. **Ethics** is the study and evaluation of what constitutes proper or correct behavior as defined by a community of people. In other words, if the answer to the question "Is this behavior acceptable to the people here?" is yes, then, ethically speaking, the behavior meets the moral standards established by the community.

Communities develop a sort of continuum, or scale, of ethical behaviors, with behaviors being viewed as tending toward higher or lower levels on that continuum. In other words, people make judgments as to whether a specific behavior is more or less ethical than other behaviors and position that behavior in their minds relative to those other behaviors. Specific behaviors that are deemed to be at the higher end of the scale, and the individuals and firms that engage in them, may be regarded as being more *socially responsible* and beneficial for the community as a whole, whereas those behaviors that cross the line set by government legislation may even be *illegal.* In between these limits are behaviors that are judged by the community to be *ethical* but of no special benefit to the community and those that are seen as *unethical,* but are still legal. Figure 4.1 illustrates the scale of ethical behavior and the community evaluation label attached to specific behaviors.

Understanding the Ethical Decision-Making Process

Whether we are examining the behavior of an individual or an organization, we must always remember that only people can actually make a decision and behave in some way. Behind the anonymity of organizational identities are the people who run those organizations. The question we will attempt to answer next is how people make decisions of an ethical nature, whether on behalf of an organization they represent or simply for themselves as users of services available on the Internet.

Figure 4.2 illustrates the three primary factors that influence an individual's ethical decision-making process. The first of these factors, and perhaps the most influential, is the *individual* him- or herself. Who and what an individual is, ethically speaking, will determine how that individual processes information and ultimately decides how to behave. An individual with strong ethical values and moral judgment enters the decision-making process equipped differently from someone at the opposite end of the moral character scale. However, we also must recognize that individuals make decisions within the context of a social situation in which they are also subject to the influences of *social environmental factors,* such as their peers, coworkers, family, and general community. Finally, we recognize that an individual's decision to behave in some manner is subject to the *opportunity* available to that individual. Someone who is alone on a desert island will have little opportunity to embark on many behaviors that might be ethically

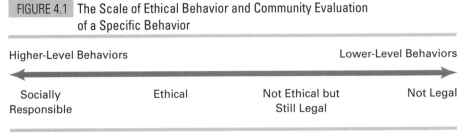

FIGURE 4.1 The Scale of Ethical Behavior and Community Evaluation of a Specific Behavior

Higher-Level Behaviors   Lower-Level Behaviors

Socially   Ethical   Not Ethical but   Not Legal
Responsible   Still Legal

Communities judge whether a particular behavior is more or less ethical than other behaviors. Highly ethical behaviors are considered socially responsible and positive, whereas lower-level behaviors may even be illegal as defined by the community.

FIGURE 4.2   Primary Factors Influencing the Ethical Decision-Making Process

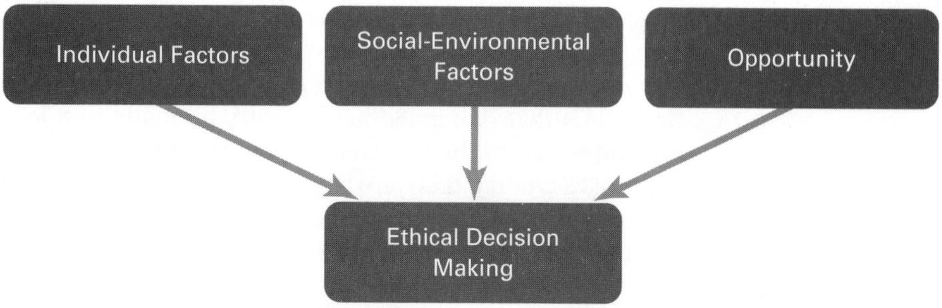

```
┌──────────────────┐   ┌──────────────────┐   ┌──────────────────┐
│ Individual Factors│   │ Social-Environmental│  │   Opportunity    │
│                  │   │     Factors      │   │                  │
└──────────────────┘   └──────────────────┘   └──────────────────┘
          ↘                    ↓                    ↙
                ┌──────────────────────┐
                │  Ethical Decision    │
                │      Making          │
                └──────────────────────┘
```

questionable. As religious leaders are apt to tell their congregants, no one worries what you will do while inside the house of God—the problems begin once you leave and face the temptations offered by the greater society outside.

Let's look at an example of how decision making might be influenced by each of these three factors and how these influences might be changed. Suppose we consider someone who would be considered a typical representative of North American culture and social values—someone who knows the basic rules of right and wrong as defined by the North American community and routinely tries to live by them. While at his place of work, he notices that most employees use their computers to reply to personal email, shop for products, and surf the Internet for questionable entertainment during the workday. No one in the firm has ever been reprimanded for these behaviors, even though the firm has a policy against employee use of its high-speed Internet connection for anything but business purposes. The culture of the firm supports a relaxed social environment, and employees often forward instant pop-up messages to one another during the day. Some of these might disturb the receiver's concentration and undermine his or her productivity. The individual we introduced at the beginning of this scenario gradually finds himself falling into the same pattern of behavior as his coworkers. He recognizes that his behavior is somewhat unethical and not particularly socially responsible, but apparently it is not illegal. His decision to follow the crowd and do what everyone seems to do is a result of his own individual character, the social environmental influences at the workplace, and the opportunity made available by his employer.

To change the level of ethical behavior of this or other employees, one or more of the three factors in the current equilibrium would have to change. First, it might be possible to strengthen the moral character of the individual and other employees so that they would resist the temptation to violate the company policy concerning Internet usage. The firm might seek out and screen for employees who it believes will be of the highest moral character to start with. Training programs covering what the firm considers to be right and wrong decisions can be launched. Second, making it known that the behavior is no longer acceptable can change the social environment and culture. Managers might issue reprimands to employees, saying that although the firm tolerated this behavior in the past, it will not do so in the future. To be credible and to have any validity with employees, this change must be adopted companywide and be applied without exception. Finally, the firm might choose to reduce the opportunities available to employees to engage in undesirable behaviors. For instance, a software program can be installed on the firm's LAN that demands that an entry be made in a log before an employee is granted access to the Internet. Knowing that the web sites visited and the activity keystrokes entered there are being recorded and possibly analyzed for violation of the firm's policy is likely to reduce employees' abusive behaviors in the future.

Needless to say, each of these approaches to changing the ethical decision making of employees is itself ethically questionable. Many critics are alarmed by the possibility that people will begin to develop psychological disorders because of the fear engendered by continuous supervision and monitoring of their behaviors. Ultimately, a balance has to emerge that reflects both the needs of the firm to regulate the activities that are taking place under its auspices and the needs of individuals to feel free in an open society.

Behavior in Online Social Environments

We have established that the individual factors that define a person, the opportunity to take some action, and social environmental factors are the primary influences on that person's decision making and behavior. The many artificially created social environments that exist in cyberspace present special circumstances for social interactions between people and may contribute to behaviors online that would not occur if it were not for the artificial reality defined by the site. For example, some people will reveal personal information about themselves and others in an online chat room that they would never tell other people in a face-to-face setting. The online social environment of a chat room, which may encourage a false sense of privacy and security through the use of temporary online user identification names, tends to precipitate this sort of behavior. When someone joins a web site exchange identified only as Bob from New Jersey, he may feel at liberty to say and do things that he might not say and do if his true identity were not shielded.

The web site chat room gives people an opportunity to behave in any way they choose. Simply put, people have an invitation to change their traditional *persona* (the face that they normally show the world) when they are online, and even if they do not do so, the effect of being online automatically changes them to some degree. Thus, they may buy things, say things, and do things that they otherwise would not buy, say, or do because of the effect of being in the virtual environment created by the Internet. None of this should be surprising. People behave differently when they are on vacation, at a party, or watching a baseball game in a stadium with thousands of other fans. The social environment that people are in—whether it is a real environment or one created in cyberspace—affects who they are at that particular moment and creates opportunities for behaviors that might not exist in other situations.

e-Business Insight

Can Socially Undesirable Online Behaviors Be Stopped?

Many people have concerns about how easily the Internet can be used to enable what they consider socially undesirable behaviors, such as online gambling and the distribution of adult entertainment. Together, these areas represent by far the greatest proportion of Internet commercial activity. The convenience and anonymity provided by the Internet are clearly the primary factors that facilitate and encourage individual decisions to become involved.

According to a Media Metrix study, 30 percent of Internet users, almost 85 percent of them men, visit adult entertainment sites each month (however, Nielsen/NetRatings reports that the figure is only 16 percent). Control and regulation are complicated by the fact that web sites may be located anywhere in the world, beyond the reach of law enforcement officials in North America. For example, the World Sports Exchange (**www.wsex.com**), the largest sports gambling web site, is located in Grand Cayman Island, and although many of its gaming activities are illegal in the United States, players can access the site with a credit card or establish an account, making control by American authorities next to impossible. In the end, without a technology to control access to foreign web sites, no government agency can hope to control what individuals choose to do on the Internet.[2]

As might be expected, a variety of issues involving privacy and the opportunity to distribute ethically questionable content and engage in ethically questionable online behaviors are likely to continue to be of concern for the foreseeable future. Most ISPs and browsers allow users to block out URLs that are identified as adult in nature, and many chat rooms are supervised so that unacceptable language or behavior can be stopped. Nonetheless, given the openness of the Internet and the relative absence of regulation, except that exercised by individuals, firms, and ISPs, each participant online will have to develop her or his own strategies for handling the difficult ethical challenges presented by the Internet.

Privacy and Confidentiality Issues

A questionable ethical practice in cyberspace is the unauthorized access to and use of information discovered through computerized tracking of users once they are connected to the Internet. There are several ways to collect data with and without the knowledge of the user, including the placing of cookies, analysis of log-file records, and data mining of customer transactions and registration records.

cookie
A small piece of software code that may allow the sender to track which pages the user visits on the site and how long the user stays at any particular page.

Cookies Track Online Behavior

A user who visits a web site may unknowingly receive or willingly accept as a condition for entry what is euphemistically referred to as a cookie. A **cookie** is a small piece of software code that may allow the sender to track which pages the user visits on the site and how long the user stays at any particular page. However, a cookie that is left on the user's computer may also continue to track the sites on the Internet that the user subsequently visits and report that information back to the site that placed the cookie. Although this ability can provide valuable information about the customer as she or he browses through an online mall, it can also be viewed as an invasion of privacy, especially since the customer may not even be aware that these movements are being monitored and analyzed.

Generally speaking, ethical web site managers will inform users as soon as they access a web site that a cookie is going to be installed on their computer and give them the choice of opting out of the offer. Cookies are often presented as shopping agents that will help users as they explore the site and, as such, may appear innocent enough. Because the cookie is software and must be recorded on the user's computer, however, the browser will display a message alerting the user to the fact that the site is attempting to write something and ask the user's permission before it allows the transfer to proceed. When there is any doubt as to the security involved, it is best to err on the side of conservatism and to refuse to download any content that might appear to be questionable. As a last resort, users can employ their browser to search the designated cookie storage area on their hard drive to locate cookies that may be residing on their computer. The cookies can then be deactivated or removed.

Surveillance and Analysis of Log-File Records

According to research by the University of Denver's Privacy Foundation Workplace Surveillance Project, more than one-third of the 40 million U.S. employees who work online—about 14 million—are under continuous surveillance by their employers, using commercially available software. Given that the average annual cost of this software is only $5.25 per employee, the number of employees who are under surveillance is likely to increase, and the debate over how much employers are ethically and legally entitled to monitor employee behavior online, versus an individual's right to privacy, is likely to intensify. The Privacy Foundation study suggests that at the very least, employers need to disclose and publicize the level of surveillance to employees and consider the corporate motivation for monitoring employees' behavior. The reason that surveillance is likely to grow is the availability at low cost of software that allows employers to monitor their employees' online actions easily. The opportunity to monitor behaviors is there, and so it is done—regardless of whether it is really productive in any way.[3]

log-file records
Files that store a record of the web sites visited.

Monitoring an employee's **log-file records,** which record the web sites visited, may be intended to help employers police unauthorized Internet use on company time; however, the same records can also give the firm the opportunity to observe what otherwise might be considered private and confidential information. This is especially true when a firm does not have a policy restricting personal use of the firm's computer resources on company time. Many firms might consider occasional personal use of the firm's LAN facilities to be an employee benefit that costs the firm little and can in fact produce greater employee satisfaction and motivation at work.

Data Mining Customer Transactions and Records

data mining

The practice of searching through data records looking for meaningful and strategically useful information.

Data mining refers to the practice of searching through data records looking for meaningful and strategically useful information. Customer registration forms typically require a variety of information before a user is given access to a site. When this is combined with customer transaction records, data mining analysis can provide what might be considered private and confidential information about individuals or groups. For example, suppose a web site offering free access to health information requires users to fill out a detailed registration form before they are granted a user identification and password. As a result of this voluntary disclosure, web site operators can easily uncover correlations between users' demographic factors, such as age and gender, and the specific health topics and issues that interest them. The web site operators could then conceivably sell this marketing intelligence to pharmaceutical firms. The information sold might suggest that there is a high level of interest in a particular type of medication that the firm manufactures among, say, a particular group of people living in Michigan. Subsequently, advertising campaigns and other marketing decisions might be changed because the firm is aware of this information.

Advocates for better control of how information about users is collected and distributed to interested third parties such as businesses point to the potential misuse of information—intentionally or otherwise. For example, if an individual frequents a web site that provides information about a life-threatening disease, an insurance company might refuse to insure this individual, thinking there is a higher risk associated with someone who wants more information about this disease. Perhaps the individual does have the disease, or thinks that she might, but perhaps she is writing a research paper for a school project or has been asked to look into this by someone she knows who does not know how to search the Internet properly. Sometimes, a little bit of information can be dangerous and can do damage to an individual. This risk is compounded if the information is incorrect or misinterpreted.

Industry Self-Regulation

To help deal with this issue and to support industry self-regulation, the U.S. Federal Trade Commission (FTC) approved the formation of the Network Advertising Initiative (NAI) in 1999. The NAI, which is made up of over 90 percent of Internet advertisers, including the industry leaders DoubleClick (**www.doubleclick.com**) and 24/7 Media (**www.247media.com**), was established to set rules and guidelines for the collection and use of personal data. The NAI prohibits the collection of personal data from health and financial services web sites that individuals are likely to visit. However, the NAI permits the cross-referencing of personal and web-collected data, provided that the user is informed that this is taking place and is allowed access to his or her records. In line with the NAI guidelines, browser software such as Microsoft's Internet Explorer is programmed to routinely prevent cookies from collecting user information without first receiving user permission through a pop-up window. By requiring the consent of users and making the process somewhat more open to scrutiny, the NAI has helped make online data collection more ethical than it used to be and lends support to the argument that the Internet can regulate itself without undue government interference.

The ability to collect and analyze personal data is critical for the industry if it is going to participate in the competition for advertisers' spending, and so it must learn to do this ethically. The great advantage of the Internet is its interactive communication features, which allow third-party vendors of products to target advertisements and other promotional messaging to small niche markets. Just as television is a mass communication medium for the delivery of messages that appeal to relatively large audiences, the Internet is attempting to carve a position in the communications industry by identifying smaller niche markets that could not be reached economically through television or other mass media and delivering highly specific and timely information to those markets. In order to achieve this position, Internet-based firms will need to analyze personal data in order to cross-reference products and services with perceived needs and wants. We will explore this topic and other marketing-related issues in Chapter 9.

Security Concerns and Cybercrime

According to research conducted by Computer Security Services Inc., 85 percent of the firms surveyed had detected online security breaches during the previous year.[4] For all intents and purposes, the Internet remains an unregulated frontier. Therefore, both individuals and business users must be cognizant of the security risks and dangers that they may encounter online.

Internet-Facilitated Fraud

In addition to the risks associated with the unauthorized use of data collected through the Internet, individual users and businesses must watch for criminal activities, including fraud and larceny. Because the Internet allows easy creation of web sites, access from anywhere in the world, and anonymity for participants, it is almost impossible to know with certainty that the web site, organization, or individuals that you believe you are interacting with are what they seem.

Consider these simple examples of fraud, which will help to illuminate the risks to unsuspecting users and illustrate how easy it is to orchestrate misrepresentations online.

First, an individual who is intent on perpetrating fraud can build a web site that falsely presents him- or herself as, say, a legitimate charitable organization dedicated to raising funds for some worthy cause. Through various online promotional efforts. such as email campaigns and banner advertising, unsuspecting individuals may be enticed to make a quick donation to the cause by entering their credit card information in an online form that is conveniently displayed on the web site or by putting a check in the mail, typically addressed to a post office box. In the former case, the web site operators are now in a position to make further illegal use of the credit card information that is now in their possession before their fraud is uncovered and authorities shut down their credit card processing capability. In any case, they may well be able to keep the donations.

A second type of fraud that is facilitated by the Internet occurs when a web site offers to sell products at an unbelievably low price, but never delivers the products, even though it collects the funds. By the time authorities are made aware of the fraud, the web site operators have usually abandoned the site and set up another that promises to deliver some other low-risk common product, such as a CD or magazine subscription. These scenarios are similar to older-style mail fraud but are more complex and difficult to control because fraudulent web sites can be set up anywhere in the world, and will often be located in areas where the authorities are reluctant to interfere with the operators.

Although online auction fraud at sites like eBay and Yahoo! occurs only rarely (less than one one-hundredth of one percent of all eBay auctions result in any confirmed case of fraud), both the Internet Fraud Commission Center and the nonprofit National Consumers League reported to a congressional committee investigating Internet fraud that auction web sites were by far the most common targets of the complaints they receive. The most popular form of fraud, and one that is difficult for auction web site operators to control, is called *shilling;* this is the bidding up of the price by people who have no intention of buying the item. These fraudulent bidders may be either the vendor or people working in cahoots with the vendor. All of the web site operators attempt to protect the integrity of their auctions by insuring transactions and monitoring activity closely. As always, *caveat emptor* (let the buyer beware) is good advice to follow, whether on the Internet or not.[5]

Network Security and Encryption

In addition to the fraudulent web site schemes that are clearly visible to users and can be avoided through investigation, businesses and individual users must also guard against nonvisible intrusion into their computer systems and the theft of data, passwords, credit card numbers, and so forth by electronic means.

In the past, businesses created **private networks,** which were secure LAN systems that were closed to outside access. Only computers that were actually connected to the private network by wires could access the information there. The only real concern was that someone with access to the system, such as an employee, might violate the system security, copy information, and remove it from the business's premises without authorization. Today, with the need to connect outside users such as customers, sales representatives, and suppliers to the firm's system, **virtual private networks (VPNs)** extend the firm's private network using secure third-party vendors' services and **encryption systems** that scramble data that are sent over the Internet.

The technological basis for a growing number of popular encryption systems today is referred to as **public-key cryptography.** The system relies on two *keys* or *codes* for **encrypting** (locking) and **decrypting** (unlocking) data transmitted by a

private networks
Secure LAN systems that are closed to outside access.

virtual private networks (VPNs)
Software-generated extensions of a firm's real private network using secure third-party vendors' services and encryption systems.

encryption systems
Systems that scramble data that are sent over the Internet.

public-key cryptography
A form of encryption that relies on two keys or codes for encrypting (locking) and decrypting (unlocking) data transmitted by a sender to a receiver.

encrypting
Locking data sent between a sender and receiver.

decrypting
Unlocking data sent between a sender and receiver.

sender to a receiver. Each party has a pair of keys, one of which is publicly available and the other of which is private. Both keys are needed to encode and decode data. The sender uses the receiver's public key to encrypt a message, and the receiver uses its private key to decrypt the message. Should an intruder capture data while in transit, that intruder would not be able to unlock the data without both keys. Public keys are also the basis for **digital signatures,** which are used to authenticate the sender of data.

To alleviate consumer concerns about online purchasing, the major credit card organizations like MasterCard and Visa have instituted various programs to protect cardholders against fraudulent use of their cards on the Internet. In addition, the effort to develop stronger encryption systems that can help prevent the theft and fraudulent use of credit card and other information continues to receive a great deal of attention. For example, the **secure electronic transaction (SET)** encryption process (**www.setco.org**), which was developed by MasterCard, Visa, IBM, Microsoft, and Netscape, prevents merchants from ever actually seeing any transaction data, including the customer's credit card number. This is accomplished by creating a system that requires the merchant, the customer, and a trusted third-party holder of shared information to exchange partial data. The system also makes use of **digital wallets,** which, as the term suggests, store consumer information, such as a consumer's name, address, credit card numbers, and so forth, and enter this information automatically when the consumer shops online. This not only saves time by not requiring the consumer to input the same data each time another transaction takes place at a different web site, but also authenticates the buyer.

Agents, Viruses, and Spamming

One of the reasons many businesses are reluctant to open their computerized records to access through the Internet is the risk that some programmer might be able to breach the security firewalls set up to protect the firm from intrusion. A programming expert who is capable of writing code that will automatically seek out information on the Internet, known as an **agent,** is likely to also be capable of writing code that can venture into a firm's computer system and retrieve records, without ever leaving a trace indicating that it was there. Therefore, it is understandable that a part of the software industry that is dedicated to security and access control features has emerged. Some firms deal with the risk of intrusion by establishing separate Internet-accessible computers that are not connected to the rest of the firm's LAN. Others make use of hosting firms that provide advanced security features or choose to distribute only what would be considered noncritical data to users over the Internet.

Computer **viruses** are computer instructions designed to disrupt normal computer and software functions. Viruses or other forms of unwanted interference with computer operations can originate from anywhere in the world. Indeed, a software security industry has emerged to protect businesses and individuals from these risks in cyberspace. Norton's AntiVirus program, distributed by Symantec (**www.symantec.com**), and McAfee's VirusScan (**www.mcafee.com**) are two

---

digital signatures
Devices used to authenticate the sender of data.

secure electronic transaction (SET)
An encryption process developed by MasterCard, Visa, IBM, Microsoft, and Netscape that prevents merchants from ever actually seeing any transaction data, including the customer's credit card number.

digital wallets
Devices that store consumer information, such as a consumer's name, address, credit card numbers, and so forth, and enter this information automatically when the consumer shops online.

agent
Software code that will automatically seek out information on the Internet.

viruses
Computer instructions that are designed to disrupt normal computer and software functions.

worm
Computer instructions that penetrate and attach to a computer's operating system before releasing viruses that cause damage to files on a network.

well-known commercial products that help to screen out incoming files containing viruses, such as the infamous LoveBug that emerged in the spring of 2000.

The Sircam series, which first appeared in 2001, is an example of a **worm,** a program that penetrates and attaches itself to a computer's operating system before releasing viruses that cause damage to files on a network. Worms do not need to be attached to any program, such as email, in order to spread, making them even more difficult to avoid. As long as undesirable data can be easily sent out, viruses and other forms of online harassment will remain a security issue and a business opportunity for firms like Symantec and McAfee, which must continuously revise their software to deal with newly created viruses.

spamming
The sending of massive amounts of unsolicited email.

Although not a violation in the same sense as releasing a computer virus, **spamming**—the sending of massive amounts of unsolicited email—may also be considered, if not a security issue, then certainly an ethical issue. Sorting through what is viewed as *junk email* is if nothing else a waste of resources that can cost individuals time and their employers money. The Internet service provider EarthLink estimates that its members receive 300 million unsolicited commercial emails each month.[6] Most email software programs and firms' mail servers have many control features that allow an individual or firm to block mail from senders that are not recorded on a list or from senders that have been identified as undesirable. Furthermore, most ISPs provide screening capability for their customers, who may choose to block any mail or connections to web sites that the ISP considers to be adult or hateful in nature. We will revisit this issue as it relates to marketing campaigns in Chapter 9 and discuss how firms that want to use the communication power of the Internet in an appropriate and socially responsible manner can do so while respecting the rights of individuals to control the volume of information they are bombarded with.

Digital Property and Distribution Rights

copyright
The inherent right of owners to be the only ones permitted to replicate and distribute material that they have created or paid someone for the rights to distribute.

A major concern for businesses that use the Internet to distribute content is control of digital property that can easily be replicated and distributed over the Internet. The legal issue of **copyright,** or the inherent right of owners to be the only ones permitted to replicate and distribute material that they have created or paid someone for the right to distribute, is best illustrated by the problems facing the music and publishing industries.

Music and Publishing

The music and publishing industries have for a long time had to deal with new technologies that allowed individuals to make and distribute copies of a firm's property. In the recent past, the music industry had to contend with unauthorized replication and distribution of its content through audiotape and CD technologies. Now, with Internet technologies such as MP3 (**www.mp3.com**) and Napster (**www.napster.com**), anyone can digitize a song into a file and then send it to someone else, without ever paying the copyright holders.

As far as the industry is concerned, every copy of a song that is passed along for free on the Internet represents a loss of sales revenue from a customer who would otherwise have made a purchase. As a means of dealing with this intrusion, some music companies have begun to sign distribution contracts with firms like MP3 and Napster (which merged with Bertelsmann AG's BMG in 2002), in order to gain a better degree of control over the distribution of their content. Others have sought a solution by establishing a software mechanism of their own making that allows the distribution of music online but prevents its free distribution by those who are unauthorized. For example, MusicNet (**www.musicnet.com**), a service set up jointly by RealNetworks, AOL Time Warner, EMI Group, and Bertelsmann AG's BMG, and PressPlay (**www.pressplay.com**), owned by Sony and Vivendi Universal Music, were established to control legal distribution of the firms' content. According to research conducted by Jupiter Media Metrix, the online music industry will be worth over $6 billion by 2006, suggesting how financially significant the stakes are for the industry.[7]

Use of Names and Trademarks

cybersquatting
Establishing a web URL name that clearly should rightfully belong to someone else.

Consider the case of Kevin Spacey, the Academy Award–winning actor, who sued a firm that used his name and identity without his permission. Spacey accused the firm of **cybersquatting**—that is, establishing a web URL name that clearly should rightfully belong to someone else—when it created a web site called **www.kevinspacey.com**. Spacey claimed that the firm uses the names of famous people to link web surfers to the firm's commercial site, located at **www .celebrity1000.com**, and thereby drive up traffic at that site for its own benefit without the permission of the people who make this possible. Furthermore, he argued, association of his name with this firm's web site undermines his ability to market himself.[8]

Currently available technology makes it quite easy to copy and use a company name or recognized trademark, like McDonald's golden arches, without permission. Most firms post information about how their highly visible and recognizable names and trademarks may legally be used and under what circumstances links to their sites can be made. However, it should be stated that there are many people who see the Internet as an open and unregulated environment, and believe that no government or company should be able to control the distribution of information once it reaches the Internet. Given these sorts of security and legal issues, it is no wonder that some firms have been reluctant to open their doors too wide to the Internet public.

Government Regulation and Taxation

For the most part, government regulators view the Internet as just an extension of the regular business activity of firms operating in their jurisdiction. They see rules and regulations as applying to all businesses, even if they exist entirely or partially online. Therefore, when it comes to the collection of sales taxes on products sold online, you would think that firms would be responsible for collecting the appropriate sales taxes and then remitting them to local governments on the basis of where the customer is located. This is not the case, and although state and local governments are working toward a uniform sales tax policy for online sales, online vendors are legally treated like mail-order companies, which collect sales taxes only if they have a physical presence or nexus in the customer's state. American buyers are expected to pay local use taxes on products bought in other states, but the responsibility for doing this is the customer's, not the selling firm's. Canadian online vendors, however, are required to collect sales taxes and remit them to both federal and provincial governments, and American firms selling to Canadian buyers can either collect sales taxes for their customers and remit them to the appropriate governments or leave them uncollected until delivery, when they are paid directly to the delivery agent by the buyer.

The absence of tax collection obviously provides an unfair benefit to those firms that can take advantage of the current law. In order to prevent the loss of potentially huge amounts of sales tax revenue, a consortium of American states is presently working to develop a uniform sales tax system so that firms will not be able to avoid collecting taxes or gain a competitive advantage over traditional bricks-and-mortar firms that are located in jurisdictions that levy sales taxes. Today, with the existence of software services designed to identify the appropriate tax authorities and their respective tax rates based on the address that products are shipped to, there is little excuse for any firm's not collecting sales taxes and remitting them to the proper jurisdictions. The online tax-free holiday will be ending shortly.[9]

Government Regulation of Restricted Products

An interesting aspect of online business is the sale and distribution of restricted products such as pharmaceuticals. In most jurisdictions, a doctor's prescription for medication must be presented to a pharmacist, who then fills the order. The Internet allows anyone to buy medications online, in some cases with only a claim to a prescription and a credit card. As a result, pharmaceuticals can be bought illegally with relatively little difficulty and subsequently sold into the illicit drug market. Just as it is in the bricks-and-mortar pharmacy on Main Street, it is legally the responsibility of the online pharmacist to verify the validity of the order and to look for abusive patterns, such as doctors prescribing unusually large quantities of certain drugs for one patient. Although it should be emphasized that most firms attempt to conduct their online activity fairly and legally, the Internet presents a great opportunity for illegal activity, for which profits can be a major motivator. In the absence of stricter government enforcement, this is both a legal and an ethical issue that will become even more pronounced in the future as more firms migrate their traditional businesses to the Internet.

The U.S. Government Electronic Commerce Policy site, located at **www .ecommerce.gov**, is the definitive portal for current information and regulation

e-Business Insight
Using the Internet to Help Nonprofit Organizations

The Internet provides a variety of means for organizations to distribute information and share expertise. Nonprofit organizations face many similar difficulties that can be dealt with through Internet-based solutions like email and web sites. Nonprofit organizations are generally concerned with raising funds, maintaining databases of donor membership lists, engaging members in dialogue, and spreading their messages to nonmembers (advocacy campaigns). Unfortunately, most nonprofit organizations are small-scale local operations with limited budgets and are highly dependent on volunteer participants to get their work done. Spending on any technology might be questionable for organizations that need to be careful about how they use donor funds.

As an example of how the Internet can be used in a socially responsible way to benefit nonprofit organizations with limited budgets, consider TechRocks (**www.techrocks.com**) of Philadelphia, Pennsylvania. The Rockefeller Family Fund has underwritten the development costs for a variety of computer-based technology solutions and made them available for free to nonprofit organizations through this Internet site. More than 10,000 organizations have downloaded copies of eBase, a software program that manages donor information.[10]

And by using customer relationship management (CRM) software, United Way of Greater Toronto generated $1.5 million in pledges from employees who were targeted with intelligent CRM-selected email. The results from targeting individuals with smart messages based on analysis of their prior giving patterns and responses to questions were impressive. Donations increased by $300,000; more than 85 percent of donations were made online; the average pledge increased from $200 to $300; and returning donors using the online method gave 5 percent more than other donors. As a result, this CRM solution, which was developed and donated by the firm Delano Technology, will be employed by United Way in Boston, Philadelphia, and several other major centers.[11]

related to online business, both within the United States and internationally. Since U.S. commercial interests drive the vast majority of Internet business, it is understandable that the focus of legal attention is on the United States. Furthermore, the U.S. Department of Justice site, located at **www.usdoj.gov/criminal/cybercrime/compcrime.html**, provides more information about the effort to police cybercriminal activities.

Public Attitudes

As for the public's view, a major year-long study of American public attitudes about accountability on the Internet by the Markle Foundation, a nonprofit group that focuses on public policy and technology, suggests a desire for the creation of a national governing commission to ensure that Internet technologies reflect democratic decision-making values in the ways they deal with privacy, quality of information, and consumer protection issues. Although these surveys, which used telephone and online polling and focus group discussions, found widespread enthusiastic support for the Internet and positive attitudes toward it, more than half of those responding had concerns about the Internet because of pornography and privacy issues and wished there was a central authority that they could contact if they felt they were victims of online fraud or scams or had other Internet-related problems. Interestingly, however, although more than two-thirds said that they wanted government regulations to protect people, about 60 percent believed that Internet rules should be mostly developed and enforced by online businesses themselves.[12]

Conclusions

Socially responsible and ethical behavior on the Internet by both individuals and businesses is a major concern that has simply extended from the general social environment to the special virtual environment of cyberspace. The individual, social environment, and opportunity to engage in unethical or even illegal behavior are primary factors determining whether unethical behavior will take place. Unfortunately, the Internet provides a shelter of anonymity and detachment for both individuals and firms, which might suggest why certain behaviors have surfaced.

CASE STUDY

RETURN TO
INSIDE e-BUSINESS

The web site for Zero-Knowledge Inc., **www.zeroknowledge.com**, provides a variety of information about encryption processes, new products coming onto the market that use new encryption processes to assure protection of information, articles promoting the need for Internet users to educate themselves about privacy issues, and links to relevant web sites related to online security. Regardless of how convincing any promotional material might be however, the fact remains that eventually all coding systems are vulnerable to someone or some organization that is willing and able to break the code. Zero-Knowledge has demonstrated this fact itself by exposing weaknesses in computer components and popular software like Microsoft Office in order to further convince users of the need to use Freedom. Like vendors of security devices of many sorts, such as car alarms and dead-bolt locks, Zero-Knowledge is selling potential customers on the idea that security can be bought. But just as in the real world, there are reasonable limits to security that individuals must recognize and learn to live with in order to function.

ASSIGNMENT
1. What are your views on the need for using online security software?
2. Should the government be able to prevent a firm from selling this sort of shielding software in order to prevent criminals from using it?

Chapter Review

SUMMARY

1. Explore a framework for understanding the ethical, legal, and social concerns related to e-business and the online environment.

The ethical, legal, and social environmental forces that are at work in e-business can be explored using the same basic models that apply to all businesses, regardless of whether or not they have any connection to the Internet. The general framework for approaching these subjects and making judgments about individual and organizational behaviors begins with an examination of ethics. Communities develop a sort of continuum, or scale, of ethical behaviors, with behaviors being viewed as tending toward higher or lower levels on that continuum. Three primary factors determine ethical decision making: the individual, the social environment the individual is presently in, and the opportunity the individual has to behave in some manner. To change the level of ethical behavior, one or more of these three factors in the current equilibrium would have to change.

2. Discuss the concerns over privacy and confidentiality.

A questionable ethical practice in cyberspace is the unauthorized access to and use of information discovered through computerized tracking of users once they are connected to the Internet. There are several ways to collect data with and without the knowledge of the user, including the placing of cookies, analysis of log-file records, and data mining of customer transactions and registration records. Advocates for better control of how information about users is collected and distributed to interested third parties such as businesses point to the potential for the misuse of information—intentionally or otherwise. However, the ability to collect and analyze personal data is critical for the industry if it is going to participate in the competition for advertisers' spending, and so it must learn to do this ethically.

3. Examine security issues and cybercrime.

For all intents and purposes, the Internet remains an unregulated frontier in business. Therefore, both individuals and business users must be cognizant of the security risks and dangers that they may encounter online. In addition to the risks associated with the unauthorized use of data collected through the Internet, individual users and businesses must watch for criminal activities, including fraud and larceny. Because the Internet allows easy creation of web sites, access from anywhere in the world, and anonymity for participants, it is almost impossible to know with certainty that the web site, organization, or individuals that you believe you are interacting with are what they seem. To alleviate consumer concerns about online purchasing, the major credit card organizations like MasterCard and Visa have instituted various programs to protect cardholders against fraudulent use of their cards on the Internet.

4. Understand the special problems related to digital property, copyright, and distribution.

A major concern for businesses that use the Internet to distribute content is control of digital property that can easily be replicated and distributed over the Internet.

The legal issue of copyright, or the inherent right of owners to be the only ones permitted to replicate and distribute material that they have created or paid someone for the rights to distribute, is best illustrated by the problems facing the music and publishing industries. With today's Internet technology, such as MP3 and Napster, anyone can digitize a song into a file and then send it to someone else, without ever paying the copyright holders. As far as the industry is concerned, every copy of a song that is passed along for free on the Internet represents a loss of sales revenue from a customer who would otherwise have made a purchase.

5. Explore the regulatory role played by government and related issues such as cybercrime and taxation.

For the most part, government regulators view the Internet as just an extension of the regular business activity of firms operating in their jurisdiction. They see rules and regulations as applying to all businesses, even if they exist entirely or partially online. Therefore, when it comes to the collection of sales taxes on products sold online, you would think that firms would be responsible for collecting the appropriate sales taxes and then remitting them to local governments on the basis of where the customer is located. This is not the case, and although state and local governments are working toward a uniform sales tax policy for online sales, online vendors are legally treated like mail-order companies, which collect taxes only if they have a physical presence or nexus in the customer's state.

REVIEW QUESTIONS

1. Describe the scale of ethical behavior.
2. What is the connection between the scale of ethical behavior and community judgment about specific behaviors?
3. Describe the ethical decision-making process.
4. What is a cookie?
5. How is the use of a cookie a security and privacy issue?
6. What is data mining?
7. How is data mining a security and privacy issue?
8. What is spamming?
9. Explain what the term *digital property rights* means.
10. Explain the issue of taxation as it relates to the sale of products over the Internet.

DISCUSSION QUESTIONS

1. Discuss the difficulties facing employers that are trying to set and administer policies concerning ethical employee behaviors.
2. Using the ethical decision-making process model, describe how you might try to change current unethical behavior in an office environment. Explain your reasoning.
3. Discuss security issues and how they can be addressed.
4. How can digital property rights be protected?
5. What are the threats to digital property rights?
6. Discuss the role of government as it relates to the regulation and taxation of e-business.

Building Skills for Career Success

EXPLORING THE INTERNET

One of the security problems related to exchanges of documentation is confirming the identities of senders and receivers. To help solve this problem and expedite the development of e-business, the U.S. government has passed legislation for a digital authentication standard called *Digital Signature Standard* (DSA). You can learn more about this important development and other topics of concern related to security and government involvement at **www.itaa.org/infosec**.

ASSIGNMENT

1. What is a current hot topic discussed at this web site?
2. How would you describe government concerns about Internet security issues?

DEVELOPING CRITICAL THINKING SKILLS

According to Internet law expert Lawrence Lessig, a professor at Stanford University in California and author of the best-seller *Code and Other Laws of Cyberspace*, innovation and creativity are threatened by attempts to regulate intellectual property. Lessig states that before the digital age, copyrights were limited rights that expired in time and allowed a certain degree of fair use by others. However, technology, which is now capable of allowing individuals and organizations to freely create and distribute content as never before, can also be designed to block and control content forever through encoding software. As a result, the necessary creative good that comes from having content in the public domain is gradually becoming more and more restricted by legislation and technology made available by firms that wish to protect what they perceive as their rights. The problem that will eventually arise, says Lessig, is a decline in overall creativity as a result of the absence of freely available—public domain—content. Lessig argues that society needs to question the very notion of copyright in a digital age and points to Disney's use of classic writer Victor Hugo's *The Hunchback of Notre Dame.* Had copyright law prevented Disney's use of Hugo's work and other such works, the world would be without the animated creations that exist today.[13]

ASSIGNMENT

1. Do you agree or disagree with Lessig's arguments on copyright protection and its effect on creativity? Explain your thinking.
2. What would you consider a fair copyright arrangement for original works?

BUILDING TEAM SKILLS

In general, government-owned or government-controlled corporations have always been considered unfair competitors to regular businesses and an impediment to industry investment. After all, the argument goes, if a government agency is going to build a business and offer products or services free of charge or at subsidized rates, how can a for-profit business expect to compete? However, a model for a compromise solution between the Canadian government and the Internet industry may have been found by way of the creation of ebiz.enable (**www.ebiz.enable.ca**) and SourceCAN (**www.sourcecan.ca**). Ebiz.enable is an information web site clearinghouse where small and medium-sized businesses can find information about moving operational processes such as supply-chain management onto the Internet. SourceCAN is an umbrella public- and private-sector e-marketplace where Canadian firms can find domestic and international buyers and sellers of services and products, participate in virtual trade shows, post and view electronic catalogs, and use applications that support online procurement, supply-chain management, and logistics services—free of charge. The site encourages Canada's large private-sector business-to-business (B2B) sites, such as Bell Canada's BellZinc.com (**www.bellzinc.com**) and Toronto Dominion Bank's TD MarketSite.com (**www.marketsite.com**), to participate. Should buyers or sellers conclude a deal with a participant that does charge a fee, the fee is paid only to that participant—not to the operators of the SourceCAN site. The result, developed after consultations with business leaders in the field, is a one-stop site for those who wish to consult a large number of competitors all at once. Considering that the development costs were only C$450,000 for ebiz.enable and C$1.4 million for SourceCAN, the strategy might be a model for governments in countries where a lack of business investment to provide online information and services is impeding e-commerce development.[14]

ASSIGNMENT
1. Describe your group's perception of the ebiz.enable (**www.ebiz.enable.ca**) and SourceCAN (**www.sourcecan.ca**) web sites.
2. Discuss the idea of government's helping to expedite the development of the Internet and report your group's position.

RESEARCHING DIFFERENT CAREERS
According to the nonprofit organization DigitalEve (**www.digitaleve.com**), whose mission is to level the playing field and encourage women to enter traditionally male career fields in technology through local seminars and mentoring programs, and Jupiter Communications Inc., women look at the Internet differently from the way men do. Whereas women relate to the communications aspect of technology, men focus on the hardware technology. There are over 10,000 organization members who belong to twenty chapters of DigitalEve in North America, Europe, and Asia.[15]

ASSIGNMENT
1. Describe how the DigitalEve web site, **www.digitaleve.com**, appeals to women.
2. Are any of the strategies used on the web site just as applicable to men?

(continued)

IMPROVING COMMUNICATION SKILLS

Although out-of-court third-party arbitration is a well-established method for solving business disputes quickly, a Toronto, Ontario, law firm believes that its Internet-based software, NovaForum (**www.novaforum.com**), can provide an even faster alternative solution. Opposing parties to a dispute anywhere in the world follow an eight-step online process that leads them to a legally binding solution rendered by the law firm within 72 hours. The $2,500 cost is a far cry from the $50,000 that clients typically need to pay for an average of 600 hours of legal services. The firm's web site provides a free-access walk through a sample case study to illustrate the process for clients.[16]

ASSIGNMENT

1. Describe the steps involved in the sample case study presented on the web site.
2. Do you think the process is as fair as a face-to-face situation? Explain your thinking.

Exploring Useful Web Sites

These web sites provide information related to the topics discussed in the chapter. You can learn more by visiting them online and examining their current data.

1. Zero-Knowledge Systems Inc. (**www.zeroknowledge.com**) is the leading provider of Internet privacy technologies and services for consumers and businesses. Its current version of its Freedom software, available as a free download over the Internet (**www.freedom.net**), provides users with the ability to create their own personal firewalls and other features.

2. The Better Business Bureau web site, located at (**www.bbbonline .org/intl/code.asp**), details an international code of ethical behaviors developed jointly with the Federation of European Direct Marketing (FEDMA) and the Association of European Chambers of Commerce.

3. DoubleClick (**www.doubleclick.com**) and 24/7 Media (**www.247media.com**) are the industry's leading online advertisers.

4. The secure electronic transaction, or SET, encryption process (**www .setco.org**) was developed by MasterCard, Visa, IBM, Microsoft, and Netscape; it prevents merchants from ever actually seeing any transaction data, including the customer's credit card number.

5. Norton's AntiVirus program, distributed by Symantec (**www.symantec .com**), and McAfee's VirusScan (**www.mcafee.com**) are two well-known commercial products that help screen out incoming files that contain viruses.

6. With Internet technology such as MP3 (**www.mp3.com**) and Napster (**www.napster.com**), anyone can digitize a song into a file and then send it to someone else, without ever paying the copyright holders. MusicNet

(**www.musicnet.com**) and PressPlay (**www.pressplay.com**) were established to control the legal distribution of copyright content.

7. Kevin Spacey sued the firm at **www.celebrity1000.com** for using his name in the URL **www.kevinspacey.com** without his permission.

8. The U.S. Government Electronic Commerce Policy site, located at **www .ecommerce.gov**, is the definitive portal for current information and regulation related to online business, both within the United States and internationally. The U.S. Department of Justice site, located at **www.usdoj .gov/criminal/cybercrime/compcrime.html**, provides more information about the effort to police cybercriminal activities. To help expedite the development of e-business, the U.S. government has passed legislation for a digital authentication standard called *Digital Signature Standard* (DSA). You can learn more about this important development and other topics of concern related to security and government involvement at **www.itaa.org/infosec.**

9. The Canadian government and the Internet industry may have found a strategy for helping to boost Internet commerce through the creation of ebiz.enable (**www.ebiz.enable.ca**) and SourceCAN (**www.sourcecan.ca**). Ebiz.enable is an information web site clearinghouse where small and medium-sized businesses can find information about moving operational processes such as supply-chain management onto the Internet. SourceCAN is an umbrella public- and private-sector e-marketplace where Canadian firms can find domestic and international buyers and sellers of services and products, participate in virtual trade shows, post and view electronic catalogs, and use applications that support online procurement, supply-chain management, and logistics services—free of charge. The site encourages Canada's large private-sector B2B sites, such as Bell Canada's BellZinc.com (**www.bellzinc.com**) and the Toronto Dominion Bank's TD MarketSite.com (**www.marketsite.com**), to participate.

10. The World Sports Exchange (**www.wsex.com**), the largest sports gambling web site, is located in Grand Cayman Island, and although many of its gaming activities are illegal in the United States, players can access the site with a credit card or establish an account, making control by American authorities next to impossible.

11. TechRocks (**www.techrocks.com**) makes software such as eBase, a program for managing donor information, which is available for free to nonprofit organizations.

12. The mission of the nonprofit organization DigitalEve (**www.digitaleve .com**) is to encourage women to enter traditionally male career fields in technology through local seminars and mentoring programs.

13. The Internet-based software NovaForum (**www.novaforum.com**) can provide opposing parties to a dispute with an alternative method of obtaining a legally binding solution rendered by a law firm.

STRATEGIC BUSINESS PLANNING FOR THE INTERNET

Module II examines the strategic business planning process in greater detail. We focus our attention on the three key components of strategic planning: research, analysis, and the formulation of an e-business plan. First, in Chapter 5 we present a structure for organizing and understanding the variety of e-business models, and we discuss how each model serves to direct the entire organization in its search to generate revenues and create a competitive advantage online. In Chapter 6 we examine these activities from the point of view of strategists working at each of the three primary organizational levels of the firm: the corporate, division/strategic business unit, and operating/functional levels. In Chapter 7 we detail the research and information-gathering process, and then in Chapter 8 we explore online communication and user behaviors. The module provides a broad base of information about what e-business models and their strategies can help the firm to achieve and how they can be incorporated into the existing organization and business plan. Managerial details and operational implications of any e-business plan will be addressed in the third module.

Developing e-Business Models

Chapter 5

INSIDE
e-BUSINESS
Napster and MP3—Pioneers in Peer-to-Peer Exchanges Online

If predictions by Forrester Research Inc. of Cambridge, Massachusetts, are close to accurate, by the year 2005 about one-third of all Internet users will be employing peer-to-peer (P2P) computing services to exchange and store personal data. P2P computing software allows anyone with a computer that is connected to the Internet to share material directly with anyone else, without going through a central computer server. This material can include music, photographs, images, movies, and other content files that they have created themselves or acquired in some other way. Under the traditional Internet transfer structure, files are generally stored on huge servers and subsequently delivered to users (clients) on demand. If too many users request copies of files at the same time, the server can slow to a crawl and waiting for files to download can be exhausting, making the user question whether the time required to complete the process is worthwhile. P2P file exchanges are done directly between the sender and the receiver, without going through any central server. A directory listing files along with a short description of their content and their location on the Internet is made available through a server, but the actual file exchange is done directly between the users through specialized P2P software.

Napster Inc. (**www.napster.com**) of Redwood City, California, was an innovative start-up software development firm that was among the first P2P Internet businesses. P2P distribution systems like Napster's would probably not have been adopted so quickly had it not also been for the timely creation of another software product called Motion Picture Entertainment Group—Audio Layer 3, or MP3 for short, from San Diego, California–based MP3.com Inc. (**www.mp3.com**). MP3 software can compress an audio file by about a

factor of twelve and still maintain satisfactory audio quality when the music is reconstructed afterwards on a user's computer or MP3 player. Stated simply, MP3 substantially reduces the amount of data that needs to be stored and transferred and therefore the time required for downloading a song or other piece of entertainment content over the Internet. As a result, MP3 has emerged as the preeminent compression software for entertainment content distribution on the Internet.

In order to build a large user base quickly, Napster made its software available for free, following a strategy established by other Internet-based businesses such as web browsers Netscape Navigator and Microsoft Internet Explorer. At its peak, Napster boasted an international base of more than 50 million users. The theory was that in order to reach this expanding market, web site operators would eventually be obliged to buy the server version of Napster to enable them to manage directories and communicate with Napster users. Eventually, once a large enough level of market saturation was reached, fees for premium services could be introduced for Napster users and vendors, or site operators might simply charge membership fees to users of their directories.

Undoubtedly, many users attracted by the approach to content distribution taken by Napster and MP3 were drawn by the ability to retrieve copies of recorded music free of charge. Critics of P2P software argue that firms like Napster violate copyright law and prevent artists who produce entertainment content from controlling the legitimate sale and distribution of their products. Others see the entertainment industries as entering a new era in which the Internet will forever transform distribution and sales promotion, causing the industry giants to redesign their established business models. Traditionally, whoever controls the server controls the distribution of the files that are stored there. The producers of entertainment content such as music, movies, and television shows would like to maintain this structure in order to better control the sales of their property. However, P2P software changes all that, and instead facilitates the exchange of files with anyone who is willing to use this software and make content available to others over the Internet.

This sort of technology exemplifies the Internet's *democratization* of business by giving greater power to small businesses and individuals. For example, an artist, such as singer Alanis Morissette, who chooses to record a song and make it available on the Internet through Napster sees this technology as an additional strategic tool to help promote the sale of her CDs, attendance at her concerts, and her career in general. Unknown performers can use Napster to generate a following and build public awareness. Instead of relying on the recording industry to launch their careers, struggling performers, animators, and writers can take control of their own product in the hope of being discovered by larger globally distributed audiences. The challenge to many businesses, especially those in the media and entertainment industries, is to develop new strategies that take advantage of emerging technologies like Napster and the distribution power of the Internet.[1]

Although Internet software products like Napster present great opportunities for new ways of approaching business thinking, a very real problem arises for the entertainment industry when an unauthorized copy of a song is illegally posted for free distribution. The recording companies argue that when this happens, they and the artists lose revenue from customers who would otherwise buy the CD. However, recent research appears to suggest that although this may be true for some customers, the net result is a greater amount of purchasing overall. This suggests that perhaps potential customers use the Napster system or one of the many similar P2P systems now available to sample music before deciding to purchase it, so that it stimulates buying in much the same way as the free play of music on radio and television does. Perhaps Napster users simply regard the software as a radio-like distribution of free music. If the Internet and P2P computing service firms are in fact catalysts to an old-economy industry like the entertainment industry, then perhaps it is possible to both increase sales and offer the consumer the opportunity to explore content without purchasing it first.

In fact, the entertainment industry had similar concerns in the early 1980s when another new technology, videotape, first entered the consumer market. Today, the industry realizes that videotape simply opened up a new source of revenue through the sale and rental of films and television programming. Ways of exploiting P2P computing services are being explored, and strategic alliances between media groups suggest that the industry will have to recognize the need to change its business planning and work with the Internet, rather than trying to fight it. Indications from the recording industry are that it will begin its own sales and distribution over the Internet as soon as compression software can be developed that works as well as MP3 but does not allow duplication. Users might pay a certain amount for each file they download or a flat subscription fee that allows them to download an unlimited number of files. Products from Liquid Radio Inc.

and the Secure Digital Music Initiative (SDMI) are efforts in that direction. According to research by Jupiter Media Metrix, the online music industry will be worth over $6 billion by 2006. Currently, two main competitors have emerged: MusicNet (**www.musicnet.com**), which is supported by AOL Time Warner, Bertelsmann AG, and EMI Group, and PressPlay (**www.pressplay.com**), formed by Sony and Vivendi Universal Music. MusicNet was created to act as an intermediary to license the member firms' music to online services using RealNetworks' secure technology. And perhaps as a sign of things to come, in the summer of 2002, after declaring bankruptcy, Napster was absorbed into Bertelsmann AG. Bankruptcy was inevitable after court action by industry giants forced Napster to cease facilitating unauthorized content distribution.[2]

Changes, opportunities, and challenges to existing strategies, and discussions about how management should respond, are best understood when they are presented in an organizing structure. For instance, what researchers and business practitioners want to learn when they look at successes like AOL and Yahoo! and celebrated failures such as Boo.com and Pet.com is a simplified description of how the business was intended to work. To answer this fundamental question, they need information about how the firm planned to earn revenues, the sources of those revenues, the identity of target customers, pricing, promotion, and other strategies that were part of the overall plan. In this chapter, we will examine a structure and related terminology that allow us to organize and analyze information and approach e-business decision making in a methodical manner.

An Introduction to Business Plans and Models

business plan

A document containing detailed descriptions of the fundamental structure of the firm and the activities within it, including sources of revenue, the identity of target customers, pricing, promotion, and other strategies.

e-business plan

A business plan or part of a larger business plan that involves a firm's Internet business activities.

Detailed descriptions of the fundamental structure of the firm and the activities within it are organized and presented in the firm's **business plan.** If the firm is an Internet-based business, like Yahoo!, or if we are examining only the part of a firm that involves its Internet business activities, like those of the Walt Disney Company, we can refer to the document as the firm's **e-business plan.** We will use the two terms interchangeably here; however, learners should recognize that the insertion of "e-" before any business term generally implies that there is a connection to the Internet in some fundamental way. So e-marketing implies a focus on marketing activities related to the firm's e-business plan and so forth.

Developing the Business Plan

The business plan is the most detailed description of what individuals within the firm are doing and what the business is trying to achieve. It should be revised as conditions and circumstances demand. A fundamental change in market prices or competition should result in a response by the firm, and a descriptive explanation or rationale for the choices that are made should be in the business plan. This allows anyone who needs to know how and why managers are making their day-to-day decisions the way that they are to better understand them.

A solid business plan is necessary for serious discussions with anyone else who is interested in the firm, including potential partners, investors, lenders, customers, and employees. Obviously, business plans can be edited to suit the circumstances and the reader's needs; a document that is presented to a potential investing partner who is interested in joining the firm is not likely to contain the same information as a document that is presented to the firm's bank manager when the firm is applying for a loan. The needs of the reader are different in each situation, and the document should reflect these needs and cater to them appropriately.

Part of the aim of this textbook is to provide learners with all the necessary tools to build and maintain an e-business plan. The topics covered in this textbook are presented in a manner and sequence that allow them to be clearly understood independently but also recognized as contributions to an e-business plan. Appendix B presents a detailed guide for researching and preparing an e-business plan, as well as giving URLs for web sites, such as that of the U.S. Small Business Administration (**www.sba.gov/starting/indexbusplans.html**), that provide elaboration on business plan preparation. For now, though, Table 5.1 presents a brief overview of the key components of an e-business plan that is more suitable at this stage and will serve to structure our exploration of the topic.

TABLE 5.1   Basic Components of an e-Business Plan

1. *Cover Page:* The cover page should include the title of the document, the name of the firm, the authors of the report, the date, and any other descriptive information that highlights the intended audience and use of the report.
2. *Introduction:* The introduction should provide a basic description of the firm and the purpose of the report.
3. *Executive Summary:* The executive summary is written last and should contain the highlights of the entire report.
4. *Environmental Analysis:* This section of the report should examine all of the relevant external and internal environmental forces discussed in the first module of the text that can affect planning.
5. *e-Business Model:* This section should present a full description of the basic nature of the business and its primary revenue streams.
6. *Marketing:* Here the plan should expand on marketing-related details such as who the targeted customers are, what we know about their behavior, and so forth.
7. *Management and Organizational Issues:* This section should provide details such as who will do what specific work, how the organization's communication system will function, and so forth.
8. *Finance:* This section of the plan will probably have three- to five-year financial projections using pro forma income statements, balance sheets, and statements of cash flows.
9. *Conclusion:* A short conclusion should bring the report to a close. Suggested actions by individuals or a timeline for action before the recommendations within the report are considered outdated might be included here.
10. *Appendix:* The appendix should contain any supplementary information that would be useful to the reader, such as sample questionnaires used to gather research data, documents used to prepare the report, and so forth.

Understanding Business Models

model
A representation of an actual device.

In order to understand how anything works, especially large-scale complicated devices like a manufacturing assembly line or warehouse distribution system, it is common to construct a **model** or representation of an actual device. Engineers build small-scale models of buildings and bridges and test them for design integrity, appearance, and other factors before committing themselves and investors to the costs of building the real thing. Much can be learned from a model. The fundamental characteristics are usually the focus of the design, and less-important details may be omitted to allow attention to be directed to the important areas alone, without complicating distractions.

Models of a particular type tend to have certain characteristics in common. For instance, most models of cars have four wheels and a steering wheel. By examining models, engineers can gain insight into the basic components that are likely to be present in their own specific designs. Precisely the same concept holds within the confines of a business model. A **business model** is a descriptive representation of the fundamental components of a business, which we described in Chapter 1 as a group of shared or common characteristics, behaviors, and methods of doing business that enables a firm to generate profits through increasing revenues and reducing costs. For example, the business model for the book retailer Barnes & Noble is similar to that of most other retail establishments: Targeted customers' reading needs are satisfied through the business activities of stocking the store shelves with desirable products at acceptable prices, and so forth. How Barnes & Noble specifically carries on its business is detailed in its business plan. But the basic model of who and what Barnes & Noble is as a business is much simpler to describe: *Barnes & Noble makes money by selling books and other products in a physical retail environment to clearly identified target customers.* Anyone else that wants to emulate this successful retail business model can study the model and replicate it with whatever additions or deletions are seen as necessary. Perhaps instead of books, another retailer might sell clothing or sports equipment. With few exceptions, the retail business model is common to a variety of individual businesses whose efforts to further customize the model are detailed in their respective business plans.

business model
A group of shared or common characteristics, behaviors, and methods of doing business that enables a firm to generate profits through increasing revenues and reducing costs.

e-business model
A descriptive representation of the fundamental components of a business that operates partially or completely on the internet.

An **e-business model** is a descriptive representation of the fundamental components of a business that operates partially or completely on the Internet. Barnes & Noble's e-business model for its online operations overlaps somewhat with its traditional bricks-and-mortar business model. Although there are similarities between the two, business operations in each model are significantly different in many ways. For example, the retail business model is based on selling and distributing a product to customers who walk into the retailer's stores. But the e-retailer can accommodate online customers who are dispersed throughout the world by using courier services for delivery and does not operate any real physical stores. All customers may enter the same "virtual door" if that is the way the online operations are designed. Alternatively, a different virtual entrance to shopping can be created for, say, young customers under the age of 11, or there can be one virtual entrance for boys and another for girls. The choice of entrances and the method of offering an online shopping experience to each target market is entirely the choice of the firm. The costs of designing multiple gateways to the Barnes & Noble online store are relatively low in comparison to the costs of building a real store and staffing it with personnel who are trained to cater to a specific target group. On the other hand, both the online and the bricks-and-mortar business operation models include equivalent warehousing and distribution logistics and costs. Regardless of whether the merchandise is sold online or at a physical retail outlet in a mall, the warehousing operation for maintaining proper inventories is going to be similar.

Although a firm's business model comprises several key features that describe how the business functions in the world, to many people, the term really means only one important thing: "How does the firm earn revenues?" Although this might be considered a somewhat myopic view, it focuses attention on the single most critical point and sheds light on the feasibility of what the firm is trying to do and whether the analyst examining the business model thinks that there is much point to continuing to investigate the rest of the firm's business model or business plan. For example, suppose that the basic premise of a business model is to make money by selling, on the Internet, used sports equipment like football and hockey pads to individuals, schools, sports teams, and organizations, and suppose that an analyst believes that this is just not a very good idea, both because people need to try out sports equipment before they purchase it and because the costs of shipping are too high given the profit margins typically available for used sports equipment. The analyst can save a great deal of time and effort by focusing immediately on the basic foundation upon which the rest of the business model and business plan rests.

e-Business Models

The list of e-business models continues to grow and has no established taxonomy. Most of these models, like the e-retailing model, are modified versions of traditional business models. In this segment of the chapter, we will examine several e-business models that have emerged and their primary descriptive characteristics. Like most interested parties looking at a business model, we will first focus our attention on the basic question of how the firm earns revenues and then explore the other descriptors related to the model.

brokerage e-business model
An e-business model that covers online marketplaces in which buyers and sellers are brought together in an organized environment to facilitate the exchange of goods.

Brokerage e-Business Model

The **brokerage e-business model** covers online marketplaces where buyers and sellers are brought together in an organized environment to facilitate exchange of goods and services. Brokerage firms often specialize in a particular product classification and may even be organized by a major supplier or vendor of these products, as is the case with the auto-parts exchange organized by General

Motors and the airline industry supply exchange set up by Air Canada. Though the vast majority of brokerage activity is conducted among businesses, the popular and profitable eBay (**www.ebay.com**) provides both businesses and consumers with access to a communications structure for buying or selling virtually anything.

Brokerages include a variety of structural designs to facilitate the exchange process, typically reflecting the real-world environment that users are already familiar with before they come to the virtual exchange. Therefore, virtual shopping malls often have a look and feel that consumers find not that different from the physical environment that they already know about, right down to the shopping cart icon for merchandise selected for purchase. On the business-to-business (B2B) side of the brokerage model, designs include regular auctions, reverse auctions, classified listings, and so forth, which also tend to reflect a buying and selling environment that users are likely to easily understand and feel comfortable with. Firms like Charles Schwab (**www.schwab.com**) and E*Trade (**www.etrade.com**) focus on facilitating the exchange of financial securities between buyers and sellers. As in all brokerage businesses, revenues are earned mostly through commission charges based on the value of the securities that are bought and sold. In addition, the brokerage firm may charge a membership fee and collect advertising revenues by selling display space on its screens. In the case of a securities brokerage firm like Charles Schwab or E*Trade, the firm earns money in traditional ways too, such as on the spread between the interest rates it charges for the money it lends to clients and what it has to pay to borrow those funds.

 e-Business Insight

Online Brokerage Firms Help Clear Surplus Inventories—Fast

According to AMR Research, less than 1 percent of an estimated $57 billion of excess merchandise is currently sold through online brokers. But that is likely to change dramatically as e-commerce sites specializing in redistributing unwanted inventories spring up to handle the task of finding buyers for these goods. AMR predicts that by 2004, about 14 percent of unwanted goods will be sold online through sites like RetailExchange .com (**www.retailexchange.com**), TradeOut.com (**www .tradeout.com**), and Overstock.com (**www.overstock**

.com), which work the inefficiencies inherent in a non-Internet-based system of finding buyers through phone calls and faxes. Often the merchandise may be slightly damaged or simply a poor-selling style or color that was overproduced by enthusiastic manufacturers. Wholesalers who overestimated demand and got stuck with too much merchandise and vendors who have declared bankruptcy make up the bulk of the oversupply industry. Huge discounts that might reduce prices to 10 percent of regular wholesale prices help to motivate buyers who believe that they have customers that would willingly buy—at the right price.[3]

A good example of a brokerage e-business model that uses the communication power of the Internet to solve logistical problems and make money where none could have been made before is Adbargains Inc. (**www.adbargains.com**), a Toronto, Ontario–based start-up serving North American media buyers and sellers. Adbargains presents an easy-to-use web site where sellers of excess advertising space in any medium can connect with buyers seeking last-minute bargains or supplementary supply to increase current advertising commitments. Like other brokerage models such as eBay, the site is automated and generates revenue equal to 25 percent of the value of any advertising space sold. Without Adbargains, media sellers would have to forgo potential sales of unsold available space and buyers would be unable to boost their current advertising campaigns.

Advertising e-Business Model

advertising e-business model

An e-business model based on earning revenues in exchange for the display of advertisements on a firm's web site.

An **advertising e-business model** is based on earning revenues in exchange for the display of advertisements on a firm's web site, in much the same way as other media such as television, radio, newspapers, and magazines earn revenues. Advertising sponsorship of distributed online entertainment or information is likely to continue to be readily accepted by audiences, which see advertising as the price they have to pay for receiving free content online. But unlike conventional media, where engaging the consumer is often problematic, the Internet provides both the advertiser and the web site content provider with the opportunity for unique design and interaction with the targeted audience.

In the near future, the biggest online content provider is likely to be AOL, since its merger with Time Warner has combined the massive audience base of AOL subscribers with the huge vault of multimedia content from the Time Warner group. However, the advertising model for the Internet has also stimulated the entry of small production studios and entertainment artists who are seeking to earn advertising revenues as well as to sell their products online. Unlike the situation with television and radio, barriers to entry are low, and virtually anyone with something that will attract an audience can get started quite easily. The advertising model has also been used by consultants such as financial advisers and lawyers, who might provide free articles about topics specific to their expertise and practice. For example, a lawyer who specializes in real estate business might set up a web site containing a variety of articles related to the legal issues that arise from the buying and selling of real property. Besides serving to advertise the lawyer's own services, the web site would also interest banks that were interested in making mortgage loans, moving and storage firms, and of course real estate agents. Although the lawyer in this case may view a professional web site as a promotional tool rather than a revenue source, there are many small start-ups that hope to find a huge global audience and the advertising revenues that go along with it. Others hope to be discovered by a larger firm that wishes to acquire their web site content as an addition to its own. From the very large to the smaller-scale firms, the advertising model can provide a financial and promotional contribution to the overall business plan.

Subscription, Pay-per-View, and Membership e-Business Models

subscription e-business model

An e-business model in which access to a site is controlled by a subscription fee.

pay-per-view e-business model

An e-business model in which access to a site is controlled by a charge to view single items.

membership e-business model

An e-business model in which access to a site is controlled by membership fees.

Web site content providers may elect to earn revenues through the use of a **subscription, pay-per-view,** or **membership e-business model,** in which access to the site is controlled by a subscription fee, a charge to view single items such as a report, or a membership fee, respectively. Often these sources of revenue are combined with advertising revenue. The subscription model, which is popular with publications and research organizations, often provides samples of the site's content free of charge and then seeks to induce interested clients to subscribe to the full range of products and services available. A common strategy is to offer a trial subscription for a limited time period and at a substantial price reduction to entice new subscribers.

Both Forrester Research Inc. and *Business Week* magazine provide free content and then attempt to sell further services through subscription. Like other magazines that display online content, the venerable *Reader's Digest* surrounds its free-access magazine articles with advertising. The hope is that the free sample will ultimately lead people to subscribe to the print version of the magazine. This approach is also common for online learning and educational institutions selling courses and programs through the Internet.

In some cases, content providers request only that users register in order to gain wider access to the providers' products and special services. IBM's small business and e-business web site, for example, will send registrants daily bulletins with links to its database of articles. The purpose of registration is to get information about the person and possibly use that information to control the number of visitors to the web site at one time. Furthermore, this information learned can be used to offer sales of products from the firm or others, if the member has agreed to this as a condition of membership.

Distribution Channel Member e-Business Model

distribution channel member e-business model

An e-business model that includes activities of retailers, wholesalers, and manufacturers carrying on business through the Internet.

The **distribution channel member e-business model** includes activities of retailers, wholesalers, and manufacturers carrying on business through the Internet. It is a natural choice for businesses that are currently active at any of these levels in the distribution system of products to end users. Taking product offerings into a global and virtual environment is easier than ever, as e-commerce software that facilitates this is available for relatively small fees from hosting firms that provide everything required to get started. Furthermore, firms can easily scale up if their initial activities produce positive results. Newcomers to the Internet might wish to place only their top-selling products in an online facility and gradually build up an entire online catalog in tandem with their bricks-and-mortar retail or wholesale operations.

Retailers such as Wal-Mart, Staples, and Sears, Roebuck provide easy and convenient online shopping experiences for virtual shoppers. In addition, shoppers may simply be using the retail web site to gather the information they need in order to make an informed decision before finalizing their purchase within the walls of one of the company's stores. Regardless of whether the web site promotes sales within the company's stores or is the primary avenue for more frequent shopping by busy or geographically dispersed customers, providing some level of online shopping assistance is considered a prudent and effective means of serving customers today.

Wholesalers and manufacturers have found that the Internet can be a productive new tool for reducing costs and finding new sales. In addition to putting their product catalogs online, wholesalers and manufacturers are increasingly making use of brokerage web sites as well as managing their own site activities. Perhaps the most celebrated Internet-related manufacturing success story is that of Dell Computer, which is credited with helping to establish a new model of tying manufacturing to orders entered online and building relationships with component manufacturers and customers.

Affiliation e-Business Model

affiliation e-business model

An e-business model that involves payments to web site operators for customers who find their way to a company's site and either buy merchandise or services or perform some other action, such as registering and providing certain information.

The affiliation concept is important for web site operators on both sides of the arrangement to consider for several reasons. The **affiliation e-business model** involves payments to web site operators for customers who find their way to a company's site and either buy merchandise or services or perform some other action, such as registering and providing certain information. This model was popularized by Amazon.com, which, like other operators of affiliate programs, has automated the process of registering and creating an online link to the destination site. Any web site operator that wants to earn a share of the revenues from books and other products sold through the Amazon.com web site to customers that the web site operator has sent there simply has to make a few clicks at the Amazon registration site. An Amazon link will then appear on the affiliate's web site. Amazon currently pays a 15 percent finder's commission for customers sent its way, which helps to explain why the program is such a success with web site operators.

This affiliation model is now commonplace for firms that are seeking to build sales through partnerships with web site operators who believe that their audience will find a reason to click on the affiliation link. Regardless of the affiliate web site operator's actual level of success, such an affiliation link costs little to try out and maintain and tends to increase the value image of the host site. The only true cost is the space on the screen that is taken up by the affiliation site icon, and this is why the programs are so attractive to both parties. Affiliation programs are really a form of advertising that is paid for only when sales are made. Thus, Amazon receives huge amounts of exposure from anyone who is willing to become an affiliate. The real costs to Amazon are practically nothing, since this is a software application that is entirely automated. For better-known brands, using affiliate programs rather than spending on massive advertising campaigns can do the job more effectively and save funds for other activities. However, an affiliation program is not likely to work well for an unknown brand unless there is no need for branding. For example, a site that specializes in the sale of science fiction titles may not be widely known, but someone who is reading an online article and sample chapter about a new science fiction book would be likely to click on the affiliation icon to order the book without caring too much about what the book distributor's name was.

Community e-Business Model

community e-business model

An e-business model built around the idea that a group of online users can be regularly brought together at a commonly used web site for commercial purposes.

The **community e-business model** is built around the idea that a group of online users can be regularly brought together at a commonly used web site for commercial purposes. The sorts of communities brought together can vary widely and include people who share an interest like playing bridge or poker, wish to exchange their opinions about politics and public affairs, or wish to find old high school classmates with whom they would like to reestablish contact.

Communities are the great growth opportunity for any individual or organization that can think of a reason why someone would be interested enough in its site to make the effort to visit it. Online communities such as those set up by educational institutions and religious organizations can be self-supporting through association with their respective larger organizations and fee structures for members or donors. These online communities are generally regarded as simply another method for members to communicate with one another and are usually free of any revenue-generating aspect. However, online communities, along with the advertising and shopping services unique to their focus, continue to flourish as a niche for small and special-interest groups. For example, Oxygen (**www.oxygen .com**), Oprah Winfrey (**www.oprah.com**), and iVillage (**www.ivillage.com**) have all developed large numbers of regular users by focusing mainly on topics that are of interest to women. Geocities (**www.geocities.com**), the build-your-own-web-site-for-free service provided by Yahoo!, provides an environment for individuals who wish to explore their own creative skills by constructing a web site. In all of these communities, advertising, affiliate programs, and online shopping provide the revenues needed to make the communities viable. The success of this model is obviously based on building awareness among interested users and spreading the word. Therefore, most site operators offer incentives such as rewards and prizes to current members who enlist new users.

---

 e-Business Insight

VerticalNet—Leading Industry Builder of e-Business Communities

Pennsylvania-headquartered VerticalNet Inc. (**www.vertical.net**) was first established only in 1995 and today is considered to be among the leading global builders of e-business communities. From dentistry to the food services industry, VerticalNet's fifty-eight industry-specific communities facilitate B2B activities among firms that come together for buying, selling, promotion, and information exchange about themselves and their industry. VerticalNet offers e-business consulting and hosting services to online community members who are seeking resources to enhance their B2B effectiveness. VerticalNet communities typically provide an e-commerce exchange service to facilitate the locating, buying, and selling of content specific to the industry, journal articles that are of interest to managers, and training and information about the industry that is of value to anyone following the industry. Students can learn a great deal about an industry, its major suppliers, and industry-specific news by visiting any of the VerticalNet sites.[4]

Infomediary e-Business Model

The **infomediary e-business model** is based on the collection and sale of online information. Many sites, especially communities, are in a position to analyze their users' online interests and behaviors and sell the results of this research to other interested parties, such as advertisers. In addition, communities can earn revenues by providing informational services from advertisers to users who accept the offer, usually in the form of email advertisements or announcements of another design. Without a community site with large numbers of users, no data collection activity is really possible unless the infomediary firm uses other methods to attract online users and motivate them to volunteer information. In some cases, this is done by providing free Internet access or free access to a web site and its content in exchange for registration and permission to collect online behavior data, send out email advertisements, and conduct other such activities. AllAdvantage.com (**www.alladvantage.com**) is an infomediary that pays users for permission to track their movements on the Internet and sell the information to advertisers and other interested parties. Users load a software program that presents intelligent advertisements directed by AllAdvantage that match their demographic profile and online behavior.

Portal e-Business Model

The **portal e-business model** is a type of infomediary that earns revenues by drawing users to its site and serving as a gateway or portal to information located elsewhere on the Internet. Some portals, such as search engines, have a wide general reach into different informational topics and are referred to as **horizontal portals,** whereas others have a narrow focus on a particular topic and are called **vertical portals.** Both types of portals can earn revenues by selling advertising, providing search services to users who are seeking merchants and products, and charging finder's fees for customers sent to a particular merchant.

Internet-Based Software and e-Business Solutions

One of the e-business models we have just examined or their many variations will generally form the core of an organization's e-business plan. In other words, a firm's selection of one or more of these models determines the basic framework for its e-business plan. In addition to these basic e-business models, it is worthwhile to examine the primary Internet-based software tools sold by vendors as e-business solutions to communication and other concerns.

In this section we will take a look at the primary Internet-based software solutions in order of their complexity and difficulty of implementation within the firm's operations. However, we will examine the strategic use of these solutions within the context of the topics to be presented in the remaining chapters of this textbook. The purpose of introducing these topics here is to point out their relationship to e-business models and to clarify the confusion that may be caused by firms that market these software products. Vendors of these products typically promote their products as the only part of an e-business plan that the buyer need be concerned about—as though e-business begins and ends with the selection of a software solution and the modification of the firm's behavior and processes to match the solution created by the software. The important thing for learners to recognize is that planning begins at a much more fundamental level—the e-business model level. Once the decision about what the firm wants to do to earn revenues and serve customers is made, software solutions can then be studied and the correct one(s) selected that will allow the organization to achieve its planned objectives. All too often, decision makers look for a software solution without regard for the overall effect the adoption of this software solution must necessarily have on the firm's business practice. Although any software solution can be "patched in" to the current business plan successfully, it is advisable to stand back and consider the bigger questions in a complete e-business plan that require answers before committing to one software solution.

Email

Today email is considered a standard communication tool for all businesspeople. Whether for internal or external communication, the benefits derived from implementing email are well established. Because it was the first Internet-based software application, email has had the longest amount of time to develop and evolve variations. Instant messaging and live online meeting capability are two examples of software that contributes to individual and group productivity. The benefits and low cost of email make it the easiest Internet-based software solution to rationalize. Every individual should have her or his own email accounts, and any communication that contains a name, address, and phone number should also provide an email address. Email allows individuals to request information and receive quick responses without other time-consuming interaction. When questions are not specific to any one person, they can be answered routinely by a rotating group of employees. For example, customer service questions could be addressed 24 hours a day, 7 days a week to **customerservice@anyfirm.com**. Experts can be hired to deal with customers' questions sent by email, relieving other employees of the firm who might have been contacted in the past, such as the sales representatives or the company's telephone receptionists, of the need to answer routine or difficult product-related questions.

Regardless of a firm's overall e-business approach, email and its many more advanced software variations, which may include calendar functions and sales force automated data sharing and messaging, are primary solutions for improving productivity and efficiency. Every firm should be employing email solutions and transforming its processes to take advantage of the improvements inherent in the adoption of email communications strategies both inside and outside of the firm.

Web Site

Every organization can benefit from the addition of a web site. As with email, the low costs and high associated benefits make the decision to establish a web site an easy one to rationalize. Also as with email, the organization's web address should be included on its stationery, business cards, press releases, advertisements, and any other form of communication. The web site serves as the organization's primary visible presence on the Internet as well as being a communication hub for customers, suppliers, investors, and the general public. How well or poorly the web site presents the organization to the world will have a significant impact on whether users decide to continue their contact. Therefore, the design, structure, and management of the site are critical to its strategic success. We will look at these strategies in the third module of this text. However, suffice it to say that even a simple and inexpensively designed web site can provide basic information about the firm, its products and services, its prices, people to contact, press releases, and other public announcements, along with an email address to write to in order to get more information.

Although a small business may look at a simple web site as little more than a low-cost, effective addition to its promotional effort, organizations that depend on large volumes of user traffic to generate either advertising revenues or user behavior information for analysis must be particularly concerned with their web sites' long-term attractiveness and appeal. The maintenance costs for continuously updating and servicing a web site are high. However, if that is what the e-business model requires, then an appropriate budget for the proper scale of web site operation needs to be included in the plan.

e-Commerce

A logical next step for sellers of products that can be readily sold over the Internet, such as books, music, DVDs, CDs, and other similar items, is an e-commerce capability. This can be part of the firm's web site and accessible through icons on the site, or it can be independent. Catalog sellers can obviously benefit by selling their products to a global marketplace over the Internet.

In the most rudimentary e-commerce system, a firm can simply use its web site to receive orders by email and then invoice its customers using its current regular procedure. However, the use of the Internet to buy and sell products is constantly evolving. Today, firms need not concern themselves with all of the complexity involved in designing and maintaining an e-commerce site. Instead, hosting firms can provide merchants with complete software services on a fee basis. Even a small business that wishes to explore global sales opportunities or better serve local and regional markets can now subscribe to a variety of simple plans. For example, a small monthly fee would typically allow the firm to post a catalog of its products, often with space for photographs and short product descriptions. The e-commerce service provider, who often is using a brokerage e-business model, generally fits the firm into one or more of the business categories that it has devised to help buyers find the vendors and products they are looking for more easily. The plan package would also incorporate credit card processing on behalf of the vendor, making the setting up of e-commerce a relatively painless process. As volumes increase, the vendor may choose to work more independently of the service provider, creating the image of having its own virtual buying environment rather than a shared one. The real task facing sellers, regardless of their size or how they first entered the e-commerce environment, is building their traffic and sales through the e-commerce site in order to make the whole effort worthwhile.

Customer Relationship Management

customer relationship management (CRM)
Software solutions that incorporate a variety of means to manage the tasks of communicating with customers and sharing this information with employees in order to create more efficient relationships.

Several large firms now sell complete **customer relationship management (CRM)** software solutions that incorporate a variety of means to manage the tasks of communicating with customers and sharing this information with employees in order to create more efficient relationships. The concept behind CRM is to establish a seamless system for handling any and all information that involves customers' interaction with the firm's employees. For example, a customer in St. Louis that sees a television advertisement for a car rental deal calls the 1-800 number to find out more. The question is whether the call-center customer service representative who takes the call will have not only all of the information needed to deal with this particular promotion, but also any additional information that might help him or her do the job better. If the customer's records can be easily retrieved from the firm's database by entering a telephone number, a complete history of that customer's prior buying behavior will be immediately available to any service representative in the network. Ideally, the service representative would have a record of important information about this customer, including the customer's request never to be put in a subcompact car regardless of the cost. The conversation could then be more personalized as well as informed and lead to more efficient service and better customer relations.

CRM software is often discussed in terms of *front-end* or *back-office* applications, with firms marketing one or both. Front-end applications involve direct dealings with customers, such as the car rental call center in the example and the e-commerce web site Flowers.com for taking orders online. Back-office applications are concerned with activities that are not visible or obvious to customers, such as accounting, warehousing, inventory and ordering management, sales force automation software, and so forth. Some smaller firms may need only part of a full CRM software package. A marketing strategy employed by vendors of CRM software is to sell users additional modules of different CRM solutions as they need them. Users understand each additional module quickly because menus and other design elements are similar across the integrated system and the users are already familiar with them. Siebel Systems Inc.(**www.siebel.com**) is the largest software solution vendor and provides an abundance of literature about CRM modules at its site, as well as the opportunity to try demonstration versions.

Supply-Chain Management

supply-chain management (SCM)
Software solutions that focus on ways to improve communication between the suppliers and users of materials and components, enabling manufacturers to reduce inventories, improve delivery schedules, reduce costs, and so forth.

Just as CRM software solutions help firms create more efficient relationships with their customers, **supply-chain management (SCM)** software solutions focus on ways to improve communication between the suppliers and users of materials and components. By providing their production requirements and planning information directly to their suppliers, manufacturers can reduce inventories, improve delivery schedules, and reduce costs, which can quickly show up as improved profitability. For example, AeorXchange (**www.aeorxchange.com**) is a B2B thirteen-member global airline procurement system set up using Oracle Exchange Marketplace software. Designed to improve members' supply chains and procurement of airplane parts and other supplies, the Dallas, Texas–based organization is being spearheaded by Air Canada. AeorXchange is a communication hub that coordinates the purchasing of parts and supplies required by all members, securing better pricing and services from vendors. Member airlines that require parts on short notice will be able to secure these from fellow members rather than needing to place rush orders with suppliers. Air Canada alone expects to save $25 million a year by using the system.[5]

Similarly, Dell Computer's B2B **Valuechain.dell.com** virtually eliminates the need for the firm to maintain any inventory, as suppliers are tied directly into Dell's new OptiPlex plant in Round Rock, Texas. Manufacturing schedules and parts orders are revised every two hours. Suppliers must keep an agreed-upon level of inventory for Dell on hand at nearby local warehouses. As a result, 95 percent of Dell's PCs are built and shipped to customers within twelve hours of their orders being entered into the system. OptiPlex has improved productivity 160 percent, increased order velocity 50 percent, and reduced errors in orders 50 percent.[6]

Fundamental Characteristics of Internet-Based Software and e-Business Solutions

In the previous section, we examined a range of Internet-based software and associated e-business solutions, from simple email to full-scale CRM and SCM systems. In this section we will examine the fundamental shared characteristics that explain why these e-business solutions are growing in popularity as firms are increasingly moving to solve their problems and improve their operations through the Internet. We will also examine how businesses can systematically make informed decisions as to whether to adopt or reject an e-business solution option.

Efficiency and Productivity

At the core of a business decision to adopt any e-business solution is the belief that more productive and efficient use of resources will result. Recall that e-business resources include human, material, informational, and financial resources. Therefore, in considering an e-business solution, the improvement in the effective use of resources should be weighed against the costs of implementing such a solution. The strategy, then, is to look at the costs and benefits of the current procedure in comparison with those of a procedure based on e-business and make an intelligent decision as to whether the change is best overall for the firm.

Let's use an example to illustrate the evaluation process. Efficiency typically means doing things at a lower cost, whether that means reduced direct costs or less time spent performing a current work activity. Suppose a firm is considering setting up a customer service bureau that will allow customers to communicate by email in addition to using the firm's 1-800 telephone number. Analysis of current operations shows that each of the twenty call-center operators working for the firm receives an average of about six telephone calls per hour. If the operator is unable to satisfy the caller's requirement, the call is routed to a technical or knowledge expert within the firm. Research suggests that an experienced operator can answer almost all of the calls within about ten minutes, since the dialogue with the customer almost always yields one of fifty common requests or inquiries that are easily retrieved on the operator's computer screen. The call center, which is located outside Chicago, operates twelve hours each business day in order to accommodate customers located in all time zones in North America. More operators are available during the peak period of the day and fewer at the start or end, when customers in different time zones may not be at work. Since the total cost of running the call center, including salaries, training for new employees, overhead, and telephone charges, is calculated to be $1.25 million per year and the firm handles approximately 3.6 million calls per year, the average cost per call works out to about $0.35.

As the firm expects to double in size within five years, it can use these figures to project the costs of serving customers. Although the firm does not intend to reduce its current call-center operation, it is anxious to know what savings can be generated by transferring the expected increase in customer service requests to a less expensive but equally effective system. Research and analysis of tests conducted to learn about directing customers to an email-based customer service bureau suggest that customer email requests would be readily understood by experienced customer service representatives and that the responses sent back would satisfy the customer's needs almost all of the time. Furthermore, the research suggests that email-based customer service representatives could comfortably handle twelve email messages per hour, twice the number handled by telephone. In addition, the research experiment, which was conducted with the help of experienced telephone customer service operators, revealed that many of the operators would prefer a break from telephone work during the day and would welcome the opportunity to switch to an email-based system for part of the time. In addition, some operators said that they would be willing to handle the servicing of email-based inquiries from home rather than at the call center, eliminating the time required for them to travel to work and providing them with the option of working hours that were more suitable to their family lifestyle. It was found that the cost of installing Internet software that would allow employee-only access from home or from the firm's premises was not significant and that the software could be programmed to record and report employees' activities whether the employees were at home or on the firm's premises. This would allow the firm to pay employees who were working from home on a per-service-call-reply basis.

Based on an analysis of the savings in new overhead for an expanded call center and the estimated number of email replies that employees who were working from home could handle, the firm arrived at the following conclusion. A new telephone-based call center would cost another $1.25 million; an email-based center on the firm's premises would cost about half that, since operators would be twice as efficient. The third possibility, employees working from home on a pay-per-call email basis, would further reduce the costs associated with the overhead for a new call center, to approximately $500,000. Based on these factors alone, the informed decision makers in the firm decided to establish a group of reliable at-home employees. To assure success, employees would have to prove their online ability by working on the company premises for a trial period before working from home. Another benefit related to this strategy is the ability to process requests from customers around the world who might not be able to telephone or converse in technical English, but would manage fine online.

Quality, Standardization, and Customization of Products and Services

A second common fundamental characteristic of Internet-based software and e-business solutions is the drive toward quality, standardization, and customization of the delivery of products and services. Software solutions usually demand a particular way of performing functions such as processing a customer's order; therefore, they lend themselves well to the establishment of performance standards for quality, time, costs, and so forth, as illustrated in the email-based versus call-center customer service bureau. Both present clear standardized processes and procedures for employees to follow. Like operations in a manufacturing environment, such work is measurable, and benchmarks based on industry standards, corporate historical records, and management goals can be employed to measure the efficiency of individual employees' performance as well as the performance of the entire organization. At the same time, because input and output screens can readily be designed to best suit individual users, software allows for a great deal of customization and adaptation to the user.

Adding Value and Creating Competitive Advantage Online

Finally, a third commonality among Internet-based software and e-business solutions is the concept of creating additional customer value. In our case example, customer value could include more convenience and less time spent communicating with the customer service center. Creating customer value is at the core of establishing and sustaining a competitive advantage over other firms in the industry. In the case of e-businesses that are attempting to outdo competitors in the eyes of current and potential customers, a competitive advantage may be created online by providing a better quality or selection of products, better order-taking and delivery choices, lower selling prices, more attractive and better online shopping environments, and so forth. Creating an online competitive advantage works in tandem with the firm's overall business strategy to create added customer value.

Conclusions

The value-adding approach to creating competitive advantage was introduced, along with a variety of solutions for creating a competitive advantage through the Internet. These solutions ranged from the introduction of simple email and group communication software to full CRM and SCM software. The chapter emphasized the creative thinking needed to understand processes as they are now and how by changing these to better online processes, the organization can transform itself into an improved needs-satisfying and value-adding company for both customers and employees. The challenge for strategists is to creatively use the e-business models and e-business tools we have just examined to build a sustainable competitive advantage in the marketplace. In the next chapter, we will explore how these concepts come together in the context of strategic planning within the firm.

CASE STUDY RETURN TO INSIDE e-BUSINESS

Whether delivered from a traditional centralized server or through a P2P network facilitated by software like Napster, the distribution of entertainment content is changing dramatically, along with the way the industry's artists and businesses will compete in the future. In short, we are witnessing a major transformation in the business plans of all industry competitors because of this new strategic tool. The Internet offers any firm the possibility of creating a competitive advantage so that it can better serve its customers and grow. Like all ways of creating competitive advantage, this means adding a perceived value-added service or product for customers that is better than that offered by other competitors. This might mean providing more convenient methods of shopping for music, the ability to create a customized CD of only the music the customer desires, information about the artist to enhance the purchase experience, or simply a lower price.

ASSIGNMENT

1. What other strategies could be used to create a greater competitive advantage for an entertainment company operating on the Internet?
2. How do you think music consumers would respond to a fee being charged for using Napster software to exchange entertainment files?
3. Do you think that eventually every major web site will provide P2P software for its users, just as online chat software and email are now made available?

Chapter Review

SUMMARY

1. Examine the meaning of a business plan and a business model and the relationship between them.

The business plan is the most detailed description of what individuals within the firm are doing and what the business is trying to achieve. It should be revised as conditions and circumstances demand. A business model is a descriptive representation of the fundamental components of a business. Although a firm's business model comprises several key features that describe how the business functions in the world, to many people, the term really means only one important thing: "How does the firm earn revenues?"

2. Explore the various e-business models.

An online broker brings buyers and sellers together, often specializes in a particular product classification, and may even be organized by a major supplier or vendor of the products. An advertising e-business model is based on earning revenues in exchange for the display of advertisements on the firm's web site. Web site content providers may elect to earn revenues through subscription fees, charges to view single items such as a report (pay-per-view), or membership fees to gain access to the site. The distribution channel member model includes activities of retailers, wholesalers, and manufacturers carrying on business through the Internet. Affiliation programs pay web site operators for customers who find their way to a company's site and either buy merchandise or services or perform some other action, such as registering and providing certain information. The community model is built around the idea that a group of online users can be regularly brought together at a commonly used web site. Infomediaries sell information such as online customer behavior to advertisers and other interested parties. The portal e-business model is a type of infomediary that earns revenues by drawing users to its site and serving as a gateway or portal to information located elsewhere on the Internet.

3. Understand the range of Internet-based software and e-business solutions.

Today email is considered a standard communication tool for all businesspeople. Whether it is used for internal or external communication, the benefits derived from the implementation of email are well established. As with email, the low costs and high associated benefits make the decision to establish a web site an easy one to rationalize. The web site serves as the organization's primary visible presence on the Internet as well as being a communication hub for customers, suppliers, investors, and the general public. A logical next step for sellers of products that can be readily sold over the Internet, such as books, DVDs, CDs, and other similar items, is an e-commerce capability. The concept behind CRM is to establish a seamless system for handling any and all information that involves customers' interaction with the firm's employees. Just as CRM software solutions help firms create more efficient relationships with their customers, supply-chain management (SCM) software solutions focus on ways to improve communication between the suppliers and users of materials and components. By providing their production requirements and planning information directly to their suppliers, manufacturers can reduce inventories, improve delivery schedules, and reduce costs, which can quickly show up as improved profitability.

4. Describe the fundamental characteristics of Internet-based software and e-business solutions.

At the core of a business decision to adopt any e-business solution is the belief that more productive and efficient use of resources will result. A second common fundamental characteristic is the drive toward quality, standardization, and customization of the delivery of products and services, and a third is the concept of creating additional customer value.

REVIEW QUESTIONS

1. What is the difference between a business plan and a business model?
2. What is the primary point of interest in a firm's business model?
3. Why is the brokerage e-business model so popular?
4. In which sort of web site is the advertising e-business model more likely to be used successfully?
5. Explain the differences between the subscription, pay-per-view, and membership e-business models.
6. How does the affiliation e-business model work to the advantage of both sides?
7. How does a community e-business model generate revenues?
8. What do infomediaries do to earn revenues?
9. Describe each of the primary Internet-based software and e-business solutions.

DISCUSSION QUESTIONS

1. Discuss the relative advantages and disadvantages of employing a payment-based e-business model versus one that is free of charge to users.
2. Do you agree that web sites that are free of charge to users are the best choice for both users and web site managers?
3. Discuss the relative importance of each characteristic that is common to Internet-based software and e-business solutions.

Building Skills for Career Success

EXPLORING THE INTERNET

A wide variety of entertainment, from music to animation, continues to find its way onto the Internet, typically aimed at smaller niche markets. Artists are finding the Internet an invaluable tool for reaching a global audience and hoping for discovery and breakthrough into the primary distribution system provided by television and radio. Explore online entertainment sites, including gateways such as Microsoft's Windowsmedia, located at **http://windowsmedia .com**, Real.com at **www.real.com**, MP3.com at **www.mp3.com**, Napster.com at **www.napster.com**, and the Broadcast.com (**www.broadcast.com**) search engine. Try to find other entertainment sites that are also catering to niche markets.

ASSIGNMENT

1. In your opinion, what are the strengths and weaknesses of one of the entertainment sites you have visited?
2. What value is contributed by these entertainment gateways to help artists?

(continued)

DEVELOPING CRITICAL THINKING SKILLS

One of the reasons that community e-business models like Oxygen (**www .oxygen.com**), Oprah Winfrey (**www.oprah.com**), and iVillage (**www.ivillage.com**) are popular is that they provide an environment in which members share a clearly defined interest of some kind. Therefore, like special-interest magazines, they deliver an audience to advertisers and vendors of products targeted to this group of potential buyers. Examine one of these online community sites or some other such site that you are more interested in.

ASSIGNMENT

1. Identify the community and then describe it in terms of how the site attracts the target audience.
2. List the community's revenue streams and your estimate of how significantly each of them contributes to total earnings. Explain your thinking.

BUILDING TEAM SKILLS

Working in a team, develop a web site concept that would serve the unique needs of people living in your neighborhood. Rather than trying to create a site that would attract users who were dispersed around the world, try to think of the sorts of things that would interest only a small group of users who lived, say, on your college campus, or off-campus in their own apartments.

ASSIGNMENT

1. Describe the concept for your web site.
2. Explain which e-business models you would employ.

RESEARCHING DIFFERENT CAREERS

Each of the e-business models discussed in the chapter would require employees with specialized content knowledge. For example, operating a brokerage site for computer components requires people with both product knowledge and knowledge of how traditional brokerage businesses operate. Brokerage sites require people with an understanding of how traditional brokerage business practices can be transferred to a web site. Examine a representative web site for one of the e-business models and any job opportunities it has posted.

ASSIGNMENT

1. Identify the site and describe the e-business model the firm is following.
2. Describe one specialized job that is specific to that e-business model.

IMPROVING COMMUNICATION SKILLS

Some e-business models seem to complement each other and fit together well, as in the case of a combination of the advertising and community e-business models. For example, since a community of alpine skiers would generally be interested in advertisements from product vendors, tour operators, and sellers of other related services, advertising would be welcomed and easily blended into a web site, just as it is in magazines. To help get a better understanding of the relationships between these e-business models, create a two-dimensional grid that shows the models listed horizontally in columns and vertically down the left-side margin as illustrated below.

	Brokerage	Advertising	Subscription	Distribution	Affiliation	Community	Infomediary
Brokerage							
Advertising							
Subscription							
Distribution							
Affiliation							
Community							
Infomediary							

ASSIGNMENT

1. Mark those combinations of models that would work well together on the grid.
2. Explain how the models in the combinations you have marked would complement each other.
3. Identify a web site that illustrates one of the combinations you have marked.

Exploring Useful Web Sites

These web sites provide information related to the topics discussed in the chapter. You can learn more by visiting them online and examining their current data.

1. Napster Inc. (**www.napster.com**) was among the first P2P Internet businesses. MP3 (**www.mp3.com**) software can compress an audio file by about a factor of twelve and still maintain satisfactory audio quality. Currently, two main music distribution competitors have emerged: MusicNet (**www.musicnet.com**), which is supported by AOL Time Warner, Bertelsmann AG, and EMI Group, and PressPlay (**www.pressplay.com**), formed by Sony and Vivendi Universal Music.

2. Brokerage site eBay (**www.ebay.com**) provides both businesses and consumers with access to a communications structure for buying or selling virtually anything. Firms like Charles Schwab (**www.schwab.com**) and E*Trade (**www.etrade.com**) focus on facilitating the exchange of financial securities between buyers and sellers. Adbargains (**www.adbargains.com**) presents an easy-to-use web site where sellers of excess advertising

(continued)

space in any medium can connect with buyers seeking last-minute bargains or supplementary supply to increase current advertising commitments.

3. Community sites like Oxygen (**www.oxygen.com**), Oprah Winfrey (**www.oprah.com**), and iVillage (**www.ivillage.com**) have developed large numbers of regular users by focusing mainly on topics that are of interest to women. Geocities (**www.geocities.com**), the build-your-own-web-site-for-free service provided by Yahoo!, provides an environment for individuals who wish to explore their own creative skills by constructing a web site. VerticalNet Inc. (**www.vertical.net**) is a leading global builder of e-business communities. From dentistry to the food services industry, VerticalNet's fifty-eight industry-specific communities facilitate B2B activities among firms that come together for buying, selling, promotion, and information exchange about themselves and their industry. AllAdvantage.com (**www.alladvantage.com**) is an infomediary that pays users for permission to track their movements on the Internet and sell the information to advertisers and other interested parties.

4. Siebel Systems (**www.siebel.com**) is the largest software solution vendor and provides an abundance of literature about CRM modules at its site, as well as the opportunity to try demonstration versions. AeorXchange (**www.aeorxchange.com**) is a B2B thirteen-member global airline procurement system set up using Oracle Exchange Marketplace software and is designed to improve members' supply chains and procurement of airplane parts and other supplies. RetailExchange.com (**www.retailexchange.com**), TradeOut.com (**www.tradeout.com**), and Overstock.com (**www.overstock.com**) find buyers online for excess inventory and unwanted goods.

Strategic Planning: A Multi-level Organizational Approach

Chapter 6

INSIDE
e-BUSINESS
Home Depot.com—Serving Customers Through Online Strategies

A do-it-yourselfer who visits the Home Depot web site (**www.homedepot.com**) for the first time might be forgiven for thinking that she has stumbled upon one of those PBS television shows' companion web sites, like Home Time (**www.hometime.com**) or This Old House (**www.pbs.org/wgbh/thisoldhouse/**). What the visitor to the Home Depot web site is likely to find is an array of handy tips and step-by-step informative instructions on anything from installing ceramic tile to remodeling an outdated kitchen. And if that isn't helpful enough, home decoration and planning ideas, such as how to make better use of a small closet space and which paint colors make a room look and feel more spacious, that Martha Stewart (**www .marthastewart.com**) might be proud of are also available free of any charge.

Of course, all of these customer informational services are also provided inside the more than 1,000 bricks-and-mortar Home Depot stores located in the United States, Canada, Puerto Rico, Chile, and Argentina through regularly scheduled employee demonstrations. Furthermore, informed personnel assist shoppers by providing answers to technical questions and suggestions to help customers solve their home decoration, renovation, and repair problems. The Home Depot web site complements this strong customer service orientation by providing free 24/7 access to the answers to service questions commonly asked by potential buyers of the firm's enormous selection of products. Customers will, of course, eventually need these products to carry out any specific project. By developing a reputation as a web site where repair and renovation projects can be researched and planned at the customer's convenience, Home Depot's web presence becomes an extension of the time-consuming preliminary services that must be provided to potential customers before they are

ready to decide on their purchase requirements. Some customers may need weeks or months of information gathering before they are ready to place their actual order, decide to hire a contractor, or elect instead to undertake the project themselves. The web site, then, helps customers and develops good will so that the customer is more likely to think of Home Depot when purchasing materials.

The efficiency of the Web in delivering a series of standardized, easy-to-understand step-by-step procedures that answer a customer's informational needs helps Home Depot continue to build on its well-deserved reputation for providing excellent customer service at competitive prices. In fact, the web site provides these services in a form that may be preferred by some customers, such as those who are unable to attend in-store presentations or who may be considering a project but have not researched important points such as cost estimates and materials and labor requirements sufficiently to crystallize what they want their project to actually be. This is especially true for larger-scale undertakings, which might include the need for financing. Conveniently, Home Depot's web site provides a loan application service, which saves the firm the cost of processing a loan in the store and provides the customer with an understanding of the budgetary limits on their home renovation project as well.

Although the Internet has opened the way for e-commerce opportunities, Atlanta–based Home Depot also plans to more than double the number of bricks-and-mortar stores it has in the Americas by 2004. Online retailing will allow customers to place orders and either pick up materials and tool rentals at local store locations or have them delivered. This time- and money-saving service is of particular value to tradespeople like carpenters, electricians, and plumbers, who must take time away from the work they do most efficiently to select and pick up the building materials they need in order to do the job. Generally speaking, a lower-paid assistant will be sent to the building supply center to get the required materials, but when it is critical that the right material is selected for the job, many tradespeople prefer to pick up materials themselves rather than risk an incorrect selection and further delay in the project. Given that the average Home Depot bricks-and-mortar store stocks more than 40,000 different kinds of building, home im-

provement, and garden products, the e-commerce facility not only becomes a way to reach more customers more conveniently, but also complements the search and selection process that customers must inevitably go through either in the store or online before they find what they need for their home project.[1]

Reprinted by permission. The Home Depot is a registered trademark of Homer TLC, Inc. (*Source:* www.homedepot.com.)

In comparison to those of many other home renovation centers, Home Depot's online services offer the advantages of lower prices, wider product selection, more knowledgeable support staff, an easier shopping environment for customers to navigate, and close ties with the company's bricks-and-mortar retail operations in many locations across North America. Together, these competitive advantages allow Home Depot to perform better than its competitors, providing superior value to customers and ultimately returning more profit for stockholders. Creating a competitive advantage over other industry competitors is the primary goal that guides the strategic planning process for any firm.

In this chapter we will see how the e-business models and tools that we introduced in the previous chapter can be used to help create a competitive advantage by finding new ways to create more customer value. We will examine how the strategic planning process is an integrated effort at all three primary organizational levels of the firm: corporate, division/strategic business unit, and operating/functional. In addition, we will explore the strategic issues facing a firm as it builds an online presence, transforms itself from an old-economy business into a new one, and considers industry-level and global positioning concerns. First, let's take a closer look at the strategic planning process, the key relationships between its components, and how creating a competitive advantage and delivering additional value to customers are incorporated throughout the enterprise.

An Overview of the Strategic Planning Process

strategic planning process
A sequence of steps taken by management to develop new plans, modify existing plans that may require revision, and discontinue plans that are no longer justified.

The **strategic planning process** involves a sequence of steps taken by management to develop new plans, modify existing plans that may require revision, and discontinue plans that are no longer justified. The strategic planning process requires first the establishment and then the maintenance of a plan of action that everyone in the organization is expected to follow. A well-managed strategic business plan is one in which each individual employee's work contribution is consistent with the goals set for the organization as a whole. The strategic planning process is about designing, monitoring, and revising a plan of action for everyone working for the organization, with the expressed understanding that deviations from planned results and any changes in the business environment are to be researched and the resulting feedback used to revise the current plan.

The strategic planning process has four key components: the mission statement, analysis, planning, and implementation. Figure 6.1 summarizes the continuous flow of activity as new strategic plans are developed and existing plans are monitored, modified, and possibly replaced if they are no longer considered a good fit with current conditions or management objectives.

Mission Statement of the Organization

mission statement
A basic description detailing the fundamental purpose for the organization's existence.

Strategic planning begins with the establishment of the firm's **mission statement,** a basic description detailing the fundamental purpose for the organization's existence. The mission statement is developed at the highest level of the firm's management and ownership structure, including its board of directors. Mission statements should be relatively stable over long periods of time and should provide a general sense of direction for all other decision making throughout the firm. The mission statement tells managers at lower levels of the firm the directions in which their strategic thinking may possibly go and those in which it should not. Opportunities for business growth and the development of competitive advantages that fit within the structure established by the mission statement will be encouraged. Those that are beyond the boundaries set by the framers of the mission statement will be rejected.

Mission statements should not change unless fundamental changes have occurred that are forcing a major rethinking of the firm's business practices. This may be due to radical changes in competition or in any other area of the business environment. For example, AOL's first mission statement was probably limited to setting a corporate goal of building a base of subscribers to its Internet connection services. In those early days of the Internet, there were a handful of competitors vying for subscribers who would pay fees for connecting to the Internet. More recently, however, especially after the merger with Time Warner, it is likely that the very essence of the firm and its long-term goals have changed to include exploiting the potential growth opportunities resulting from the merger. Not surprisingly, then, AOL's web site (**http://www.aoltimewarner.com/about/mission.html**)

FIGURE 6.1   The Strategic Planning Process

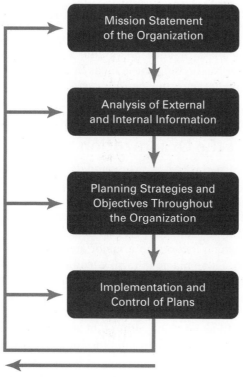

Feedback Flow of Results

After the organization's mission statement has been established, analysis of relevant information leads to the development of strategic plans and their subsequent implementation by the firm. Feedback links assure the continuous incorporation of new information at all steps of the process.

analysis
The study and evaluation of both external and internal factors to the firm that are considered important environmental forces acting upon customers, current strategies, and new plans still under development.

external factors
Sociocultural, technological, legal and regulatory, political, economic, and competitive forces.

currently states that the firm's mission is "to become the world's most respected and valued company by connecting, informing, and entertaining people, everywhere in innovative ways that will enrich their lives." Other broad descriptors of AOL's mission, such as its social responsibility, help to frame the company's direction for management and interested publics.

Analysis of External and Internal Information

Information is derived from the **analysis** of factors, both external and internal to the firm, that are considered important environmental forces acting upon customers, current strategies, and new plans still under development. **External factors** include sociocultural, technological, legal and regulatory, political,

internal factors
The organization's human, material, informational, and financial resources; structure; operational style; culture; and other characteristics that are at work within it.

economic, and competitive forces. **Internal factors** include the organization's human, material, informational, and financial resources; structure; operational style; culture; and other characteristics that are at work within it. Any new plan will have to reflect the reality of both the external world and the internal dynamics of the organization. We examined these environmental forces that affect planning and business practice in Module 1 of this text. Chapter 7 presents methodologies for researching these areas and staying in front of continuously and rapidly changing events that can affect current and future planning activities.

Planning Strategies and Objectives Throughout the Organization

planning
Organizing and detailing all of the strategies that will be undertaken throughout the firm and their expected or targeted objectives and results.

corporate-level planning
Planning that determines the overall direction for the firm.

division- (strategic business unit [SBU]-) level planning
Planning that focuses on a major area or group of related products offered by the firm.

operating- (functional-) level planning
Planning that occurs within specific departments of the organization.

Planning is concerned with organizing and detailing all of the strategies that will be undertaken throughout the firm and their expected or targeted objectives and results. Planning is organized hierarchically from the top down, and therefore **corporate-level planning** and objectives that determine the overall direction for the firm become the starting point for **division- (strategic business unit [SBU]-) level planning,** which focuses on a major area or group of related products offered by the firm. These plans, in turn, become the starting point for **operating- (functional-) level planning,** which involves more local plans within specific departments of the organization. For example, when Home Depot corporate-level planners decided that the firm would have an Internet presence, the decision precipitated planning activities within a team at the divisional/SBU level of the firm that would be charged with fulfilling the task. Within this divisional/SBU-level team, many operating or functional groups, such as web designers, e-commerce customer service representatives, software administrators, and others, would then be expected to develop specific plans for their areas that were consistent with the planning laid out at the divisional/SBU level.

Implementation and Control of Plans

implementation
The actual tasks that must be carried out in order to realize a strategic plan.

control
How well an intended objective is likely to be realized.

feedback
The evaluation of activities that are reported back to management decision makers.

Implementation refers to the actual tasks that must be carried out in order to realize the plan. This includes a control and feedback system that can direct useful information to the various levels of the firm that are involved in the ongoing planning process. **Control** refers to how well an intended objective is likely to be realized, given current conditions. Control strategies may simply involve evaluating daily reports of web site activity in order to assess the success or failure of the current strategy. If the expected volume of web users and the number of transactions are in line with expectations, then the plan is judged to be under control. **Feedback** refers to the evaluation of activities that are reported back to management decision makers. Reports to management may trigger decisions to stay the course or to make changes. In this way, progress toward the successful achievement of the plan can be measured and information that may be useful to the development of emerging plans can be directed to those who can incorporate these findings. We will explore these topics in greater detail in Chapter 12.

Strategic Planning at the Three Primary Organizational Levels of the Firm

Developing an understanding of the complexities of strategic planning is perhaps best begun by examining the activities that are undertaken at each of the three primary organizational levels of the firm. Although one might focus on the planning at one particular level, it is critically important to recognize that management must make an effort to integrate strategies consistently across all levels of the organization in order to assure success.

Corporate-Level Planning

Planning at the corporate level answers fundamental questions about the nature of the business. What business are we in? What is our business model? What is our mission statement? How will our corporate plans be understood and carried out by the division/SBU teams in our firm? Who are our customers? What sorts of products are we selling? Will we operate globally? Will we have strategic alliances, and if so, with whom? These questions and their answers can be summarized at the corporate level into a few generic competitive strategies that the firm may choose to employ in pursuit of growth and profitability.

strategic alliance
An arrangement in which the strategic planning of one firm is dependent on the cooperative strategic planning of another firm.

Let's first examine the use of strategic alliances and partnerships with other firms. A **strategic alliance** exists when the strategic planning of one firm is dependent on the cooperative strategic planning of another. For example, IBM (**www.ibm.com**) maintains a strategic alliance with Siebel Systems Inc. (**www.siebel .com**), the largest developer of customer relationship management (CRM) software. In essence, IBM chose to enter into a strategic alliance with Siebel Systems and to sell Siebel Systems' products rather than developing its own. Why would the venerable IBM choose such a course of action, and what's in it for Siebel Systems? The answers are quite simple. Advantages accrue to both firms. In the case of IBM, the firm does not have to develop, continuously update, and maintain a software solution that would be only one of many. Instead of directing resources to what would be a costly SBU focused on competing with Siebel Systems and other firms that produce CRM software solutions, IBM can instead sell CRM solutions from several vendors. Should Siebel Systems' products lose their appeal in the marketplace, IBM can switch to other vendors' products. Siebel Systems wins because a strategic alliance with IBM gives it access to IBM's client base. IBM's endorsement of Siebel Systems' products adds value to these products in the customer's eyes, and Siebel reaches a larger potential client base through IBM's network of sales teams than it would ever be able to reach independently.

An important point should be included here. Although software sales are a significant part of revenue for both IBM and Siebel Systems, most revenues are earned from installation and software customization programming. For IBM, the game is won by getting a contract to install a solution—regardless of which software is used to create that solution.

partnership
An arrangement that is viewed as more permanent and longer-term commitment between firms than a strategic alliance.

The difference between a strategic alliance and a partnership is one of degrees. A **partnership** is viewed as a more permanent and longer-term commitment between firms, whereas strategic alliances are generally considered weaker arrangements that may not receive the same level of involvement by the firms. For example, Lotus Development Corporation offers a partnership program to firms that wish to act as local representatives of the firm and its products. In essence, when a prospective customer contacts Lotus and asks for information or a sales presentation about Lotus software solutions, the firm notifies a local partner and that partner takes over the responsibility on Lotus's behalf. Local Lotus partners may undertake the sale of any product, installation, or training. Thus, Lotus does not need to maintain sales representation offices everywhere and can make use of the goodwill, reputation, and knowledge of its local partners. This is particularly important in international markets, where the vendor needs information on a variety of local issues and details in order to conduct business properly. Should the local partner be unable to handle the entire project, there are other partners that may be more skilled in a particular part of the job that can join the "Lotus team" in order to complete the task. In this way, local firms gain the competitive advantage of having access to a variety of skills and knowledge that they might require in order to secure certain contract work for their clients.

AOL Time Warner, the world's biggest media company, invested $200 million into a strategic partnership with Legend Holdings Ltd., China's biggest personal computer manufacturer, to codevelop Internet services. There are currently an estimated 30 million people who regularly log on to the Internet in China, and analysts estimate that there may be more than 100 million users within the next few years. Although China is the world's most populous country, with more than a billion people, there are concerns about whether enough of the Chinese will be able to afford AOL's Internet services and content. By partnering with Legend Holdings, AOL shares the risk and opportunity with a knowledgeable firm that is able to help guide its strategy.[2]

merger
The combining of two more or less equal firms into a new firm.

acquisition
A larger firm buying a smaller operation and taking it into its organizational structure.

Another generic competitive strategy at the corporate level is the decision to merge with or acquire another firm. A **merger** suggests the combining of two more or less equal firms into a new firm, whereas an **acquisition** usually implies that a larger firm has bought a smaller operation and taken it into its organizational structure. Sometimes a merger or acquisition is not apparent to clients and employees because the firms continue to operate independently, much as they did before. The motivation for acquisitions varies, but it is generally related to the perception that the competencies of the acquired firm will contribute to the acquiring firm's value in some way. Rather than trying to generate these competencies on its own, the acquiring firm may consider it more economical, efficient, and practical to simply buy another firm that has these competencies and resources. For example, IBM merged with or acquired, depending on how one views the relationship, Lotus Development Corporation. IBM, which was not known for its smaller computer software solutions, saw an opportunity in joining with the leader in the field. On the other side of the deal, Lotus could capitalize on IBM's large global computer client base and reputation. Perhaps more fundamentally, Lotus's principal owners and managers realized an opportunity to convert the years of work they had put in to develop the firm into personal riches and to move on.

Mergers and acquisitions are a common route followed by smaller firms that have grown to a size that makes them attractive to larger organizations. Often start-up firms have a potentially great-selling product or have a customer base, skills or expertise that another firm may desire or need. Sometimes, in order for a firm to grow, a variety of elements are needed, such as capital and global geographic sales representation. Instead of moving to the next level by conventional means such as internally generated growth, strategic alliances, and partnerships, management may choose to be bought outright by a larger firm that can supply these needs and thereby expedite continuing growth to the next level. In these situations, the management of the acquired firm may join the larger firm and the acquired firm may continue to operate as a divisional SBU. Senior executives from each division would probably be part of corporate-level planning committees, where synergies between divisional operations of the firm can be examined for mutual benefit. This can be seen in AOL's mergers with Netscape, ICQ, and more recently Time Warner; each of these combinations has rewarded both firms by providing AOL with new competencies and providing the firms that chose to merge rather than continue growing independently with greater growth opportunities.

vertical integration

A strategy of growth based on taking on more activities either further up or back along the production line.

Vertical integration refers to a strategy of growth based on taking on more activities either further up or back along the production line. For example, many Internet retail vendors focus their effort on selling products to customers and contract with another firm for warehousing and shipping services. If they established their own distribution services, these firms would be able to earn the revenues associated with providing these services as well. As to why a firm would not wish to seek growth through vertical integration, the answer may be as simple as a decision that the added value or contribution to profitability does not justify the use of the firm's resources in this way. In order to be successful in some of these areas, a large-scale operation may be required. If the firm's scale of operation is too small, it would be counterproductive for the firm to attempt to include that operation in the channel. Consider that for many firms it is generally more advantageous to use computer hosts for e-commerce than to maintain their own software and maintenance operations. Instead, the firm's resources are directed to those areas where the firms can best exploit them for optimal value creation and profitability. Similarly, it should not be surprising to learn that Atlanta, Georgia–based United Parcel Service (UPS) (**www.ups.com**) generates over $30 billion of revenues and continues to grow by using Internet technologies to handle logistical solutions for its customers. UPS delivers more than half of all goods ordered over the Internet, a major portion of the 13 million packages it delivers each day, and maintains warehousing logistics for many of its customers.[3]

As these broad-based questions suggest, corporate-level strategic planning takes a wide and long-term view of business operations. The fundamental identity of the firm is decided at this level, and the decisions taken here determine which divisions or strategic business units will be established for the firm and what their individual mandates will be. For instance, a decision to create a web site with e-commerce services to customers will generally result in the establishment of a division or SBU responsible for achieving the objectives set by corporate-level planners. Exactly how those objectives are to be achieved are set by planners at the SBU level.

Division/Strategic Business Unit–Level Planning

The division or strategic business unit level of the firm concerns itself with those items that we generally consider when we think about the "nuts and bolts" meaning of planning. What products will we sell, and to whom? What price will we charge, and how will the product be delivered? These are fundamental marketing issues, and we will explore them in greater detail in Chapter 9, but here let us emphasize that the focus is placed on fundamental strategic questions concerning the competitive advantages enjoyed by the firm. Generic strategies available to the firm include cost leadership, focus on a particular target market, and differentiation of its products.

cost leadership
A strategy that implies that the firm is able to channel its distinctive competencies into lowering its costs of operations.

A **cost leadership** strategy implies that the firm is able to channel its distinctive competencies into lowering its costs of operation and thereby gain competitive advantage by being able to sell its products or services to customers at lower prices or by selling at the market price and benefiting from the extra profit. For example, Dell Computer's success is mainly attributed to its ability to reduce costs in several areas, including order taking, inventory, and selling. By producing excellent-quality products at competitive, but not the cheapest, prices, Dell has established itself as the premier online computer vendor for both industry and consumer markets. Dell's just-in-time delivery scheduling with suppliers and its strategy of producing products as customers enter orders on Dell's e-commerce web site have produced a model of manufacturing excellence that is used as a benchmark both inside and outside the computer and technology industries.

focus
A strategy that is based on creating value by satisfying the wants and needs of specific targeted groups of customers.

Market segmentation analysis might suggest that certain target groups are more profitable and better matches for the distinctive competencies of the firm than others. A **focus** strategy is based on creating value by satisfying the wants and needs of specific targeted groups of customers. For example, web-based magazines such as Businessweek.com and retailers such as Gap.com focus on a particular target customer. In most situations, the firm's Internet-based strategy is an obvious extension of its primary strategy. This niche approach to marketing can permit higher selling prices when customers are seeking specialized products and can't easily find alternative sources of supply.

differentiation
A strategy in which the firm directs its distinctive competencies into differentiating its products from those of its competitors.

In the third generic strategy, **differentiation,** the firm directs its distinctive competencies into differentiating its products from those of its competitors. By creating a unique product, the firm is able to more readily distinguish itself in the marketplace and either charge higher prices for its products or simply draw a customer base that is attracted to its unique offerings. For example, online providers of content such as information, articles, animation, and music enjoy a competitive advantage if the content they produce is perceived by customers as being of value. The more distinctive the content provided on the web site, the more likely it is that the content-providing firm will be able to carve out a niche market that is willing to pay premium dollars to view the content. This can be offered on a subscription or pay-per-view basis, or, if the web site is sponsored, the firm can profit from higher advertising revenues. Forrester Research Inc., for example, sells reports costing as much as several thousand dollars each that can be downloaded from its web site on a demand basis. Businessweek.com online subscribers have access to a variety of content that is not available in the free viewing public areas that are advertising-sponsored and are supplemental to the print version of the magazine.

Combinations of differentiation, focus, and cost leadership strategies are common and should be employed whenever possible, as they allow the firm to transform more competencies into specific competitive advantages. For example, iVillage.com, like many content providers on the Internet, differentiates itself and its products by focusing on a niche market of women and providing a wide range of information and services that either generate revenues directly or provide the opportunity to charge higher advertising rates. CDNow (**www.cdnow.com**) and Egghead (**www.egghead.com**) compete by both using a cost leadership strategy and offering differentiated products at low prices. Although one of these three generic strategies may be emphasized at the SBU level, it is common to find that a combination is employed to carve out a position in the marketplace.

Operating/Functional-Level Planning

efficiency
Doing things at a lower cost.

At the operating or functional level of the firm, the work of building competitive competencies is channeled through the effort to provide superior efficiency, quality, innovation, and customer responsiveness. **Efficiency** means doing things at a lower cost. For example, processing orders through e-commerce can reduce costs by reducing or even eliminating the time that employees spend in entering and processing orders. Superior efficiency can be generated by improving employee training and providing employees with software solution tools such as CRM. This, in turn, can help to reduce the rate of customer attrition (loss). Keeping existing customers longer, increasing the number of customers, and increasing the effective service provided to those customers reduces the average fixed costs of any business operation, such as the installation of an e-commerce system or CRM software. The opportunities to improve efficiency through management and leadership techniques, performance bonuses for employees, and interdepartmental cooperation are just a few areas for management to explore.

quality improvement
Making a better product and, in so doing, delivering increased customer-perceived value.

Quality improvement means making a better product and, in so doing, delivering increased customer-perceived value. This can be achieved in a variety of ways, including better manufacturing and automation and using superior components, which are affordable despite their higher prices because of efficiencies derived from economies of scale. Dell Computer is recognized for its excellent quality and reliability, which in turn generates more sales and customer loyalty.

innovation
The idea of creating new products, designs, styles, and other features that are attractive to customers.

Related to issues of quality is **innovation,** which refers to the idea of creating new products, designs, styles, and other features that are attractive to customers. Innovation is critical for a firm's survival in many businesses, especially for a computer manufacturer like Dell or a content web site such as Businessweek.com.

Without continuous refreshment of magazine content, customers will become bored and move on to other sites.

Customer loyalty is a major concern and a reason for a focus on customer responsiveness as a means to create competency. **Customer responsiveness** refers to how well the firm is serving and responding to the needs of its customers. Once again, a CRM software solution may be considered part of an overall effort to improve customer responsiveness and efficiency. For example, providing excellent online customer support can be a critical part of selling CDs on CDNow.com. Without efficient and high-quality customer attention provided by customer service representatives who are tied in to the web-based selling effort, the overall strategy would be unlikely to succeed.

To briefly summarize this section, then, the effort to develop new competitive competencies is generally a mix of many different functional-level activities, not all of which are necessarily Internet-based activities and concerns. Most strategic planning involves an overlap between functional areas and departments. Senior management must make a concerted effort to tie together all the participants in the overall plan and to ensure that a consistent objective is shared and integrated throughout the three primary levels of the firm.

customer responsiveness
How well the firm is serving and responding to the needs of its customers.

Strategic Planning and the Value Chain

Harvard Business School professor Michael Porter's seminal thinking about the firm's value chain and management's need to be vigilant in monitoring the five forces in the business environment that create both opportunities and threats to the firm's competitive advantage provides a guiding framework for managers to employ in the strategic planning process. In a recent look at e-business, Porter uses the same five-forces model, which highlights (1) the risk of entry by new competitors, (2) the level of rivalry among established competitors, (3) the bargaining power of buyers, (4) the bargaining power of suppliers, and (5) the threat of substitute products or services, to examine how the Internet is affecting existing competitive arrangements (see Figure 6.2).

Porter points out the obvious empowerment of buyers, who can use the Internet to find better sources of supply at lower prices, and of suppliers, who can also readily seek buyers around the world and use the Internet to reduce their operating costs. In addition, the Internet has low barriers to entry, allowing virtual firms to enter the market and meet any fulfillment gaps through strategic alliances with other firms, such as the arrangement between AOL and AutoNation (**www.autonation.com**), in whichAutoNation allows AOL to share in the huge and growing online market for the sale of new and used autos, and AOL provides AutoNation with exposure to AOL's database of customers. Not surprisingly, Porter sees increasing competitive rivalry among players and increasing numbers of substitute products and services available online.

According to Porter, understanding and properly deploying Internet strategies are critical if firms are to remain competitive. Porter suggests that every activity in the firm essentially involves the movement of information, and that since the

FIGURE 6.2   The Five-Forces Model

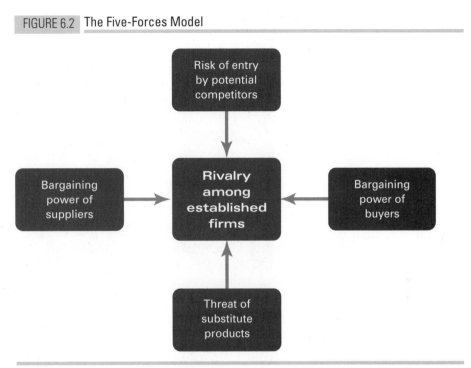

Internet has the special ability to link previously separate activities in real time, it plays a vital role in the entire value chain. Successful deployment of Internet-based solutions from supply-chain management activities on one end to customer relationship management on the other will strengthen the company and its brand. The challenge for managers will be to break the traditional structural barriers within the organization so that cross-functional solutions involving people in all company departments can be developed.[4]

Much strategic planning effort focuses on the task of finding ways to add customer-perceived value in the value chain. The **value chain** refers to a view of the firm as an organization of activities concerned with transforming inputs into customer-valued outputs (see Figure 6.3). The underlying thinking that guides strategic planning is to select activities that are superior to other choices and, in so doing, deliver superior customer value. Superior value will, in turn, provide the firm with a competitive advantage and thereby lead to greater profitability.

value chain

A view of the firm as an organization of activities concerned with transforming inputs into customer-valued outputs.

Primary Activities in the Value Chain

The primary activities in the value chain are research and development, production, marketing and sales, and service. Next, let's examine these value-creating opportunities in greater detail and look at the opportunities for creating competitive advantage in the marketplace that they give the firm.

FIGURE 6.3   The Value Chain

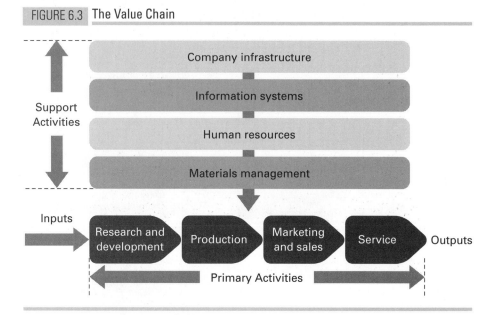

From Charles Hill and Gareth Jones, *Strategic Management,* Fifth Edition. Copyright © 2001 by Houghton Mifflin Company. Reprinted with permission.

Research and Development
Research and development focuses on generating innovative products and services that are recognized as offering superior value to customers. For example, online securities trading services offered by innovative firms like Charles Schwab provide investors with an alternative method of trading and monitoring their investment portfolios. Furthermore, online brokerage firms differentiate themselves through various unique online services, such as information and advice about current economic and investment conditions.

Production
Production is concerned with the creation of a product or service. A bank web site can provide quick processing and approval of a loan application based on information entered by customers online. In a sense, the production of the loan is accomplished on the web site. The web site provides a more efficient means of production, creating value by reducing costs and saving time for both parties. Rather than a loan officer of the bank sitting in front of the same data input screen and asking a customer questions over the telephone or in the bank's offices, the entire activity is automated and customer-controlled. The bank saves on the costs of the loan officer and on overhead and processing costs. The customer saves time, can access his or her bank accounts at any time it is convenient, and probably will benefit from the bank's savings through lower, more competitive interest charges as well.

Marketing and Sales

Marketing and sales activities allow firms to distinguish themselves from their competitors and create unique customer-perceived value in a variety of ways. For example, AOL, the leading Internet service provider, stands out in the industry by providing its subscribers with special products and services that are not available to others on the Web. *Business Week* magazine gives subscribers to its print edition access to an extended online version. Marketing and sales activities can also provide useful customer information, such as user behavior and preferences, that the research and development staff can use in developing future products and activities.

Service

Providing superior customer service is a popular focus for adding value and distinguishing the firm from competitors. For example, online retail customers may abandon the purchasing process if information and assistance are not readily available when they need it. If the buying process is stalled at some point, a quick exchange over the telephone with a customer service representative who can see the current screen being used by the customer may be needed to solve the problem. In that case, a firm like Dell Computer (**www.dell.com**) that provides this service will be perceived as superior and as having a competitive advantage. Given the importance of providing high-quality service, CRM software solutions are commonly deployed by firms that can afford the relatively high cost of operating them. Customer expectations are an important part of the decision as to whether or not to deploy a full CRM solution as part of a web strategy. Large firms that provide superior customer quality in their bricks-and-mortar operations will be expected to at least match that quality level in their web site activities. Smaller firms or those that are unknown to customers may be given some grace as the web effort is unfolded; however, if there are competitors that are already established and are providing high-quality service, management should be concerned with erosion of customer loyalty and the reputation of the corporate brand. It might be advisable to delay a public web effort until there is confidence in the quality of the service rather than risk the damage that might be done by a poor solution.

Support Activities in the Value Chain

In addition to the primary activities in the value chain that we have just examined, there are also support activities, which include the company infrastructure, information systems, human resources, and materials management. Support activities facilitate the primary activities in the value chain.

Company Infrastructure

company infrastructure
Those things that define the structure within which the value-chain activities take place, such as the firm's culture, leadership, organization structure, control systems, and other such activities.

The **company infrastructure** refers to those things that define the structure within which the value-chain activities take place, such as the firm's culture, leadership, organization structure, control systems, and other such activities. A firm that encourages innovation and rewards initiative can develop superior competency in a variety of activities, such as research and development and marketing and sales. Firms that fail to innovate and develop a competitive advantage may find that their problem lies here and that a shake-up of long-established managerial methods of thinking and practice is required. Creative thinking can be learned, but doing so is affected by the environment in which any such effort takes place. Establishing a good supporting environment that encourages risk taking and thinking out loud in meetings (where rejection can easily be personalized) is a major challenge for all organizations that are hoping to create new value.

Information Systems

The firm's various information systems engage in a broad range of activities involving intelligent decision making that can lead to competitive advantage. Information that produces better understanding of warehousing and distribution strategies and customer-related information about products and prices are only a few of the information support activities that tie in with the primary value-chain activities. Sales force automation software is one solution that provides a network of databases and cross-referenced information about customers, products, and sales activities to assist the sales and marketing management team by providing superior communication and knowledge.

Human Resources

The human resources activities needed to contribute to the firm's value chain concern the maintenance of an appropriate number of trained, skilled, motivated, and properly rewarded employees to carry out the primary activities in the value chain. The sales force needed to assist customers in completing online orders at the firm's web site needs to have a great deal of information about the firm and its products and services, as well as knowing online customer selling strategies. Training, CRM, and other web-based software solutions can help distinguish the firm from its competitors by enhancing the abilities of its human resources.

Materials Management

materials management (logistics)
A support activity that involves the procurement, production, and distribution of physical product throughout the value chain.

Materials management (logistics) is a supporting activity that involves the procurement, production, and distribution of physical product throughout the value chain. For example, Amazon.com must order and warehouse inventories of books, CDs, and other products in order to be able to distribute them to customers quickly. One way to differentiate one online retailer from another is by the quality and efficiency of this activity. Poor materials management may mean lost customers, who will not purchase again if the delivery of their orders is delayed. On the other hand, good materials management can translate into better customer service, lower costs, and other savings as a result of more efficient logistic operations. As demonstrated by both Dell and Amazon.com, real-time transaction of orders, automated customer-specific agreements and contract terms, and customer access to delivery status are web-based strategies for creating a competitive advantage.

Creating and Sustaining Competitive Advantage

The value chain provides strategic planners with a map of the primary and supporting activities that are carried out by the firm as inputs are transformed into customer-valued outputs (products and services). Next, we will look at how the value-chain concept provides a structure for identifying opportunities for creating a competitive advantage over competitors and more profits for the firm. As illustrated in Figure 6.4, the model suggests that the firm's resources (human, material, informational, and financial) and capabilities (skills and abilities to make productive use of available resources) lead to the development of **distinctive competencies,** or the ability to provide superior efficiency, quality, innovation, or customer responsiveness. Superiority in these areas can permit the firm to differentiate its products, lower its costs, or both and thereby create a valued competitive advantage over competitors in the marketplace that generates higher profits.

Let's look at an example to illustrate the process. Radio Shack's ubiquitous chain of retail stores and its e-commerce web site operations were recognized as significant resources that could allow the consumer electronics distributor to create a distinctive competency. One of the advantages that Radio Shack (**www .radioshack.com**) enjoyed over most of its web-based competitors was the ability to make use of any local Radio Shack retail location to better serve customers who might want to pick up the merchandise that they had ordered online instead of using a delivery service. Besides saving on the delivery charges, customers who wanted to see the merchandise before they finalized their purchase could simplify the order-processing procedure by using the e-commerce web site to place their orders. Furthermore, many shoppers are reluctant to buy online because of concerns over the return of unwanted or unsatisfactory merchandise. Once

distinctive competencies

The ability of the firm to provide superior efficiency, quality, innovation, or customer responsiveness.

FIGURE 6.4 Creating Competitive Advantage

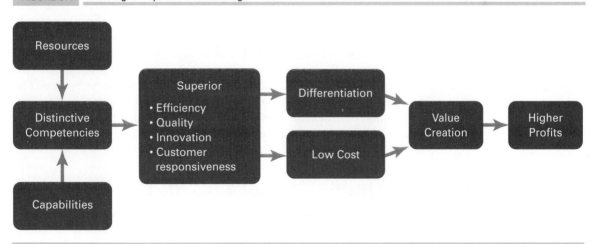

From Charles Hill and Gareth Jones, *Strategic Management,* Fifth Edition. Copyright © 2001 by Houghton Mifflin Company. Reprinted with permission.

e-Business Insight
Just Send Flowers.com

When Flowers.com added Internet-based ordering, consumers had the new value-added option of placing their orders over the Internet rather than through a retail store or through a 1-800 telephone number, which were two other value-added services supplied to customers. By using the Internet web site and e-commerce facility to place their orders, customers can view available floral arrangements and then select one that suits their taste, eliminating the time and inconvenience of finding and going to a retail store. Furthermore, the e-commerce order-taking process costs considerably less than order taking by either a telephone operator or a retail store clerk. Because the customer is the only participant in the order-placing procedure online, the only cost is that of the software and web site maintenance, which becomes lower and lower with each transaction and approaches relatively insignificant levels in high-volume operations. Selling flowers over the Internet works especially well because the product is well known to buyers and because online advertising and visual displays can readily trigger impulse buying.

---

competitive advantage
A benefit that originates with the firm's distinctive competencies, which allow it to provide superior efficiency, quality, innovation, and customer responsiveness in the value chain.

benchmarking
A firm's comparing itself to performance standards established by other firms inside or outside of its industry.

again, the local Radio Shack retail stores facilitate the human contact, which provides a value-added service to those customers who perceive this as a critical part of their buying decision.

The superior services that Radio Shack can provide its online customers allows the firm to differentiate itself from its competitors and perhaps also offer products at lower selling prices because of savings on the handling of returned merchandise and reduced inventories. All of these value-added services ultimately result in a competitive advantage for the firm and higher profitability.

Competitive advantage originates with the firm's distinctive competencies, which allow it to provide superior efficiency, quality, innovation, and customer responsiveness in the value chain. In order to sustain a competitive advantage for the long term, however, the firm must continuously work at cultivating new resources and capabilities that feed the development of new distinctive competencies—something that is easily said, but is challenging for any firm to carry out. In addition, the firm needs to maintain a high level of focus on ways to continuously improve its efficiency, quality, innovation, and customer responsiveness and seek excellent practices. By **benchmarking** or comparing itself to performance standards established by other firms inside or outside of its industry, the organization can measure its progress toward the goal of sustaining its competitive advantage.

Building an Online Presence for an Existing Business

So far in this chapter, we have expanded on the understanding of the e-business models and Internet-based software tools and solutions that were introduced in the previous chapter by adding the concept of creating value and developing a competitive advantage in the marketplace through superior competencies. In addition, we have looked at the planning process that takes place within the firm at the three primary levels of the organization, emphasizing the relationships between the three levels. Although these concepts apply to any business, whether it is a new venture that intends to operate exclusively online or an existing operation with bricks-and-mortar investments, it is particularly important to recognize the unique planning concerns related to introducing web-based solutions into a currently functioning operation. In this section of the chapter, we will examine how an existing business firm should frame the development of its online presence, which critical factors need to be weighed, and which guidelines planners should use as the planning process is carried out at each level of the firm.

Complementing Existing Non-Internet-Based Plans

The development of the firm's online presence should be guided by one key objective: to complement the existing non-Internet-based business plan. Whatever the firm's objectives, the e-business plan must be in line with them, supporting and, it is hoped, enhancing the current plan. If customer responsiveness is considered a weakness that can be solved by bringing a companywide CRM solution into play, then this strategic option will require planning at each of the three levels of the firm in order to properly integrate it. Clearly the worst situation for a firm is one in which a local- or department-level effort to use the Internet is being made, but people in other areas of the firm who need to be part of the total effort are left out of the planning process. For example, if one SBU is using a CRM solution to increase customer responsiveness and other SBUs are not, customers may be confused by the lack of consistency across the operations of the business. The same would follow with the introduction of a web page that promotes one SBU but not others in the firm.

 e-Business Insight
Yahoo!'s Strategy for Success

The dot-com story written by Yahoo.com established the basic e-business recipe for success: First, create content that can continuously attract an audience, and then sell advertising space to businesses that are interested in reaching this audience. In the case of Yahoo.com, success was based on an early lead, providing users with an Internet search engine that would help them to find sites in a complex and rapidly expanding universe of web sites. Since then, hundreds of firms have entered the market with variations on the algorithm for locating web sites in the directories developed by the search engine. Most web sites provide a search engine to serve their audiences. They can either develop their own, create a link to an outside web site that provides the service, like Yahoo.com, or buy the software and give it their own brand identification. Given the choice, efficiency arguments suggest that firms should concentrate on creating the content they are best suited to produce and acquire those other services that their e-business plan requires through purchase, licensing agreements, or other partnership arrangements.

Complexity and Time Concerns

In addition to having a consistent overall companywide policy toward building the e-business plan, the firm must also be concerned about complexity and time. Solutions such as introducing email or a simple company web site to help the staff of all SBUs communicate better with suppliers, customers, and one another can be developed and installed without undue delay, cost, or disruption of current work responsibilities. However, as the complexity of the plan increases, so too does the amount of time required to design, install, and test the new solution and then train the staff to use it. All of this is further complicated by the need to educate customers and suppliers, who will be expected to change their current behavior and shift to a new, perhaps unfamiliar method of placing orders, making requests for information, and so forth. For example, although Internet banking is growing in popularity with every passing day, there is a learning curve that customers moving to this method of recording transactions for the first time must pass along. A strong customer support system is critical to help those customers who may be confused about the online screen menus, computer and connection problems, and anything else that they may need assistance with at a particular moment. The telephone contact channel of a complete CRM solution should allow the service representative to view the same screen seen by the customer. Furthermore, the customer service representative needs to be knowledgeable and skilled not only with the bank's online software, but with computer systems and their common problems as well.

A good overall e-business plan requires research into and an understanding of the behaviors demonstrated by users of web sites and Internet-based solutions. For example, how long will it take the typical bank customer to adapt to the online banking system? What behavioral problems can planners anticipate and prepare for in order to assure successful acceptance of the system by potential users? These behavioral issues and other important topics related to online communication will be examined in greater detail in Chapter 8.

Motivating Acceptance of e-Business Plans

A business that already has a physical location (bricks and mortar) and a customer base generally looks at e-business as a way to expand sales to current customers and to add new customers who are beyond the reach of the firm's geographic location. Firms also look to improve their operations through the development of superior competencies that are available as part of an Internet-based software solution. For example, retail firms like Radio Shack, Sears, the Gap, Barnes & Noble, and many others have turned to the Internet to sell more products through e-commerce or to lead customers to a local bricks-and-mortar store to finalize a purchase. Both customers who are seeking the convenience of shopping online and receiving delivery and those who are simply using the web site to view a retailer's catalog of merchandise and promotions before buying in their local store outlet can use the firm's web site to satisfy their personal shopping needs. These retailers can improve efficiencies and customer responsiveness by combining web site content with CRM solutions.

Every business must be prepared to allow sufficient time for customers, suppliers, and staff to adapt to the new methods of operation necessitated by the installation of e-business solutions. If the newly introduced solution is seen as an improvement—for example, if it reduces employees' workload by increasing their efficiency and making their tasks easier and more enjoyable—then planners might expect motivated users who are eager for the transition to the new system. The message here is simply that planners must recognize the motivation level of those involved. The more that an e-business plan complements existing operations and improves life for individual users, the more likely it is that it will be well received, learned quickly, and adopted. Even though the firm sees installation of the new system as a positive course of action, if the users' perception of the planned changes is negative, the firm can expect resistance to the installation and a desire to maintain familiar behaviors. This was the case when banks first introduced automatic teller machines (ATMs) in the 1980s. Many customers were hesitant to exchange lining up to transact business with a live teller for the time-saving efficiency of the ATM. Although ATMs were first offered as a way to extend bricks-and-mortar banks' operating hours, it was not until the ATMs were networked, so that far more locations were available, and in some cases charges were levied for transactions conducted at a teller that the general population switched over to ATMs in large numbers. The lessons learned seem to have been applied with the introduction of online banking, as banks generally provide online banking services as a further service, in addition to telephone and ATM banking, for clients who really do not need the services of a teller and can manage autonomously.

Industry- and Global-Level Issues Related to e-Business Planning

The strategic planning process model that we have presented focuses on the strategic choices that are available to management at each of the three corporate levels of the organization and the interconnection of decisions. But just as the decisions taken at the corporate level set the stage for the selection process at the divisional level and on to the operational level, we recognize that the firm must view itself as a member of an industry and that industry as part of a global network of organizations competing within and across national borders. In this closing section of the chapter, we will examine the nature of both environments and the corporate-level strategic choices that must reflect the influences of these environments on the firm's e-business plan.

supply chain
The firms along the distribution channel that deliver valued services as the product is processed and moved along a path to the final buyer.

The Industry Supply Chain

Just as the firm can be viewed as a value chain of activities that transform inputs into customer-valued outputs, the organization can also be viewed as a contributing member of the industry supply chain. The **supply chain** refers to the firms along the distribution channel that deliver valued services as the product is processed and moved along a path to the final buyer. So just as there is a value chain within a single firm, we can recognize an industry-level chain involving suppliers, producers, service providers, and so forth, who in combination deliver value to the final customer.

The logistical concerns of warehousing, sorting, packaging, and transportation are only a few examples of the many activities in the chain that add value. The focus for businesses here is always, "What new and better customer-perceived value can be added to the current arrangement?" Current and potential participants in the supply chain compete to uncover a new value-added service or a better way to manage the current supply-chain activities. Obviously, any activity that reduces costs along the channel will be of benefit to final customers. For example, a brokerage firm that facilitates the exchange process among all industry suppliers by providing an easy-to-use web site is contributing a value-added service to the supply chain that delivers products to business customers. This service might result in lower prices or a wider selection of products for others farther down the supply chain. Regardless of the value added to the supply chain, the service is judged to be an improvement to the way the supply chain was operating previously. By looking at itself as a component of a larger infrastructure (the supply chain), the firm can expand on its internal view of its own value chain.

A Fragmented Industry Environment

fragmented industry
An industry in which there are a large number of small and medium-scale firms that typically employ a focus strategy at the SBU level of their organizations.

Corporate strategic planning should also reflect the environmental competitive conditions present in the industry. Industries can be classified as fragmented, growth-oriented, mature, or declining. A **fragmented industry** is one in which there are a large number of small and medium-scale firms that typically employ a focus strategy at the SBU level of their organizations. The strategic focus may be based on specialized products or services, a particular target audience, or a particular geographic area. On the Internet, many industry environments can be considered fragmented, with the customer often having difficulty differentiating one firm from another and therefore selecting one firm over another. For example, consider online retailing of CDs, books, clothing, and other consumer products. Just as consumers may have dozens of bricks-and-mortar retail locations to choose from in their geographic area, the Internet creates even greater fragmentation problems for vendors of these easily compared products. To take advantage of the organizational strategies inherent in Internet solutions, firms will tend to graduate toward some sort of online organizational structure, such as an online mall, that can consolidate this fragmented situation and thereby take advantage of economies of scale and cost savings. This is precisely the same reason why local firms will join in strategic alliances and partnerships with larger-scale firms, as was described earlier in the Lotus partnership program. In short, the solution for managers in a fragmented industry is to seek a unifying organization on the Internet that can bring shared economies and other benefits to smaller firms that are trying to expand their operations online.

Industry Life Cycle Issues

industry life cycle

The stages that an industry and its firms pass through over time as their product sales soar in growth, level off in maturity, and finally decline.

The **industry life cycle** refers to the stages that an industry and its firms pass through over time as their product sales soar in *growth,* level off in *maturity,* and finally *decline.* Characteristics of a *growth industry* environment usually include the introduction of innovative products and services by firms that hope to capture higher prices for their inventions and solutions. The strategic choices for an innovative firm in a growth industry are to either go it alone, if the firm possesses the competencies needed to properly exploit the available opportunities, seek a strategic alliance or partnership, or license the right to distribute or produce its product. For example, the online entertainment industry is certainly a growth environment, with innovative products and services emerging every day. In the area of peer-to-peer file-sharing software that allows superior Internet distribution of music, there is likely to be the development of more partnerships between software firms and industry giants in order to quickly exploit the technology before another takes its place.

A few dominant large-scale firms with established, long-selling familiar products and brands typically characterize *mature industries.* On the Internet, these firms might be retailers like Amazon and Barnes & Noble. Whether the Internet presence of these firms is mature or not is not the point. What is important is the perception of the products and services being sold to customers. The primary strategy for vendors of mature commodity products like books and CDs is to focus on cost-reducing efficiencies and superior customer responsiveness. Price reductions and other promotional efforts can also help to better position the firm and its brand association.

In a *declining industry,* where sales are falling and some competitors are leaving the market, the surviving firms can develop strategies for picking up abandoned customers and focusing on niches in the marketplace that are considered still viable. Although we have already witnessed a major shakeout of so-called dot.coms or Internet-only firms, it would be inappropriate to identify any industry as an example of a declining online industry. However, as is the case with mature industries and their products, any declining industry with products to sell may find that the expanded opportunities and efficiencies that are available through the Internet provide a new venue for finding and serving customers.

Global-Level Strategic Planning Issues

international strategy

An attempt to benefit through transferring the firm's competencies to markets that lack them while providing a minimal amount of customization to suit local conditions.

multidomestic strategy

A strategy that recognizes the need to customize the firm's operations to reflect selected local conditions.

The Internet opens the door to global strategic planning opportunities for even the smallest of organizations. An **international strategy** is an attempt to benefit through transferring the firm's competencies to markets that lack them while providing a minimal amount of customization to suit local conditions. Developers of online game sites may customize their entry screens with instructions and advertising in the local user's spoken language, but the rest of the game display is likely to be unchanged, especially since the game display is visual and the added sound effects are readily understood across cultures and language barriers. A **multidomestic strategy** recognizes the need to customize the firm's operations to

global strategy
A strategy in which the firm sets up some operations in foreign countries to take advantage of local economies.

transnational strategy
A strategy in which a firm combines a variety of operations in different countries to create the firm's overall operations.

reflect selected local conditions. For example, Microsoft's network, msn.com, has more than a dozen versions using different languages and customized for different regions in the world. A firm with a more involved **global strategy** would set up some operations in foreign countries to take advantage of local economies, and a firm with a **transnational strategy** combines a variety of operations in different countries to create the firm's overall operations. For example, many high-tech American-based firms have established their programming operations in India, where expertise is available at lower costs.

To conclude, global-level Internet-based strategies should reflect the corporation's degree of commitment to the globalization of the firm's other operations. The Internet can provide cost-effective means for drawing together strategic alliances, partners, and divisions of the firm that are scattered across geographic distances.

Conclusions

In this chapter, we presented the strategic planning process as a methodical approach to understanding and building an e-business plan of action for any organization. We emphasized that the planning process takes place within the firm at the three primary levels of the organization. Understanding the relationships between the three levels is critical to overall successful planning. Planning objectives set at the corporate level set the conditions for planning at the divisional level, and this in turn sets the conditions at the operational level. We explored the basic thinking behind the strategic planning model, which sees as its primary objective the delivery of value to customers and developing competitive advantage through superior competencies. Furthermore, we recognized the position of the firm within its industry and global planning as sources of influence on the planning process. In the next chapter, we will examine the research process that planning should follow as information is collected, analyzed, and used to create and maintain the strategic planning process.

CASE STUDY
RETURN TO INSIDE e-BUSINESS

Home Depot's Internet presence is clearly designed to assist customers with their home improvement planning before they enter the stores. Besides providing important information about interior design and product selection, the site acts to develop and nurture long-term relationships with customers. In many ways, the web site's design and style are not unlike those of the sites associated with not-for-profit PBS shows like Home Time and This Old House. All sites clearly must have a commercial aspect that will generate revenues or be sponsored instead; otherwise their business model cannot work.

ASSIGNMENT
1. What design additions would you make to the Home Depot site to increase perceived customer value? Explain your suggestions.
2. Does the Home Depot enjoy any online competitive advantage that is not presently being exploited through its web site? If so, what would you suggest it do?

Chapter Review

1. Describe the fundamental characteristics of the strategic planning process.

The strategic planning process involves a sequence of steps taken by management to develop new plans, modify existing plans that may require revision, and discontinue plans that are no longer justified. After establishing the organization's mission statement, analysis of relevant information leads to the development of strategic plans and their subsequent implementation by the firm. Feedback links assure the continuous incorporation of new information at all steps of the process. The strategic planning process requires first the establishment and then the maintenance of a plan of action that everyone in the organization is expected to follow. A well-managed strategic business plan is one in which each individual employee's work contribution is consistent with the goals set for the organization as a whole. The strategic planning process is about designing, monitoring, and revising a plan of action for everyone working for the organization, with the expressed understanding that deviations from planned results and any changes in the business environments are to be researched and the resulting feedback used to revise the current plan.

2. Examine the strategic planning process at each of the three primary organizational levels of the firm.

Planning is organized hierarchically from the top down, and therefore plans and their objectives at the corporate level become the starting point for planning at the next lower level, the division or strategic business unit level, and plans approved here become the starting point for creating plans at the local operating or functional level of the organization. Most strategic planning involves an overlap between functional areas and departments. Senior management must make a concerted effort to tie together all the participants in the overall plan and to ensure that a consistent objective is shared and integrated throughout the three primary levels of the firm.

3. Define the value chain and ways to create competitive advantage.

The value chain refers to a view of the firm as an organization of activities concerned with transforming inputs into customer-valued outputs. The primary activities in the value chain are research and development, production, marketing and sales, and service. In addition to these primary activities, there are also support activities, which include the company infrastructure, information systems, human resources, and materials management. Support activities facilitate the primary activities in the value chain. The underlying thinking that guides strategic planning is to select activities that are superior to other choices and, in so doing, deliver superior customer value. Superior value will, in turn, provide the firm with a competitive advantage and thereby lead to greater profitability. Opportunities identified within the value chain can be turned into a competitive advantage and more profits for the firm. The firm's resources (human, material, informational, and financial) and capabilities (skills and abilities to make productive use of available resources) lead to the development of distinctive competencies, or the ability to provide superior efficiency, quality, innovation, or customer responsiveness. Superiority in these areas can permit the firm to differentiate its products, lower its costs, or both and thereby create a valued competitive advantage over competitors in the marketplace that generates higher profits.

4. Explore issues related to building an online presence for an existing business.
The development of the firm's online presence should be guided by one key objective: to complement the existing non-Internet-based business plan. Whatever the firm's objectives, the e-business plan must be in line with them, supporting and, it is hoped, enhancing the current plan. As the complexity of the plan increases, so too does the amount of time required to design, install, and test the new solution and then train the staff to use it. A business that already has a physical location (bricks and mortar) and a customer base generally looks at e-business as a way to expand sales to current customers and to add new customers who are beyond the reach of the firm's geographic location. Firms also look to improve their operations through the development of superior competencies that are available as part of an Internet-based software solution. Businesses must be prepared to allow sufficient time for customers, suppliers, and staff to adapt to the new methods of operation necessitated by the installation of e-business solutions. If the newly introduced solution is seen as an improvement, then planners might expect motivated users who are eager for the transition to the new system.

5. Explore the industry- and global-level strategic planning issues facing the firm.
Just as the decisions taken at the corporate level set the stage for the selection process at the divisional level and on to the operational level, we recognize that the firm must view itself as a member of an industry and that industry as part of a global network of organizations competing within and across national borders. Corporate strategic planning should reflect the environmental competitive conditions present in the industry. Industries can be classified as fragmented, growth-oriented, mature, or declining. Global-level Internet-based strategies should reflect the corporation's degree of commitment to the globalization of the firm's other operations. The Internet can provide cost-effective means for drawing together strategic alliances, partners, and divisions of the firm that are scattered across geographic distances.

REVIEW QUESTIONS

1. Explain each of the key steps in the strategic planning process.
2. How is planning different at each of the three primary organizational levels of the firm?
3. Explain the meaning of the value chain.
4. What are the five forces that influence a firm's competitive thinking?
5. What is meant by competitive advantage? Describe some examples.
6. What advantages does a bricks-and-mortar business have as it develops its e-business plan?
7. What industry-level issues should e-business planning consider?
8. What global-level issues should e-business planning consider?

DISCUSSION QUESTIONS

1. The strategic planning process is an integrated business effort across the firm. Discuss.
2. Discuss how the value chain relates to the strategic planning process.
3. How are e-business models and Internet-based software solutions related to the strategic planning process?
4. Is it easier or more difficult for an existing firm to create an e-business strategic plan in comparison to a business that is just starting up?

Building Skills for Career Success

EXPLORING THE INTERNET

Microsoft's central web site operation at **www.msn.com** is the firm's gateway for contact with global users seeking sources of news, chat rooms, communities, links to other Internet web sites, and a variety of other valued content and services. Content distributors like Microsoft and the British Broadcasting Corporation (**http://www.bbc.co.uk/**), the most popular site in the United Kingdom, can easily modify and customize their display screens to better serve the global marketplace, which wants content that is culturally and linguistically suited to their needs. Taking the theme of customization one step further, both sites provide users with a variety of personalization choices, including the ability to select local news and weather services by entering a postal code. The Microsoft site allows users to select the magazine article title links that they prefer to see each time they load their personalized web page. The ability to interact with individuals and offer them independent control of what they see on their screen is a prime attraction of the globalization effort.

ASSIGNMENT

1. Select a web site that allows customization by the user. What sorts of options are provided to users?
2. How beneficial do you believe this strategy to be for the web site you have selected, in terms of attracting and keeping loyal users?

DEVELOPING CRITICAL THINKING SKILLS

Michael Porter's value chain and five-forces model play an important role in the strategic planning process. By examining the current situation facing a firm and the industry it competes in, planners can develop an inventory of opportunities for growth to consider and can better understand the threats to any competitive advantage they may enjoy. Use the Internet to learn more about a firm that currently enjoys a competitive advantage in its industry.

ASSIGNMENT

1. Describe the reasons for the competitive advantage that the firm currently enjoys.
2. How much risk to this advantage from the entry of new competitors is there? From substitute products?
3. Describe the level of rivalry among established competitors.
4. Describe the bargaining power of buyers and suppliers.   *(continued)*

BUILDING TEAM SKILLS

The SBU level of the firm concerns itself with those items that we generally consider when we think about the "nuts and bolts" meaning of planning. What products will we sell, and to whom? What price we will we charge, and how will the product be delivered? Generic strategies that are available to the firm include *cost leadership, differentiation,* and *focus on a particular target market.* Search the Internet together and select three web sites, each representing one of these generic strategies.

ASSIGNMENT

1. Describe each of your selections and how it conforms to the definition of the generic strategy.
2. Which was the easiest site to select? Which was the most difficult? Explain why you think this is so.

RESEARCHING DIFFERENT CAREERS

Learning Tree International (**www.learningtree.com**) is a leading private information technology (IT) training organization, providing courses on software, systems design, and so on in both teacher-led and multimedia student-controlled learning environments. The typical two- or three-day seminars held in hotels around North America are usually bundled with CD-ROM packages and online learning that continues after the learner has completed the seminar. You can learn about IT careers and the knowledge requirements demanded of IT personnel by examining the course descriptions and promotional material provided for targeted learners. You can also learn about some of the current software used by IT professionals by exploring Learning Tree's promotional site at **www.GetTechTips.com**.

ASSIGNMENT

1. Describe the categories of courses offered by Learning Tree.
2. What software training programs seem to be popular, and who are the target learners?

IMPROVING COMMUNICATION SKILLS

Benchmarking involves comparing an organization's performance to standards established by other firms inside or outside of the industry. Performance standards can cover a wide range of activities, from how well customer services are provided to the visual quality of the firm's web site. Understanding the criteria that are both useful and informative for benchmarking can be as important as the actual data describing a firm. Select a firm that you are familiar with, such as a search engine or a news site.

ASSIGNMENT

1. Identify the selected site and list its competitors in its industry.
2. List the criteria that you believe would allow a comparison between the chosen web site and its competitors.

3. Create a scale or some other measurement that allows you to score the firms on each criterion you have selected. For instance, you might use a scale of 1 through 5, where 1 represents a low and 5 a high degree of performance.

4. Present the criteria and your scores for the site and the industry in the form of a grid. Indicate whether the firm was above or below the industry standard scores and to what degree by placing an asterisk on the grid line.

Exploring Useful Web Sites

These web sites provide information related to the topics discussed in the chapter. You can learn more by visiting them online and examining their current data.

1. The Home Depot (**www.homedepot.com**), Home Time (**www.hometime.com**), This Old House (**www.pbs.org/wgbh/thisoldhouse/**), and Martha Stewart (**www.marthastewart.com**) web sites provide handy tips and step-by-step informative instructions on anything from installing ceramic tile to remodeling an outdated kitchen.

2. The Internet has low barriers to entry, allowing virtual firms to enter the market and meet any fulfillment gaps through strategic alliances with other firms, such as the arrangement between AOL and AutoNation (**www.autonation.com**).

3. One of the advantages that Radio Shack (**www.radioshack.com**) enjoyed over most of its web-based competitors was the ability to make use of any local Radio Shack retail location to better serve customers who might want to pick-up merchandise ordered online instead of using delivery service.

4. IBM (**www.ibm.com**) maintains a strategic alliance with Siebel Systems Inc. (**www.siebel.com**), the largest CRM software developer.

5. United Parcel Service (UPS) (**www.ups.com**) generates over $30 billion of revenues and continues to grow by using Internet technologies to handle logistical solutions for its customers.

6. CDNow (**www.cdnow.com**) and Egghead (**www.egghead.com**) compete by both using a cost leadership strategy and offering differentiated products at low prices.

7. Microsoft's central web site operation at **www.msn.com** and the British Broadcasting Corporation (**http://www.bbc.co.uk**), the most popular site in the United Kingdom, can easily modify and customize their display screens to better serve the global marketplace, which wants content that is culturally and linguistically suited to their needs.

8. Learning Tree International (**www.learningtree.com**) is a leading private IT training organization. Learning Tree's promotional site at **www.GetTechTips.com** provides informational tips on popular software.

Researching and Analyzing Opportunities for Growth

Chapter 7

INSIDE e-BUSINESS
Forrester Research Exemplifies e-Business Industry Growth

Forrester Research Inc. of Cambridge, Massachusetts, is among the leading Internet-industry research firms that analyze the future of technology change and its impact on businesses, consumers, and society. Forrester's success in this highly competitive field is reflected in the respect and status it has earned as a primary resource center for e-business clients wishing to make informed decisions and develop better strategies. Forrester is led by a dynamic personality, following unconventional management rules in a new industry that had very few rules to start with.

Forrester Research Inc. was established in 1983 and taken public in 1996 by its founder and driving force, chairman and CEO George F. Colony. Since then, the fast-growing Nasdaq-traded (FORR) star of the Internet-research industry has more than doubled the number of clients it serves, from 885 to 1,793. Today's 576 employees, more than four times the 134 employed in 1996, provide clients with research and guidance as they transform their operations and adapt to the new Internet-based economy. Revenues, which have grown at a compounded rate of 52 percent since the company went public, continue their stellar performance. Unlike many other new firms in the industry, Forrester has consistently earned a profit, which reached $20 million on $159 million of revenues in 2001.

It is probably safe to say that George F. Colony's leadership and management styles are both unconventional and a primary explanation for the success of the firm. By building a culture that supports both individuals and collaborative work groups that are determined to deliver creative excellence for their clients, Colony supports an open management style that encourages people to voice their opinions, rewards accomplishments, and holds individuals accountable for their work through goal setting and quarterly reviews of performance.

At the same time, Colony, like other leaders of new-economy firms, believes that people work best when they enjoy the work they do. Therefore, although Forrester provides competitive pay and benefits, the corporate culture includes the idea of having fun and socializing with fellow workers as part of the work environment. At Forrester, a work team that is responsible for a specific research project shares a large common office area, without office walls that keep people in physical and spiritual isolation. Access to others can be as easy as standing up and walking over to their desk, since nobody, including Colony, has a traditional office.

Like the clients it serves, Forrester is not immune to the rapidly changing forces in the e-business environment and has recently transformed its entire business model. The new model places a greater emphasis on electronic formats and distribution to clients that take advantage of the Internet, new products, and the development of strategic partnerships for collecting and reporting research. For example, to build on its reputation and continue its successful growth pattern, Forrester entered into a strategic alliance with the National Association of Purchasing Management (**www.napm.org**) to produce a new product called the NAPM/Forrester Report on eBusiness. The quarterly report will track the adoption of Internet-based purchasing by both manufacturing and nonmanufacturing organizations through a jointly developed survey of business-to-business (B2B) e-commerce activity. This valuable resource will help more than 47,000 supply management NAPM members and the business community in general understand the impact of e-commerce on their operations and plan accordingly.

With the addition of the NAPM/Forrester Report on eBusiness, e-business researchers will have one more reason to look to Forrester's web site, **www .forrester.com**, as a reliable source for industry information collected by both traditional methods and the inventive online strategies that we will explore in this chapter.[1]

Information is a primary business resource that is necessary for individual and collective decision making throughout any organization. Information, like other assets, has value, and like any other tangible asset of the firm, it must be created. Somehow, somewhere, somebody has to invest time and effort to learn about something, organize the relative importance of the facts and their interpretation, and then prepare a summation of that information for others in the firm to use. Many of the clients that firms like Forrester Research serve are planners and decision makers who need to know a variety of often fast changing and complex information, especially when it comes to the e-business area.

In this chapter, we will examine the complex challenge of researching e-business and explain how managers might begin the process that leads to discovering, evaluating, and finally adopting specific e-business solutions. We will structure our approach by first examining the fundamental reasons for e-business research and then look at a common model of the research process as it applies to e-business concerns and activities.

Primary Reasons for Conducting e-Business Research

In the absence of complete and perfect information, all decision making involves a certain degree of risk. However, additional information can lower the risk that a specific plan or decision being taken will be wrong or a poor choice. Researching and maintaining a continuous flow of useful information to those who need to know it is a vital part of any good organizationwide **management information system.** Research can be thought of as the principal activity that provides information for this system and helps management make better-informed decisions. This is particularly important in the growing effort to find e-business solutions and incorporate them into overall strategic plans.

There are a variety of often overlapping reasons for conducting e-business research and maintaining, as part of a larger management information system, a more narrowly defined **e-business information system.** We will structure our discussion by focusing on three primary purposes: gathering business intelligence, managing problem solving and decision making, and discovering new opportunities for growth.

management information system
A system for researching and maintaining a continuous flow of useful information to those in the organization who need to know it.

e-business information system
A more narrowly defined system that serves the needs of the organization as part of a larger management information system.

Gathering Business Intelligence

A good e-business information system will provide managers at each level of the organization with timely and pertinent data and information through reports that are written in a style and format that is appropriate for the intended user. Business intelligence requires continuous gathering and reporting of information about a firm's industry, suppliers, competitors, or customers, or even background data on a single potential client. A good system will not overload the user by providing a volume of information that is too large to digest or information that is

Search Results of "Business" from college.hmco.com

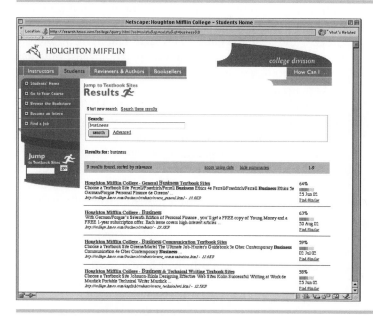

Reprinted by permission of Houghton Mifflin Company. (*Source:* http://search.hmco.com/college/ query.html?col=colstu&qc=colstu&qt=business&B.)

superfluous given the user's current research needs. In addition, in order to be an effective and productive tool, the system must anticipate the likely search behavior pattern of users. For example, to help them focus their search of the many reports and databases available, clients of Forrester Research first fill out a descriptive profile of the sorts of research they are most likely to find useful. In addition, the support system recalls which reports a user selected in the past and can make intelligent decisions that identify other related reports that may also be of interest to the user. Furthermore, Forrester provides a search engine that can employ key words and phrases to intelligently help to guide clients to the information they seek.

Most e-business information systems that are designed to help users to quickly find information online provide a search engine, especially those systems that hold a large and complex volume of stored data. The firm can choose from among many search engines used on popular web sites, then add key words, names, and phrases associated with the contents of the company's collection of data. Search engines typically provide a ranking of each found item returned to the user's screen based on an intelligent evaluation by the software of how closely the search criterion entered matches the listed item. This is often displayed as a percentage figure such as "95%," suggesting that the software believes that the item is highly associated with the search criterion and is "95% certain" that the user will find it useful. The screen shot shown above displays a screen of data received from the Houghton Mifflin search engine after the firm's database catalog was searched for "business" books.

competitive intelligence (CI)

A type of business intelligence that focuses on continuously gathering information on clients and competitors and then incorporating this information into the firm's strategic decision-making process and business plan.

A special type of business intelligence referred to as **competitive intelligence (CI)** focuses on continuously gathering information on clients and competitors and then incorporating this information into the firm's strategic decision-making process and business plan. CI involves searching publicly available databases and journals; interviewing suppliers and employees; and using other intelligence-gathering strategies in order to maintain an awareness of what industry competitors are up to. California-based Palo Alto Management Group Inc. estimates that the global market for CI currently exceeds $100 billion and will continue to grow. You can learn more about CI from the Society of Competitive Intelligence Professionals (**www.scip.org**), a nonprofit organization that offers training seminars and acts as a network for its 6,750 worldwide members. There are hundreds of private-sector firms that specialize in CI services, such as Fuld & Company of Cambridge, Massachusetts.[2] Entering the term *competitive intelligence* as the search criterion in the Forrester Research web site search engine will yield a list of reports tagged with the term, allowing clients to find and purchase needed reports quickly and easily. This primary strategy for gathering business intelligence online is a basic starting point for researchers who need to learn techniques for successfully searching both their firm's information system and externally available sources.

Managing Decision Making and Problem Solving

management decision-making process

A continuous activity that requires a creative approach to understanding the problems or opportunities at hand and generating solutions or means to take advantage of opportunities that might not last for long.

A second primary purpose for carrying-out e-business research and maintaining an e-business information system is to help management make intelligent decisions and solve problems. To do this, management must be committed to the **management decision-making process,** a continuous activity requiring a creative approach to understanding the problems or opportunities at hand and generating solutions or means to take advantage of opportunities that might not last for long. The logical connection between the firm's business information system and the building of an organizational culture that nurtures individual contributions to a creative problem-solving and decision-making process should be readily seen: Without a good system in place, the organization's ability to carry out any problem-solving and decision-making effort will be weakened. For example, the open-style culture nurtured by Forrester Research founder George Colony is regarded as a fundamental reason for the firm's rapid growth and success as it seeks ways to serve clients' research and information needs. Rather than simply presenting reports and databases on its web site for clients to access, Forrester's staff work with clients as part of the total research team. If a Forrester service representative is unable to find existing documents that would serve a client's needs, then the option of beginning a new research report might be suggested, providing new growth for Forrester. For another example, Eastman Kodak Company's recent entry into digital films—projection, editing, and distribution to theaters and movie studios—which, when announced, helped boost the firm's sagging share value 5 percent in one day, illustrates how looking at e-business solutions can revitalize a firm that many believed was unable to make a break from its original but aging technology.[3] Whether Kodak manages the shift to digital technologies in film and photography that will facilitate the distribution of entertainment content over the Internet or fails in this endeavor remains to be seen. However, investors perceived the decision as a positive move by management to change strategies to reflect customers' needs. Clearly other firms have failed to respond properly to technological changes, littering the business landscape with disappointments. For example, Polaroid failed to deal with its aging instant photography technology because management was unable to make proper decisions to revitalize the firm. Surely the Polaroid brand could have found a place in digital photography had better decisions been taken in time. To help managers think creatively and differently about solving problems and recognizing opportunities to improve current business operations, we will examine the steps that are typically recommended, as presented in Figure 7.1.

FIGURE 7.1   The Management Decision-Making Process

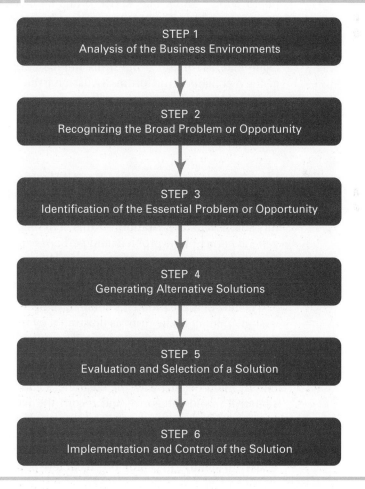

STEP 1
Analysis of the Business Environments

STEP 2
Recognizing the Broad Problem or Opportunity

STEP 3
Identification of the Essential Problem or Opportunity

STEP 4
Generating Alternative Solutions

STEP 5
Evaluation and Selection of a Solution

STEP 6
Implementation and Control of the Solution

Step 1: Analysis of the Business Environments

The first step in the process is the ongoing analysis of business environments both internal and external to the firm. Managers involved in decision making need to be well-informed about trends in their industry, recent strategic moves by competitors, technological developments, and so forth. Contributing to the firm's e-business information system and using it on a regular basis automatically stimulate management participation in the first step of the process. Individuals and groups that are responsible for specific products or perhaps operating divisions within the firm will often maintain their own online discussion forum focusing on the development of a greater common understanding of the changes occurring within the firm or in the industry. For example, how will the trend toward greater use of wireless communication technologies like phone sets and other palm-held devices affect access to our web site and our e-commerce business? And now that digital photography has shifted activity away from centralized photo-processing labs to desktop computers and printers, how should traditional photo supply firms like Kodak and manufacturers of printers like Hewlett-Packard respond? The forum can be a place for comparing ideas and floating thoughts or suggestions in an environment that should encourage creative thinking. A forum monitor should regularly prepare short summary reports on the dialogue and add these to the firm's database, or perhaps send a monthly email giving highlights of the forum discussion to an "interested-parties" list. An examination of the archived summaries in the firm's database would provide a quick history of the sequence of discussions on the topic to anyone who needed to know this information.

Step 2: Recognition of the Broad Problem or Opportunity

Eventually, the analysis step of the process will allow an individual, a group, or the firm as a whole to recognize a problem that demands a solution or an opportunity that awaits exploitation. At this step, management will recognize only the general nature of the problem and perhaps express it in descriptive terms such as "our customer satisfaction ratings are falling," "customers do not consider our prices as competitive as they used to," or "we don't have a competitive online presence in a growing new market."

The first of these problems could have been recognized through an analysis of customer email to the firm, as illustrated by the graphical presentation in Figure 7.2, where the trend in the number of complaints has been upward and the number has clearly reached a level that is above the acceptable benchmark performance level set by the firm. To generate this sort of data, after reading an email message and dealing with the customer's concerns, the customer service representative would categorize and record the nature of the email. An alert report might be automatically triggered if the acceptable benchmark level is exceeded for more than two consecutive days. To better understand the reasons behind the complaints, management would probably want to read recent email messages and try to identify any common characteristics.

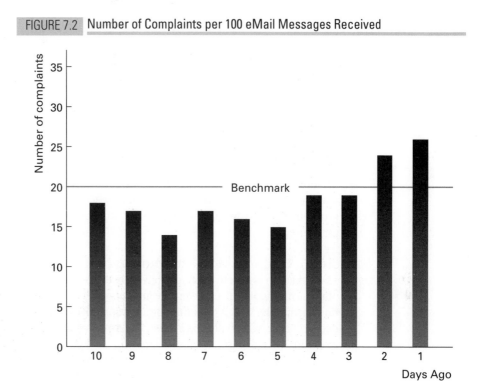

FIGURE 7.2   Number of Complaints per 100 eMail Messages Received

Step 3: Identification of the Essential Problem or Opportunity

In this step, the specific nature of the problem or opportunity is established. For instance, research into a fall in customer satisfaction ratings may discover that the fall is directly attributable to excessive time required to receive responses to questions about use of the firm's products, and that there are no complaints about the products themselves. Before any serious amount of time and effort is devoted to generating solutions, decision-makers must be confident that they have clearly identified the true problem. Otherwise, any solution taken may be misdirected at the very least and completely off target in an extreme situation. For example, if this problem can be solved through new and better training of employees, then the process will have succeeded. However, if the source of customer dissatisfaction is in no way related to employee behavior, then any effort spent on training will be wasted, as the problem will remain unsolved. The execution of a solution is usually the more expensive portion of the process. Management needs to be satisfied that the problem has been clearly defined and pinpointed before proceeding with a solution; however, as is the case with all decision making, even after substantial research effort and expert opinion, there remains the risk that the understanding of the problem may be incomplete or wrong.

Step 4: Generation of Alternative Solutions

A belief that the true problem is known leads next to the creative work of generating alternative solutions that can solve the problem. Here managers will assemble assumptions about current and future conditions and the likely costs and benefits associated with each potential solution. Perhaps more customer service staff should be hired to deal with the workload, or perhaps better computer-assisted problem-solving software needs to be developed to improve employee productivity and thereby reduce the time it takes to respond to customers. Of course, the alternatives available to management will be constrained by the need to make a decision within a reasonable amount of time given the relative importance of the problem at hand and the limitations on resources such as staff capabilities and money. Undoubtedly, Kodak's management recognized the severity of the problem facing the firm as increasing numbers of customers shifted to digital photography.

Step 5: Evaluation of Alternatives and Selection of a Solution

The next step is where management proves its worth to the firm, for decisions are often not obvious or clear-cut. Management must evaluate the alternative solutions available, weigh the consequences of selecting each one, and then make the decision as to which choice is best. Perhaps improved training of staff really is the solution in this case. Perhaps, because of high staff turnover, the benefits of allocating extra funds for better training will have a short life, and therefore computer-assisted problem-solving software will better serve the firm. For example, in addition to assisting full-time staff, the investment in software might make the use of part-time employees more attractive, since average training costs and time can be substantially reduced if the software is used by many employees instead of just a few.

Step 6: Implementation and Control of the Solution

Once a solution is selected, a plan of action needs to be laid out, complete with a timetable and an identification of who will be responsible for carrying out specific actions in the plan. Checkpoints set on a calendar can allow management to track whether planned actions are unfolding as scheduled and help guide the successful rollout of the intended solution. Information learned during the implementation of the plan can provide new data for the firm's e-business information system and contribute to decision making in the future, when another similar situation might arise.

Discovering New Opportunities for Growth

The third primary purpose for carrying out e-business research and maintaining an e-business information system is to help management identify and assess new opportunities for growth through e-business solutions. This means employing and extending the management decision-making process into an aggressively creative research force that is on the prowl for good ideas that will increase revenues and reduce expenses. Often research into current market activities, and especially what are considered clear successes by competitors, will uncover ideas that management will wish to follow. For example, although IBM is well known today for its effort to sell a variety of services to small businesses, historically the firm was more associated with providing large-scale computer hardware and software solutions to large-scale organizations. IBM recognized that it did not have to abandon its traditional markets in order to reach out to new ones, but that it would have to change its business thinking and strategies if it wished to serve small-scale business operations, where a sole proprietor may be operating a business alone from an office set up in his or her own home. To reach this market, IBM and other firms that are interested in the same market make greater use of mass media (television, magazines, and newspapers) than they ever did in the past. Online e-business strategies such as e-commerce and web site service centers that focus on small business needs are designed to help serve niche markets in conjunction with mass media advertising campaigns. IBM was not the first to follow this route and probably borrowed strategies from successful competitors like Dell Computer, which paved the way by selling directly to businesses and proved these techniques would work.

The e-Business Research Process

Now that we have established why e-business research effort is so important to the good management of an organization, we will focus next on a model of the research process that explains how this process should be carried out. In order to understand the tasks involved, the assignment of staff to these tasks, and the status of work in each area, it is useful to view the research process as a sequence of steps, as illustrated in Figure 7.3. As in marketing or general business research, the labels for each step are fundamentally the same. What is distinctive in our discussion here are the details related to e-business that apply within each step.

Step 1: Define What Information Is Needed

The research process is goal-directed. This means that every research project should have a stated purpose, even if that purpose is expressed simply in terms of the continuous gathering of useful intelligence about the current state of the industry and the market, competitors' and customers' behavioral trends, or changes in market prices for products. For example, e-retailers like the Gap and Sears, Roebuck need to conduct ongoing research so that they can modify their selling strategies as circumstances warrant. However, research projects may also be of short duration, rather than continuous, if the need for information concerns a one-time decision. For example, Sears may need to know whether a line of power tools would sell well to online gift-buying shoppers. If the study returns a positive result instead of a negative one, suggesting that the firm should go ahead and introduce the product line to its web-based shopping catalog, the need for this particular project will have been satisfied and the project completed. The results of a research project will often precipitate new needs

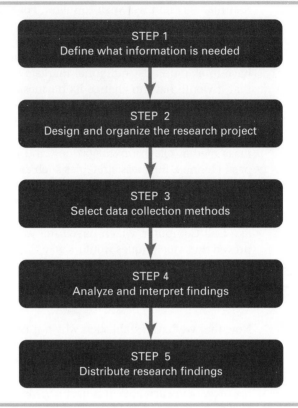

FIGURE 7.3   The e-Business Research Process

STEP 1
Define what information is needed

STEP 2
Design and organize the research project

STEP 3
Select data collection methods

STEP 4
Analyze and interpret findings

STEP 5
Distribute research findings

assessments and trigger new research projects aimed at supplying more information. For Sears, this might focus on the best way to market the line of tools, pricing and promotional strategies, and so forth.

Step 2: Design and Organize the Research Project

The best way to design and organize any given research project will depend on a variety of factors, such as the nature of the information, its importance to the firm, what the costs and benefits of the research effort are to decision-makers, and the relative need for reliability and validity in the data collection process. The basic research design may focus on the testing of a **hypothesis,** which is simply a statement that we want to prove true or false, based on the data collected. For example, the statement "men and women are equally comfortable navigating our web site" is a hypothesis that we can show to be true or false, and the *null hypothesis,* "men and women are not equally comfortable navigating our web site," suggests that there may be a gender bias favoring one group of users.

To gather data, researchers may elect to conduct **exploratory research,** seeking out appropriate information related to a research question or hypothesis, if

hypothesis
A statement that we want to prove true or false, based on the data collected.

exploratory research
Research that seeks out basic information related to a research question or hypothesis.

descriptive research
Research that focuses on helping to shed descriptive light on some area of interest.

causal research
Research that attempts to determine whether there is a causal relationship between two variable items.

one has been formulated. Exploratory research often leads to the clarification of a hypothesis, which then triggers more research targeted more precisely at the question. **Descriptive research,** as the term suggests, focuses on helping to shed light on some area of interest. For instance, the research question "how do men navigate our web site?" might be answered through descriptive research. A skilled researcher who is capable of explaining the observed behavior of men using the web site would probably prepare a descriptive report. A third type of research, **causal research,** attempts to determine whether there is a causal relationship between two variable items—for example, "Would the display of a photograph of a star athlete change the daily volume of traffic on our web site?" To test the hypothesis, we would first establish a benchmark or current traffic volume level and then compare it with the traffic level after placing a photograph on the web site for a trial period of time, say three months. If the results showed no statistically significant difference in traffic after the placing of the photograph, we would conclude that it had no effect on traffic. Of course researchers are generally interested in finding out what does attract more traffic and might conduct exploratory research to first gather ideas. Then descriptive research might be employed to help formulate an understanding of what web content and techniques are popular on web sites in general and web sites of firms like their own in particular. Lastly, causal research might be used to test for the right mix of specific content that best suits the target audience for the firm's site and generates the greatest traffic.

reliability
A measurement of the ability of the research method to report what it is intended to report each time it is used.

Reliability is a measurement of the ability of the research method to report what it is intended to report each time it is used; it is generally regarded as a critical element of design quality. A wooden ruler is usually a very reliable instrument for measuring length, as it returns the same length for a given item each time it is used. In e-business research, we are interested in discovering and using methods of data collection and measurement instruments that will return more or less the same results in successive trials. For example, an online survey that attempts to measure customers' satisfaction with their online purchase experience would be considered very reliable if the results are shown to be about the same each time another sample of customers is surveyed, within the time frame established for data collection, which should be one within which the results would not be expected to change. If, say, between 68 and 70 percent of all randomly selected samples of 1,000 customers returned a positive customer response, the research team would be likely to be satisfied that the method (survey) and the instrument (questionnaire) being used to measure customer satisfaction levels are reliable.

validity
A measurement of how accurately the research method and instrument measure what they are intended to measure.

Validity is a measurement of how accurately the research method and instrument measure what they are intended to measure; this is also regarded as a critical design quality factor. For example, if a question on the survey is misunderstood by a large number of the customers that answered it, then even though the results may be reliable (the same results occur with each sample), they do not necessarily measure what the researchers wanted to know. Selecting good methods and designing reliable and valid measuring instruments such as survey questions is a complex field of study that is beyond the scope of this textbook. Reliability and validity are mentioned here simply to draw students' attention to the importance of questioning the results of any research project they may be presented with and asked to pass judgment on. If the design and organization of the information-gathering process is suspect, then it follows that the value of the rest of the research process will be questionable too.

Step 3: Select Data Collection Methods

Although there are a variety of research methods and techniques that can be used to gather data about e-business, surveys, experiments, observation, web site content analysis, focus groups, and individual interviews with customers and suppliers are the methods most commonly used because of their ability to deliver good-quality results within a relatively short time span and on a limited budget. In addition, these conventional methods can be adapted to online data collection, so that the firm can take advantage of the automated data collection tools established at various customer "touch points," or moments when customers are in direct contact with the firm. These would include data entry by customer service personnel who take orders, provide product information, or receive complaints from customers by email or telephone or through the regular mail. Furthermore, retail bar code scanners at the check-out counter and credit card purchase data provide information on the quantities and types of products purchased as well as data that are useful for creating customer purchasing profiles and patterns. Interviews can often take the form of unstructured conversations with randomly selected sample groups of customers about their experiences using a firm's web site, and the dialogues provoked within focus groups of six to eight people can often reveal information that would not be uncovered through one-on-one interviews. Surveys can be done online, by telephone, or by email, and this method is familiar to the subjects providing the data as well as to the researchers. Surveys can direct subjects' responses through multiple-choice, true-false choices, or fill-in-the-blank selections, use open-ended complete-the-sentence statements, and so on. We will examine each method in greater detail later in this chapter.

Step 4: Analyze and Interpret Findings

Once the raw data are collected, the tasks of organizing, analyzing, and interpreting what they mean to the firm and to decision-makers in particular begins. **Information** can be defined as data that have been transformed into a form that is meaningful to users. A long list of data, such as thousands of reported ages entered on a questionnaire at an online site for a magazine, can be summarized using statistics. A **statistic** is a calculated measurement that summarizes a characteristic of a large group of numbers. Suppose that the survey data that were entered by users seeking a password for access to the online magazine resulted in the following statistics. The **mean** (arithmetic average) age of the respondent was 19.5 years old, the **mode** (the age with the most entries) was 19 years, the **median** (the age at which half of the total number of entries, arranged in order, are higher and half are lower) was 19 years, and the **standard deviation** (a measure of the rel-

information
Data that have been transformed into a form that is meaningful to users.

statistic
A calculated measurement that summarizes a characteristic of a large group of numbers.

mean
The calculated arithmetic average of a group of numbers.

mode
The group or class of data with the most entries.

median
The data item at which half of the total number of entries in an ordered list are higher and half are lower.

standard deviation
A measure of the relative difference between each data entry and the mean for the entire group.

ative difference between each entry and the mean for the entire group) was only 0.23. These statistics indicate that the age distribution of users is quite narrowly clustered around 19 years and that there are very few entries by users whose age deviates substantially from the group mean.

What this information might mean for the web site content developer and the marketing manager can be quite different. To the web site content developer, the information helps create a better profile of the users' characteristics. By extrapolating what is known in general about 19-year-olds and their lifestyles, interests, and motivations, the web site developer can possibly create a more attractive site that will generate greater satisfaction and loyalty. The marketing manager might consider this information to be a sort of alarm bell if the intended target audience of the magazine is 18- to 24-year-olds. These statistics would indicate that only a narrow part of the entire target audience is exploring the site. Further research might then be called for to determine why this is the case. Perhaps potential readers above and below the age of 19 don't like the look of the site or don't know about it. Whatever the reason, the information can now stimulate an appropriate planned action response by management.

Step 5: Distribute Research Findings

The distribution of research findings can follow one or more of the many methods employed by firms intent on building a solid knowledge-based organization. Generally speaking, the research findings, the methods used to collect and analyze data, the assumptions made, recommendations for actions to be taken, and so forth will be documented in a full written report. Typically, full reports can run from a few pages long to more than a hundred pages.

executive summary
A shorter version of a longer report that highlights only the key points.

An **executive summary** is a shorter version of a longer report that highlights only the key points of concern. Executive summary reports will normally be no more than two or three pages long. High-level managers are busy people and prefer a well-written short version. Should they desire or need to read the details, the full version should be readily available to them through a link to the firm's computer-based **documentation warehouse,** which stores and catalogs cross-referenced reports for easy retrieval. For instance, after reading the full report, an executive might wish to call up a list of any other reports that contain the client's name. Lotus Development Corporation's popular trademark software Lotus Notes, in combination with its Document.com software, facilitates the storage, retrieval, and management of documentation and attached multimedia files.

documentation warehouse
A facility that stores and catalogs cross-referenced reports for easy computerized retrieval.

In a simplified distribution system, reports and their executive summaries may simply be circulated through email lists and specialized email group discussion software such as Microsoft Corporation's Outlook Express. Corporate web sites and electronic newsletters are also popular methods for distributing documents. To help direct the circulation of new information to individuals who need to know it as soon as possible, software systems typically use a categorical coding approach when storing the documents, so that anyone who has registered to receive documents in a particular category is assured of email notification immediately.

Researchers generally expect to present their findings in person to their superiors or peers at meetings that have been arranged specifically to share information and stimulate discussion about strategic reactions to the findings. These meetings may be regularly scheduled on a weekly, monthly, quarterly, semiannual, or annual basis or may be called on demand when the findings are deemed urgent enough to call for convening such a meeting. Strategic planning committee meetings are often the setting for PowerPoint multimedia presentations about research findings related to a targeted brand, customer perceptions, industry developments, and so forth. The PowerPoint slides prepared for presentation at committee meetings are often posted on the firm's internal information web site along with the research report documents. If they are designed well, the PowerPoint slides should convey the essential characteristics of the actual presentation and often may contain audiovisual recordings of the exchanges between participants and recorded notes. Microsoft Corporation's NetMeeting is one of many popular tools used for facilitating the exchange of information by participants dispersed in different locations.

Understanding the Types of Research Data Available

Data that are collected during the e-business research process are classified on the basis of, first, whether they originate externally or internally to the firm and, second, whether they are primary or secondary in character. The significance of each classification is examined next.

External and Internal Sources of Data

External sources of data include a variety of Internet-based and traditional publishing sources, such as research firms and government agencies that provide databases and published reports of e-business industry facts, conditions, and trends. Often some of the research data are published and made available for no fee as a marketing strategy to publicize the research firm and attract clients interested in the collection, analysis, or reporting of more specific data. For example, Forrester Research (**www.forrester.com**) and Media Metrix (**www.mediametrix.com**) are two well-known sources of free Internet-based information. Like most research firms, they provide a regular newsletter highlighting recent findings that can be received by those who have signed up at the firms' respective web sites. The research firms are motivated to do this by the belief that brand awareness can be built up over time and that when the time comes for a firm that has been receiving the newsletter to hire a research organization, Forrester or Media Metrix will be at the forefront of the potential client's mind. This strategy is also followed by a variety of firms selling all sorts of products and services, including industry giants such as IBM and Oracle as well as smaller-scale management consultants. Every firm that can publicly publish data and reports, and so create a portrait of expertise in the potential client's mind, should do so to take advantage of an inexpensive means to promote its business activity and build its brand identity.

In order to take advantage of this wealth of externally and usually freely available data and reports, researchers should assemble their own personal list of the web sites they find worthwhile. The next step should be the creation, with other researchers, of a common web site that pools the researchers' lists. In this way, duplications can be eliminated from a master list, and an annotated description of what sort of information can be found and why it is considered useful can be part of the firm's e-business information system and web site. This gives the firm the opportunity to share a categorical listing of useful external sources with whoever else may be interested, both within the organization and outside of it. To publicize its own business through the Internet, the firm may choose to make its research site accessible to its clients, suppliers, and other parties who might also be interested in this valuable service. The web site for this textbook contains our list of good sources of research data and is designed to serve a broad audience interested in learning about e-business.

Internally generated data and reports can originate from the firm's own research and data collection activities. The firm's computerized accounting system can provide a variety of facts, lists, charts, and profiles about customers,

 e-Business Insight
Research into B2B e-Commerce

Finding high-quality information that can be trusted and used as the basis for planning e-business strategies is a daunting challenge. Executive decision makers are continuously bombarded by advertising hype and anecdotal references suggesting that organizations that do not get on board the Internet revolution today will be left behind forever. Knowing how far ahead or behind your business practices are in relation to those of competitors and other industry players is important. The quarterly survey and report of manufacturing and nonmanufacturing members of the National Association of Purchasing Management, prepared in collaboration with Forrester Research Inc., sheds a high-quality light on the behavior patterns that are emerging in the B2B e-commerce field.

The first issue of this report showed that only about half of the firms surveyed are even at a very early stage of adapting to new Internet technologies and to the buying processes that are available through the Internet, such as e-commerce and other procurement activities. However, these firms view the Internet as an important part of their future procurement planning, suggesting that B2B adoption is still at a very primitive stage of development, with much growth still to come. For example, only about 40 percent of organizations bought their direct manufacturing materials online, and only 15 percent used online auctions during the three-month period studied. The survey also found that organizations were using the Internet to identify potential new suppliers and for collaboration with current suppliers. Meanwhile, only 20 percent of organizations reported satisfaction with their suppliers' online capabilities, suggesting that these suppliers need to improve or face losing customers to other suppliers who can provide better online services.[4]

products, and sales staff performance. External sources tend to be broader in scope and to be applicable and useful to both the firm and its competitors, whereas internal sources tend to be specific to the firm and not generally in public distribution, unless the firm wishes to make them so. The firm is likely to have a greater degree of confidence in the quality and interpretation of its own data and reports than in those produced by external sources for a wider interested public and intended also to promote the image of the research firm.

Sales representatives are valuable sources of information about the firm's clients, trends in the sales of specific products and categories of products, and so forth. A good research site will collect this information and prepare summary reports by divisional team members so that everyone in the firm can share in the development of a company view of customers and markets.

Primary and Secondary Sources of Data

primary data
Data that have been collected through the original efforts of the firm and presented in reports.

primary research
Research effort that produces primary data and original information.

secondary data
Someone else's primary research and data.

secondary research
The use of someone else's primary research and data.

Data that have been collected through the original efforts of the firm and presented in reports are called **primary data,** and the work involved is called **primary research.** This original research data and research effort are referred to as **secondary data** and **secondary research,** respectively, when they are used by a second party, such as a researcher from another firm who reads the report and makes use of the original data, analysis, and so forth. It is generally preferable to make use of secondary data and reports whenever possible because these are generally a less expensive (possibly even free) means of deriving information than company-led primary research. Large-scale research studies that look at common industry trends and characteristics, such as consumer behavior issues, are generally expensive and time-consuming to produce. Purchasing a copy of a report written by a research firm that has conducted broad-based research in the field is almost always a preferable strategy. For example, the NAPM/Forrester Report on eBusiness, which tracks organizations' adoption of Internet-based purchasing, can provide a wealth of information at relatively little cost because its contents are of interest to many subscribers who effectively share the cost of developing it. Furthermore, firms may be able to purchase only those portions of certain reports that are most important to them. On the other hand, reports on broadly focused topics, whether offered for free or sold for fees, are not likely to contain the detailed information that is important to the firm. In these situations, the firm will probably weigh the costs and benefits of conducting its own primary research to satisfy its information needs. Often, large research organizations can be hired to do research on behalf of a client for that client's confidential or exclusive use, thus preventing competitors from knowing the client's business intelligence.

The need for research on broad-based e-business topics that are common to the industry as a whole is most likely to be satisfied through the use of secondary research. In practical terms, these topics are the dynamic environmental forces that, as discussed in Module 1 of this textbook, will strongly influence the strategic planning process and as such should be monitored and used on a continuous basis.

Methods for Successful e-Business Research

The decision to select any particular research method over the alternatives is generally a reflection of the perceived advantages and disadvantages inherent in the selected method. Among the research methods available for understanding e-business, the use of surveys, particularly online surveys, stands out from the rest in terms of the benefits offered. In this segment of the chapter, we will examine the online survey method, introduce the online research survey located on the web site for this textbook, and discuss how you can contribute to and supplement your use of the survey results for your own research projects. First, we will briefly examine several other research methods and their application to e-business research.

Observation

Watching what the subjects in a research study are doing can provide information that those subjects might not consciously understand. For example, how long would you wait for a web page to download over the Internet and appear on your computer screen before canceling your effort and moving on to another site? This is an important question for web site managers, who must weigh the value of providing entertaining or revenue-generating content such as advertisements as part of the web page against the quick reflex action of the user's finger on a mouse button. Although high-speed Internet access is growing in popularity, most users are still using slower modem connections, and so web site managers must consider the slowest common denominator in their design or risk losing a large portion of the global Internet audience.

A popular belief holds that web pages must be able to load on a user's computer screen within 8 seconds in order to minimize the risk that the user will become frustrated with waiting and simply move on to another site. Research has uncovered something that web site designers and site managers have long known intuitively: that superfluous downloads that slow the process are often not welcome and can be the cause of lost viewers not only for the offending page, but, by association, for the entire site as well. As a result, producing designs that are simple, quick to download, and created with the intended user in mind is the best strategy to follow. Although snappy animations may be possible and might look better, they are useless if the viewer has already left the page.

One way to find this and other information related to user behavior is through observation of targeted users. A computer lab at a school or library and volunteer subjects who don't object to the researcher's monitoring their behavior will provide acceptable data on a variety of behavior patterns. Although only a stopwatch is needed to measure the time spent waiting for a page to load, the research technician's time may be a significant cost for this type of research, especially if several technicians are needed to observe many subjects.

Observation research also has more serious drawbacks, though. There is the error risk associated with technicians not accurately recording the start and stop moments. Measuring short time frames is particularly problematic when the range is measured in seconds. A better solution would be to have a computer-assisted measuring instrument built into the computers that would accurately record the time required for a page download and the amount of time the user waited for an incomplete download before moving on. Another major concern inherent in this method is the behavior demonstrated by subjects while they are working under conditions that have been set up to efficiently observe them and collect primary data. Is an individual behaving normally? That is to say, is any subject under observation behaving as he or she would in front of the computer screen at home or in the office? There are a host of issues that can distort the value of the data collected using this design; however, as with any research effort, the researchers must weigh these risks against the real value derived. If the results of this method seem to be consistent with those derived through other methods, then those results can be used with a higher degree of confidence.

Observation research is highly dependent on the skill of the observer. In this situation, we were concerned only with the technical skill needed to identify the start and stop moments. What skill would the research technician need if we wanted a descriptive report on users' emotional responses to web pages? Were the subjects having fun? Did they seem to be enjoying themselves? Were the pages entertaining enough to create long-term good will for a particular site? The more complex the research questions, the more skills the research technician will need to have in order to recognize the behaviors and then interpret their meaning. And at what point do we trust the individual researcher's interpretation of the observed situation? Did the 6-year-old subject rush away from the computer screen out of frustration over navigating the page, or did he have to get to the washroom quickly? The more we rely on research on observed behavior, the more we need to know about the people who prepared the data and reports. In a sense, this triggers the need for an underlying faith in the validity of the researcher, or at the very least a cursory review of the researcher's credentials, before attributing value to the report.

Interview

The interview process is also a relatively inexpensive method that is highly dependent on the technical skills of the researcher. To follow the same example introduced in the discussion of the observation method, the interviewer could simply talk to subjects before, during, and after they used web pages in order to uncover their attitude toward waiting. Using this method, the researchers might not hear a simple answer. For example, when asked, "How long would you wait for a page to download before moving on to another?" subjects might say, "It depends on the site, how busy I am, how tired I am, my mood, what's on television," and so forth. Interviews allow the researcher to explore a theme with the subject and to pursue information that might be difficult or impossible for the subject to formulate independently. A good interviewer can uncover a wide range of information by skillfully navigating a list of directional conversational questions.

Long-term studies of behavior changes and learning are particularly well suited to this method, since the individual subjects are generally known to the researcher and can be remunerated for their time and effort. For a small cost, usu-ally under $100 for a one-hour session, a research firm can track changes in the online behavior of regular research subjects over time. Furthermore, paid sub-jects will generally feel an obligation to be truthful and "earn" their payment by helping the researchers find what they are looking for.

Focus Group

In much the same way that interviews can uncover online attitudes toward wait-ing, focus groups can stimulate the flow of information through interaction among the members of the focus group. Because there is the opportunity for in-teraction among members of the group, individual responses may differ from what the same people would say in an interview. For example, suppose a subject in the focus group started the discussion by saying, "Anyone who waits more than 5 seconds for a web page to appear is a fool. I never wait, and ever since I got hooked up at home to my high-speed Internet service I won't use anything else that is slower." How might others in the focus group react to these statements? Would a user of older technology hide the fact out of embarrassment or concoct totally false information about his or her behavior to conform to the group atti-tude that emerges through the discussion? On the other hand, focus groups can provide great opportunities for generating ideas for improving a web page and site. Simple leading questions about what the subjects like best and dislike the most can open up a cornucopia of creative ideas for improving the design and content of a site.

Experiment

Experimental methods can also be used to answer the research question of how long subjects will wait for a web page to download before abandoning the page and moving on to another. One way to ascertain this information would be to conduct experiments in which the length of time spent waiting is measured un-der controlled conditions. Suppose the researchers set up a site that they believed would be interesting to targeted research subjects. For instance, if it was a site de-signed to focus on a variety of topics related to Alpine skiing, the research sub-jects chosen would qualify only if they were ski enthusiasts. As the subjects progress through the simulated and controlled web site, the researcher reduces the download speed of each of the pages as the subject requests them, in 1-sec-ond intervals. Therefore, the first page would appear in 1 second, the second in 2 seconds, and so forth. The software is designed to record the moment at which a subject first interrupts a page download and moves on to another page instead.

A variety of analytical techniques can be applied to the list of subjects and the number of seconds each of them waited before abandoning the page download. Suppose the research results showed that subjects waited an average of 8 sec-onds, suggesting a strong measure of consistency with what was assumed before the experiment. Additional information could be derived by analyzing a fre-quency distribution showing how many subjects abandoned downloads at any

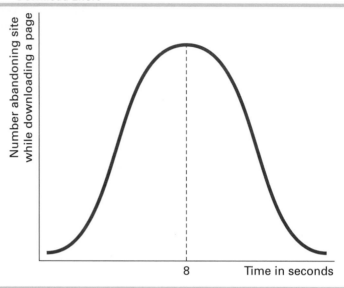

FIGURE 7.4   Frequency Distribution of Waiting Times Before Abandoning a Web Page Download Effort

given second. The distribution illustrated in Figure 7.4 appears to be normal, with few subjects having very low or high waiting times and the mass of subjects being bunched together at about the average wait time of 8 seconds.

Content Analysis

Content analysis is concerned with understanding the nature of the content in some medium, including a web site. For example, researchers for a small corporation who are considering the design of a web site for the corporation might want to know what content is typically presented by other firms of similar size in the same industry. A fair and systematic method for selecting web sites would be used, and data on the content found would be gathered. Suppose over 90 percent of the web sites surveyed provided an email link to facilitate contact with the firm and information about the company and its products, but only 30 percent provided e-commerce services to facilitate the online purchasing of the firm's products and services. Information on how much content is static, or basically not changed very often, and how much is replaced or updated daily, weekly, monthly, or on some other schedule is important to know. These facts, along with descriptive reports on the web site designs that were found to be easy to navigate and artistically pleasing, would be useful in guiding the firm in its design approach. As with other methods that depend on researchers' ability to accurately report what is often a personal value judgment, there are error risks that should be considered before any reports prepared using this research method are accepted.

e-Business Insight
Training Robots and Sharing Research on the Internet

Finding exactly the information you want on the Internet is growing more difficult with each passing day. For although more and more information is being posted online, much of it is not quite what the researcher is looking for. Now, however, the task of sifting through the volumes of articles, reports, and web pages that may be located anywhere in the world has been made easier and more effective through the use of a new type of search engine based on peer-to-peer file sharing.

OpenCola Limited (**www.opencola.com**) is a Toronto- and San Francisco–based software start-up whose peer-to-peer file-sharing technology combines capabilities similar to those of Napster and Gnutella with the intelligence of a search robot that will seek out relevant files from other OpenCola users. Here is how it works. Suppose, for example, a researcher wants to find information on "peer-to-peer software." After the researcher creates a folder to receive information on the subject, the OpenCola software would launch a robot to search out files associated with descriptive key words connected to the topic. The robot initially searches the Internet on the basis of one or more files that the researcher has placed in the folder. The robot simply seeks other information that it thinks is associated with the files that are currently in the folder. If a file is removed, the robot understands this action to mean that the user does not want files like those.

Any information that is found on the Internet is collected in this folder, including other files that may have been organized by other OpenCola users. Therefore, someone else on the Internet who may have been at this much longer can make available his or her findings on the same topic. The best part of this sort of technology, besides the quick sharing of someone else's research effort, is that the robot's intelligence grows and it becomes more sophisticated with time. This occurs as the user rewards or punishes the robot for the files that have been found. Based on the researcher's feedback, the robot learns more clearly what the folder should contain and even ranks the files according to their value to the researcher. The robot then looks for more files based on these rankings. Gradually, what develops is what OpenCola calls a "smart folder" holding only the sort of information that the researcher really wants in one location.[5]

Survey

Researchers using the survey method may collect data over the telephone, through face-to-face contact with the subject, on paper forms sent through the mail, or online through electronic forms. The questionnaire may limit respondents' choices by asking true-false or multiple-choice selections, or it may be open-ended and allow written answers to incomplete sentences. These and other style and format techniques for using this well-established research tool are available to e-business researchers, but the most interesting are online research designs that take advantage of the fact that subjects are momentarily connected to a site or are subscribers, clients, or suppliers of the firm.

Just as mailing lists facilitate the distribution of paper survey forms, email lists can be compiled from the firm's internal sources of data or purchased from external sources. There are businesses that prepare and maintain updated categorical lists of email addresses of people who have indicated a willingness to receive solicitations online. The lists are often created through online advertising and promotions at popular web sites, which usually reward participants by entering them in a contest in exchange for filling in a profile data sheet and agreeing to receive other solicitations through email. A popular form of data collection and means of building an emailing list is the online survey questionnaire that customers are generally required to fill out before they can gain access to the firm's web site, documents, and services. By providing information such as gender, family income level, educational level, achievement, and so forth, web site users trade valuable information about themselves and their online behavior each time they navigate the site. When done in an unobtrusive manner, short surveys that demand little of a user's valuable time and attention can become great sources of current information that is useful for improving the firm's marketing to targeted customers. Consider the online survey form on the screen shot on this page and note the information that must be provided in order to gain access to the site.

Although online surveys are inexpensive to launch and easy to distribute, they are often suspect for many reasons, including the quality of the questions that are asked; how the respondents were selected or came to be presented with the sur-

Online Form Used by IBM to Screen for Potential Small Business Clients

Reproduced by permission from www.ibm.com. Copyright © 2002 by International Business Machines Corporation. (*Source:* http://isource.ibm.com/cgi-bin/world/wnewsub.)

vey form; the large number of potential respondents who ignore emailed requests or pop-up surveys that interrupt another activity online and thus refuse to participate; the danger of bias when a benefit is offered to respondents to entice their participation; and the risk of multiple entries by a motivated individual.

Our Online Survey

In order to better understand how online surveys are structured, written, analyzed, interpreted, and then reported, we have created an online survey targeted at learners like you, who probably are using this textbook and are interested in e-business strategic thinking. The questions cover a wide range of subjects' interests and online behaviors. Long-term trend analysis will allow us to monitor and report the changing characteristics of respondents over time. Our reports will help to illustrate the challenging art of data analysis, data reporting, and information display. Because the survey is online, we can present a larger variety of visual presentations of data in the form of tables, charts, and graphs than can be accommodated in a textbook. Each of these will be accompanied by a short, easy-to-understand explanation of what the item means and how it can be used by strategic planners. More importantly, we will present a comprehensive summary of what all of the survey data mean in terms of e-business opportunities for online entrepreneurs who are interested in targeting this market.

We will be updating our reports regularly and modifying the questions we ask as you the users suggest. Along with the rest of the web site for this textbook, these web-based learning materials should be regarded as your research gateway to the Internet. While conducting your own research, feel free to use the data and reports we have prepared and, of course, to supplement them with research of your own. You may use the same questions to learn about a target audience that is of particular interest to you, such as your classmates. You may benefit as well by modifying the questions slightly to find out other information that is not included in the survey. Before you do any data collection, however, it would be a good idea to have your instructor or some other expert review the quality of your questions and your research design. You may reach the survey on the *e-Business* web site at **http://college.hmco.com/business/students/**.

Conclusions

This chapter has presented a broad overview of the research process and the reasons for maintaining an active and up-to-date e-business information system. The tasks involved in research, the sources of information available, and the methods used to find, analyze, and distribute reports were discussed, along with the importance that must be placed on the quality of the information produced.

CASE STUDY

RETURN TO
INSIDE e-BUSINESS

Strategic alliances such as the one between Forrester Research and the National Association of Purchasing Management are popular tools for growth among e-businesses. The synergistic goals of these organizations support this strategic alliance. The task of collecting good-quality research data is often the single most difficult issue facing research firms. Response rates of randomly solicited participants are often quite low, which may compromise the usefulness of the data and reported findings. By partnering with NAPM, Forrester gains access to a large membership that is more likely to participate voluntarily in research efforts. On the other side of the alliance, NAPM benefits from the expertise Forrester brings to its research program and taps into the historical base of knowledge that Forrester has already established. By co-operating with Forrester, NAPM fulfills its mandate to provide members with education and research resources to help expand their professional knowledge and improve their business practices.

ASSIGNMENT

1. What other benefits for these two firms do you see emerging from this strategic alliance?
2. What other strategies can you think of that could help Forrester Research continue its successful growth?

Chapter Review

SUMMARY

1. Examine the primary reasons for conducting e-business research.

Research is conducted in order to gather business intelligence, manage problem solving and decision making, and discover new opportunities for growth. Since information can lower the risk that a specific plan or decision being taken will be wrong or a poor choice, e-business research can help improve a firm's activities in all three of these areas. In the absence of good information, managers lack an understanding about what their competitors are doing in the marketplace, how best to select one solution to a problem out of many possible solutions, and how to maintain the firm's competitive position through the discovery of new business opportunities for growth. Researching and maintaining a continuous flow of useful information to those who need to know it is a vital part of any good organizationwide management information system. A good e-business information system will provide managers at each level of the organization with timely and pertinent data through reports on the firm's industry, suppliers, or competitors, or background data about a particular client.

2. Identify the steps in the e-business research process.

The e-business research process follows these consecutive steps. First, the researcher defines what information is needed. Next, the research project is designed and organized; data collection methods are selected; and data are gathered, analyzed, and interpreted. Finally, the research findings are distributed to those who need to know them.

3. Describe the types of research data available.

Data that are collected during the e-business research process are classified on the basis of, first, whether they originate externally or internally to the firm and, second, whether they are primary or secondary in character. External sources of data include a variety of Internet-based and traditional publishing sources, such as research firms and government agencies that provide databases and published reports of e-business industry facts, conditions, and trends. Internally generated data and reports can originate from the firm's own research and data collection activities. The firm's computerized accounting system can provide a variety of facts, lists, charts, and profiles about customers, products, and sales staff performance. Data that have been collected through the original efforts of the firm and presented in reports are called primary data, and the work involved is called primary research. These original research data and effort are referred to as secondary data and secondary research, respectively, when they are used by a second party, such as a researcher from another firm who reads the report and makes use of the original data, analysis, and so forth.

4. Examine the methods used for successful e-business research.

The decision to select any particular research method over the alternatives is generally a reflection of the perceived advantages and disadvantages inherent in the selected method. Among the research methods available for understanding e-business that are considered most likely to produce successful results are observation, interviews, focus group interviews, experiments, content analysis, and surveys.

REVIEW QUESTIONS

1. What is an e-business information system?
2. What role should an e-business information system play in management?
3. Explain the meaning of business intelligence gathering.
4. List the steps in the management decision-making and problem solving process.
5. List the steps in the e-business research process.
6. Explain the differences between external and internal data.
7. Explain the differences between primary and secondary data.
8. List the primary methods used for successful e-business research.

DISCUSSION QUESTIONS

1. Describe the primary reasons for conducting e-business research. Discuss the relative importance of each reason.
2. Discuss the reasons for conducting primary and secondary research. Provide situations in which one would be preferable over the other.
3. Discuss the problems facing researchers when they analyze and interpret secondary reports.

Building Skills for Career Success

EXPLORING THE INTERNET

In addition to the current display on the home pages of industry research firms like Forrester Research and Media Metrix, learners can find a great deal of information about the recent activities of these firms from their press releases and briefs. These items, which generally contain key bits of useful information such as statistics or critical findings about changes or new breakthroughs, are usually accessible from the sidebar menu. The information that is freely displayed helps to promote the firm's products, services, and expertise to potential clients. By examining this material, potential clients can better assess whether the research firm will be able to help them with their research needs. Often enough, the purchase of full reports or paid subscription to periodic summary reports can serve the information needs and fit within the budget constraints of smaller firms. You can find links to several web sites of research firms that are good sources of e-business information on the information gateway for this text, located on the *e-Business* web site at **http://college.hmco.com/business/students/**.

ASSIGNMENT

1. Examine the home web page for one of the research firms and describe some of the areas currently being studied.
2. Select a research firm that presents its press releases and briefs in chronological order. What can you learn about e-business from these items? About the firm?

DEVELOPING CRITICAL THINKING SKILLS

The e-business research process described in this chapter sets out the steps required to conduct research systematically. Select a problem or question that you consider worth exploring. For instance, is there a difference between the way men and women shop online? You may choose to test a hypothesis or write an exploratory report. The choice is yours as you follow the research process and prepare your report.

ASSIGNMENT

1. Briefly describe your research problem or question.
2. Following the recommended structure for the research process, write a short report that describes what you would do at each step.

BUILDING TEAM SKILLS

Select a question to research that is of interest to all members of your group. For instance, how do students in your class divide the time they spend online? How much of the time is spent checking email, in chat rooms, doing research for class assignments, and so forth? Discuss the methods of research that are available and select two methods that you consider to be better than the rest. Divide your group equally and assign one method to the first team and the second method to the other. Working independently, conduct the required research and then compare the results from each group.

ASSIGNMENT
1. Present the two reports to your class and compare the results.
2. Explain why you believe the results turned out to be the same or different.

RESEARCHING DIFFERENT CAREERS

A career in research requires good conceptual, analytical, and communication skills. Researchers need to be able to recognize business problems, select effective methods of information gathering, and report their findings effectively. These skills develop and improve with experience. Competitive intelligence focuses on gathering information about competitors and buyers in an industry. The answers to questions like "Which new products or services would customers want to buy?" and "What new products are competitors planning?" are important pieces of information to firms that wish to stay up to date. The Society of Competitive Intelligence Professionals is a nonprofit organization that offers training seminars and acts as a network for its 6,750 worldwide members.

ASSIGNMENT
1. Explore the Society of Competitive Intelligence Professionals web site, **www.scip.org**.
2. Describe the information you find there that you would consider useful to someone interested in a career in research.

IMPROVING COMMUNICATION SKILLS

Conducting interviews and focus groups can uncover a great deal of information. Often these research methods can be excellent exploratory tools for understanding complex behaviors and decision-making processes. Organize a focus group to discuss some complex issue, such as how people use the Internet for shopping or researching information before they shop in a bricks-and-mortar store. Then interview one member of the focus group alone to review the results of the focus group discussion.

ASSIGNMENT
1. Briefly describe the research question that you want to explore.
2. Describe the characteristics of the focus group you have selected.
3. Prepare a report that summarizes what was communicated during the focus group.
4. What, if any, new information was uncovered by conducting an interview with only one member of the group?

Exploring Useful Web Sites

These web sites provide information related to the topics discussed in the chapter. You can learn more by visiting them online and examining their current data.

1. Forrester Research (**www.forrester.com**) entered into a strategic alliance with the National Association of Purchasing Management (**www.napm.org**) to produce a new product called the NAPM/Forrester Report on eBusiness. The quarterly report will track the adoption of Internet-based purchasing by both manufacturing and nonmanufacturing organizations through a jointly developed survey of B2B e-commerce activity.

2. Media Metrix (**www.mediametrix.com**) is a well-known source of free Internet-based information.

3. The web site for this textbook contains our list of good sources of research data and is designed to serve an audience interested in learning about e-business. You can help build this site and receive acknowledgment by emailing your own recommendations along with a brief annotative description of the site and why you believe it can help fellow researchers in e-business studies. You may reach our *e-Business* web site at **http://college .hmco.com/business/students/**.

4. Our online survey site on the *e-Business* web site at **http://college.hmco .com/business/students/** provides a variety of information about Internet usage and suggested questionnaire design. Our information gateway on the *e-Business* web site at **http://college.hmco.com/business/students/** provides links to information sources on the web.

5. The Society of Competitive Intelligence Professionals (**www.scip.org**) is a nonprofit organization that offers training seminars and acts as a network for its 6,750 worldwide members.

6. OpenCola Limited (**www.opencola.com**) offers peer-to-peer file-sharing technology that combines capabilities similar to those of Napster and Gnutella with the intelligence of a search robot that will seek out relevant files from other OpenCola users.

Understanding Online Communication and Behavior

Chapter 8

INSIDE e-BUSINESS
Jupiter Media Metrix— Measuring Internet Activity One Click at a Time

Although Media Metrix Inc. (**www.mediametrix.com**) of New York only began operations in 1996, today it is considered a global leader in Internet user behavior research and measurement reporting. The first to launch an Internet audience measurement and meter-based tracking service, the firm provides information to more than 900 clients worldwide, including advertising agencies and web site operators who wish to know more about specific online usage behavior patterns. Through internally generated growth and mergers with industry-related research firms such as AdRelevance Inc. (**www.adrelevance.com**) and Jupiter Communications Inc., the recently emerged Jupiter Media Metrix group (**www.jmm.com**) has become a dominant industry research organization focusing on the measurement of audience traffic and usage, web site ratings, advertising impact, and e-commerce activity—so much so that in 2002, Jupiter Media Metrix was itself acquired and merged with the operations of the Reston, Virginia–based research firm comScore Networks Inc. (**www.comscore.com**). Without the critical information that is independently gathered, analyzed, and reported by firms like Jupiter Media Metrix, little would be known about the success or failure of the strategic plans for any given web site, what advertisers should be willing to pay for display space, and which sites are more likely to produce the desired results.

Jupiter Media Metrix collects data from a sample of more than 100,000 globally representative Internet users. The firm's database is constantly fed by tracking of the click-by-click behavior of users who have been categorized by demographic, geographic, and other criteria. The sample is composed of randomly recruited individual and business users who have agreed to allow a software program to track their online behavior and report the data back to Jupiter Media Metrix. A variety of data are recorded, such as the identity of the user, determined through a log-on procedure; which sites the user's browser visits; how long the user stays; the number of pages viewed; and even whether the user switches to other digital activities such as a spreadsheet or word processor. By analyzing these data, web site developers can test the appeal of various types of online content, how much time and information customers require to make their buying decisions, and whether customers leave the site and are lost after any particular screen is displayed, suggesting perhaps a flaw in the design or presentation of that screen.

Using information gathered through its proprietary software and research methodology, Jupiter Media Metrix was able to report that the merger of AOL and Time Warner had boosted the new firm to a dominant position in the rapidly converging Internet entertainment industry. While AOL Time Warner was enjoying the top-ranking spot, Microsoft's MSN.com moved ahead of Yahoo.com to take over second place. According to Jupiter Media Metrix, AOL Time Warner accounted for more than one-third of all online activity in the United States during January of 2001. Time Warner's popular news and business web sites CNN.com, CNNFN.com, and CNNSI.com had at-home penetration to nearly three-quarters of all U.S. households and almost the same percentage of business users. Today, AOL Time Warner remains in the top position, with the same two rivals not far behind. These early results helped investors judge the merger a success, guided advertisers' site selection, and suggested a strategy for competitors to consider.[1]

The Internet is a relatively new interactive medium for users and content providers, as well as for researchers who are interested in understanding both individual and group online behaviors. Although the Internet is similar in many ways to older and more established media such as television, radio, and print journals, it provides the unique capability of allowing user interactivity and two-way communication. This critical difference changes the design considerations completely from those used with the passive approach employed by noninteractive media such as television, which simply "talks" to an audience. Advertisements on television, for instance, generally hope to attract the audience's attention for a few moments and then, ideally, to generate a positive response to the advertisement at a later time when the viewer makes a purchase at a retail store. On a web site, the design objective is more likely to be to provoke an immediate user response, which occurs when the viewer clicks through to the next screen or on a link taking her or him to another site. Ultimately, the design of an e-commerce web site is intended to lead the user to make a purchase online; however, all commercial web sites try to keep viewers for as long as possible and to make them as loyal as possible. Consider, for example, what your home or opening web browser screen is and why you have chosen to return to it each time you start your computer. Chances are that it is one of the top three sites we mentioned in the profile that opens this chapter.

The online behavior of customers, staff, and suppliers must be better understood if strategic plans are to have any chance of succeeding. In order to accomplish this task, we will build on the popular Shannon-Weaver model of communication and explore the primary factors that can influence the online behaviors of suppliers, employees, and others who use the Internet to communicate with one another. Finally, we will examine a series of related psychological theory–based models that provide a framework for understanding moment-to-moment online behavior and help in the development of new strategic plans to direct future online behaviors.

Understanding the Online Communication Process

online communication process
A sequence of steps that successfully transfers multimedia content and information from one person to another through the Internet.

The **online communication process** model involves a sequence of steps that successfully transfers multimedia content and information from one person to another through the Internet. The model is built around several component points of reference: the *sender of a message,* the *encoded message* that the sender intends to send to the targeted receiver or audience, the *medium* used to distribute the message, the *decoded message* that is actually received and interpreted by the targeted *receiver of a message,* and finally the *feedback* response by the receiver to the sender reflecting the reaction to the message received. Figure 8.1 presents a graphic illustration of the structure of the model and the flow of communication that helps us to focus on the reasons for both successful and unsuccessful communication. We will further examine the model's architecture and bring into our discussion strategic details related to online communication at the same time.

FIGURE 8.1   The Online Communication Model

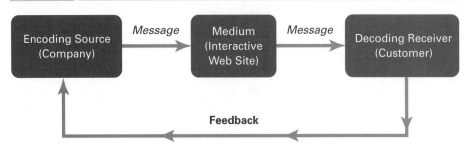

From Carol H. Anderson and Julian Vincze, *Strategic Marketing Management Theory*. Copyright © 2000 by Houghton Mifflin Company. Reprinted with permission.

Sender or Source of a Message

sender of a message
The initiator or source of a message; in most online communications this is the individual or group that is responsible for preparing the organization's online content and Internet presence.

The **sender of a message** is the initiator or source of the entire communication process. In most online communications this is the individual or group that is responsible for preparing the organization's online content and Internet presence. In a simple situation, the sender could be someone who composes an email message or posts a web page of information describing the attributes of a product or service that the firm is selling. In more complex situations, there are usually designated individuals who are responsible for designing and developing content for distribution through the Internet.

A managerial structure is in place to control the production of content. The designers and developers of content will often work in tandem with someone else—a content expert or a division in the organization that wishes to create communication for a specific strategic purpose, such as providing marketing support to sales representatives in the field or posting press announcements to generate public awareness of the organization and present its official response to information about it that is being circulated by others. In situations like these, it is critical to successful communication that the design team and those who wish to send out the message work well together. This is especially critical in the design of the firm's web pages and the posting of content. Once active, the communication between the firm's web pages and Internet users is generally automated, and any content errors can be costly in terms of sending confusing or incorrect information to the public. The possible damage to the firm's brand equity and goodwill makes the careful design of the web site a critically important first step in the online communication process.

Encoded Message

encoded message
The many different ways in which the sender may prepare a message for the targeted receiver, using appropriate and meaningful images, symbols, and jargon.

The **encoded message** component of the model refers to the many different ways in which the sender may prepare a message for the targeted receiver. Just as advertising messages for children's television are different from those for adults, so too should Internet-delivered messages reflect the sociocultural specifics of the targeted receivers. Obviously, this means encoding messages in the language understood by the receiver and using appropriate images, symbols, and jargon. In this respect, the design and encoding of Internet-based messages is not all that different from the design and encoding of messages for other media. Consider how different the encoded messages are for the broad-based target audience for MSN (**www.msn.com**) and the much narrower target audience for Warner Bros. entertainment (**www2 .warnerbros.com/web/hipclips/index.jsp**). Whereas MSN presents a more conservative image of news and information in a magazine-style format, Warner Bros. uses bold visual images of highly recognizable actors from its recent film and television productions to attract users and generate an exciting online environment.

The specific purpose and function of the message the sender intends to send to the targeted receiver should be identifiable. Is the message supposed to inform, persuade, or elicit a specific reaction or response from the targeted receiver? If these basic questions are unclear, then the design of the message is likely to be unclear as well. Whether it is a basic text message or sophisticated audiovisual content in an interactive web page, each message can be viewed as an effort by designers to transfer specific information to the intended receiver. Consider the home page for Yahoo! (**www.yahoo.com**), which presents a broad range of multimedia content, including links to online shopping sites, along with an interactive screen of information categories and a search engine to assist researchers. The page design and the words chosen to describe the categories of databases that Yahoo! has organized for searching are simple and relatively stable, so that users can gradually learn how to use the Yahoo! site to find the information they seek. The hierarchical structure within the categories is consistent with a model of the way people organize and remember information, further facilitating the search procedure and making use of the web site a comfortable and nonfrustrating experience. The relatively large amount of print information as opposed to graphics allows the site to jam a great deal of information into the starting screen. This is in contrast to MSN (**www.msn.com**), which makes greater use of graphics to attract users to articles on a wide range of topics, often related to general interests such as home decoration and health care. Visitors to Yahoo! are motivated by the desire to use the site to search the Web for information. Visitors to MSN, on the other hand, are perhaps more likely to see the site as an online magazine and will come back often if the site provides a satisfactory balance of real news and what can be called *entertaining news.* The motivation of each design team is fundamentally the same—to draw and retain users. The demographics of users of Yahoo! and MSN might also be quite similar; however, they expect fundamentally different interaction from each of these sites. The lesson to be learned is not to try to be *all things to all people,* but instead to create and support your brand presence and clear identity. It would be an error for Yahoo! to try to be a magazine as well as a primary search engine. The brand identity that Yahoo! wishes to reinforce with each subsequent visit is that it is the user's search engine of choice.

Medium

The **medium** is the vehicle that delivers the message to the receiver. The online communication medium includes the Internet and the network of communication devices such as desktop and laptop computers, interactive television, and

medium
The vehicle that delivers the message to the receiver; online, this includes the Internet and the network of communication devices such as desktop and laptop computers, interactive television, and wireless telephones that use the Internet.

wireless telephones that use the Internet. Because of the convergence of technologies, content that is traditionally associated with one device can now be accessed by other devices. For example, users can check their email messages on any of these devices that may happen to be most convenient at a particular moment. As a result, when Internet-based securities trading firms like E*Trade and Charles Schwab send out email alerts on stocks held by their investors, these alerts may be viewed on any of these devices.

Designers need to consider the device that receivers will use to access Internet-based information. A large-screen display on a computer monitor or television works well for reading text and scanning colorful images; however, only short messages or menus may be practical for a small display area on a wireless telephone. The 1970s media guru Marshall McLuhan's famous observation that "the medium is the message" takes on new meaning in the age of the Internet. How users see the Internet and the information transmitted through devices tied to the Web influences their understanding of the messages they receive. Some users may view the Internet as simply a source of entertainment and do not use it for any business transactions such as banking or online shopping. For others, the Internet is a practical business tool, saving time and money. Knowing the manner in which any targeted audience views the medium is critically important before beginning the message encoding and web page design process.

Decoded Message

decoded message
The message that is understood by the targeted receiver.

The **decoded message** is the message that is understood by the targeted receiver. Using whatever perceptual, conceptual, and intellectual skills and knowledge they possess, receivers will create in their minds a model of what they believe was the intended message. Whether their perceived model of the message and the intended message are in fact the same is a matter that generally will require verification. Suppose MSN (**www.msn.com**) uses a photograph that shows a child playing with a puppy. The image can communicate a wide range of information and emotion for many viewers, perhaps even standing out from much of the content on the rest of the screen for some. However, while this image might be attractive and appealing to, say, a mother with young children who are about the same age as the child depicted in the photograph, it might be quite uninteresting to an unmarried older male business executive; in fact, he might not even notice the graphic display.

Consider also how a pop-up advertisement that unexpectedly appears and overlays a large portion of the user's screen might be decoded. Suppose the advertisement offers the user a free trial subscription to a parenting magazine. The young mother we just mentioned is a potential new subscriber and may welcome the ad, leading to the desired outcome—a new subscriber. On the other hand, the older businessman may perceive the ad as an annoyance or even as an obstruction or intrusion into his personal space. Knowing how the communication effort will be decoded or understood by the receiver is critical to its successful utilization and placement.

Receiver of a Message

receiver of a message
The targeted audience of a message; in most online communications, this is the individual receiver of email or the group that views the organization's web content, such as customers, suppliers, and employees.

Much of the success or failure of any communication effort will be determined by the comfort and degree of familiarity message designers have with their targeted audience—the individual **receiver of a message**. The research methods presented in Chapter 7, such as focus groups and surveys, can help designers gain this familiarity. The mother and the older business executive that we mentioned earlier might both use the same MSN web site, but they are very different people who are likely to use quite different sociocultural references for interpreting the images displayed. Therefore, each is likely to derive different meaning from them, which will consequently trigger different responses. It is incumbent upon designers to know the targeted receivers of their messages well so that they can better direct successful image and message creation. However, it is also important that they be aware of the fact that many diverse users in addition to the intended target audience may be exposed to the message. Designers must be careful not to create messages that might be well received by the target audience but are considered offensive by others visiting the same web site. The results might prove to be counterproductive to the overall communication effort.

Feedback

feedback
Responses from the message receiver that are communicated back to the original sender.

The model suggests that communication is an ongoing process, with **feedback** responses from the receiver being communicated back to the sender. Feedback tends to drive the next round of communication, as the feedback demands a response from the original sender. A lack of response from the receiver can also be interpreted as feedback. If viewers are expected to click on the graphic image of the child playing with the puppy and few of them do so, then this feedback, in the form of a low click rate, is a clear indication of poor message design for the intended audience or some other flaw. Often repetition of the message is needed because of noise. **Noise** is any disturbance in the environment that prevents the receiver from fully receiving the intended message. The phone ringing and displacing the user's attention from the computer screen is a form of noise, as is a pop-up advertisement window overlaying the screen being viewed. More likely, the feedback will indicate successful communication of the message and a shared understanding with the target audience. However, when feedback indicates that communication has been unsuccessful, the next round of communication should be designed in such a way as to incorporate this vital piece of feedback into the process.

noise
Any disturbance in the environment that prevents the receiver from fully receiving the intended message.

Content analysis of customer feedback, such as email and other CRM inputs through customer contact opportunities, can provide the firm with insight into the success of its design effort. Often the comments made or the way the user expected to navigate the web site can indicate where the design failures or successes lay. According to researchers at Greenfield Online Inc. (**www.greenfieldonline.com**), online polls are an inexpensive and popular strategy for creating feedback and interactivity with viewers. People like expressing their opinions and comparing themselves to others. Furthermore, online polls are good for generating content and entertainment for virtual communities. According to an online poll (about online polls), about half of the respondents said that they were an amusing diversion. Although highly unscientific, such polls can also be successfully used to generate traffic at web site communities and direct users to chat rooms to discuss the results.[2]

Clearly, the best chance for successful communication starts with an understanding of the characteristic makeup of the targeted receivers of the message. Designing web sites that communicate successfully with potential customers requires an understanding of those customers' buying processes, our next topic.

Consumer and Organizational Buying Processes

Both the consumer and organizational buying processes follow similar steps, which logically resemble the management decision-making process that was discussed in Chapter 7. After all, the whole point of the process is to make a good buying decision for oneself or one's organization. In either situation, the decision is driven by the desire to optimally satisfy needs or wants through the particular buying decision that is being taken. For example, online buyers might be motivated to save time or money when shopping for products or services. Other common reasons for buying online include convenience, delivery services, and selection. A starting point for any understanding of why customers are or are not shopping at a firm's web site is the answer to the fundamental question about why they have chosen to be there instead of at any one of the other e-commerce sites or bricks-and-mortar options that are available. Failure to satisfy that basic need will logically undermine any other positive effort to attract customers and keep them coming back.

Step 1: Problem or Need Recognition and Defining Specifics
As illustrated in Figure 8.2, the buying decision process begins with the *problem or need recognition and defining specifics* stage, in which potential customers must first become aware of a need or want and then define the specifics of that need as much as possible to help narrow the scope of the task they face. This stage can be stimulated automatically, as when an organization's inventory reporting system indicates low levels of supplies, or spontaneously, as when a consumer decides it's time to plan a summer vacation. The problem recognition stage includes defining as specifically as possible just what the problem or need is and what purchase will be required to satisfy the need. Generally speaking, the more clearly defined the need is in the buyer's mind, the easier it will be to find a purchase solution. However, consumers are often not clear about what they want—and may not know what they wanted until after they have found it. Web sites that encourage browsing or that make suitable gift suggestions can generate customer loyalty if the shopping experience is satisfactory, whereas frustrated browsers are unlikely to return. Sites like Amazon (**www.amazon.com**) keep track of what customers have bought in the past and direct them to possible new purchases intelligently related to past buying preferences.

FIGURE 8.2   The Consumer and Organizational Buying Process

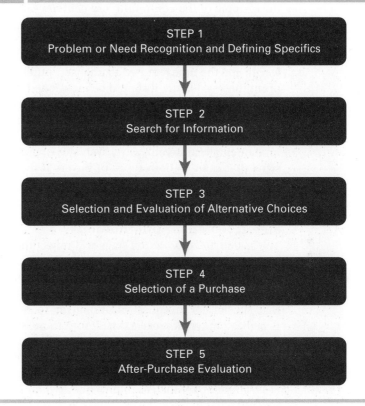

STEP 1
Problem or Need Recognition and Defining Specifics

STEP 2
Search for Information

STEP 3
Selection and Evaluation of Alternative Choices

STEP 4
Selection of a Purchase

STEP 5
After-Purchase Evaluation

It is useful to categorize the buyer's perception of the purchase in terms of its complexity and the level of buyer involvement in the purchase decision. *Routine* or *simple purchases* require minimal search and analysis effort. For example, re-ordering paper and ink cartridges for office printers and photocopy machines is generally automatic. Typically the specifications of the needs are known and suppliers are routinely contacted when more is required. Often long-term relationships are established with certain suppliers to take advantage of discounts and minimize transportation charges, and prices are generally not a major part of the decision process. According to office supplies retailer Staples (**www.staples.com**), the average spending by bricks-and-mortar small-business customers increased from $600 to $2,800 when they shifted to the firm's web site. As a result, online sales have risen to more than 5 percent of the overall $10 billion earned each year.[3]

An example of a *moderately complex purchase* with moderate buyer in-volvement would be a product, such as a computer, that is acquired less frequently. The buyer probably has a great deal of information from previous pur-chases and experiences with vendors and brands, but the existence of many new technological features may make the current decision a bit complex. Finally, on the extreme of the continuum are *complex purchases* and buying situations that demand a high level of buyer involvement. For example, buying a Caribbean cruise package or selecting an e-commerce host for the firm for the first time is no small undertaking for most people. There are many issues and concerns to weigh, and the time required to finalize a purchase decision will reflect the degree of complexity. Finally, it should be mentioned that what may be a simple, routine buying decision for one person or organization may be quite the opposite for another. Someone who routinely takes cruise ship vacations in the Caribbean and a first-time buyer may both end up on the same ship but make their decisions in fundamentally different ways. Web site operators must be concerned with designs that cater to both types of buyers if they are to succeed at satisfying the needs of each type of customer.

Step 2: Search for Information

The *search for information* stage will reflect the buyer's prior knowledge and experience. If a buyer's prior experiences at certain sites were positive, it is likely that the buyer will at least begin by revisiting those sites. For instance, a buyer might choose to visit the site where she booked her last Caribbean cruise (a site that specializes in cruise vacations) or to begin at Microsoft's travel central, Expedia.com (**www.expedia.com**). From there, if the search proves unsatisfactory, the buyer may back up to a more general search environment by entering a few descriptive keywords into a search engine. The organizational buyer who is reordering paper and office supplies might simply search the e-commerce site of the firm's supplier to determine whether there are new products or price changes that might influence the purchase decision before entering the order online. There are also a wide range of influences and sources of information in addition to what a potential buyer might find online. We will explore these factors later on in this chapter.

Step 3: Selection and Evaluation of Alternative Choices

After the buyer is satisfied with the available information and understands the decision required, the *selection and evaluation of alternative choices* stage begins. In this stage, the potential buyer must first select the alternative choices considered worthy of evaluation and then evaluate the advantages and disadvantages of each. It is at this stage that the important motivational factors directing the purchase decision will emerge and the vendors will have the opportunity to differentiate their products. Perhaps price is truly the key issue determining which purchase will be made in the end, or maybe the delivery dates available from various suppliers will be more important. Ultimately, in order to be successful, an online strategy must reflect whichever factor or factors are considered pivotal at this point in the process. Online agents can search the sites selected by potential buyers or search the Internet seeking close matches with a set of specified criteria. The results of the search can help sort out the large number of potential alternative choices. Commercial web sites such as those at IBM and Dell Computer allow visitors to enter the criteria for the sort of computer system they need and provide online direction and answers to commonly asked questions. Together, all of these online strategies help potential customers make an informed and satisfactory needs-driven decision.

Step 4: Selection of a Purchase

When the buyer is satisfied with the decision or the time available to continue the search and evaluation of alternatives runs out, the *selection of a purchase* takes place. How the firm handles the recording and completion of the sale is critical to determining whether the sale will in fact be finalized. If the web site confuses the buyer or if the buyer requires online support to complete the forms required, the firm must be sure to provide proper customer service and support or it risks losing the sale. It is here that a good CRM solution helps tie together the total selling strategy, as telephone-based customer support staff can not only talk to the buyer while she or he is entering information on the firm's screen but also see exactly what the buyer sees at the same time.

A variety of statistics have been published suggesting that large numbers of online sales have been lost because customers drop out of the process as a result of online frustration. No doubt few of those who abandon a purchase effort at this stage of the process are likely to return to the site again. The permanent damage from the loss of potential customers cannot be overstated. Designers and e-commerce managers must provide the support required not only by new customers with first-time navigation problems but also by regular customers who need assistance. Finding customers and bringing them to the web site for the first time is a difficult and costly task. It is tragic if customers are lost because of a lack of the support needed to keep them.

Step 5: After-Purchase Evaluation

The *after-purchase evaluation* stage reflects the buyer's experience with not only the product or service but the entire buying experience as well. If the cruise was a vacation dream come true and the online booking process was simple to understand and to navigate, then the buyer can be expected to repeat what was essentially a totally positive experience. If there were problems with the online booking process, then the buyer might choose to take her business to another online site or perhaps a bricks-and-mortar travel agency the next time she is considering a Caribbean cruise vacation. The purchase experience will be feedback into the repertoire of knowledge with which the buyer will begin the process the next time around. Therefore, it is critical that online vendors monitor just what buyers are learning about their products and online support, and any other vital information that can lead to strategic improvement in the future. This is especially important for organizational vendors where routine and highly automated B2B buying is the basis of their business, and losing one customer to a competitor can translate into large revenue losses.

Sources of Influence on Buyer Behavior and Decision Making

Now that we have established the sequence of steps that buyers take as they make their way to a purchase decision, we will turn our attention to some of the major influences or factors that can affect buyers' decision making and how businesses can use this knowledge to better develop their online strategic presence. Influences on buyer behavior fall into three primary categories: social, personal, and psychological factors.

Social Factors

social factors
Cultural and social influences on individual buyers' behavior; these can include an individual's social roles and the influence of family, peers, opinion leaders, and reference groups.

Social factors are cultural and social influences on individual behavior; these can include an individual's social roles and the influence of family, peers, opinion leaders, and reference groups. Social roles are associated behaviors that an individual person engages in in the context of some social situation or environment. A manager, whoever else he or she might be outside of the workplace, is expected by his or her superiors, subordinates, and customers to behave in some particular manner that is consistent with the role or position he or she has within the firm. This may mean, for instance, that the manager is expected to solicit advice about which CRM system the firm should acquire before making a final decision. Similarly, the manager might be influenced by family members, peers, industry opinion leaders, and managers in other departments in the firm who constitute a reference group from which the manager seeks advice and guidance.

 e-Business Insight

College Students' Online Shopping Behavior

A recent study sponsored by the College Stores Research and Educational Foundation, the research arm of the National Association of College Stores, uncovered a variety of interesting facts about college students' online buying behavior. First, college students are highly influenced by the college environment itself and quickly become comfortable with online shopping once they have left home. More than half shop online, spending only about $330 a year on music (38 percent), books (34 percent), travel (33 percent), concert (22 percent) tickets, and computer software (18 per-

cent). Also, the survey reveals that low prices, best selection, and personal knowledge of the brand sold are the top three reasons that students select one online retailer over another. About 60 percent of students find out about a web site through an online search engine, of which the leaders are Yahoo!, AltaVista, and Excite. Interestingly, recommendations from socially relevant others such as friends and family were a distant second source of information about where to shop. Although students were generally satisfied by the service provided, the survey reported that they cited difficulties in locating online stores and navigating their web sites.[4]

From a communications point of view, it is important to understand what sorts of social influences might be affecting and guiding an individual's behavior and decision making. It should not come as much of a surprise to find advertising or other marketing efforts directed at a buyer that incorporate advice from the sources of influence that are significant to that buyer. For instance, an advertisement for a CRM software solution might try to direct management decision making to that solution by simulating a meeting of peers or emphasize an endorsement from an industry opinion leader.

Personal Factors

personal factors
Those general characteristics that are closely associated with the individual buyer; they can be categorized as *demographic, lifestyle,* and *situational.*

Personal factors are those general characteristics that are closely associated with the individual buyer; they can be categorized as *demographic, lifestyle,* and *situational.* Demographic factors, which include individual descriptive characteristics such as age, gender, occupation, income, and so forth, are traditional tools that strategists use to help them understand customers and their behavior. For instance, knowing that married couples between 25 and 55 years old make up a large part of the cruise ship travel market suggests how the designers of the Celebrity Cruises Inc. (**www.celebritycruises.com**) web site might consider communication with the likely visitors to the site. The images that appeal to this target group and how comfortable its members feel navigating the Web can easily be researched through focus group studies. Similarly, lifestyles or psychographic factors that describe people in terms of their categorical activities, opinions, and interests can help strategists identify special niche markets of visitors to their site. For example, Celebrity Cruises might design web pages that are of particular interest to frequent cruise vacationers, scuba divers, adventurers, and other lifestyle-defined groups. Researchers must also recognize the importance of situational factors that can influence individual buyer behavior. For instance, while an individual is examining free access to *Business Week* magazine online, a pop-up promotional advertisement for a highly discounted cruise of the Caribbean may influence that person to take some positive buying action at that particular moment. Although the individual had not been intending to consider a cruise ship vacation, the situation presented conditions that could precipitate a sale.

Psychological Factors

psychological factors
General types of behavioral influences that can influence individual buyers' behavior that are widely shared by individuals, including motivation, perception, learning, attitude, personality, and self-concept.

Psychological factors include general types of behavioral influences that are widely shared by individuals regardless of any individual characteristics they may have, such as their demographic or lifestyle circumstances. Psychological factors that influence human behavior include motivation, perception, learning, attitude, personality, and self-concept.

Motivation is what we call the force that drives an individual toward the achievement of goals associated with the fulfillment of his or her needs, wants, and desires. In social situations, individuals generally seek to satisfy their needs for *power, achievement, affiliation,* and *control.* For example, researchers who are seeking to understand the motivation of visitors to the online lifestyle community iVillage.com might discover that all of these needs are being satisfied in one way or another through the activities and interaction with others on the web site. The job for web designers is to maintain a steady supply of online content that can regularly meet the need requirements of visitors and thereby keep them coming back.

Motivated behavior is often explained as an attempt to satisfy a combination of these needs simultaneously. For example, shopping online at a web site for the first time might be explained by the shopper's need to express power by proving that she can locate merchandise, click where she must, and conclude a purchase—something that not everyone can do with confidence. The ability to then tell all her friends about this shopping experience allows her to share her personal sense of achievement and to feel that she belongs to a relatively small community of special people who know about Internet shopping firsthand. Finally, the shopper might also feel that she has learned to control her life just a bit more by demonstrating to herself that she has the ability to control technology rather than having technology control her. Managers need to be tuned into the needs that are important motivators for online behavior and develop web sites accordingly.

Perception, which refers to the ways in which an individual selects, organizes, and understands information and thereby creates personal meaning about the world, is important for successful web communication. For example, web designers need to understand just how viewers of a particular site will perceive those ubiquitous interrupting pop-up advertising promotional boxes. Perhaps there are moments when the advertised offers are more likely to be well received than at other moments. It is commonly accepted that much banner advertising is not even noticed by viewers, let alone read or acted upon. Research into breaking the protective barriers that individuals naturally erect to prevent themselves from being overwhelmed by information overload is relatively weak. Our understanding of online perception is fairly limited and provides a wide-open opportunity for research.

Learning is considered to have occurred when a change in individual behavior can be attributed to acquired experience or knowledge. Web designers should consider what they are teaching users through their online learning experiences. Are customers gaining valuable insight into an important purchase decision, or are they learning that the web site operators know little about their product? Often the impression that the customer comes away with will be a lasting one. A poorly designed opening screen that looks unprofessional may be all that a new visitor to the firm will ever see. First impressions are important, and web page designs need to be given the attention and budget that they rightly deserve if the firm is to create good first-time learning experiences for web visitors.

Attitude can be thought of as a combination of factors, including an individual's knowledge, understanding, or beliefs (cognitive factor); feelings (affective factor); and likely behavior or tendency to act (behavioral factor). For instance, someone who believes (cognition) that he would not enjoy a cruise ship vacation in the Caribbean and feels uncomfortable (affective) about the idea of being on a ship far away from the sight of land is unlikely to even search out a web site with information on cruises (behavior), let alone book a vacation online. In short, this person's attitude toward cruise ship vacations is not a positive one and there is a consistency or equilibrium between the three component factors that make up his attitude toward cruise ship vacations. How attitude is formed and can be changed is beyond the scope of this textbook. However, it should be apparent that changing one of the component factors that make up a current attitude structure, would provoke a change in the others. For example, providing information about a web site (cognition) can provoke a change in the motivation to examine a web site and thus in behavior. We will revisit this important part of understanding individual behavior later in this chapter.

Personality refers to individual characteristics and consistent behavioral tendencies in a particular situation. For example, employees working online at a call center may demonstrate aggressive behaviors and other personality quirks that they do not normally demonstrate when they are communicating face-to-face with customers. Trainers need to recognize that an individual's personality can vary widely as the social situation changes, possibly resulting in undesirable behaviors. Furthermore, the notion of *self-concept* is closely related to personality and refers to how the individual views or perceives him- or herself and how the individual thinks others see him or her, especially in particular social situations. Thus, an online call center customer service representative can be trained to adopt a particular personality and to see herself, at least while answering the phone, in a way that is highly effective for the organization's purposes.

e-Business Insight
Research Shows Teens Search Online but Shop Offline

Recent research by Jupiter Communications, part of the Jupiter Media Metrix group, suggests that the Internet serves primarily as a source of information for preteens and teenagers, with purchases being made later at a bricks-and-mortar store. The survey of 2- to 17-year-olds suggests that this group is likely to spend $4.9 billion annually online by the year 2005, but will spend $21.4 billion at regular retail outlets after first researching the purchase decision on the Internet. According to the survey, girls are more likely than boys to be influenced by online marketing efforts directed toward brands and so should be the preferred target of online advertising effort. Boys seem less interested in following brand names online. Since teens' main online activities are instant messaging, chatting, and searching, marketers are advised to incorporate viral or word-of-mouth communication strategies, which let teens share their opinions about brands and products with other teens by sending messages to their friends that include links to brand web sites.[5]

A Framework for Understanding Moment-to-Moment Online Behavior

Explaining and understanding users' online behavior is certainly facilitated by the study of the social, personal, and psychological influences affecting the individual. What is still required, however, is a model that can help guide research into online user behavior and an understanding of that behavior, especially while it is occurring from one moment to the next. For example, one might rightly feel confident in suggesting that women choose to visit iVillage.com because it reflects a lifestyle community that appeals to a class of women in the general population and satisfies a variety of their needs. However, what is perhaps more difficult to measure and explain is why an individual woman chooses to behave the way she does from moment-to-moment while she is navigating the iVillage web site. Rather than simply seeking to explain how and why a web site can attract its targeted user audience, we will conclude this chapter by presenting a series of related psychological theory–based models that attempt to provide a framework for understanding why an online visitor to a web site chooses to make the next selection that he or she makes—whether that is to click on a pop-up advertisement, read content, or perhaps leave the current site completely.

Value-Expectancy Theory

value-expectancy theories
Theories based on the belief that the individual rationally weighs the advantageous and disadvantageous outcomes associated with a specific behavior and the expectancies of each outcome occurring as a result of their behavior.

All of the models we will examine are derived from value-expectancy theories of human behavior. **Value-expectancy theories** are based on the belief that the individual rationally weighs the advantageous and disadvantageous outcomes associated with a specific behavior and the expectancy that each outcome will occur as a result of her or his behavior. In other words, the individual asks him- or herself, "What is the likely outcome of this behavior, and how valuable is it to me?" The individual is expected to maximize the value of that decision by choosing the behavior that represents the greatest measure of outcome benefit or the least amount of loss.[6]

Table 8.1 illustrates a user's value-expectancy-based decision to remain at a current web site or switch to the next one. She is researching information for a class term paper and is progressing down a list of potential sites that a search engine has produced. In this highly simplified situation, her behavior is restricted to only two possible choices: remain or switch to the next site on her list.

First, a list of outcomes is created for each behavior. Here, researchers find that the same two outcomes apply to both behaviors: a belief that the site will provide useful information and that it will be easy to find that information. A 7-point bipolar scale is used to allow the individual to weigh the value or importance of each outcome associated with remaining at the current web site and switching to the next. For instance, placing a "3" value for "Will provide useful information" indicates a high value level for this particular outcome. This means that the individual places a great deal of value and importance on this particular outcome, and therefore it is an important motivating factor for the user.

| TABLE 8.1 | Value × Expectancy Decision Structure for Deciding to Remain at the Current Web Site or Switch to the Next Web Site on a List |

Outcomes	Value × Expectancy = Score				
Remain at Current Site					
- Will provide useful information	3	×	3	=	9
- Will be easy to find information	−2	×	3	=	−6
Total value of choosing this behavior					3
Switch to Next Site					
- Will provide useful information	3	×	1	=	3
- Will be easy to find information	−1	×	3	=	−3
Total value of choosing this behavior					0

Strongly Negative		Neutral		Strongly Positive		
−3	−2	−1	0	1	2	3

Similarly, the individual uses the same bipolar scale to indicate the expectancy that the behavior will actually deliver the outcome. The 3 indicates that the individual user has a high level of expectation that remaining at the current web site will in fact provide useful information. The combined score of 9 for the value-expectancy of the first outcome indicates that the user has a high level of confidence that remaining at the current site will deliver the information she is seeking. Why she believes this to be true to the degree indicated is another matter. Perhaps she has been to this site previously and has been successful in finding information, or perhaps her professor has suggested that it is a good source of information for the topic she is writing about. Regardless of the reasons, the model helps researchers focus on the user's motivation at a particular moment. Will the score remain the same if the user has not found any useful information after an hour of searching the site? One would expect not.

Let's examine the other scores that help predict what the decision-making behavior will be. The second outcome score (−6) is derived from a strong expectation (3) that finding information at this site is not going to be easy (−2). The combination of the two scores (3) suggests that there is a relatively strong positive chance that this behavior will be selected. But we cannot predict which of the two behaviors will be chosen until we consider the scores for the only other choice. The second behavior has a lower positive score associated with the user's belief that the web site will provide the information she is seeking (3). Although the value of the outcome (3) is the same for both behaviors, and logically it should be the same for any site the user selects, the user's expectancy score (1) changes. Perhaps the user has never been to the next web site on the list and has no real way of knowing what the likelihood is of finding the information she seeks. Whatever the reason, on this factor, the first behavior wins by a difference in score of 6 points. However, with respect to the belief about how easy it will be to find information on the web site, the score is less negative (−3) for the next web site on the list than for the current site (−6). On this factor, the scores suggest a movement toward switching to the next web site.

To predict which choice will be made, we need to compare the total scores for the different behaviors. According to the total value-expectancy scores for this individual, remaining at the current web site would deliver a higher result (+3) than switching to the next site (0) on her list. Hence, the model would predict that this rational decision maker would opt for remaining at the current web site on the basis of her self-reported measure of the value to be gained. The message for web site designers is to research the important outcomes and their respective expectancies for a user group and develop strategies that improve the scores for those factors that will contribute to positive online behaviors, such as remaining at the site longer, and reduce the scores for alternative behaviors, such as switching to another site. We will examine these strategies in more detail in Chapter 9.

The principles of value-expectancy theory form the basis for more elaborate models used for predicting rational decision making and behavior. In a sense, other value-expectancy models have evolved out of the generic form just described. We will examine several other theories in order to further develop our understanding of this area and its utility in online behavior research.

Theory of Reasoned Action

The theory of reasoned action is a widely used technique for predicting and explaining behavior in a variety of social situations, including those involving consumer behavior.[7] The simplicity of the model and its ease of use make it well suited to many research situations in which prediction of behavior is desired. The theory of reasoned action is a value-expectancy model in which outcomes, beliefs, expectancies, the strength of the beliefs, and the opinions of socially influential others are organized into two groups, or factors. The first group measures attitudes toward the behavior and is composed of measures related to outcomes attributed to the individual performing the behavior. This part of the model is similar to but not exactly the same as the original value-expectancy model we have just examined. The second part of the model measures the opinions of important sources of social influence representing socially normal behavior for the individual—referred to as the subjective norms.

Mathematically, behavior (B) is expressed by the equation

$$B = BI = w_1(A) + w_2(SN)$$

The theory behind this model suggests that the closest antecedent, or prior state, to actual behavior (B) is behavior intention (BI), meaning the intended behavior of the individual at some moment. Behavior intention in turn is dependent on two weighted factors (weights w_1 and w_2), attitude toward the behavior (A) and subjective norms (SN) about the behavior. The calculation of the weights for these two factors can be derived through research or established more simply by making an educated guess as to how much decision making in the particular social situation under study is influenced by the individual and how much by his or her social environment. For instance, assigning a weight of 70 percent to w_1 and 30 percent to w_2 suggests that social sources of influence have a lesser effect on decision making in this particular situation, regardless of the individual scores for each factor.

Attitude Toward the Behavior

Mathematically, attitude toward the behavior measures both the strength of the person's belief that performing the behavior will result in a specific outcome and the individual's evaluation of the outcome, as expressed by the following equation:

$$A = \sum_{i=1}^{n} b \times e$$

where A = the attitude toward performing the behavior

b = the strength of the person's belief that performing the behavior will result in outcome i

e = the person's evaluation of outcome i

n = the number of relevant outcomes

The individual's attitude toward the behavior (A) is explained by the strength of his or her beliefs about the action and the result of taking the action as well as by his or her evaluation of the outcome. For example, an individual who strongly believes that her action of searching a web site (b) will lead to finding useful information (i) and who evaluates the outcome of finding useful information (e) as a very positive outcome will have a strong positive attitude toward the action of searching the web site.

Consider the hypothetical data for an individual given in Table 8.2, which illustrate the relationship between the individual's beliefs (b), evaluations (e), and attitude.

The first attitude component, or outcome, which is based on the belief that the web site will provide products that the user wants to buy, contributes a relatively high positive score (6), since the belief is strong (3) and the user's evaluation of the importance of finding products also has a relatively high positive score (2). However, the fourth attitude component counters the first because the user does not believe shopping at Amazon.com will save him money (-3) and this factor is given the same importance (2) as the first factor. Therefore these two forces contributing to the total measurement of the user's attitude toward shopping at Amazon.com effectively neutralize each other.

TABLE 8.2 Measurement of Attitude

Outcomes of Shopping at Amazon.com	b	e	score
1. Will provide products I want to buy	3	2	6
2. Will be easy to find products	−1	3	−3
3. Will save me time	2	1	2
4. Will save me money	−3	2	−6
Total attitude score			−1

The second attitude factor, based on the belief that products will be easy to find, contributes a negative value (−3), while the third attitude factor, based on the belief that shopping at Amazon.com will save time, contributes a positive value (2). On the whole, we would evaluate this individual's attitude score (−1) as relatively neutral. The positive attitude would be weaker if the individual did not hold strong beliefs about the likelihood of the web site's being able to provide the products he wanted to buy or if this were not evaluated as an important outcome. To produce a more positive attitude score and thereby increase the probability of keeping this customer, web site designers should focus on increasing the scores on those beliefs that are important to the user. Positive experience using a web site will strengthen the user's scores, whereas frustration or poor shopping results are likely to result in scores so low that the customer might not return.

Subjective Norms

Mathematically, the individual's subjective norm score is measured by summing the products of beliefs about whether a significant source of social influence approves or disapproves of the individual's performing the behavior and the strength of the individual's willingness to comply with the norms set by these sources, as expressed by the following equation:

$$SN = \sum_{i=1}^{k} b \times m$$

where SN = the individual's subjective norm regarding the behavior

b = the belief that social influence group or person i thinks the individual should or should not perform the behavior

m = the person's motivation to comply with the norms set by social influence i

k = the number of relevant sources of influence for this behavior

Consider the hypothetical data for an individual given in Table 8.3, which illustrate the relationship between beliefs about what socially important others think about the behavior (b), the strength of the individual's motivation to comply with their view (m), and the resulting measurement of subjective norms.

TABLE 8.3   Illustration of Measurement of Subjective Norms

Social Influence	b	m	bm
1. Parents	−2	−2	+4
2. Peers	+1	+2	+2
3. College professor	+2	+2	+4
4. Best friend	−2	+2	−4
Subjective norm score			+6

Although both parents and the person's best friend (sources 1 and 4) equally think shopping at Amazon.com is a bad behavior choice (-2), the negative motivation to comply with parents (-2) results in a $+4$ score, in comparison to a -4 for the best friend. Given that these two sources mathematically cancel out each other's influence, the remaining positive scores from peers and college professor combine to create a strong positive $+6$ subjective norm score.

Interpretation of Scores

The attitude toward the behavior score (-1) is not as strong a force determining behavior intention as the subjective norm favoring the behavior ($+6$). The final predictive value of the model requires the weights for each factor, which would probably have been derived from preliminary studies using linear regression and are beyond the scope of this text. If they were 0.7 (70 percent) for w_1 and 0.3 (30 percent) for w_2, then

$$B = BI = w_1(A) + w_2(SN)$$

$$= 0.7(-1) + 0.3(+6)$$

$$= -0.7 + 1.8$$

$$= 1.1$$

This final score indicates a low probability of shopping at Amazon.com. The relative strength of the BI for one person or one group can easily be compared with that for another by examining this score. For example, a score of 2.5 would indicate a higher probability of shopping at Amazon.com than one of 0.4.

Self-Regulatory Theories of Behavior

Self-regulatory models regard behavior as being goal-directed; that is to say, an individual's behavior is activated in order to achieve a perceived desirable goal. Action is taken to close the perceived gap between what is and what is desired. A feedback mechanism actively compares the individual's present circumstances with the desired future state and activates behaviors that work toward eliminating the perceived discrepancy in reality. Understanding is therefore achieved by identifying the goals and the processes connected with the behaviors undertaken to reach those goals.

The social settings in which behaviors take place are fluid, presenting a continuously changing environment for individuals to navigate. Although previously learned behaviors may be routinely activated, the opportunity to select alternative, nonroutine behaviors is always present.[8] It is at this level that the theories attempt to understand individual social behaviors by trying to explain why some choices are made and not others.

Research into cognitive psychology and information-processing theories suggests that long-term memory has a hierarchical structure made up of clusters or nodes of related items.[9] In addition to the factual component of a node, it is useful to acknowledge an affective or emotional dimension as well. For example, the emotional affect of frustration that is experienced by an individual who cannot find the product he or she wishes to buy online is likely to contribute to a long-term negative association with the web site and other related nodes in the situation.

Similarly, associated with factual and affective knowledge are stored "scripts" or behavior sequences, which are part of an individual's complete cognitive network.[10] Hence, the procedure for logging on to the Amazon.com web site and reviewing the current list of suggested products of interest to the buyer can be treated as a memory unit of related nodes.

Festinger suggested back in the 1950s that people generally undertake behaviors that are consistent with their attitudes. When there is a discrepancy between the two, then dissonance is suffered until the attitude-behavior consistency is reestablished. This is usually accomplished by changes in attitude to fit the expressed behavior.[11]

Bem's self-perception theories, which date from the 1960s, argue that cognitive dissonance works only when the individual has strong attitude-behavior definitions. When they are weaker or undefined, he argues, attitude may be rationally defined after the behavior has been performed.[12]

Regardless of which philosophical approach is taken, the common theme of consistency or congruence between behavior and attitude is remarkable in its simplicity and utility. The task becomes one of choosing which of the two is easier to change or whether an attack on both would expedite the transition process. Festinger suggests that given a change in attitude, behavior will fall into line in order to eliminate the stress of dissonance. Likewise, should an intervention strategy force or persuade individuals to adopt a different behavior first, Bem suggests that attitudes will fall into line later.

This research suggests that managers need to know whether the current attitude-behavior relationship is firmly rooted or relatively weak. Consumer marketing strategies have successfully applied these theories by advertising the need for consumers to try the product in order to know what to think about it. To get consumers to try products when their attitudes toward those products are weak or relatively undefined, firms can provide a free trial membership or access to a web site. Managers recognize that generating the motivation to pay for something requires providing the first step toward the formation of a positive attitude. This approach is certainly a well-used strategy for firms like AOL, which regularly attract new clients with free trial membership offers.

Self-regulatory theories of behavior suggest that the difficulty will be greatest with people who are strongly entrenched in an alternative attitude-behavior relationship. Weakening these bonds will require offering a variety of alternative behaviors that can disrupt the existing strong support for the present behavior. In general, a person's behavior, such as shopping, can be explained in terms of a goal, in this case finding and buying desired products. The cognitive network of factual information, behavior pattern, and goal achievement is common to cognitive information processing models of behavior.[13] The question of why some behaviors are attempted and others not, and why some are completed while others are not, is the subject of much debate and theorizing. Ajzen has transformed the theory of reasoned action into what he calls the theory of planned action to underline the gap between the present behavior intention and the point in time when the behavior can be carried out or actualized. As the gap in time closes, Ajzen points out, the strength of the behavior intention increases. Ajzen explains the problem in terms of intervening or interrupting factors that interfere with the original behavior intention. Ajzen argues that there is a continuously active cognitive processing of information by the individual up until the very moment when the behavior is actualized. He leaves the discussion on this point: the closer one is to the moment of actualizing the behavior, the greater the probability of its execution, since there is less time, and hence opportunity, for influences to change the intended behavior.[14]

Action Control Theory

Although Ajzen helps to narrow the focus of the issue by suggesting the importance of the time dimension, he does not attempt to explain the cognitive competition that is going on within the mind of the decision maker except to say that some "thing" may act to strengthen or weaken the intended behavior. Julius Kuhl and Jurgen Beckmann developed a cybernetic (feedback) explanation for why people often fail to complete their intended actions, such as shopping at a web site. This body of cognitive psychology, called action control, focuses on self-regulatory mechanisms, which mediate the formation and enactment of behavioral intentions. A distinguishing feature of the theory is the attention it pays to action intention formation and change.[15]

According to action control theory, whether a current behavior intention will be carried out depends on the difficulty of carrying out the behavior relative to the efficiency of the self-regulatory processes involved. The difficulty of carrying out the behavior is determined by the strength of the external forces working against the behavior, such as social norms; the strength of the internal forces working against the behavior, such as competing action tendencies; and the individual's predisposition toward change-prevention (state-oriented) or change-inducing (action-oriented) behavior.[16]

According to Kuhl, an individual's predisposition to behave in a particular way in some situation lies somewhere between two extreme reference points, referred to as action and state orientation. A person is action-oriented to carry out some behavior when all four of the following conditions are met: The person is focused on (1) his or her present state or condition, (2) a future state or condition, (3) a discrepancy between the two states, and, finally, (4) an action that can eliminate the perceived discrepancy. If any of these four conditions is lacking, the individual is classified as being state-oriented—that is to say, incapable of action.

This simple structure provides management an understanding of how to discourage undesirable actions and encourage alternative choices. For example, suppose research confirms that there is a failure to perceive a gap between a present state and a more desirable future state (conditions 1, 2, and 3). If the subject responds with, "I see no advantage to shopping online at Amazon.com and have no desire to change my current practice of shopping at the local mall," then Amazon's management may be able to initiate change by creating awareness of the advantages of shopping at Amazon.com. Or suppose research confirms that the issue is not a lack of awareness, but instead the absence of buyer strategies (condition 4). By providing needed advice through CRM solutions that meets individual needs and responds to concerns or doubts about self-efficacy, management intervention can promote change.

The action environment is a defined subset of the larger environment with which the individual interacts. For example, an individual who is visiting iVillage .com is in a clearly definable social environment that involves many previously learned, hierarchically arranged nodes of useful information and behavior patterns (scripts), such as talking to people in chat rooms, reading articles, and examining merchandise that is for sale. Every action environment has its own goals, which are subjectively and normatively defined. That is, each person at the site has her or his own definition of the goals or purposes of being at the site and the shared understandings with people who are sources of social influence. For example, most people would agree that the site is a place to find useful information about products and events of interest. In addition, each person holds a personal definition of the goal or purpose of the action environment. It is likely that the subjective and normative definitions will be closely related, but some situations may produce great differences between the two.

According to Kuhl, the action environment or situation is composed of competing action tendencies. An action tendency is a behavioral predisposition to carry out an action that is goal-directed in a specific action environment. For example, an individual who feels confused might adopt an action tendency that involves first the intention and then the action of using the help menu on the site. The goal is to eliminate the current state of confusion, and the action sequence necessary to succeed at this has probably been learned through experience at other sites or observation of others.

While the individual is engaged in this particular action tendency, any one of several other action tendencies may interfere with the successful completion of the intended action. For example, while exploring the help menu for information, the individual might notice the 1-800 CRM number and choose instead to telephone a site representative who is available to assist visitors. At this point, the strength of the competing action tendency (talking to the CRM representative) may win out and therefore replace the initial action tendency (searching the help menu).

The strength of an action tendency relative to competing action tendencies determines whether the action tendency will be interrupted or will reach its goal. Action tendencies are protected from interference by alternative action tendencies in order to achieve goal completion. However, expectancy theory would suggest that the value of goal completion is continuously being weighed against the appeal of alternative goals in the network.[17]

Another way to think of an action tendency is as the strongest behavior intention associated with some social environment, or the one with the highest probability of being invoked. An action tendency does not occur in a vacuum; it emerges as a possible course of behavior in the context of an action environment. Asking for help while shopping may occur as an action tendency at a retail location or online at Amazon.com. This action tendency is one of several possible action tendencies that might occur at any moment in the particular action environment. Whether it will emerge is primarily a function of its strength relative to that of other familiar and unexpected action tendencies that are present at the time.

One action tendency may be programmed to trigger the activation of another so that the second action tendency emerges dominant at the completion of the first. For example, the familiar and strong action tendency of checking email or updating virus screening software is likely to be cued by sitting down at one's computer for the first time that day. The more linked the action tendencies, the more familiar and stronger they are.

The task for managers, then, is to understand the complex structure of an action environment of competing behavior patterns and networks of cognitive decision rules. In essence, the question becomes, how does one support positive action tendencies and disrupt negative ones through interventions?

The simple, heuristic answer is based on research findings indicating that an action tendency will remain in effect until it is completed or replaced. Therefore, the strategy for managers should be to build informative and persuasive campaigns supporting positive action tendencies and to attempt to disrupt negative action tendencies by offering alternative/competing action tendencies or by weakening the cognitive/affective network that supports the action tendency.[18]

If, as Kuhl argues, disruption of only one of the four components that identify an individual in an action environment, is required in order to create a state orientation, then a strategist might seek ways of disturbing the existing formation if it is associated with an undesirable action tendency and then maneuvering an alternative action tendency to replace it.

Researchers should be looking for "new" substitutes and components that will alter the strength of the present action tendency. Success is likely to be quicker with action tendencies that are familiar and that are strong in other action environments. The idea of crossover is a popular one in commercial advertising and can be readily explained in the context of this approach. Also, people are more easily moved to take small steps away from a familiar behavior. Therefore, moving a bank customer to full Internet banking is likely to be easier if the customer has already made the move away from the bricks-and-mortar branch and is using the automatic teller machines. The next step to online banking is not that great for those who have already taken the first step. Similarly Home Depot's online information services prepare customers for the next step, which is actually shopping online.

The selection of an action tendency may be based on the belief that that behavior will best satisfy a multitude of goals in the action environment. For example, in making the decision to shop at Amazon.com, the goal may comprise an improved self-image, saving time, feeling empowered, and so forth. In a sense, the selection of an action tendency may go beyond the achievement of the immediately perceived goal and the present action environment. In terms of reasoned action theory, the online shopper may be making his or her choice of behavior based on a desire to optimize time or mental energy. Online shopping may emerge as the "best" activity to engage in at the moment, in order to satisfy a variety of needs.

Conclusions

This chapter has attempted to construct a comprehensive model of online user behavior to help guide management's strategic decision making. We started with the communication process and the primary sources of influence on individual behavior, and were then able to consider a variety of psychological theories of individual behavior. Given the importance of knowing how and why online users choose to make their next decision the way that they do, the series of value-expectancy models provided a framework for understanding the moment-to-moment choices that individuals make while online. Though ideally we would like to be able to reduce individual decision making to a few simple factors, such as economic gain or self-image enhancement, we recognize the complexity of human behavior and the motivation to achieve goals that often may not even be perceived by the individual, let alone the researcher.

The next module of the text will explore the micro-level of strategic planning, where detailed marketing, management, and financial strategies are planned out and mechanisms for implementation and control of the overall e-business plan are set.

CASE STUDY — RETURN TO INSIDE e-BUSINESS

Fortunately for student researchers, Jupiter Media Metrix makes many of its key research findings available on its web site as a promotional tool to attract potential clients. For example, their web site highlights recently revealed that more than 14 million online department store shoppers did most of their buying at the top four retail sites—Walmart.com, Sears.com, JCPenney.com, and Target.com. Other online retailers were far behind these leaders, who were bunched up well ahead of the rest.

ASSIGNMENT

1. Report some of the content and structures used at Jupiter Media Metrix web sites.
2. What changes would you make to improve the sites and increase the chances of attracting new customers? Explain your suggestions.
3. Why do you think these bricks-and-mortar retailers are so popular online?

Chapter Review

SUMMARY

1. **Examine how the communication model can be used to understand online communications.**

The online communication process involves a sequence of steps that successfully transfer information from one person to another through the Internet. With respect to online communications, we generally think in terms of people and machines communicating text, images, and sounds with each other. The model is built around several component points of reference: the sender or source of a message, the encoded message that the sender intends to send to the targeted receiver, the medium used to distribute the message, the decoded message that is received and interpreted by the targeted receiver, and finally the feedback response by the receiver to the sender reflecting the reaction to the message received. The model suggests that communication is an ongoing process, with feedback to the sender acting to drive the next round of strategic effort to either repeat or modify what was communicated previously. Often repetition of the message is needed because of noise. Noise is any disturbance in the environment that prevents the receiver from fully receiving the intended message.

2. Explore the similarities and differences between consumer and organizational buying processes.

Both the consumer and organizational buying processes follow similar steps, which logically resemble the management decision-making process. After all, the whole point of the process is to make a good personal buying decision or one for the organization. In either situation, the decision is driven by the desire to optimally satisfy needs or wants through the particular buying decision that is being taken. The sequence of steps is (1) problem or need recognition and defining specifics, (2) search for information, (3) selection and evaluation of alternative choices, (4) selection of a purchase, and (5) after-purchase evaluation.

3. Examine the sources of influence on buyer behavior and decision making.

Influences on buyer behavior fall into three primary categories: social, personal, and psychological factors. Social factors are cultural and social influences on individual behavior; these can include an individual's social roles and the influence of family, peers, opinion leaders, and reference groups. Personal factors are those general characteristics that are closely associated with the individual buyer; they can be categorized as demographic, lifestyle, and situational. Psychological factors include general types of behavioral influences that are widely shared by individuals regardless of any individual characteristics they may have, such as their demographic or lifestyle circumstances. Psychological factors that influence human behavior include motivation, perception, learning, attitude, personality, and self-concept.

4. Explore a framework for understanding moment-to-moment online behavior.

A series of value-expectancy-theory-based models were presented in an attempt to provide a framework for understanding why an online visitor to a web site chooses to make the next selection that he or she makes. Value-expectancy theories are based on the belief that the individual rationally weighs the advantageous and disadvantageous outcomes associated with a specific behavior and the expectancy that each outcome will occur as a result of her or his behavior. In other words, the individual asks him- or herself, "What is the likely outcome of this behavior, and how valuable is it to me?" The individual is expected to maximize the value of that decision by choosing the behavior that represents the greatest measure of outcome benefit or the least amount of loss. The theory of reasoned action is a value-expectancy model in which outcomes, beliefs, expectancies, the strength of the beliefs, and the opinions of socially influential others are organized into two groups, or factors, that predict the behavior. Self-regulatory models regard behavior as being goal-directed; that is to say, an individual's behavior is activated in order to achieve a perceived desirable goal. Action is taken to close the perceived gap between what is and what is desired. A feedback mechanism actively compares the individual's present circumstances with the desired future state and activates behaviors that work toward eliminating the perceived discrepancy in reality. Understanding is therefore achieved by identifying the goals and the processes connected with the behaviors undertaken to reach these goals. According to action control theory, whether a current behavior intention will be carried out depends on the difficulty of carrying out the behavior relative to the efficiency of the self-regulatory processes involved. The difficulty of carrying out the behavior is determined by the strength of the external forces working against the behavior, such as social norms; the strength of the internal forces working against the behavior, such as competing action tendencies; and the individual's predisposition toward change-prevention (state-oriented) or change-inducing (action-oriented) behavior.

REVIEW QUESTIONS

1. Explain the communication process in terms of the flow of information from a sender to a receiver.
2. How is the Internet like other media? How is it different?
3. What is feedback?
4. Describe the steps involved in the consumer and organizational buying processes.
5. Referring to the categories described in the text, which sources would be likely to influence a manager's decision on whether or not to advertise the firm on the Internet?

DISCUSSION QUESTIONS

1. Why is it so important to know how the receiver is likely to decode a message?
2. How are the consumer and organizational buying processes similar? How are they different?
3. Discuss the main sources of influence on buyer behavior and decision making.
4. Discuss the basic concepts involved in the value-expectancy model and their ability to explain individual online behavior.
5. What are some competing behavior intentions that might be at work while an individual is searching a web site?

Building Skills for Career Success

EXPLORING THE INTERNET

The VALS (Values and Lifestyles) survey, which categorizes U.S. adult consumers into mutually exclusive groups based on their psychology and several key demographics, is probably one of the best known surveys of its type and can provide students with a great deal of understanding of how large-scale surveys are designed and their results interpreted. The survey organizes respondents into psychographic types and identifies specific attitude statements that have a strong correlation with a variety of consumer preferences in products and media. Recent research by SRI International (**www.sri.com/**), the nonprofit research organization based in Menlo Park, California, that administers VALS, has helped to explain attitudes toward technologies and the Internet. You can contribute to the database of responses and learn about the VALS survey at **http://future.sri.com/VALS/VALSindex.shtml**.

ASSIGNMENT

1. Describe your impressions of taking the VALS survey questionnaire.
2. What are the types or categories that VALS has identified?
3. What did you learn from the site that can help you to better understand online behaviors?

DEVELOPING CRITICAL THINKING SKILLS

The online communication process model presented in this chapter provides a guided structure for explaining the flow of information between a web site and the target audience. Select a web site you are familiar with and consider the communication effort directed at viewers.

ASSIGNMENT

1. Identify the web site you have chosen and describe the likely target viewer.
2. Prepare a report describing the communication process, using the steps in the model.

BUILDING TEAM SKILLS

The model of the consumer and organizational buying process that is presented in this chapter provides a structure for explaining how individuals and organizational decision makers make their purchases. Select a product that all of the members of your team would normally be motivated to purchase, such as a laptop computer or cellular telephone. Make a group decision to purchase the product that satisfies the most people.

ASSIGNMENT

1. Using the model as a guide, prepare a report that describes how your group arrived at the purchase decision.
2. What were some of the most influential factors that determined the choice?

(continued)

RESEARCHING DIFFERENT CAREERS

Online behavioral research is an emerging specialized field of study. Social scientists such as psychologists and sociologists are likely to lead the research effort to understand and predict online behaviors. Management research will also have to expand its traditional limits of study to look at how employees communicate using technologies that are rapidly emerging.

ASSIGNMENT

1. Describe the sort of work social scientists would be expected to do that is related to online behaviors.
2. Describe one emerging work-environment problem that might require the professional services provided by social scientists.

IMPROVING COMMUNICATION SKILLS

Using one of the value-expectancy models presented in the chapter, conduct a survey to measure and predict the likely behavior of your entire class. To do this, just calculate average scores in the model you use for analysis. For instance, you might try to predict whether or not the class would book travel reservations online using Expedia.com.

ASSIGNMENT

1. Which model did you choose to use? Why?
2. Prepare a report that explains the results you derived from the survey, using the model structure to help communicate your thinking.

Exploring Useful Web Sites

These web sites provide information related to the topics discussed in the chapter. You can learn more by visiting them online and examining their current data.

1. Jupiter Media Metrix (**www.jmm.com**) has become a dominant industry research organization focused on measuring audience traffic and usage, web site ratings, advertising impact, and e-commerce activity. It was formed through the mergers of Media Metrix Inc. (**www.mediametrix.com**), AdRelevance Inc. (**www.adrelevance.com**) and Jupiter Communications Inc.
2. Expedia.com (**www.expedia.com**) is Microsoft's online travel center.
3. SRI International (**www.sri.com/**) is a nonprofit research organization that administers VALS. You can contribute to the database of responses and learn about the VALS survey at (**http://future.sri.com/VALS/VALSindex.shtml**).
4. Greenfield Online Inc. (**www.greenfieldonline.com**) is a research firm.

Module III

IMPLEMENTING THE
e-BUSINESS PLAN

In Module III, we join the strategic thinking concepts examined thus far to the specific *marketing, management,* and *financial* plans of action. These three functional components are universally recognized as the core foundations for any strategic business plan. Therefore, we incorporate each of these subject matter areas into our study of the design and creation of the complete e-business plan while examining related issues that affect e-business strategy. Additionally, each chapter can help to guide e-business planners toward the development of detailed answers to questions in each of these core subject areas. The final chapter in this unit concludes our discussion of the entire planning process by looking at how the e-business plan can be integrated into an organization's current structure, and then controlled, measured, and evaluated for future decision making.

Creating the Marketing Mix

Chapter 9

INSIDE
e-BUSINESS
Office Depot—Creating Online Business Communities

When Office Depot Inc. of Delray Beach, Florida, was founded, in 1986, it had only a single retail outlet to serve the office supply needs in the Fort Lauderdale vicinity. Today, it is the world's largest seller of office products and an industry leader in every distribution channel, including stores, direct mail, contract delivery, the Internet, and business-to-business electronic commerce. Office Depot can serve its customers 24 hours a day, 7 days a week anywhere in the world. Customers can shop for more than 14,000 products—anything from furniture to paper supplies—by phone, fax, or the Internet and at 1,020 retail stores in nine countries. Most people know that Amazon.com (**www.amazon.com**) is the biggest online retailer, but some might be surprised to learn that Office Depot is the second biggest. Its online retail operations, located at **www.officedepot.com**, were established in 1998 to complement its existing direct mail catalog, telephone call centers, and retail outlets, and today generate about $1 billion of sales—at a profit.

Since Office Depot already had good relationships with customers and suppliers and had in existence proven logistical distribution (fulfillment) systems made up of its own vehicle delivery and warehousing network, the addition of Internet retailing was not as difficult an undertaking as it would probably have been for an entirely new firm, which would have faced the multiple tasks required to create an infrastructure from scratch. For Office Depot, the Internet was an additional tool to serve its existing and growing customer base and was readily integrated into the existing business plan, which had already been tested by years of experience.

The web site not only provides convenient online shopping for busy customers but is also an online community where customers are encouraged to create their own web sites, promote their businesses, and network with potential customers. Managed in collaboration with Microsoft's bCentral (**www.bcentral.com**), the site provides businesses with a rich selection of information through posted articles and links to other useful sites that provide such things as guides for writing business plans, research, and so forth.

Rather than just providing another convenient method for placing orders, **www.officedepot.com** provides customers with additional reasons to return to the web site. As a result, the brand recognition, which was strong from the start because of Office Depot's long-established retail and catalog distribution system, has been successfully transferred to the Internet, an important lesson for other firms seeking to develop successful Internet strategies. Furthermore, the web site provides the firm with additional opportunities for nurturing customer goodwill through value-adding informational services that might be tied to partnerships with vendors of office products and services. An endorsement by Office Depot can assure customers that products with lesser-known brand names are to be trusted and represent good value for the money charged—otherwise they would not be offered to Office Depot's valued customers.

This transparent cooperative marketing strategy between an established and trusted Internet brand that can deliver large numbers of potential customers and firms whose products have lesser-known brand names that are seeking customers is likely to produce results superior to those that could be generated simply by placing advertisements on the Internet. We are likely to see the continued use of this strategy, in which an established and well recognized brand like Office Depot manages its web site in such a way as to develop an online community of attractive shoppers for vendors of the products it markets. Instead of buyers just searching the web for products and services from any site, we will probably see trusted brands like Office Depot serving as the endorsing gateway for buyers who want assurance of what they are actually buying and from whom.[1]

Up to this point, we have explored what might be called the *macro level* of topics related to e-business strategic thinking and planning. Beginning with this chapter, we now turn our attention to the *micro level,* where planning decisions must be made within an individual firm. We will start by exploring the "nuts-and-bolts" decision-making process that takes place within strategic marketing and ways in which e-business considerations can be accommodated as part of overall planning. As we do this, the guiding structure that should be followed in order to properly develop the marketing strategies within the e-business plan will become evident.

marketing management process

The comprehensive term used to refer to the ongoing planning, organizing, and controlling of marketing activities that the firm's personnel are engaged in at all levels of the organization.

e-marketing

Those marketing management activities that are mainly associated with the use of the Internet.

The **marketing management process** is the comprehensive term used to refer to the ongoing planning, organizing, and controlling of marketing activities that the firm's personnel are engaged in at all levels of the organization. This includes **e-marketing**, or those activities that are mainly associated with the use of the Internet. Although the marketing management process is by definition a continuous series of activities, new projects, such as the Office Depot web initiative, must begin somewhere. Logically, a firm needs to first identify potential markets and then select those customers that will be targeted for the marketing effort. Then a marketing mix of strategies related to product, price, place, and promotion is developed in order to successfully reach each targeted group. This chapter will examine the steps in the marketing management process that are central to the preparation of an e-business plan.

Identifying and Describing Potential Markets

At the heart of any good business plan are well-thought-out, detailed answers to basic marketing questions. e-Business planners need to first identify and then select markets of potential buyers that will be the targets of their strategic effort. An important consideration for planners who are looking at developing an online strategy to complement their existing business is whether the market that can be reached online is fundamentally made up the same people the firm is presently dealing with in its bricks-and-mortar operation. In some cases, a firm may be reaching out to new markets that are geographically dispersed and quite different in a variety of ways from the customers the firm is used to dealing with locally or in its physical stores. The more complex the different market characteristics, the more challenging will be the task of developing appropriate strategies that will appeal to each targeted group. For instance, besides the obvious differences in language usage, a web site selling a product like clothing or footwear must be sure to give sizes in the forms that are used in the different markets around the world. Furthermore, designing a web site that can successfully communicate to each market and cater to individual online behavior raises additional challenges for online vendors that are far greater than simply assuring the display of proper size references to customers.

Defining Broad Markets

market
A group of customers with a common need or desire to acquire some product and an estimated amount of dollar or unit sales over some period of time.

A **market** is characteristically defined by customers with a common need or desire to acquire some product and the estimated amount of dollar or unit sales over some period of time. For example, we might describe the market for high-speed Internet service access in terms of all individuals and organizations, including businesses and governments, that desire fast Internet connection services. Firms like Cisco Systems, Nortel Networks, and others whose sales of products and services are directly linked to the growth of this market adjust their strategic plans based on an estimate of the current number of subscribers and the expected market growth over the next few years. For firms like Cisco, the market is primarily made up of telecommunications firms that use Cisco's computer products to deliver high-speed service to individual customers, and larger organizations that need Cisco's products to handle these connections and deliver data to the individual users who are connected to the organization's LAN. Cisco Systems' sales are considered bellwethers by other firms in the industry, and announcements that Cisco intends to either expand or reduce the production or inventories of its products can trigger an industrywide response by competitors and other firms selling related products.

consumer markets
Markets composed of individuals making purchases for their own use.

organizational markets
Markets composed of businesses, governments, the military, nonprofit groups, and any other group where purchasing is done by an individual or a committee on behalf of the entire organization.

market segments
Identifiable groups of customers within the larger consumer and organizational markets that share characteristics such as a common lifestyle or demographic.

In broad terms, markets are classified by the type of buyer making the purchase decision; **consumer markets** are composed of individuals making purchases for their own use, whereas **organizational markets** are those composed of businesses, governments, the military, nonprofit groups, and any other group where purchasing is done by an individual or a committee on behalf of the entire organization. British children's author J. K. Rowling made good use of the Internet to launch her international marketing effort for *Harry Potter and the Goblet of Fire*. The book launch became an event, with a previously unheard of advance sales of 5.3 million copies in the first international print run. Many of these sales took place through Amazon.com and Barnesandnoble.com, as customers ordered online and had the books shipped as gifts to children for their summertime reading enjoyment.[2] On the other hand, Dell Computer built its online B2B business by serving the growing number of technically knowledgeable organizational buyers and then, more recently, making an effort to appeal to the individual consumer.

Market segments are identifiable groups of customers within these larger consumer and organizational markets that share characteristics such as a common lifestyle or demographic. For example, we have identified the market for iVillage.com as being a community of women who are brought together online by shared interests in health education, financial issues, lifestyles, and so forth. Carefully examining the attractiveness of the market segments that make up a larger market facilitates the selection process and the development of the marketing mix of strategies that will be used to cater to their interests and needs. Marketers use segmentation criteria to help define these segments.

Using Market Segmentation Criteria

The principal consumer segmentation criteria (also referred to as *variables* or *factors*) that are used to define market segments are demographic, geographic, psychographic, and behavioristic criteria. Regardless of which primary market the firm intends to deal with, segmentation of the broad market using these basic descriptive criteria will help create a clearer understanding of the identity of each group of potential customers within that market.

Demographic criteria reflect descriptive characteristics of consumers, such as their age, gender, family status and size, social class, religion, occupation, educational level achieved, and so forth. For example, families that can afford a home computer and high-speed Internet access are likely to have a higher-than-average income, and the parents are likely to have higher levels of education and to place a higher value on the need to provide this service to improve their children's academic performance. *Geographic* criteria describe where individuals are physically located, the density of the local population, climatic conditions, and so forth. Cost-effectiveness considerations suggest that densely populated urban areas are likely to receive fiber-optic cables and other high-speed infrastructure installations from telecommunication firms like WorldCom and AT&T before less densely populated suburban and rural areas do. *Psychographic* criteria include lifestyle, personality traits, and psychological factors such as motivation. For example, part of the personal lifestyle statement for many Internet users is to have the latest computer gadgets and technology. This psychological characteristic generally leads these people to want the fastest Internet connection service available. This segment can be trusted to be the first to graduate to the latest high-speed service as new technology is introduced into their geographic market. Finally, *behavioristic* criteria can be thought of in terms of how individuals use a product or service, such as heavy versus light usage, their intended purpose for using the product, and the benefits they seek. One might assume that heavy users of the Internet, as defined by the amount of time spent uploading and downloading data, are more likely to be customers for high-speed access because of the benefits of faster data transfer rates, greater work productivity, and less frustration waiting for screen displays.

The principal criteria used to define large organizational market segments are similar to those used for segmenting consumer markets and may include *geographic, type, size,* and *product usage* variables. For example, Dell Computer manufactures Internet computer servers for large, high-usage firms as well as lower-capacity units. Each machine is designed to best suit the different needs of a particular market segment.

Defining Markets According to Size

mass market
A market that is large, with little, if any, important differentiation among segments and offering great potential for revenue generation.

niche market
A market that is smaller in size and more specialized in character than a mass market.

After segmenting the broad market into identifiable segments, planners will then be able to organize and rank them in order of size and potential sales value. A **mass market** is characteristically large, with little, if any, important differentiation among segments and offering great potential for revenue generation. A **niche market**, on the other hand, is smaller in size and more specialized in character. A niche market tends to encompass consumers who have in common a single lifestyle characteristic or issue, such as teenagers interested in science and technology or weekend campers in Wisconsin. We can distinguish, then, between e-business strategies employing web sites that appeal to a mass market of teenagers and those appealing to the more narrowly defined niche market of teenagers motivated to learn more about science and technology, career choices, and so forth.

The potential for revenue enhancement derived from serving a mass market tends to attract many competitors who have different market share strategies to draw customers. For example, AOL Time Warner is the largest Internet service provider in a mass market of customers seeking basic connection and services. In order to compete with AOL Time Warner, competitors will have to offer something outstanding to draw away satisfied customers. AOL Time Warner has differentiated itself from its competitors by offering access to exclusive online content that other providers do not have. Meanwhile, some competitors have responded by offering lower-priced services to draw customers who are more attracted by cost savings than by exclusive online content.

On the other end of the size continuum, the Internet has lowered the barriers to identifying globally dispersed niche markets of customers, who now have a powerful medium for communication and distribution of a wide array of products and services. As we have emphasized throughout this text, the Internet has become the "great equalizer," allowing smaller businesses to compete on a global scale and allowing niche markets of customers to receive better service from firms using web tools such as web sites, e-commerce sales presentations, and so forth.

Although North America is still the dominant commercial market in the world, its market share continues to shrink as Internet usage in other areas grows. According to the study "A Nation Online: How Americans Are Expanding Their Use of the Internet," published by the *National Telecommunications and Information Administration* and the Economics and Statistics Administration, more than half of the American population, approximately 140 million people, now use the Internet regularly, and usage is growing at the rate of 2 million people every month. Furthermore, although the most popular use for the Internet is still email, which is used by 45 percent of the overall population, approximately one-third of Americans use the Internet to search for product and service information (36 percent, up from 26 percent in 2000), and among Internet users, 39 percent are making online purchases and 35 percent are searching for health information. According to research by Goldman Sachs, Harris Interactive, and *Nielsen/NetRatings*, Americans spend about $5 billion online every month and the average order is for $91.

e-Business Insight

Forrester Research Offers New Organizational Segmentation Variables

Segmenting organizational markets into groups with clearly identifiable characteristics related to their willingness to spend funds on new technologies, attitude and progress toward the use of new technologies, and buying style has been more difficult for e-business markets than it traditionally has been for consumer markets. The conventional categorical variables such as industry type, size, and location generally do little to explain or predict how businesses make their decisions. To meet the need for better understanding, Forrester Research Inc. of Cambridge, Massachusetts, has introduced a new system for predicting how and why businesses make their technology buying decisions and what decisions they will make. Based on a survey of more than 1,000 senior business and information technology executives of firms with revenues greater than $1 billion, the firm's *Business Technographics* segmentation focuses on three key dimensions of e-business culture: risk tolerance, executive commitment, and buying style. A combination of these dimensions can identify a segment that might, for example, be more risk-tolerant buyers of newer technology, with strong backing from executives and a coordinated buying process for products like supply-chain and wireless applications. Other segments might be slow to adopt new technologies but maintain a coordinated buying process for new products. To market successfully, vendors need to know which segments they are dealing with and then use appropriate strategies for each one—regardless of whether the market segments are consumer or organizational.[3]

But the trend is clearly toward more international business growth along with the expansion of commercial use of the Internet. By 2003 more than two-thirds of all Internet users are expected to log on from outside the United States, and the non-American share of e-commerce is predicted to reach 56 percent, more than double the 26 percent share in 1998. European consumer e-commerce is expected to grow from $5.6 billion in 1998 to $430 billion by 2003, and Japanese online buying is expected to expand twentyfold over five years, from $3.2 billion in 1999 to $63.4 billion in 2004. Whether or not these predictions turn out to be overly optimistic, the numbers clearly suggest a belief in the emergence of opportunities for firms with an online global capability.[4]

Analyzing Markets and Targeting Strategies

The process that leads to decisions about which market segments will be selected and which will be passed over involves management's ability to weigh risks and rewards and assess the firm's likelihood of succeeding with each possible available choice. After a satisfactory degree of analysis, an overall targeting strategy will emerge that reflects the number of markets that will be selected and the level of sales expected for each. We will begin this section of the chapter by examining the use of SWOT analysis in the selection of markets and targeting strategy.

Using SWOT Analysis

SWOT analysis

An acronym referring to the firm's self-study and evaluation of its overall *strengths* and *weaknesses,* along with the *opportunities* and *threats* it faces in the marketplace.

SWOT analysis is an acronym referring to the firm's self-study and evaluation of its overall *strengths* and *weaknesses,* along with the *opportunities* and *threats* it faces in the marketplace. A SWOT analysis should be undertaken before market selection decisions are made in order to better enable the firm to choose those available opportunities that offer it the greatest reward relative to the accompanying risks. In essence, marketers should select opportunities that fit well with the firm's strengths, increasing the chances that the firm will be successful. At the same time, marketers need to be vigilant and guard against threats from competitors that might take advantage of the firm's weaknesses in the marketplace. Eastman Kodak, Canon, Hewlett-Packard, and many other digital technology firms have recognized the opportunities presented to them by the growth of digital photography. According to Info Trends Research Group of Boston, in 2000, consumers spent about $1.2 billion on digital cameras, which allow them to edit their photographs, create online albums, print pictures on their own printers, and email images over the Internet.[5] However, a Gartner Group Dataquest study predicts that digital camera penetration will reach about 17 percent of U.S. households by the end of 2002 and exceed 50 percent by 2006.

Smart business strategists can use SWOT analysis to help them identify who their target market should be and the viability of catering to any particular segment in the larger market. For example, suppose a well-know print-based publisher like the National Geographic Society was considering the introduction of an online publication that focused on science and technology. The firm enjoys a strong reputation for educational publications across a broad range of readership. Suppose preliminary research suggested that there are many market segments that currently are not being well served in this area and might be receptive to the effort. For example, a publication dedicated to the needs of secondary school children and one aimed at community college students might be only two of many specific market segment possibilities. The task for marketers is to select the best one.

Before committing major resources to any online effort, however, the organization needs to determine whether there are sufficient potential viewers in the target market to make the project viable. Furthermore, given that there are many potential niche markets, it is important to conduct research studies to establish the range of possible market segments and the potential benefits that can accrue by serving each one before committing to any individual market segment. Using a SWOT analysis framework, the organization might conclude that it has many *strengths,* such as strong brand recognition among both students and educators, a knowledgeable staff that is capable of handling this new project, and a large inventory of multimedia content that can be used for the intended online publication. However, *weaknesses* also exist, such as limited experience working in an online environment, the challenges related to the product design, and the difficulty setting prices given that online users are not used to paying for information. Finally, there are the *threats* from other publications that might replicate design of this publication and fragment the market further. Since barriers to entry are weaker in the online marketplace than in the print world, National Geographic can expect many more competitors to consider entering the market. All of these factors must be properly weighed so that management can move forward with fuller awareness of the risks and benefits associated with the *opportunities* it may select.

Targeting Strategies

concentrated targeting strategy
A marketing strategy that focuses on only one market from among many.

After identifying each of the available market segments and conducting a SWOT analysis, a firm may opt for a **concentrated targeting strategy** and choose to focus only on one market. The selected single target market might be a niche market with little appeal for larger competitors, thus providing a good opportunity for a firm that wishes to be left alone. Selling prices in such a market might be higher than they would be in larger markets where competitors vie to attract customers. Concentrating on a neglected niche market is often considered a good way to get started in business and is sometimes associated with entrepreneurial activity. Most online communities like iVillage.com are examples of e-business start-ups that were looking for a way to cater to the growing number of niche markets that wanted information, products, and services tailored to their needs to be delivered to them through the Internet. Interestingly, many of these firms gradually came to offer traditional printed versions of their product to customers who wanted to view this content at times and places where computer access was not available. Similarly, television show personalities like Oprah Winfrey have found new product development, distribution, and promotion opportunities online through sites like **www.oprah.com** and **www.oxygen.com**.

undifferentiated targeting strategy
A marketing strategy that basically treats everyone as a member of one mass target market.

A second choice for marketers is an **undifferentiated targeting strategy**, which basically treats everyone as a member of one mass target market. The argument made here is that although individuals have different characteristics, they behave fundamentally in the same way when it comes to the particular product or service. For example, for the most part Internet search engines and directories are designed to be easily manageable and intuitively navigated by a wide range of people who are seeking information. The hierarchical structure and layout of, say, Yahoo.com is similar regardless of which branch in the directory the user is scanning. So whether you are looking for fishing lodges in Wisconsin or wedding gifts, the site navigation tools allow you to comfortably explore all of Yahoo!'s lists.

differentiated targeting strategy
A marketing strategy involving the selection of more than one identifiable market segment and the creation of a unique marketing mix of strategies tailored for each segment.

A third alternative strategy for selecting market segments is perhaps the most common of the three. A **differentiated targeting strategy** involves the selection of more than one identifiable market segment and the creation of a unique marketing mix of strategies tailored for each segment. Cable News Network (CNN) serves several identifiable market segments that are linked to its main web site at **www.cnn.com**. Customers of its Financial News Services can also access that site directly at **www.cnnfn.com**. Similarly, the Sporting News Network provides branches to a variety of niche markets of sports news and information through its web site at **www.tsn.com**.

Developing Sales Forecasts

As part of the market selection process, management will need to estimate the market potential of each market segment, or the total amount of sales that might be available to all firms competing in that segment. A segment that has forecasted sales of $10 million annually is going to be more attractive than a smaller niche market that might only provide $1 million. Obviously the calculated value can vary depending on many factors and on the methods used. It should be stated here that as fundamental as sales estimation is to the entire strategic e-business planning process, it is at best an art and is open to wide margins of error. To help them plan, many firms have taken to using customer-driven web sites. For example, to satisfy its customers' needs for information, Ford Motor Company has joined up with Microsoft's Carpoint web site (**http://carpoint.msn.com/home/New.asp**) to help consumers find decision-critical information about Ford's products and dealers from the comfort, convenience, and privacy of their own homes and offices. Ford and Microsoft hope to transform the site into a complete build-to-order system that will link customer orders for options directly with Ford's supplier system. This way, customers get the products they want and Ford reduces the risks associated with guessing the inventories of cars its dealers should stock.[6]

Some of the key factors that can influence sales forecasts include the e-business model adopted by the firm, the number and types of revenue streams employed, the number and types of customers in the market segment selected, the firm's marketing mix of strategies and allocation of resources, reactions by competitors in terms of their effort to compete with and counter the firm's marketing effort, and changes in the economic and other environmental forces that were presented in Chapter 2 of this text.

Popular categories of forecasting methods include the *executive judgment* of experienced or knowledgeable experts whose opinion is trusted, *surveys* of customers' behaviors that can indicate future sales and responses to the firm's marketing effort, *time series analysis* of historical sales data for the firm or industry to establish sales trends and cycles, *regression analysis* to find the mathematical relationship between historical sales and a predictive factor or factors such as the number of families with high-speed Internet access or changing levels of disposable family income, and *market tests* in which products and services are actually marketed on a test basis to help assess the overall success of a national market launch. In general, firms are likely to use more than one method of forecasting to help them form an estimate that they can have greater confidence in.

Let's use a simple example to illustrate several factors that can influence a sales forecast and the forecasting methods that might be used. Take the case of a firm that wishes to establish an online professional journal for engineers. The firm currently publishes several professional journals in print form, and it believes, based on surveys of current subscribers and focus group discussions, that there is an opportunity to create an online journal that will be of interest to about 30 percent of the subscribers to the firm's current printed journals. The firm believes that it can reach a potential global audience of 100,000 stable subscribers after three years of marketing effort. The figure is derived by looking at other niche publications, both online and in print, and from surveys of subscribers to competing professional journals and focus group studies with potential subscribers to assess their willingness to subscribe, the price they would be willing to pay, and the content they wish to read. Current economic and competitive conditions suggest that a niche publication could be established with a subscriber base as low as 10,000 readers, and research and opinions expressed by those familiar with the current competitive situation suggest that the trend is clearly toward specialized online publications. If subscribers were to pay $100 annually for access to journal content, as 95 percent of those surveyed indicated they would, the market potential would conceivably total $10 million. This figure would be modified to reflect any advertising revenues that might be part of the firm's e-business model and any other factors that could affect the initial sales forecast.

Online Product Development and Thinking

After completing the market selection process and identifying the firm's target market or markets, management will need to develop a full marketing mix of strategies designed to achieve the sales forecast estimate for each target market. These strategies fall into the four categories familiar to marketing students—product, price, place, and promotion—which are generally referred to as the *4Ps of marketing*. All new strategies should be developed in conjunction with existing plans so as to build a consistent overall business plan for the firm. To begin developing marketing strategies, management should logically first focus its attention on understanding the nature of the product or service to be sold, followed by pricing, place, and promotion decisions.

Defining the Scope of Online Products and Services

We define a *product* as anything tangible—or, in the case of a *service*, intangible—that is provided to customers in an exchange. What is given in exchange is usually money, but it might also be a customer's time and attention. For example, web sites using an advertising e-business model, such as Yahoo!, provide an Internet search facility in exchange for the user's willingness to view advertisements placed on his or her screen. Lack of expertise is not a barrier to firms' using the Internet for marketing activities, as a huge online services industry has developed to help them with those areas where they lack resources. For example, according to research by IDC Inc., revenues from hosting a firm's web site and providing product information for that firm on the host's computer system in return for a monthly fee are expected to grow from $1.8 billion in 2000 to $18.9 billion in 2004.[7]

At the core of understanding the motivation for the exchange process is the recognition that products and services are bought because of an expectation that they will satisfy purchasers' wants and needs. High-speed Internet access service that slows noticeably during peak periods of demand will disappoint users, who will identify the service as being poor in quality and therefore unsatisfactory be-cause of expectations created by the service provider's marketing strategies, which promise fast speed always—not most of the time. Before anything else, the firm must be clear about what its product or service—or combination of the two—actually is and what it is not. It must also learn what its customers believe they are being sold and develop strategies that are consistent with those belief systems.

Before we expand on our general understanding of product strategies, let us first examine several special characteristics of those intangible products that we call services. Services may be sold or may be provided as part of the purchase of a tangible product. However, the Internet lends itself to the sale of a plethora of services, and so special attention must be given to the unique ways in which cus-tomers may perceive the delivery of services online. For instance, because serv-ices are intangible, customers may have greater difficulty assessing their quality and price-value relationship. What one customer may consider excellent service, another might think is mediocre. Just how fast does an Internet service con-nection need to be for a home-based customer to consider it *fast*? As with tangi-ble products, experts can offer ratings and opinions to help evaluate and rank services, but the very nature of services presents unique issues for marketers to consider.

In addition to being intangible, services cannot be stored for later delivery, which presents problems when business activity is high. Since services are often deliverable only by specially trained employees, as in the case of a consulting firm that bills for the time its employees spend on a project, the question facing man-agement is whether the current growth in the demand for services is likely to con-tinue. If it is, then the expense of hiring and training more personnel is justified. However, if the growth in volume is a temporary phenomenon that will ease shortly, then expansion would be a mistake. Employees who are not providing billable services for customers are a drain on a firm and are generally released if they cannot be kept working. It is always preferable to minimize the need to reduce staff, but doing so is a necessary function of properly managed service-oriented firms.

Services, being delivered by people, are also quite difficult to control. A physi-cal product can be evaluated more readily, machinery adjusted, and substandard production set aside. However, an employee who delivers a specific service on be-half of the firm is unlikely to repetitively provide exactly the same service in every respect. In order to minimize the variations in quality and other deliverables as-sociated with the services being rendered, firms must carefully train and monitor the performance of service employees. Furthermore, the delivery of the service is inseparable from the employee delivering the service—consulting services pro-vided by one employee cannot simply be transferred to another employee if the original employee should happen to leave the firm. People cannot be substituted for one another as readily as physical products. The quality of the relationship an employee has developed with a customer is paramount in determining the firm's future ability to maintain a long-term working relationship with that customer.

Product Description and Classification Schemes

There are many other ways to describe, define, and classify products that produce useful direction for further strategic market development. For example, we can classify products and services in terms of their intended target markets—*consumer* and *organizational*. This classification can be clarified even further if we examine the segmentation criteria used to define the markets. An IBM computer server that is designed to rapidly retrieve files and transfer them on demand to users over the Internet is a product that will probably be of interest only to organizational markets. On the other hand, a laptop computer might have market segments in both consumer and organizational markets and require multiple marketing strategies aimed at each segment individually. IBM, Dell Computer, and other manufacturers commonly advertise in daily newspapers in order to reach both markets but will also advertise in business and trade journals in order to reach specific organizational markets in which large-scale purchases are often common. For consumer markets, these firms will target students with back-to-school specials in the autumn and prepare product models with features and software that are more appealing to students.

Marketers generally speak about three primary classes of consumer products—*convenience, shopping,* and *specialty*—each reflecting the consumer's attitude toward and view of the purchase. *Convenience products* are generally bought with little expected effort by consumers, at low prices, and with little price differentiation among different retail locations. Newspapers and magazines like the *Wall Street Journal* (**www.wsj.com**) and *Business Week* (**www.businessweek.com**) are good examples of a convenience product that is available online as well as at traditional retail stores. Products and services that might be considered exclusively online convenience products may be difficult to identify today, but the trend is clearly toward the development of more such products as well as the continuing migration of traditional convenience products and services onto the Internet. Retailers of office supplies such as Office Depot (**www.officedepot.com**) offer their customers added convenience through web sites that provide catalog shopping and delivery service. According to eMarketer's *U.S. eBanking Report,* although only 5 to 10 percent of the customer base now uses online services, consumer banking is expected to grow from12.2 million users in 2001 to 18.3 million by 2004.[8]

Impulse products are a subcategory of convenience products. As the term suggests, they are bought with little time spent on the decision. Pop-up advertisements and banner advertisements promote impulse purchases such as sending flowers to someone or subscribing to a magazine. Often links lead to other *unsought products,* meaning products that the customer was not originally considering and probably would never have considered purchasing had the advertisement not been placed on the screen.

Shopping products require some level of information gathering and investigation on the part of the customer before a purchase decision can be made. Most consumer products that are available online are in this category and are well served by the ability of the Internet to provide a storehouse of consumer information along with a customer service call center to help close sales online. Everything from computers to automobiles can be bought online as firms seek to reach customers through the Internet. In some cases, consumers may simply use the Internet to gather information and narrow their search before selecting certain retail outlets. For instance, using the Internet to examine fashions, furniture, and automobiles is a sensible first stage in the buying process but is no substitute for sampling the product by trying on clothing, sitting on sofas to see how comfortable they actually are, and test driving a car to see how it feels on the road in your neighborhood.

Traditional retailers need to estimate how much of their current customer base and how many new customers that they currently do not serve with their bricks-and-mortar business can be drawn to an online effort. For example, retailers such as Sears, Roebuck and Borders bookshops hope to increase sales by reaching customers who are unable or unwilling to shop at the firms' current retail store locations. The question at the heart of a strategy in which a bricks-and-mortar firm migrates to the Web is how many current customers will simply transfer their buying to the web site. If sales on the web site are simply counterbalanced by reduced sales at physical store locations, then there may not be much economic incentive to mount a retail web presence. The whole idea of going ahead with online retailing is to increase the volume of buying by current customers and to add new customers who might never shop at the stores. Otherwise, the venture makes no economic sense.

Finally, the Internet is best recognized as a tool to help vendors reach niche markets of customers anywhere in the world who are interested in buying *specialty products,* such as special effects digital imaging camera equipment or computer hardware and software. Even hard-to-find books that might be available only at specialty book retailers in major cities are readily available online. Online sites such as eBay allow buyers and sellers to market just about anything and have opened the door to artists seeking a way of selling their own unique works.

Organizational products classes include *raw materials, major equipment, accessory equipment, component parts, process materials, supplies,* and *services. Raw materials* such as wood, steel, and other commodities are used to manufacture products such as furniture and filing cabinets or components of final products such as door handles. Raw materials are sold by grade and are increasingly being sold through web-based contracting sites where firms can post their needs and suppliers can bid to deliver materials accordingly. Firms are also increasingly making use of the Internet for other procurements of needed organizational products, and to create better links with their customers' inventory and warehousing systems. And, as we've discussed elsewhere in the text, firms are increasingly seeking ways to build better relationships with their customers through the Internet by opening their ordering and inventory control systems to suppliers so that operational activities and costs are somewhat transferred to them, freeing employees to focus on generating revenues.

Major equipment includes large capital purchases such as computer systems or manufacturing machinery, whereas *accessory equipment* is not directly involved in the production of the firm's output but may be used to make it or be part of the office work environment. *Component parts* are used to complete production (for example, disk drives that are added to a computer assembled at one of Dell Computer's plants), and *process materials,* such as specialized resins and glue, are not readily identifiable as components but are incorporated into the manufacturing process. Finally, *supplies,* from photocopier paper to toner cartridges, are continuously needed for smooth operation of both the manufacturing and administrative areas of the firm.

Product Mix Issues

product mix
The total number of different products a firm makes available; it is used to compare the relative variety of the products available from a company.

The term **product mix** refers to the total number of different products a firm makes available; it is used to compare the relative variety of the products available from a company. For example, IBM has a larger product mix than Dell Computer, as IBM produces several models of large-scale computers and supercomputers that are not part of Dell's product mix.

Given the variety of Internet-based products and services to choose from, it is interesting to note that changes in the conventional concept of a wholesaler who bundles together a mix of products for a customer are already well under way. For example, Redmond, Washington–based InfoSpace Inc. works with providers of all sorts of Internet content, from weather services to news and information sites, to put together specific content mixes for customers' sites.[9]

product line
Related products that a firm sells that can be thought of as being part of a group.

Related products that a firm sells can be thought of as being part of a group referred to as a **product line**. Both IBM and Dell Computer produce a line of specialized Internet file servers as well as other lines of personal computers, laptops, workstations, and so forth. Furthermore, we can describe a firm's product mix in terms of how many lines the firm has (the *product mix width*) and the number of individual product items within one line (the *product mix depth*). Companies will expand their product mix when they believe that offering more variety will increase customer satisfaction and the firm's profitability. Likewise, management may choose to reduce the product mix depth and seek economies of scale by concentrating on producing only a few models within a product line, but at lower costs. For example, when Nortel Networks Inc. sold off its DSL high-speed production division in 2001, this decision reflected a change in management's view of the value of putting any further resources into an aging line of technology as opposed to focusing entirely on the new frontier defined by fiber optics.

Strategically, a firm may choose to market only certain products online because the selling characteristics of these products lend themselves to an online environment better than those of the firm's other products. In some cases, selecting certain products for sale exclusively online, leaving the existing products for sale only inside the firm's retail stores, may be strategically sensible. For example, a jewelry retailer like Zales might choose to sell a diamond bracelet exclusively on its web site (**www.zales.com**) if the firm could only secure a limited quantity of the item that was insufficient for national distribution in each of its retail stores. Furthermore, the bracelet might be considered an excellent choice for an online, highly discounted, promotional collection of jewelry that drives traffic to the web site and helps promote the retail store as well.

Understanding Product Strategy Decisions

There are many conceptual models that can help marketers understand and frame the strategic decisions before them. In this section of the chapter, we will examine the product life cycle concept, product differentiation, and product positioning, three important and popular conceptual models, and their utility to planners in an online strategic environment.

Product Life Cycle

product life cycle

A concept that suggests that products follow a life cycle pattern of clearly identifiable stages that coincide with changing sales, profits, and environmental selling conditions.

The **product life cycle** concept suggests that products follow a life cycle pattern of clearly identifiable stages that coincide with changing sales, profits, and environmental selling conditions. As a product ages and passes from stage to stage, marketing managers need to adjust their plans to reflect the conditions that the product faces in the marketplace and prepare for its inevitable abandonment and replacement with newer products. For example, semiconductor manufacturers like Intel always have new computer chips waiting to be introduced into the marketplace, but they delay the decision to begin production until management believes it is strategically best to shift resources to the newer technology. Several factors might indicate when it's time to make the shift; for example, sales of the older chip may be declining rapidly, indicating that the market is reaching the limits of demand for the current chip, or perhaps that competitors have introduced a better chip and the firm will lose market share if it does not bring out an equivalent product. Intel might also choose a time to launch the next chip in order to maintain its image as a technology leader and not a follower. The product life cycle for Intel's Pentium chips averages about two years, meaning that management and customers anticipate new product introductions about every two years.

The product life cycle, as illustrated in Figure 9.1, has four basic stages: introduction, growth, maturity, and decline. It is important to note that Figure 9.1 cannot reflect the actual length of time that each stage lasts, since this will be different for each and every product. The figure merely helps to illustrate the relative relationship of two critical factors: sales and profits.

In the *introduction stage,* a firm will traditionally experience losses, as the firm is spending more money than it is receiving in sales revenue. Start-up costs associated with infrastructure investments, switchovers to new production, and the high promotional costs necessary to inform customers are common strains on the resources of a firm that is launching a new product. Sales may increase quickly if the product is an instant hit with customers, or the firm may be burdened with a longer, more costly start-up period before the critical mass of customers takes form. At Amazon.com, it took several years before sales reached a level sufficient to cover the costs connected with establishing the web site and warehouse delivery infrastructure needed to offer the service. At the other extreme, sales can increase quickly for, say, new software or a software update that

FIGURE 9.1   The Four Stages of the Product Life Cycle

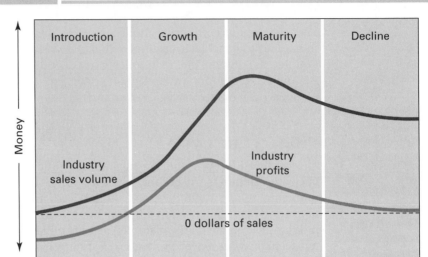

From William Pride, Robert Hughes, and Jagdish Kapoor, *Business,* Seventh Edition. Copyright © 2002 Houghton Mifflin Company. Reprinted with permission.

is made available to an established customer base through the firm's web site. For example, software firms like Microsoft depend on selling a large number of software upgrades quickly to a significant portion of their customer base, who will generally respond to improved features that offer additional value. This process is facilitated when the product upgrade can be promoted inexpensively through direct email to the registered customer base and customers can complete the transaction easily by clicking on icons displayed on their screens. The close of the introductory stage is marked by crossing over from losses to profits.

The Internet is fast becoming an important vehicle for launching new products. For example, best-selling author, spiritualist, and pioneer of alternative medicine Deepak Chopra set up an Internet site called **www.HowToKnowGod.com** as a companion to help promote his book by the same name. People who did not have access to the book but did have a connection to the Internet could read about the seven stages of God consciousness—free. Chat rooms on Yahoo.com, Amazon.com, CNN, Borders, iVillage, and barnesandnoble.com with links to his site helped to launch the book onto the bestseller list.[10] Similarly, Michael Gellert, the author of the philosophical book *The Fate of America—An Inquiry Into National Character,* illustrated once again how the Internet is a great equalizer by using a similar online strategy at **www.thefateofamerica.com**.

The *growth stage* is a period of dramatically increasing sales and profits, along with the entry of new competitors who are drawn by the product's noticeable success during the introductory stage. In addition, there is likely to be more variety in the product mix, and some specialty products that cater to niche markets are likely to emerge. For example, during the growth stage of the wireless communications market, cellular phone makers such as Nokia and Motorola raced to introduce new devices with more features while Research In Motion entered the market with the Blackberry, a smaller and less expensive device that allows mobile users to send and receive email messaging. To keep up in an ever more crowded marketplace, manufacturers of cellular phones and hand-held personal digital assistants like Palm have added email communication features to their products as well.

The *maturity stage* is marked by a steady decline in profits while sales reach their peak and then also begin to decline. This period can last a long time as customers grapple with the question of how much value continues to be offered by an aging product and firms make decisions about the adjustments required to remain actively involved in this market. Some firms will leave the market to other competitors if they feel that they have too little to gain in return for the effort required, while others with strong brand recognition may simply cull their product mix and abandon products selectively. Generally speaking, the levels of marketing expenditures and manufacturing costs will not be as great as they were in earlier stages, and as a result profits can remain satisfactory for many years. This is also the stage in which mergers or acquisitions among industry competitors is most likely to take place as the industry rationalizes its resources in what is euphemistically termed a *shakeout*.

Finally, the *decline stage* represents a gradual and often extended period of gradual reductions in both sales and revenues as fewer and fewer competitors remain active. By then, newer technology has made the deficiencies in older technology more obvious, and few buyers are likely to want the product any more even at extremely low prices. For example, when Intel's Pentium IV chips were introduced to the marketplace in the spring of 2001, the Pentium III series was clearly entering the latter part of the maturity stage and the Pentium II series and older versions were already undesirable for the mass market, since they lacked the speed that was considered necessary for multimedia software and faster Internet interaction.

Short life cycles for hardware can create special problems and lead to creative solutions. According to technology research firm Stanford Resources Inc., about 500 million personal computers will be considered obsolete by 2007. Because of toxic materials used in computer components, which must be treated as hazardous waste, California no longer allows personal computers to be dumped in landfills, presenting a severe problem of what to do with aging technology components. To help deal with the problem, the recycling plant in Roseville, California, set up by technology manufacturer Hewlett-Packard charges break-even prices ranging from $13 to $34 to handle each item. Whatever cannot be repaired and recycled is mined for usable components or sold to smelters for blending into other products. Rather than attempting to generate any real revenues, the firm is simply attempting to deflect general criticism directed at itself and its industry for manufacturing products that cannot easily be disposed of. Both IBM and Gateway operate similar recycling and disposal programs.[11]

Product Differentiation

product differentiation
Efforts to distinguish a firm's products from those offered by competitors by its design, color, style, quality, price, brand, and any other element recognized by the customer.

As we discussed in Chapter 6, the firm's overall e-business plan must focus on creating added customer value and a sustainable competitive advantage. Often, this effort begins with the product sold. **Product differentiation** refers to efforts to distinguish the firm's products from those offered by competitors. A product can be differentiated by design, color, style, quality, price, brand, or any other element recognized by the customer. For example, Intel's Pentium IV chips are faster than both its earlier models and competing chips from other semiconductor producers such as Advanced Micro Devices, and Apple computers are instantly recognizable because of their styling and their clear and candy-flavored colors, as well as their high-quality multimedia technology capability.

According to consultant Patricia Seybold (**www.patriciaseybold.com**), coauthor of *The Customer Revolution,* the Internet has permanently transformed the relationship between buyers and sellers by providing opportunities for firms to distinguish themselves from their competitors by offering *mass-customization* services. The 30,000 commercial-free radio stations available at **www.live365.com** and manufacturers like Dell Computer (**www.dell.com**) and handbag maker Timbuk2 Designs (**www.timbuk2.com**) that allow customers to construct their purchases online before any order is sent to production illustrate this logistical competitive approach. Besides bypassing traditional cost-heavy distribution systems and dealing directly with manufacturers, customers now control this part of the marketing function, creating new challenges for managers who are trying to compete and satisfy customer needs.[12]

Product Positioning

product position
How customers perceive the relative value of a product in comparison to its competition, using important product differentiation criteria.

product positioning
Management activities and efforts aimed at changing the product position of an existing product or establishing one for a new product.

perceptual map
A grid that illustrates the relative position of competing products as perceived by customers.

How customers perceive the relative value of a product in comparison to its competition using important product differentiation criteria is referred to as the **product position.** Management activities and efforts aimed at changing the product position of an existing product or establishing one for a new product are referred to as **product positioning.** The simplest way to understand product positioning is through the use of a grid called a **perceptual map** that illustrates the relative position of competing products as perceived by customers. Figure 9.2 displays the hypothetical customer perception of the relative positions of several computer manufacturers with respect to price and quality. This information has been fabricated in order to allow us to illustrate how strategic thinking about product positioning is done; however, for an actual perceptual map, the relative position for each manufacturer would have been generated through survey-style Likert questions in which customers are asked to use numbers to express their opinion about each manufacturer. For example, the question might be, "On a scale from 1 through 7, where 1 indicates Very Low, 2 Low, 3 Below Average, 4 Average, 5 Above Average, 6 High, and 7 Very High, what scores would you give IBM for price and quality?" The scores would be averaged and the average scores would be used to locate each firm on the perceptual map of the perceived relative differences between them. For example, our hypothetical grid shows that Dell

FIGURE 9.2   Hypothetical Perceptual Map Illustrating Product Positions of Major
Computer Manufacturers

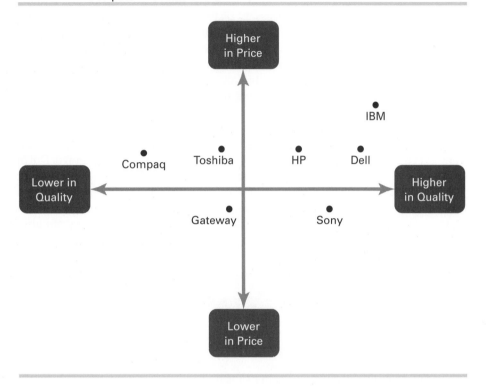

Computer is perceived as less expensive than IBM and a bit lower in quality. If in fact IBM were lower in price than Dell, then IBM management might decide to advertise this incorrect perception and gain market share. Or perhaps another result of this information would be that Compaq would undertake a major effort to improve the quality of its product and then emphasize this effort as part of a renewed marketing strategy. And finally, suppose another manufacturer recognizes the absence of any firms selling a high-quality but low-priced product and hence sees an opportunity to market such a product. Perhaps a new breakthrough production technology can allow this firm to realize what would clearly be a competitive advantage and capture this corner of the market.

Completing the Marketing Mix of Strategies

Although decisions related to product strategies are generally dominant in most planning situations, the planning process is incomplete without the incorporation of the other key decision areas, pricing, place, and promotion. In this final segment of the chapter, we will explore issues related to these important components of the marketing mix.

Pricing Strategies

pricing strategies
Strategies for setting and managing prices

Pricing strategies are concerned with both setting and managing prices. The exchange process is facilitated by the customers' ability to pay a given dollar amount for a product or service. High-speed Internet access for home-based customers is worth whatever people are willing to pay, just like telephone service or an airplane flight from New York to Los Angeles. The forces of supply and demand suggest that any product or service that is in high demand and short supply will have higher market prices and that the opposite conditions will result in falling market prices. However, many factors besides these basic market forces influence prices. For example customers expect new technologies to emerge periodically and learn to follow a product life cycle pattern in which a newer product might be introduced every two years on average. During this time period, the older technology will generally fall in price as newer and presumably better technology replaces it. For instance, faster computers and semiconductor chips routinely replace older and slower models. Those customers who need or simply want the latest and fastest computer technology are also generally prepared to

e-Business Insight

e-Banking: No New Sales or Customers—Just Lower Costs

Consider another strategic argument for building a web presence: simply transferring current customers online in order to serve them better and reduce costs. Research by the firm Yankee Group Inc. suggests that Internet-based banking transactions are by far the least expensive for banks, costing 1 cent per transaction, in comparison with 32 cents for ATMs, 62 cents for telephone banking, and $1.29 for retail customer service at a local branch. By shifting customers to the Internet, banks may not increase their sales revenues, but they can increase their profits by reducing costs. According to the North America–wide survey, 46 percent of respondents said that they would be switching to Internet-based banking over the next two to three years—doubling the number that were already being served by the banking industry in this way. The results suggest continued expansion of Internet activity by the banking industry as it answers the demand by technologically comfortable customers for more convenient services. Interestingly, Canadian banking customers, representing 15 percent of all North American customers, are three times more likely to use Internet-based banking services than Americans are. This is attributed to greater willingness to adopt the use of technology such as ATMs and debit cards and the fact that the six largest nationwide Canadian banks, which dominate the industry, have historically been heavy promoters of moving their customers to the use of cost-saving technologies through incentives and higher fees for services provided at bank branches. The trend toward more e-banking is clearly established, with competition for online bill payments and other simple repetitive transactions likely to develop not only within the banking industry but also from other organizations such as the postal service that can act as intermediaries for the delivery and storage of statements and the transfer of funds for payments.[13]

pay a premium price for the newer technology, whereas those who have delayed their purchases have the added incentive of lower prices for the slightly older technology.

cost–benefit analysis
A form of analysis that provides the purchaser with an understanding of what benefits can be gained in exchange for the price paid.

For any purchase that is being considered, a **cost–benefit analysis** provides the purchaser with an understanding of what benefits can be gained in exchange for the price paid. Sales representatives can also use cost-benefit analysis to persuade customers that the value they will receive from the purchase is sufficient to justify the price. For example, it might be argued that switching from a lower to a higher Internet access speed can actually save the firm money by saving employees' time and thereby increasing their productivity. The use of wireless email devices such as Research In Motion's Blackberry is highly regarded because, among other selling points, it is considerably less expensive for mobile employees to use than laptop computers.

shopping agents
Intelligent software tools that will seek out pricing and other product information and report it back.

Buyers can take advantage of **shopping agents**, intelligent software tools that will seek out pricing and other product information and report it back. After the buyer fills in a short questionnaire, the agent uses the criteria indicated there to locate web sites containing matches. For example, Microsoft's Expedia (**www .expedia.com**) flight reservation system will help users locate airline, hotel, car rental, and other related services online. The use of agents and search engines and the ease with which customers can exchange information among themselves through the Internet have all contributed to a more knowledgeable and price-sensitive customer. Customers who want a clearly identified product can easily retrieve lists of web vendors selling the product ranked according to the offered selling price. To reduce the effect of price on customers' selection of a vendor, the product can be bundled with other products or services to obfuscate the description. However, where customer decision making is driven by price alone, vendors need to be careful about how they present product descriptions. Furthermore, given the power of the Internet to facilitate communication among existing and potential customers, products that are perceived to be unsatisfactory in some way or simply not worth the current market price are likely to come under price reduction pressure as a result of weakening demand.

The Internet makes comparing prices relatively easy for users. Perhaps not surprisingly, the biggest-selling consumer product on the Internet currently is computer hardware. However, if trends continue, online airline transactions will fly right by it to an estimated $17 billion by 2004, more than $1 billion higher than computer hardware. In 1999 about 5 percent of airline ticket transactions were conducted over the Internet, but this figure is expected to grow to 18 percent by 2004 as customers seek lower prices and convenient shopping for what is fast becoming a commodity item.[14]

Regardless of how much money customers are willing to pay for products and services, over the long run firms must employ pricing strategies that generate sufficient revenues to exceed their costs of production and produce a profit. Failure to deliver profits will affect the viability of the organization and undermine the ability of management to compete for employees, develop new product and services, and secure access to external sources of financing necessary to expand the firm. We will explore these topics in greater detail in Chapter 11.

Place Strategies

Place (distribution) strategies are concerned with making the product or service available when and where customers want it. As a distribution tool, nothing beats the Internet in terms of its ability to create *time* and *place utility* by delivering digitized products on demand 24 hours a day, 7 days a week, anywhere in the world where a device is available to the customer. Research analysts at International Data Corp. (IDC) estimate that as more and more customers around the world connect to the Internet, any product that can be digitized and thereby delivered on the Internet will contribute to an explosion in e-commerce sales. According to IDC, worldwide e-commerce spending grew 68 percent between 2000 and 2001, reaching more than $600 billion in 2001, and is projected to reach $1.5 trillion by 2003.[15] The Walt Disney Company has a clear advantage over many of its competitors, since much of its content is animation. Animation is the easiest non-still content to transfer to the Internet, and the vast majority of Internet users have access only to narrow-bandwidth transmission, which delivers a reasonable-quality image of animation. As access to wider bandwidths expands, Disney is expected to be ready with a vault full of prerecorded film and video content.[16]

As more devices enter the marketplace, customers will enjoy the flexibility and convenience of receiving many more products online, such as e-books, music, and video programming on demand. According to BiblioMondo Inc. (**www.bibliomondo.com**), whose software allows any private or public library to manage and sell its digital content on the Internet, the world's 712,000 libraries will be joining a growing list of online vendors like netLibrary (**www.netlibrary.com**) and ebrary (**www.ebrary.com**) that are seeking methods for managing their business and earning revenues through online sales. The firm's management suggests that in the future, buyers will see libraries as quality points of purchase which have screened for the best selections for their clients and created a brand identity as the source for specific information.[17]

Bricks-and-mortar retailers and firms with highly recognizable brand names such as The Walt Disney Company (**www.disney.com**) continue to expand their reach into global markets by setting up online retail shopping sites. According to research by the Boston Consulting Group, it costs an online retailer about $82 to generate a single customer, whereas it costs an established bricks-and-mortar retailer only $12. This is mostly due to the customer's recognition of the store name and established associations in the customer's mind.[18] Furthermore, according to some experts, it costs between $15 and $25 million to build a top-notch web site but at least $150 million to build a warehouse and distribution system. The Internet component represents only 10 percent of the investment for online retailing, giving existing bricks-and-mortar organizations with existing brand recognition such as the Gap and Radio Shack a sizable advantage.[19] Regardless of how great a web presence a firm plans to have, it will also have to incorporate sufficient online customer support. According to Forrester Research Inc., 37 percent of all online buyers request customer service while shopping online.[20]

Distribution is rarely direct from the manufacturer, however. As illustrated in Figure 9.3, *intermediaries* or *middlemen* help to increase exchange efficiencies by reducing the number of contacts that both producers and buyers need to deal with by forming a *marketing distribution channel.* The typical marketing distribution channels are illustrated in Figures 9.4 and 9.5.

In addition, intermediaries facilitate the exchange process by buying and selling, creating assortment, and negotiating prices. Traditional intermediaries (retailers and wholesalers) also operate online, providing physical supply services such as handling, transporting, and storing products and facilitating activities such as consulting services, financing, grading, and providing market information.

The term *supply-chain management,* which was introduced in Chapter 6, refers to the effort to nurture partnerships among channel members, with the goal being to continuously increase efficiencies in the distribution channel. The Internet provides a variety of solutions that contribute to improvements in

FIGURE 9.3 Efficiency in Exchanges Provided by an Intermediary or Middleman

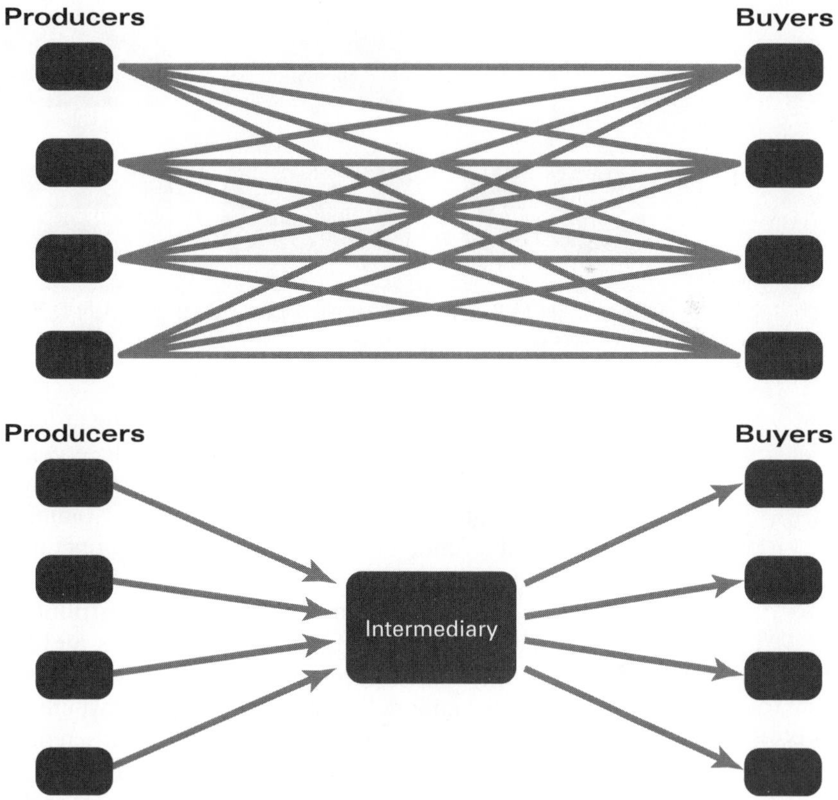

From William M. Pride and O. C. Ferrell, *Marketing* 2000e. Copyright © 2000 by Houghton Mifflin Company. Reprinted with permission.

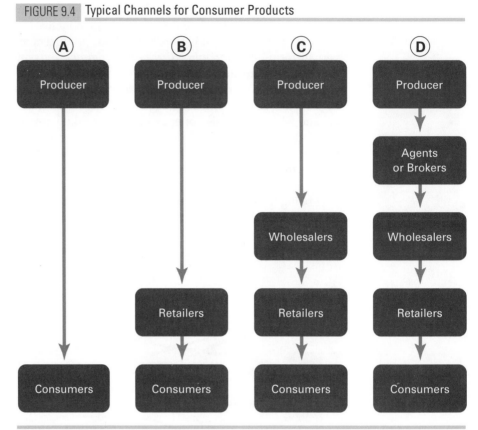

FIGURE 9.4 Typical Channels for Consumer Products

From William M. Pride and O. C. Ferrell, *Marketing* 2000e. Copyright © 2000 by Houghton Mifflin Company. Reprinted with permission.

supply-chain management such as online buying groups, auctions, reverse auctions, and facilitating communications software—ranging from customer relationship management software to simple email—to assist buyers and sellers. Whether through cost reductions or increased customer satisfaction, the Internet is considered a fundamental tool for improving operations in the supply chain. However, the Internet can also contribute to *channel conflict,* since geographic boundaries that would normally set limits on distributors' behaviors are absent. For example, products such as pharmaceuticals and health-related items that would traditionally have been sold through local retail stores can now be bought through online vendors by customers living anywhere. Manufacturers' ability to control prices in different markets is significantly reduced by the power transferred to online buyers. The financial threat to traditional local distributors is real and is likely to grow in the future as more customers seeking lower prices become increasingly comfortable with ordering products online. As Dell Computer did, firms may decide to eliminate intermediaries completely and rely on their own direct marketing effort with customers. Other firms that feel that they need local

FIGURE 9.5   Typical Channels for Business Products

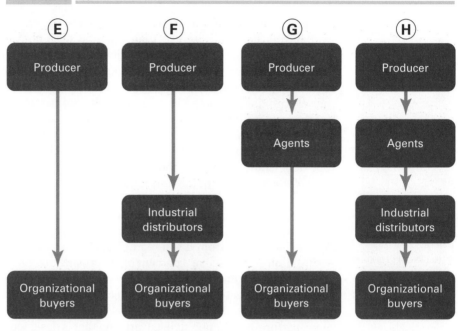

From William M. Pride and O. C. Ferrell, *Marketing* 2000e. Copyright © 2000 by Houghton Mifflin Company. Reprinted with permission.

bricks-and-mortar geographic representation are likely to require new strategies for tackling the channel conflicts that will continue to grow as customers' use of the Internet grows.

Promotion Strategies

promotion

Any communications activity that is designed to positively influence the buying decision-making behavior of customers; it includes advertising, personal selling, sales promotion, publicity, and public relations.

Promotion is any communications activity that is designed to positively influence the buying decision-making behavior of customers; it includes advertising, personal selling, sales promotion, publicity, and public relations. Coordinated into a single driving force, these activities are collectively referred to as the firm's *integrated marketing communications strategy* or *promotional mix*. For example, according to brand marketing expert Will Novosedlik of San Francisco, California–based Organic Inc., large-scale global firms like Volvo will continue to blend their traditional media with Internet media marketing strategies as they go after technologically comfortable consumers online. Volvo's launch of the S60 model, for instance, was built around a contest that awarded a new S60 to the winner. Consumers could enter the contest by providing data about themselves at a web site that provided promotional information about the car. Contestants could use PDAs and wireless devices to monitor developments, which helped the company measure the interest of the users of each group of communication devices. Banner advertising on CBS Sportsline (**www.sportsline.com**) and its sponsorship of the NCAA basketball March Madness tournament were combined with other on-line and televised promotions designed to bring audiences to the web site.[21]

Many marketers use the Internet to expand their channels of communication with buyers. Research suggests that consumers will not visit a consumer product site without a motivating reason. Understanding why consumers visit web sites drives their design and use by marketers. For example, Unilever Inc., makers of Wisk laundry detergent, has integrated consumer information about stain re-moval with the product's label and web site. Consumers can check the web site for the extra information, which is a value-added utility in the marketing mix.[22]

All promotional strategic thinking is guided by the communications and be-havioral decision-making models presented in Chapter 8. Here we will expand our understanding of promotion by looking at specific characteristics of each area of the integrated marketing communications strategy.

advertising

Any paid nonpersonal communication that is distributed to a target market through a medium such as television, radio, newspapers, journals, or, of course, the Internet.

Advertising is any paid nonpersonal communication that is distributed to a target market through a medium such as television, radio, newspapers, journals, or, of course, the Internet. According to Forrester Research Inc. of Cambridge, Massachusetts, far from declining in importance, online advertising is expected to rise from an average of 8 percent of advertising budgets in 2000 to 15 percent in 2003 and 25 percent by 2005, when it will reach about $63 billion. However, there is likely to be a switch toward more direct email marketing campaigns that will in-clude contests and other promotional interaction with customers rather than poor-performing banner-style advertising that is designed to attract attention but has an estimated clickthrough rate of about half a percent. IBM directs about $50 million of its $760 million advertising budget to online advertising, and other tra-ditional, non-dot-com companies like Toyota, MasterCard, and Disney have also begun to develop closer communication ties and information exchanges with current and potential customers through advertising strategies that engage cus-tomers over the Internet.[23]

The Internet is an attractive medium because it allows customers to interact with advertisements. Customers can enter data such as names and phone num-bers, and web sites can be designed with menu control selections that allow the customer to self-direct navigation of the site. Instead of mimicking television ad-vertising, which is generally regarded by viewers as an interruption of program entertainment, Internet advertising that attempts to assist motivated shoppers is likely to be more successful. Interestingly, online advertising is also extremely concentrated. Only ten companies received 70 percent of all revenues. Among these firms, the top three, AOL, Microsoft, and Yahoo!, earned more than half of the revenues.[24]

Regardless of the attractiveness and power of Internet advertising, however, the advertising e-business model is generally regarded as a weak one to depend on because viewers often disregard banner advertisements when they visit web sites or receive them as email. Furthermore, the increasing use of software that blocks the downloading of advertising makes the whole area of Internet advertis-ing challenging, to say the least. For example, WebWasher (**www.webwasher.com**) and AdSubtract (**www.adsubtract.com**) are programs that are designed to recognize incoming advertisements by analyzing page formats and looking for standard banner advertising shapes. These software programs typically fill the advertising space by restructuring the desirable page content or simply replacing advertisements with blank spaces. The delays are often worthwhile to users in that they reduce the time spent in downloading unwanted images.

The task facing marketers who are using the Internet is to design advertisements that are likely to engage interested and motivated viewers, such as someone searching for information about digital cameras and photography. According to a study by researchers at NPD Group Inc., building brand awareness by paying search engines to place the advertiser's name among the top positions displayed is three times more effective than a banner advertising strategy.[25]

According to Michele Slack, an analyst at Jupiter Communications Inc., Internet advertising that is placed at an appropriate point in an online presentation, such as at the end of a round of an online game, is more acceptable to the audience. Since such placements resemble the placement of television advertisements, which interrupt programming at regular intervals, this is also a familiar structured experience for the user. Furthermore, according to Erick Hachenburg, president and CEO of pogo.com, an advertisement-sponsored free Internet multiplayer gaming site, sites like pogo.com draw an audience that regards the placed advertising differently from the way most Web users regard it. Instead of wanting to move on as quickly as possible, players welcome advertisements displayed between sets in the game as a respite and do not rush off to another site. Pogo.com players spend an average of 45 minutes at a time playing a variety of Java versions of word puzzles, checkers, and card games like Hearts. Given the 300 million impressions (exposures to a viewer) per game per month served on the web site, and advertising revenue that doubled every quarter in 1999, pogo.com and other game sites appear to be offering a marketable content site that is interesting to advertisers. As a result, the *cost per thousand (cpm)* exposures ranges from $15 to $30, and above-average industry click rates (players clicking on an advertisement) of about 1 percent suggest that game sites are likely to find niches of viewers.[26]

According to Forrester Research Inc., online advertising will grow to $6.4 billion by 2007. The report suggests that multichannel campaign feedback will help set budgets as advertisers move toward a greater degree of integration of online with traditional advertising media.[27] Research by New York–based eMarketer reported a drop in online advertising from $8.2 billion in 2000 to $7.3 billion in 2001, reflecting the fallout from reductions in dot-com advertising and the fortunes of those like Yahoo! that relied heavily on online advertising. However, the survey suggested that recovery in 2002 would bring advertising spending back to $8.2 billion, and that spending would then grow to $9.2 billion in 2003.[28]

Although banner-style advertisements account for 40 percent of all advertising, this is down from higher levels in the past as marketers continue to shift toward what is considered more effective online marketing such as direct email sales promotions, building databases of information online for future communication with potential customers, and e-commerce partnerships.[29] As a result, the cost per thousand exposures of banner advertising has fallen dramatically. The cpm can vary from pennies to hundreds of dollars, depending on the size of the banner, the web site, the market it can deliver to advertisers, and so forth. A survey by Ad Resource (**www.adresource.com**) suggests that the average cpm is probably about $30 for a typical web site with high-quality content and the capability of delivering an audience for the advertisers.[30] The cpm is the metric that allows advertisers to compare the advertising costs of different media in creating their budgets. Advertisers can expect to pay twice the normal exposure rate for any actual clicks on the banner advertisement, and many share their sales revenue from whatever is sold on the Web with the web site presenting their advertising. Rather than trying to place their advertising on web sites themselves, advertisers can use the services of firms like Doubleclick (**www.doubleclick.com**) and 24/7 Media (**www.247media.com**) to select web sites and target specific viewers with sophisticated smart software.

personal selling
Paid communication that relies on personal contact with an individual representing the firm to convey information and persuade customers.

Personal selling is also a form of paid communication, but it relies on personal contact with an individual representing the firm to convey information and persuade customers. The equivalent of the sales representative in the bricks-and-mortar world is the online customer service representative that assists customers with pre- and postsale services. The Internet has introduced new challenges to traditional strategic thinking that has worked well for a long time. For example, after being reluctant to move from a face-to-face sales approach to a less personal web site approach, Allstate began taking what some consider to be small, catch-up steps by creating an Internet presence to support its established sales force and channels. Firms like eCoverage.com that have exclusively web-based strategies are expected to take a big share of the estimated $4 billion Internet insurance sales market.[31]

sales promotion
Activities and offers that can help motivate positive buyer behavior, including contests, samples, coupons, rebates, and so forth.

Sales promotion refers to activities and offers that can help motivate positive buyer behavior, including contests, samples, coupons, rebates, and so forth. The Internet is a cost-effective facilitator, distributing sales promotion offers to customers and potential customers through email campaigns and pop-up and banner advertising on selective web sites. However, according to the research firm Jupiter Media Metrix, the number of commercial emails received by the average U.S. consumer will grow to 1,600 by 2005, and Forrester Research Inc. predicts that marketing firms will send more than 200 billion commercial emails by 2004, inundating users and crowding out any messages that may be of interest to recipients.[32]

The Internet is especially effective when the sales promotion offer is a digitized item that can be distributed online.

publicity
Any unpaid nonpersonal communications activity designed to generate a favorable and positive image for the firm and its products.

Publicity is any unpaid nonpersonal communications activity designed to generate a favorable and positive image for the firm and its products. Publicity includes the preparation of press releases, participating in press conferences, providing a company representative to be interviewed by news reporters, preparing articles for publication on issues the firm is considered knowledgeable about, and so forth. Publicity can be thought of as a strategy for getting out a positive word about the firm and its products through the mass media without having to pay for it. In order to accomplish this, the firm has to have something of value that reporters will find useful and therefore worthwhile repeating. For example, the release of a new edition of AOL software or Microsoft Windows generally qualifies for freely distributed publicity for these firms. Needless to say, negative publicity about the firm, such as a report on a drop in the value of its stock or on unhappy shareholders voicing discontent with what they consider excessive executive compensation packages while stock values fall, can be a problem.

public relations
Paid efforts to manage the various publics that the firm deals with, such as customers, suppliers, governments, share-holders, employees, and the media.

Public relations refers to paid efforts to manage the various publics that the firm deals with, such as customers, suppliers, governments, shareholders, employees, and the media. Public relations activity is concerned with managing the firm's publicity. For example, negative publicity concerning a dramatic fall in the value of the firm's stock might be counterbalanced by a news conference announcing a new strategic alliance with a partner that is expected to boost sales revenues in the near future. A popular public relations strategy is the preparation and dissemination through the firm's web site of white papers and research reports on topics of wide interest to selected target markets. For example, any major firm such as IBM publicizes itself, its industry, and the products it is promoting to a variety of markets through freely available articles and press releases posted on its web site. Even small businesses can take advantage of the Internet to generate publicity by posting articles of interest and advice on their web sites. Given the relatively low costs involved, Internet-based public relations campaigns can be effective tools for generating good relations on behalf of the firm.

Conclusions

This chapter helped to provide a bridge between conventional marketing theory and practice and strategic e-business planning. Established marketing models such as the marketing management process, market segmentation, and the marketing mix were presented in such a way as to illustrate how marketing strategies should be structured to contribute to the e-business plan. In the next chapter we will explore how management theory and practice can be strategically applied to the firm's e-business planning process.

CASE STUDY RETURN TO INSIDE e-BUSINESS

Office Depot's marketing strategy, which incorporates the building of an online community of buyers for the products it distributes, illustrates the ways in which the Internet can be used to build better customer relationships and sell more products at the same time. Well-known brands may have less difficulty attracting online shoppers. Lesser-known brand names can take advantage of the implied value-exchange fairness suggested by web site distributors like Office Depot.

ASSIGNMENT

1. What other collaborative efforts can a web site operator like Office Depot develop with vendors because of its highly recognized and valued brand name?

2. What risks are associated with this collaborative marketing approach for Office Depot? for vendors?

Chapter Review

1. Identify and describe potential markets of online customers.

Although the marketing management process is by definition a continuous series of activities, new firms or new projects within an established firm must begin somewhere. Logically, a firm needs to first identify potential markets and then select those groups of customers that will be targeted for the firm's marketing effort. A market is characteristically defined by customers with a common need or desire to acquire some product and the estimated amount of sales in units and dollars over some period of time. In broad terms, markets are classified by the type of buyer making the purchase decision; they are divided into consumer and organizational markets. These in turn can be segmented into smaller groups of various sizes using descriptive criteria allowing for the identification of large-scale mass markets as well as smaller niche markets.

2. Examine the process for analyzing and selecting target markets.

The process that leads to decisions about which market segments will be selected and which will be passed over involves management's ability to weigh risks and rewards and assess the firm's likelihood of succeeding with each possible available choice. After identifying each of the market segments available and conducting a SWOT analysis, a firm may opt for a *concentrated targeting strategy* and select to focus only on one market; an *undifferentiated targeting strategy,* which basically treats everyone as a member of one mass target market; or, perhaps the most common of the three, a *differentiated targeting strategy,* which involves the selection of more than one identifiable market segment and the creation of a unique marketing mix of strategies tailored for each segment. As part of the market selection process, management will need to estimate the market potential of each market segment, or the total amount of sales that might be available to firms competing in that segment.

3. Discuss topics related to the development of online product strategies.

To begin developing marketing strategies, management should logically first focus its attention on understanding the nature of the product or service to be sold. At the core of understanding the motivation for the exchange process is the recognition that products and services are bought because of an expectation that they will satisfy purchasers' wants and needs. Before anything else, the firm must be clear about what its product or service (or combination of the two) actually is and what it is not. The firm must also learn what its customers believe they are being sold and develop strategies that are consistent with those belief systems. There are many ways to describe, define, and classify products that produce useful direction for strategic market development. For example, we can classify products and services in terms of their intended target markets—*consumer* and *organizational.* This classification can be clarified even further if we examine the segmentation criteria used to define the markets. Finally, product mix considerations can contribute additional useful information for the development of online product strategies.

4. Describe product strategy decision making using popular conceptual models.
The product life cycle concept, product differentiation, and product positioning are three important and popular conceptual models that can help planners understand and frame the strategic decisions before them. The product life cycle concept suggests that products follow a life cycle pattern of clearly identifiable stages that coincide with changing sales, profits, and environmental selling conditions. As a product ages and passes from stage to stage, marketing managers need to adjust their plans to reflect the conditions that the product faces in the marketplace and prepare for its inevitable abandonment and replacement with newer products. Product differentiation refers to efforts made to distinguish the firm's products from those offered by competitors. A product can be differentiated by its design, color, style, quality, price, brand, or any other element recognized by the customer. How customers perceive the relative value of a product in comparison to its competition using important product differentiation criteria is referred to as the product position. Management activities and efforts aimed at changing the product position of an existing product or establishing one for a new product are referred to as product positioning.

5. Explore the development of pricing, place, and promotion strategies.
Although decisions related to product strategies are generally dominant in most planning situations, the planning process is incomplete without the incorporation of the other key decision areas, pricing, place, and promotion. Pricing strategies are concerned with both setting and managing prices. Many factors besides basic market forces influence prices. Cost-benefit analysis provides the purchaser with an understanding of what benefits can be gained in exchange for the price paid. Sales representatives can also use cost-benefit analysis to persuade customers that the value they will receive from the purchase is sufficient to justify the price. Place (distribution) strategies are concerned with making the product or service available when and where customers want it. As a distribution tool, nothing beats the Internet in terms of its ability to deliver digitized products on demand 24 hours a day, 7 days a week, anywhere in the world where a device is available to the customer. Promotion is any communications activity that is designed to positively influence the buying decision-making behavior of customers; it includes advertising, personal selling, sales promotion, publicity, and public relations. Coordinated into a single driving force, these activities are collectively referred to as the firm's *integrated marketing communications strategy* or *promotional mix.*

REVIEW QUESTIONS

1. Define the marketing management process.
2. Describe what part e-marketing plays in a firm's marketing strategy.
3. Describe the market segmentation variables.
4. What does the term *SWOT* mean to a marketer?
5. What does the term *market potential* mean?
6. What are the key product classifications for consumer products? Provide an example of each one.

7. What are the key product classifications for organizational products? Provide an example of each one.
8. What is the product life cycle?
9. What is product differentiation?
10. Explain what a perceptual map is and the concept of product positing. Use an example to illustrate your point.
11. What is cost-benefit analysis?

DISCUSSION QUESTIONS

1. List the market segmentation variables that might be used by an Internet-based firm and discuss why you have chosen them.
2. Discuss the key differences between differentiated, undifferentiated, and concentrated targeting strategies.
3. Why might a firm choose a concentrated targeting strategy?
4. Describe how marketing managers might develop some sense of market potential.
5. Describe how product classifications can be used to market products.
6. Describe how the product life cycle can be used to develop marketing plans.
7. Using an example you have created, discuss which strategies might emerge from the examination of a perceptual map.
8. How can cost-benefit analysis be used to set the price for a product?
9. Discuss the advantages and disadvantages of one type of promotional strategy available to a firm.

Building Skills for Career Success

EXPLORING THE INTERNET

Yahoo.com uses an undifferentiated market strategy, whereas Tom's of Maine (**www.toms-of-maine.com**) uses a concentrated niche market strategy to sell all-natural toothpastes and other health products on its web site. Many opportunities exist for smaller web site operators like Tom's of Maine, who are interested in serving the growing number of Internet users seeking specialized products, services, and information. Many niche markets have also emerged out of what were once larger undifferentiated markets. This is especially true when a mass-market web site attracts large numbers of viewers and then gradually loses some users to web sites that cater to their more narrowly defined niche markets of needs and interests.

ASSIGNMENT

1. Locate, explore, and describe a web site that uses a mass-market strategy and one that is catering to a specialized niche.
2. Compare the similarities and differences between their respective strategies.

DEVELOPING CRITICAL THINKING SKILLS

The top ten web sites dominate the online advertising business. Among these, AOL (**www.aol.com**), MSN (**www.msn.com**), and Yahoo! (**www.yahoo.com**)

earn more than half of all advertising revenues. Examine these sites looking for commonalities that might explain their strengths as compared to their competitors.

ASSIGNMENT

1. Explain why you believe AOL, MSN, and Yahoo! dominate the online advertising industry.
2. How might a competitor attempt to wrest market share from any of these giants?

BUILDING TEAM SKILLS

Building an online presence for an established bricks-and-mortar firm with a recognized brand name is facilitated by many things. First, there is an existing customer base that knows about the firm, so the company does not have to create an identity from scratch. Second, the firm has a warehouse and physical infrastructure along with a supply-chain system already in place and financially supported by current operations. Select a local firm that has little if any web presence at the moment.

ASSIGNMENT

1. Briefly describe the firm's business, markets, competitors, products, and distribution system.
2. Create a web presence that would be complementary to the firm's current operations without being too disruptive.

RESEARCHING DIFFERENT CAREERS

Designing web sites and online advertising requires a blend of creative skills and marketing knowledge about the product and the customer. You can learn a great deal by examining well-designed web content created by others. Select a web site or promotional email that you believe represents excellent design and creative work.

ASSIGNMENT

1. What message is being communicated, and to whom?
2. Is the communication effort successful, in your opinion? Explain your answer.

IMPROVING COMMUNICATION SKILLS

Digital photography, in which a camera creates digital images that can be stored and later printed, displayed on web sites, sent as attachments with email, and so forth, is a good example of a new technology that is also well suited for marketing on the Internet. Web sites such as Megapixel.net (**www.megapixel.net**) and Digital Photography Center (**www.dpreview.com**) provide a buyer's guide to understanding how to select the right camera without the pressure of a retail sales representative. In addition to price and

(continued)

the number of megapixels (thousands of dots per square inch) produced by the camera, these sites provide a variety of useful information to help potential buyers. For example, to produce a good-quality 4-inch by 6-inch color print, the camera should have at least 2.3 megapixels.

ASSIGNMENT
1. Describe the marketing communication strategies on one of these sites.
2. Are the strategies weak in any way?
3. How would you improve the site?

Exploring Useful Web Sites

These web sites provide information related to the topics discussed in the chapter. You can learn more by visiting them online and examining their current data.

1. Most people know that Amazon.com (**www.amazon.com**) is the biggest online retailer, but some might be surprised to learn that Office Depot (**www.officedepot.com**), which generates about $1 billion of sales—at a profit, is the second biggest. Managed in collaboration with Microsoft's' bCentral (**www.bcentral.com**), the site provides businesses with a rich selection of information through posted articles and links to other useful sites that provide such things as guides for writing business plans, research, and so forth.

2. Television show personalities like Oprah Winfrey have found new product development, distribution, and promotion opportunities online through sites like **www.oprah.com** and **www.oxygen.com**. Cable News Network (CNN) serves several identifiable market segments that are linked to its main web site at **www.cnn.com**. Customers of its Financial News Services can also access that site directly at **www.cnnfn.com**. Similarly, the Sporting News Network provides branches to a variety of niche markets of sports news and information through its web site at **www.tsn.com**.

3. Newspapers and magazines like the *Wall Street Journal* (**www.wsj.com**) and *Business Week* (**www.businessweek.com**) are good examples of a convenience product that is available online as well as at traditional retail stores.

4. According to consultant Patricia Seybold (**www.patriciaseybold.com**), the Internet has permanently transformed the relationship between buyers and sellers by providing opportunities for firms to distinguish themselves from their competitors by offering *mass-customization* services, as illustrated by the 30,000 commercial-free radio stations available at **www.live365.com** and manufacturers like Dell Computer (**www.dell.com**) and handbag maker Timbuk2 Designs (**www.timbuk2.com**).

5. Microsoft's Expedia (**www.expedia.com**) flight reservation system will help users locate airline, hotel, car rental, and other related services online.

6. BiblioMondo Inc. (**www.bibliomondo.com**) software allows any private or public library to manage and sell its digital content on the Internet. The world's 712,000 libraries will be joining a growing list of online vendors like netLibrary (**www.netlibrary.com**) and ebrary (**www.ebrary.com**) that are seeking methods for managing their business and earning revenues through online sales.

7. Bricks-and-mortar retailers and firms with highly recognizable brand names such The Walt Disney Company (**www.disney.com**) continue to expand their reach into global markets by setting up online retail shopping sites.

8. Banner advertising on CBS Sportsline (**www.sportsline.com**) and its sponsorship of the NCAA basketball March Madness tournament were combined with other online and televised promotions designed to bring audiences to Volvo's web site.

9. WebWasher (**www.webwasher.com**) and AdSubtract (**www.adsubtract.com**) are programs that are designed to recognize incoming advertisements by analyzing page formats and looking for standard banner advertising shapes.

10. Rather than trying to place their advertising on web sites themselves, advertisers can use the services of firms like Doubleclick (**www.doubleclick.com**) and 24/7 Media (**www.247media.com**) to select web sites and target specific viewers with sophisticated smart software.

11. Tom's of Maine (**www.toms-of-maine.com**) uses a concentrated niche market strategy to sell all-natural toothpastes and other health products on its web site.

12. Web sites such as Megapixel.net (**www.megapixel.net**) and Digital Photography Center (**www.dpreview.com**) provide a buyer's guide to understanding how to select the right camera without the pressure of a retail sales representative.

Organizational and Managerial Issues

Chapter 10

INSIDE
e-BUSINESS
Google.com—Small-Business and Entrepreneurial Success Story

Google.com (**www.google.com**) began operations in 1998, shortly after two Stanford University graduate students, Larry Page and Sergey Brin, conceived the search engine algorithm in a school project they had worked on together. Generally considered the third most popular search engine, Google.com serves more than ten million unique users each month. Users generate an average of 150 million search queries each day through the database of 2 billion URLs that Google has categorized and listed.

Today, entrepreneurs Page and Brin still lead an effective, creative, and forward-thinking company in an increasingly competitive environment that forces firms to carefully monitor their managerial resources in an ever-changing business climate. There are literally dozens of freely available popular web search engine sites vying for the attention and loyalty of Internet users. Almost all of them, like the industry leader Yahoo!, base their business model mostly on generating banner-advertising revenues. Many small start-up free-use dot-com sites base their businesses entirely on generating sufficient revenues from advertisers. According to Harvard Business School professor Michael Porter, this is a major error in judgment that cannot help a firm sustain a competitive advantage. Fortunately, Page and Brin have managed to avoid this pitfall.

The attraction of advertising revenue for a small start-up site is easy to understand. Given that web searches are the next most popular Internet user activity after email, any site that can attract and keep a loyal audience will be able to generate huge amounts of advertising revenue from vendors that wish to communicate with their users. Success is limited only by the momentous task of attracting users and keeping them at the site in what can only be described as a highly competitive environment with few barriers to entry. Consider the fact that Page and Brin were still students when they entered the fray.

Managing a search engine site is not an easy task. The firm must distinguish itself from its competitors and deal with a variety of psychological factors, such as users' dislike for online advertising and for the delays caused by downloading advertising images along with search data. Many users have even adopted screening software to block the downloading of advertisements, bringing into question the effectiveness of banner advertising. Managers of most sites have expanded their basic search services, attempting to create a personal and preferred Internet portal for users. Free emailboxes, file storage, personal web pages, stock market portfolio tracking, and so forth are now common valuable product strategy additions to sites. The strategic thinking behind these offerings is to make the site an attractive home base for users and thereby increase advertising revenues further.

The use of a business model based on banner advertising is a guiding strategy for many firms, so it may come as a surprise to some people that Google.com distinguishes itself by not selling banner advertising. Nonetheless, the firm has managed to generate sufficient revenues from other forms of advertising as well as other sources of revenue to break even during a time when many competitors have had difficulty just staying in business. Google's core source of revenue is two- and five-line text-based advertising links to sites directly related to the search keywords entered by users. For example, someone who is searching for information on cars will be presented with text-based advertising links to car sites. However, because these are text only, the time required to download them is a fraction of what would be required for graphic advertising. Furthermore, they are less obtrusive for users and are less likely to distract them from their search activities. However, because the advertisements are highly targeted and relevant, the clickthrough rate on Google's text-based advertisements is four times the industry rate, allowing the firm to charge higher rates. Google also earns revenues by providing search services to other web sites—including Yahoo!.

Google distinguishes itself further in the market by providing searchers with superior technology that maintains databases on more than 1.3 billion ranked web pages. Unlike some search engines, which sell listing positions, Google software analyzes the popularity of pages in terms of how many other pages are linked to them and then delivers the ranked list of web pages. Thus, users know that a web site appears at or near the top of the Google results page because it is a popular choice based on the number of links, not because the advertising client paid to have it placed there.[1]

Google.com's strategic efforts to distinguish itself from its competitors and thereby create a sustainable competitive advantage are reflected in the culture of the organization, which sees itself as being in close partnership with its users. Google.com is essentially designed the way users wish an ideal free-use search engine to be designed, but it manages to also satisfy the needs of advertisers. Without this compromise between users and advertisers, the site could not generate sufficient revenues to survive. Another entrepreneurial success story uses a somewhat different revenue approach to create a sustainable competitive advantage. Monster.com (**www.monster.com**) manages more than half of the entire online-recruitment market and earns quarterly profits of more than $100 million by charging employers to search through the 8.9 million job résumés it stores in databases.[2] Both of these companies exemplify successful e-business strategic thinking and practice and have shaped their organizational and managerial plans to reflect their respective operating environments.

In this chapter, the second dealing with micro-level decision-making issues within the firm, we will explore how companies should approach the development of organizational and managerial strategies within an e-business environment. Although we acknowledge that the entire body of management knowledge applies to all organizations, including those focusing on e-business strategic planning, we also recognize that within an e-business environment there are several important and sometimes unique considerations. We will explore these as we establish a guiding structure for preparing the management component of an e-business plan, beginning with an overview of the principal subject areas of management and their connections to e-business.

An Overview of Management and e-Business

management process
The ongoing planning, organizing, and controlling of all sorts of activities that personnel throughout the organization are engaged in, including marketing, finance, production and operations, human resources, and so forth.

The **management process** is the ongoing planning, organizing, and controlling of all sorts of activities that personnel throughout the organization are engaged in, including marketing, finance, production and operations, human resources, and so forth. The word *process* suggests that these activities are continuous and never-ending. In a simple sense, then, these activities are the work that people do to keep the enterprise moving toward its identified goals with purpose and direction. The management process focuses on the detailed planning issues that need to be addressed within the firm. You will use much of the terminology we will explore in this chapter to explain how you intend to execute your strategic e-business plan, which organizational structures you will use, how employees will be led and motivated, and so forth.

Planning, Organizing, and Controlling Activities

planning
The setting of goals (longer-term) and objectives (shorter-term) to strive for at each of the three primary organizational levels of the firm (corporate, divisional/ strategic, and operating/ functional) and the development of activities to achieve them.

organizing
The grouping of activities and the marshaling of the necessary resources (*material, human, financial,* and *informational*) in order to achieve specific goals and objectives.

controlling
The monitoring, evaluating, and adjusting of activities to assure the successful achievement of the targeted goals.

The management process begins with **planning**—the setting of goals (longer-term) and objectives (shorter-term) to strive for at each of the three primary organizational levels of the firm (corporate, divisional/strategic, and operating/ functional) and with the development of activities to achieve them. You will recall from Chapter 6 that corporate-level planning establishes the framework and, more importantly, the specific goals for the divisional/strategic level of the firm, and this level, in turn, establishes specific goals for the operating/functional level.

Organizing is the grouping of activities and the marshaling of the necessary resources (*material, human, financial* and *informational*)–in order to achieve specific goals and objectives. After the planning process has established *what* the firm intends to do, organizing answers the questions of *how* it will be done, by *whom*, and with *which resources*. Organizing requires the development of a structure or framework such, as the creation of a new division, and the selection of managers with the appropriate leadership and motivation skills to accomplish the necessary tasks.

Controlling involves the monitoring, evaluating, and adjusting of activities to assure the successful achievement of the targeted goals. For example, suppose planned sales revenues for a new division of the firm were estimated at $10 million for the following year, with incremental growth of 30 percent in each of the following two years. If in fact sales for the first year were disappointing and came in 20 percent lower than was anticipated, managers would have to modify their strategies to take into consideration this failure to achieve a planned objective. Perhaps a change in advertising strategy is called for or perhaps more specialized human resources should be hired. Identifying all the possible decisions that might be taken is beyond the scope of this short discussion. The important point to understand is that if feedback suggests that longer-term goals are not likely to be achieved unless a change in strategy occurs and the direction of current activity is changed, then managers at each level of the organization must adjust their current e-business plans appropriately. We will explore these issues in greater detail in Chapter 12.

Organizational Structures and Issues

Organizational structures define the way in which individuals work together—how they solve problems, make decisions, communicate, and share responsibility, authority, and power with one another. We will describe several types of organizational structure here. It is likely that a firm will employ more than one of these structures over time and that different parts of the firm will use different structures at the same time. So, for instance, a large management-consulting firm like Siebel Systems Inc. might use a bureaucratic organizational structure at its corporate level and organic, matrix, and cross-functional team structures at the divisional and operational levels. According to Eric Schmitt, an analyst at Forrester Research Inc., organizations are in the midst of reorganizing themselves and changing the way they do business as they adapt their corporate structure to an online presence based on interaction with customers and suppliers over the Internet. For example, Cisco Systems Inc. uses Ariba Inc.'s software to run its online purchasing system, which connects its 20,000 employees with more than 3,000 suppliers. The result has been an estimated 10 to 20 percent savings.[3]

Bureaucratic structures tend to have more rigidly defined structural arrangements, a high degree of job specialization, and formal patterns of communication and relationships among employees. The finance department of a firm might be expected to use a bureaucratic structure where management decisions about which customers will receive credit and how much credit they will receive would follow standardized rules. Overriding the set rules would be likely to require special procedures and multiple approvals from supervisors. For example, an online brokerage firm like E*Trade would normally follow rigid rules for establishing the margin-trading limits for its online clients. This would be especially important for more speculative trading in options, where small changes in price can result in enormous swings in investors' portfolio values.

An *organic structure*, in contrast, would have much more loosely defined structural arrangements among employees, who would tend to collaborate on work and use informal rules to guide their behavior. Authority would tend to be based on an individual's expertise rather than on his or her title in the organization. Organic structures tend to be used in project work, where creative collaboration is needed among employees who bring various types of knowledge and skills to the team. For example, a group that is designing and programming new computer solutions or a web page for a client is likely to employ an organic structure.

A *matrix structure* is a step up in complexity and combines more than one level of authority within a work project. Matrix structures are common in e-business. When a client commissions a job, a project manager might be assigned responsibility for assuring the successful completion of the entire job, but several specialized teams of employees from different departments would probably be brought together in a matrix structure as they are needed. While working on any given project, employees would report to both their respective team supervisors and the project manager. For example, after a request from the account manager responsible for maintaining CRM software for an existing client, Siebel Systems might initially send in a team of employees to conduct a needs analysis. Next, the details of the project work would be written up in a contract, which would be duly signed, and then several other teams of employees would be scheduled to contribute to the project according to an agreed-upon timetable. First a new hardware installation might be required. Then the software would have to be configured and adapted to ensure there is no interference with existing software or hardware with which the new installation has to interact—a common problem for new installations. And finally, the client's employees would have to be trained in how to use the new installation by yet another team of consultants. As each group completes its tasks, the group members would be assigned to other projects. Typically, the project manager (leader) would see the project through to its conclusion and act as the liaison between the firm and its client. While the work is being done, employees report to their supervisor as well as to the project manager. Often, the supervisor would be the channel used to deal with any problems that might arise with the project or the project manager.

An *organizational chart* is a schematic diagram illustrating the relationships between key positions in the organization and the chain of command or line of authority between individual positions; it gives some insight into the firm's organizational structure. For instance, the chart might show that the organization is using a wide *span of control* (management), with each manager overseeing the work of a large number of employees. This is often the case in organizations that have clearly defined procedures and objectives and employees who are competent and self-directing. For instance, a call center might have a single supervising manager for dozens of customer service representatives who have been well trained and know how to handle what are generally routine calls. On the other hand, a narrower span of control is likely to be used when the work demands continuous interaction between managers and their subordinates. Furthermore, the organizational chart would illustrate whether the firm's structure is *flat*, with project managers likely to be working alongside their staff; or *tall*, indicating that there are layers of bureaucratic managers that receive progress reports from their subordinates and generally do not participate directly in the work that is being done.

Production and Operations Management

operations management
The process of coordinating all the activities related to the production of the products and services that the organization provides to its customers.

Operations management involves the coordination of all the activities related to the production of the products and services that the organization provides to its customers. Clearly in some cases, such as in a CRM consulting firm like Siebel Systems, virtually everything that the firm does can be considered part of operations management; however, in general, we consider the fundamental areas on which operations management focuses to be the manufacturing processes, including facilities, capacity, purchasing, inventory, quality control, use of technology, and employees' skills.

The objective of operations management is to deliver planned production of products and services within set cost limits. Operations management is continually seeking ways to reduce costs and improve the quality of the products and services produced. This is accomplished primarily through the study of how work is organized and done so that efficiencies and other improvements can be introduced. For example, the introduction of an automated web-based information distribution system at a bank might reduce the number of customers who need to speak to a customer service representative. By simply making menu selections on their screen, customers can retrieve commonly requested information such as current account balances independently. As a result, more of the existing customer service representatives are available to deal with those people who call a firm's center needing unique information or answers to complex questions. Because automated telephone-based and web-based information retrieval systems are so cost-effective, their use is almost always incorporated into the logistics of the e-business plan.

Productivity and Efficiency

productivity

The amount of output that an individual worker can produce within a set period of time.

Productivity refers to the amount of output that an individual worker can produce within a set period of time. Productivity is influenced by a variety of things, including the efficiency and skills of the employees, the tools they have to work with and the training they have received, and the organization structure and management methods, including leadership and motivation, that are in place. For example, the number of orders received on the firm's web site that a customer service representative can process involves all of these things. According to Cisco Systems' management, 68 percent of its orders are placed and fulfilled over the Internet and 70 percent of service calls are resolved online. As a result, the firm has reduced its manufacturing costs by 7 percent, or more than $1.4 billion annually.[4] Furthermore, a recent survey indicated that there are about 400 electronic trading communities, including auctions, exchanges, e-procurement hubs, and multisupplier online catalogs, made up of businesses selling to other businesses. According to the investment bank Goldman Sachs, all major industries are expected to begin transforming their processes over the next 5 to 10 years, resulting in increased productivity through reducing inventory, shortening cycle time, and using human effort more efficiently.[5] As a result, IDC Inc. predicts that B2B online selling will grow about 50 percent each year, reaching a level of more than $2 trillion by 2006.

Productivity improvements are expected to increase dramatically as more economic activity is transferred onto the Internet, reducing the costs of servicing customers and handling routine ordering. According to a Jupiter Communications study, the frequency with which human intervention is needed to help online customers rises substantially as the product price increases, from 8 percent at low price levels to nearly 30 percent as the product price crosses the $100 point. If e-commerce efforts are to succeed, decentralization of authority to the level of the online service representative must be put in place.[6]

The savings of time and money that result from productivity improvements allow businesses to increase their profits and turn their efforts to other business opportunities. According to Alan Greenspan, chairman of the Federal Reserve, American labor laws and culture allow for the quicker replacement of unneeded workers with others whose skills are more in demand than do labor laws in other countries, where it tends to take longer for the change to occur. As a result, the Internet and high technology in general are contributing to a greater increase in worker productivity in the United States than in Asia and Europe.[7] However, just as technology can help improve productivity, it can also retard productivity if the volume of communications becomes unmanageable for employees. According to a Gartner Group survey of U.S. businesses, employees reported that 34 percent of the email they received was unnecessary and that they spent 49 minutes each day managing their email; 24 percent of them spent more than an hour.[8]

If a firm wishes to increase the productivity of its workers, it can do this in one or more ways, such as increasing workers' motivation through financial incentives or introducing improved training methods that help them deal with difficult calls. Questions about operations management and productivity are central to the firm's planning decisions. First of all, the firm has to decide how to put the e-business plan into operation. Basic questions about how the work will be organized and managed and how employees will be distributed within the firm need to be resolved. In many situations, the decision may be to outsource certain operations to other organizations that can deal with them more efficiently because they are handling only a limited and very specialized area of work. For example, rather than maintaining a computer system to service the firm's web site, many firms will opt to purchase hosting services from an organization whose only concern is maintaining computer facilities for its clients. In many cases, this choice is motivated not only by cost savings and efficiency but also the need to keep trained staff on hand to maintain specialized operations, security concerns, and the faster access speeds generally provided by hosts, who are often close to a major artery of the Internet. According to the Information Technology Association, an industry shortage of skilled knowledge workers at the peak of e-business activity in 2000 was a driving force behind the outsourcing of computer system needs. By using Internet-based hosts that provide all software and technical services for a monthly fee, firms avoided the need to fill many highly specialized jobs. The association estimated that there were about 850,000 unfilled technology jobs, and that the shortage of workers was exacerbated by the strong growth in e-business activities.[9] Interestingly, although the shortage of skilled workers has eased considerably during the industry downturn that began in 2000–2001, many firms continue to outsource rather than hire their own staff to meet their needs. Similarly, to improve their purchasing system, aerospace giants Boeing, BAE Systems, Lockheed Martin, and Raytheon jointly developed an online exchange that links more than 37,000 suppliers, hundreds of airlines, and national governments into a single web-based marketplace for parts estimated to be worth more than $400 billion in annual sales. It also reduces administrative costs and speeds procurement for private and government aerospace and defense concerns worldwide.[10]

Leadership, Motivation, and the Corporate Culture

Businesses that are operating in the fast-changing environment of the Internet need a corporate leadership approach that can motivate employees and support trust and risk taking. Creating a culture of trust within an organization can lead to increases in growth, profit, productivity, and job satisfaction. A culture of trust can help a firm retain the best people, inspire customer loyalty, develop new markets, and increase its creativity. Critics suggest that IBM inadvertently developed a culture that punished those who took reasonable risks and then failed in their endeavors. As a result, up until the early 1990s, the organization became overly bureaucratic and people gradually stopped taking competitive risks in order to avoid failure. Today IBM's leadership approach is vastly different, reflecting the new age of creative thinking about ways of managing organizations.[11]

Corporate Leadership and Influence

Arguably more than any other factor, the leadership exhibited by a firm's management can have a dramatic influence on whether the firm achieves its goals. Success for both the firm and individuals is generally acknowledged to be highly determined by strong leadership qualities that filter down throughout the entire organization so that everyone is unified in their sense of purpose and direction. Microsoft, GE, IBM, Dell Computer, Sun Microsystems, and Oracle are only a few of the celebrated firms led by dynamic and charismatic leaders who built their empires by uniting everyone from highly ranked executives to lower-level employees, as well as bankers, investors, suppliers, and other players. In each of these great e-business success stories, an outstanding leadership figure and an overall leadership style that emanated from the top can be pointed to as an important factor contributing to the firm's success. For instance, Larry Ellison, chairman and CEO of Oracle Corporation of Redwood Shores, California, built the firm's annual revenues up from a mere $282 million in 1988 to an estimated $9.7 billion today—an incredible increase of more than 3,350 percent. Much of that growth has taken place since 1994 as Oracle capitalized on its global leadership in Internet software in addition to its base in information management software. As a measure of its growth, Oracle now has more than 23,000 employees in 144 countries in addition to the 21,000 working in the Unites States.[12]

In general, e-business activities require a large number of self-motivated individuals, and such people will not flourish in a working atmosphere led by someone with an authoritarian leadership style. Besides realizing that highly skilled personnel can readily leave and find work at other firms where they will be treated better, employers recognize the need for a free-thinking, creative work environment where new ideas can more readily emerge. Since much of the work that is done is measurable, such as the number of lines of computer programming code written, web pages created, or new sales contracts written within some set time period, both management and employees are cognizant of employees' ability to reach targets. Furthermore, employees can help with adjustments to current strategies, since they are the ones who are closest to the action and can shed the greatest amount of light on the possible reasons for the failures and what to do about them.

Motivation, Recognition, and Compensation Issues

motivation

In a business environment, the drive that individuals feel to perform their assigned tasks.

Motivation in a business environment refers to the drive that individuals feel to perform their assigned tasks. Research suggests that employees are likely to be more motivated in the work they do when the firm has clearly defined goals and realistic objectives for them to strive for. These expectations can be communicated through meetings with supervisors and by giving employees edited portions of the business plan or the full plan. People who are directly involved in decision making and the preparation of those business plans will feel a greater sense of ownership and a greater drive to realize them.

Needless to say, compensation and recognition of achievement are important motivational factors. Employees expect fair monetary compensation and might be more motivated by bonus payments for successfully reaching targeted individual and group objectives that are part of the e-business plan. Higher-level managers traditionally seek performance bonuses for leading a division or project successfully. Stock options (which we will discuss in greater detail in Chapter 11) and revenue- or profit-sharing plans are also common motivational tools. As a means of motivating top executives and, increasingly, middle-ranking managers working long hours for what are generally considered poor salaries, many Internet-related firms provide *stock options* as part of the employee compensation package. A stock option is simply the right to buy shares of the firm within a prescribed time at a set price. If the firm does well, and its stock price rises past the set price (presumably at least in part because of all the work being done by the employee), the employee can exercise the option and immediately sell the stock to cash in on the company's success. For example, Joseph Galli was lured away from Black & Decker to take the president's post at Amazon.com. Along with an annual salary of $200,000, Galli was given 3.9 million options on Amazon.com stock. When Amazon's stock soared, those options rose to a theoretical value of more than $200 million, but they fell to no value as the stock market turned on Amazon. Time will tell whether Galli's options turn out to be worthless or make him a fabulously rich man.[13]

After the industry shakeout in 2000, the perceived value of an equity stake in an e-business has fallen dramatically as employees have come to view stock options as promises of corporate riches that may never be achievable. Therefore, demands for higher salaries today are likely to increase as stock option plans fall from favor. Looking at the successes of celebrated industry leaders, we can easily understand the strength of the financial incentives. Even after the huge fall in technology share values in 2000–2001, Bill Gates, the chairman of Microsoft

Corporation, was still the richest man in the world for the seventh year in a row, with an estimated $60 billion of assets. Paul Allen, Microsoft's cofounder with Bill Gates, was third at $30 billion; Larry Ellison of Oracle Corporation fourth at $26 billion; and Michael Dell of Dell Computer twenty-seventh.[14]

Recognition through public acknowledgement, especially among peers, can produce great motivation, and, more importantly, the absence of proper acknowledgement or acknowledging the wrong people can be counterproductive. Organizations can promote their successes and the people that made them happen through giving them awards and publicizing their achievements. Sometimes a very small expenditure, such as for a photo and an article in the firm's newsletter, can boost the ego-sensitive motivation that is lying dormant in most of us. Maslow's hierarchy of needs theory suggests that most employees are motivated by social and ego needs. A firm with a work environment that is unfriendly or that does not support these needs will have difficulty finding and retaining highly motivated individuals. Senior management may be driven by their personal desire to contribute to building an enterprise from scratch. Given the widespread publicity and accolades for individuals and firms like Microsoft and Yahoo!, many individuals came to see e-business as a new frontier, without the barriers or limits that were traditionally found in older, more established industries. Many saw this work environment as a once-in-a-lifetime chance to create a business monument that they could be forever associated with and simultaneously to be rewarded richly with huge salaries, stock options, bonuses, and so forth.

All of us want to feel that we matter and that our work is recognized and properly rewarded. Of the major motivational theories employed in an attempt to understand the e-business working environment, equity and expectancy theories should be considered quite useful. *Equity theory* suggests that people are motivated by their personal *sense of equity* in a situation. In brief, this means that if an individual perceives that he or she is well treated and rewarded, then that individual will complement this belief with an appropriate level of motivation and effort to perform his or her work. By contrast, if someone perceives that he or she is being less well treated and rewarded, the theory suggests that that person will adjust his or her motivation and perform accordingly. Somewhat similarly, *expectancy theory* (also discussed in Chapter 8 to explain buyer behavior) suggests that motivation is associated with how much an individual wants to achieve the objective presented and the degree to which she or he believes it can be achieved. The message of expectancy theory is that management must be sure to make the accomplishment of the assigned tasks both important to the individual employees and achievable in their minds. Weaknesses in either one of these factors will undermine the individual's level of motivation to complete the set tasks successfully.

In deciding how best to motivate employees, the developers of the firm's e-business plan must be confident that they are not compensating employees beyond what their contribution truly is worth and what the firm can realistically afford to pay. Criticism of excessive compensation packages for high-tech executives was not common when stock market prices were soaring but poured out into the press as disgruntled stockholders saw their investments collapse in value. For example, when retiring Nortel Networks Inc. CEO John Roth stepped down in the spring of 2001, he did so after having exercised stock options that earned him $135 million. This was during a year in which the firm's stock value had fallen more than 80 percent from the previous year's high.[15]

Corporate Culture and the Informal Organization

The term *corporate culture* refers to the general values and behaviors that are considered normal within the firm. As we discussed in Chapter 4, corporate culture sets the tone for ethical behavior. In addition, corporate culture sets the tone for leadership, decision making, risk taking, and the communication behaviors that are generally used within a particular group of employees and across the entire firm.

Part of the corporate culture is the *informal* organization that exists within the *formal* organizational structure and often explains how the organization really functions. For instance, although decisions may be made formally at committee meetings called expressly for that purpose, people may meet informally in smaller groups and exchange email messages to discuss their decisions before the meetings take place. Informal communication can take place outside the organization as well. For example, in response to their personal experiences of burnout, Steve Baldwin and Bill Lessard launched a New York–based web site aptly called Netslaves (**www.disobey.com/netslaves**). The two are driven to demythologize the media image of work in the Internet industry and to provide a forum where other managers can exchange stories about the difficulties of working in a dot-com world.[16]

The use of communication technologies is generally associated with positive outcomes, but research suggests that there may be a growing negative impact on corporate culture as well. According to research, the use of technological tools such as email can contribute to dysfunctional work-related problems, including stress, loneliness, anger, and even depression. Because email is convenient and ubiquitous, it may reduce the amount of face-to-face human interaction to below the level that people have come to accept as normal. Communicating through email can frustrate both the receiver and the sender because it does not allow individuals to communicate in subtle humanistic ways, such as eye contact, gestures, body language, and voice tones. And email creates the expectation of instant answers to questions leading to the feeling that work never seems to have an end.[17]

Ironically, the same technology that may contribute to dysfunctional behaviors and work-related problems may also provide solutions. One of North America's largest employee assistance program providers, the Warren Shepell Company (**www.warrenshepell.com**) of Toronto, Ontario, has over 1,000 e-counselors who use email to help more than 3 million employees at 1,300 corporate clients. The use of e-therapy as a method for dealing with employees' personal problems is in addition to conventional face-to-face and telephone-based sessions. However, research has shown that, in addition to saving client firms money and providing faster service to employees, asynchronous email benefits clients by giving them the time to contemplate their exchanges with counselors as much as they need to before they formulate a response.[18]

The Internet presents new challenges for firms whose employees enjoy easy access to sites through convenient high-speed connections at work. An employee's behavior online can be viewed as offensive to coworkers and can possibly be illegal. As a result, research by Websense and the Center for Internet Studies revealed that nearly two out of three companies nationwide have disciplined employees and nearly one out of three have fired employees for Internet misuse in the workplace.[19] Interestingly, today's high-technology and Internet-based firms rank relatively high when it comes to environmental issues, working conditions, the representation of minorities and women in upper management, animal testing, and charitable donations. According to the New York watchdog group called the Council on Economic Priorities, which examines more than 700 of the country's largest companies annually, the cultures of new-economy firms tend to be rated better than average, but they are not immune from criticism either.[20]

Topics in Management

In this final section of the chapter, we will explore three important topics in management: human resources management, small-business management and entrepreneurial issues, and management consulting services. Although there is a large body of knowledge on each topic, we will introduce these topics only briefly and then highlight several important connections to e-business planning.

Human Resources Management

human resources management
All of the activities related to acquiring, maintaining, and developing the people who do the work in the firm.

Human resources management is concerned with all of the activities related to acquiring, maintaining, and developing the people who do the work in the firm—the firm's *human capital*. Acquiring the employees needed to do the tasks involved in running the firm requires planning for future human resources needs, creating descriptions and analyses of the jobs that will need to be done, finding and hiring employees for those jobs, and integrating the employees into the firm.

Evaluating Skills and Knowledge
In order to evaluate the true value of an applicant's or employee's skills and knowledge, continuous assessment and certification are likely to grow in importance, since the assessment of the firm's human resources is so strongly related to the speed with which knowledge ages. For example, ten years of experience in programming old and outdated software is of little value to a firm if it requires programmers who are knowledgeable about Internet and e-commerce software programs that are in use today.[21]

Finding Specialized Employees
Finding qualified specialized employees can require a number of strategies, many of which are rather traditional. According to Michael Boyd, senior HR analyst at IDC, Internet-based sites such as Monster (**www.monster.com**), CareerPath (**www.careerpath.com**), and CareerMosaic (**www.careermosaic.com**), which hold millions

of résumés for employers to choose from, are not the primary connections for successful high-tech job hunters. In fact, only 8.1 percent of those hired were recruited through web-based employment services. Boyd's studies suggest that the complex social networks of human interaction such as word-of-mouth and employee referrals still account for more than a third of high-tech recruiting. Even job fairs, print and TV ads, and old-fashioned headhunters are better than online agencies.[22]

Employee Dissatisfaction on the Job

The high level of dissatisfaction at high-tech firms, especially among employees at dot-com start-ups, is a growing reality as many people who are working long hours, often without much social contact outside of the workplace, have decided that career advancement does not make up for the absence of a personal life.[23] Once employees have become part of the human resource infrastructure of the firm, they represent a valuable investment in terms of the time and money spent to get them there. Replacing them is an additional cost that does not contribute to profitability. Internet software solutions firms like SAS Institute Inc. of Cary, North Carolina, work hard to find and keep good high-technology workers. Interestingly, by promoting a normal workweek that takes into consideration the importance that employees place on spending time with their families, relaxing, and participating in other things in life besides work has helped to create a more content and motivated workforce. As a result, employee turnover is an astonishingly low 4 percent, compared to a 20 percent industry rate.[24] For some jobs, though, such as customer service representatives employed in a call center, the turnover of employees is high; employees may not last more than a few months, and those that suffer from burnout and cannot be promoted to other tasks are lost. Firms can attempt to maintain employees through good treatment, good working conditions, fair compensation, and other benefits.

Developing Skills and Knowledge

Developing the skills and knowledge of existing employees is recognized as both a factor in determining whether an employee stays or quits and an important means of producing employees with the skills needed at higher organizational levels within the firm. A by-product of the boom in Internet and information technology employment is the high demand for highly skilled workers in a fast-changing work environment. Interestingly, many high-technology workers fear losing their jobs and, with them, access to the ability to learn about new knowledge and skills. The result is somewhat of a counterbalance to the salary and wage demands in this sector of the economy.[25] In addition to these dynamics influencing highly skilled employees and employers, there is the industry slowdown that began in 2000–2001.

Since many jobs require cumulative skills and knowledge, it would be logical for a firm to build on the employee base it already has rather than hiring from outside as new jobs requiring more advanced skills are generated. Not only is this motivational for the employees, but the firm will also benefit by being in a position to mold the knowledge and skills accumulated by each employee over time.

Thus the firm's human resources planning can be directed toward internal training and development.

A recent report prepared by the American Society for Training and Development (ASTD), an industry association that monitors and also promotes employee-learning strategies, revealed the value of employee education programs. The report found that for an added $600 investment made by the firm in the education of each employee, the firms surveyed experienced a 57 percent increase in sales per employee and a 37 percent increase in gross profit. In dollar terms, this means that for every $100,000 in sales per employee and gross profit per employee, the added investment returned $157,000 in net sales and $137,000 in gross profit. Driven by savings in cost, travel, and time, online learning, either alone or in conjunction with face-to-face situations, is a strong alternative strategy.[26] Recent estimates suggest that the corporate market for e-learning in the United States could surpass $11 billion in 2003.[27]

Online Learning Systems

Training and development costs are increased by the fact employees are not working at their regular responsibilities while they are away at training seminars or conferences or taking Internet-distributed courseware. Internet-distributed courseware is growing in popularity for many reasons, particularly its flexibility and its adaptability to the learning style and needs of the learner. Courseware is generally divided into small modules, each of which may take only 10 or 15 minutes to complete. Employees can therefore explore several modules in sequence if they have time. And while they are traveling on business, employees can pass long evenings in their hotel rooms more productively by completing many modules at one sitting. Often, courseware modules are retrievable from directories for *just-in-time learning*, so that the user can call up a module or two to help with a particular learning situation. This is common in IT training, where the knowledge requirements for software tasks generally emerge over time as user expertise increases. Therefore, it makes more sense to train employees to *find* the information they require than to expect them to learn everything and retain that knowledge indefinitely.

Online learning systems are a cost-effective way to initiate new employees into company procedures, regulations, and policies. Popular and repeated questions can be designed as a self-service listing of frequently asked questions (FAQ) or what to do if . . . or who to speak to for something. Furthermore, online learning systems work well to familiarize employees with the firm's executives and with one another through personal web pages that typically contain biographical information and photographs of the people within the organization.

Once a company decides to adopt online learning as part of its overall training and development effort, selecting the best learning management system for the particular firm is still a complicated task. The term *learning management system* refers to the software that contains the learning content; it may allow sophisticated authoring of online course content, testing, tracking of employee development, and analysis of employee skills along with advice on individual training needs and courses. There are more than 100 competing learning management systems with various strengths and weaknesses. They are not all compatible with one another, and content developed on one may not be readily transferable to another. Vendors may also host learning systems and charge clients according to the number of employees, number of courses, or hours spent accessing the system. According to consultant and e-learning expert Brandon Hall, firms are well advised to look for a good fit between the system and the firm's business processes. Furthermore, the firm should be sure to properly organize learning groups and facilitate continuous communication among all participants.[28]

In addition to setting up internal organizational learning systems for employees, many firms have established formal online learning courses that meet at scheduled times and are organized into work and study groups. Some organizations have developed working relationships with academic institutions in which these institutions provide online learning courses that allow the organizations' employees to earn academic credits. Hybrid courses can involve some classroom lecture time in combination with an online learning component. Many universities are competing in this growing market segment, even offering fully accredited undergraduate and graduate degrees. In all of these cases, the learning system must prove itself worthwhile through measurable results such as test scores upon completion of a module or entire course, appraisal feedback by the learners, and assessments of the learners by their supervisors when they return to work and apply their newly acquired skills and knowledge.

 e-Business Insight

Continuing Growth of Internet-Delivered Corporate Learning

According to research by International Data Inc., the corporate market for e-learning in the United States is expected to grow more than 500 percent—from $2.2 billion in 2000 to more than $11 billion in 2003. The reasons are well established by now: convenience, lower costs of delivery, reduced need for travel, immediate delivery of learning to large numbers of employees at the same time, flexibility in design to accommodate different learning styles, and so forth. For example, since Circuit City moved its sales training course online, 90 percent of its 55,000 plus staff have taken more than 400,000 courses, each lasting about 30 minutes to an hour. Not only are these courses popular with employees, but the firm is able to measure learning through online tests and then compare the scores with changes in sales performance and employee turnover. American Airlines flight attendants are now able to take part of their annual certification training online as an alternative to classroom-based instruction. The courses review emergency, security, and other procedures and are approved by the Federal Aviation Administration. Finally, after taking part in a pilot program, 94 percent of MasterCard International employees responded positively to online training, indicating that they would prefer that all or part of their training be provided online. Given that it costs MasterCard $10 to have each learner take a sexual harassment course online in comparison to the $150 cost of classroom-based delivery, it is highly likely that all employees will be seeing more continuing education and training services delivered online.[29]

Small-Business Management and Entrepreneurial Issues

According to a 2002 report prepared by American Express, 66 percent of the small businesses surveyed had already integrated the Internet as a tool to help them run their businesses by making travel plans and purchasing office supplies, equipment, or other business services (tied at 36 percent), conducting industry or market research (34 percent), marketing or advertising (29 percent), networking with other entrepreneurs (24 percent), purchasing goods from wholesalers (22 percent), and managing accounts and making payments (16 percent). Furthermore, 51 percent viewed the Internet as more cost-effective than other marketing methods, and 29 percent stated that the Internet is the most cost-effective method. Considerably fewer respondents considered direct mail, newspapers and magazines, or Yellow Pages advertising to be the most cost-effective marketing strategy. Finally, growth in small-business Internet-based solutions is likely, given that 77 percent of these businesses agree that a web site is a "must have" for small business; 60 percent said that they wish they had built a web site for their business sooner; and 85 percent would also advise other small-business owners to have a web site.[30]

The Internet has been a boon to small-business and entrepreneurial efforts for thousands of people around the world. The reasons are simple: The traditional barriers to entry that exist for most businesses are far lower for small e-business start-ups. e-Business start-ups do not require large amounts of capital, many employees, and established distribution relationships with suppliers and customers. They can be, have been, and continue to be launched on a shoestring budget, sometimes by one person using a home office; the only critical tool is a computer with access to the Internet.

Recognizing the opportunity to capitalize on the needs of small businesses with limited cash, firms like BigStep (**www.bigstep.com**) provide small businesses with the opportunity to create their own web site for free, a service that generally would cost about $250 a month from other web site service firms. Backed by partnerships with Sun Microsystems, Washingtonpost.com, and Newsweek Interactive, BigStep makes its money from sponsorships and fees for optional services.[31]

What Can Small Businesses Do?

Small e-businesses often thrive because they provide services to larger firms on a contractual basis. Once the work is completed, they are free to pursue other contracts with other firms. The larger firms save money by doing this because they need not hire permanent personnel for what might be a short-term project and are not obliged to pay a variety of employee taxes and benefit costs, such as insurance and pension programs.

Common services provided by small e-businesses include the design and setup of web pages, writing simple applications in a computer software program code like Lotus Notes, training employees (particularly on the use of software), research into new products and markets, and the preparation of business plans for internal use as well as for external parties such as lenders and investors. Often, an innovation made by a small business contributes to an established industry by adding some valuable service, as demonstrated by San Mateo, California–based MakeOverStudio (**www.makeoverstudio.com**), founded by Lori Von Rueden. The firm's free Internet service allows users to upload a digital photo of themselves and then experiment with the latest product styles and colors available from cosmetics vendors who license the product. Customers can change their hair and lipstick color a thousand different ways with just a click of their mouse. When customers at the vendors' sites purchase the products that have delivered their online look, the firm earns a percentage of the online sales generated.[32]

Formula for Success

According to entrepreneur Bill Tatham, the founder of Janna Systems of Toronto, Ontario, the most important advice for start-up firms to follow is to focus on those strategies that will generate revenue the fastest and to target a market with at least $1 billion in annual sales. After Janna Systems' sales doubled each year for six years in a row, its biggest rival, Siebel Systems, acquired it for $1.76 billion in 2000. Janna Systems' CRM software was particularly popular with Wall Street firms and fit well within the Siebel organizational structure. Tatham acknowledges that the firm made mistakes in the beginning by chasing after the wrong customers. It was only after it changed the focus of its plan to seeking profitability that business began to really change for the better. Tatham suggests that after the competitive shakeout of 2000–2001, e-business strategy will have to be different; in order to raise capital, a firm will need to rely much more heavily on a proven management team, a distinct product, and profitability.[33]

Web Threatens Small Business

Although the Internet has given rise to many new opportunities for small businesses, it has created many challenges as well. For example, according to the American Society of Travel Agents, the industry shift to Internet-based operations has been nothing short of catastrophic for small-business travel operators. The number of agents fell from 33,000 in 1994 to 24,000 in 2002—a drop of more than 27 percent.[34] Motivated by customers and industry vendors who are seeking ways to cut their costs, online operations are being transformed by firms like **www.travelocity.com** and **www.expedia.com**.[35]

Management Consulting Services

According to research, the U.S. market for IT consulting services is estimated to be over $3 billion.[36] The Internet has been a boon to the management consulting industry, as the same services that are widely provided for small businesses are also provided on a greater scale to large organizations. Creating a web site and setting up an online retail service for a client that only needs a few hundred hours of services from a knowledgeable consultant might be a simple enough task for a small business. However, considering what would have to be done when a large retailer like Sears or the Home Depot decides to establish an online presence, how work processes would have to be changed to accommodate the

e-Business Insight
A Board of Directors Can Help Establish Start-ups

According to Richard Bertrand, president of the technology consulting firm Ithink Inc. and a member of the board of directors of several small start-up firms that he has helped direct toward successful acquisition by larger e-businesses, venture capital firms are rightly interested in a firm's management and how the organization will be governed. After the firm's strategic thinking and technology, as described in its e-business plan, passes inspection, venture capitalists next need assurance that the plans they have agreed can suc-ceed will in fact be properly managed. This is where the firm's board of directors can help build credibility and confidence. Rather than looking at the board of directors as a necessary evil to ac-commodate investors, Bertrand advises, start-up firms should utilize the experience, wisdom, in-sight, and, most importantly, the network of peo-ple and other e-businesses that board members can bring to the young firm's management. Citing the example of his success as chairman of the board of start-up Northwood Technologies, which he helped sell to Marconi Corp. for $42 million, Bertrand believes that the formula for small busi-ness start-up success is clear.[37]

new structure, and so forth, it is safe to say that a variety of services were needed to help management work through the process and launch the site. In few if any cases can large-scale organizations roll out an e-business effort without the coor-dinating and research help provided by consulting firms with the talented and knowledgeable employees needed to manage the project. Complex projects can run on for years as various divisions of the organization are gradually brought on-stream according to a planned schedule. Even the installation of popular pro-grams such as CRM software from firms like Siebel Systems, which is modular in design and can be built in stages as the client firm grows, is a complex affair re-quiring a variety of corporate resources that only larger management consulting firms will be able to provide.

Today, e-business management consulting services have attracted a variety of seemingly unrelated companies whose clients are demanding e-business serv-ices. Rather than see revenues and possibly clients lost to competitors, a variety of large-scale enterprises have established management consulting divisions or entirely new independent businesses to go after the growing market for e-business management consulting services. Accounting firms (Ernst & Young), computer hardware vendors (IBM), telecommunications firms (AT&T), and established management consulting firms (Accenture) are all competing for what appears to be a great growth opportunity. Accenture Corp. (**www.accenture.com**) is the world's leading provider of management and technology consulting services and solu-tions, with more than 70,000 people in 46 countries delivering a wide range of specialized capabilities and solutions to clients across all industries. Accenture operates globally, building a network of businesses that can meet the full range of any organization's needs—consulting, technology, outsourcing, alliances, and venture capital. The company generated revenues of $9.75 billion for the fiscal year 2000, and $5.71 billion for the first six months of 2001.[38]

Conclusions

In this chapter, we explored the ways in which firms can approach the organizational and managerial issues related to strategic planning in an e-business environment. A variety of important subject areas were examined, including the components of the management process, organizational structures, production and operations, and productivity and efficiency issues. We saw how leadership and corporate culture play an important role in operations and employee motivation, and, finally, we examined e-business issues related to several key areas of management decision making, including human resources management, small-business management, and consulting. In the next chapter, we will examine financial planning and investment in an e-business environment.

CASE STUDY

RETURN TO
INSIDE e-BUSINESS

Google's management and its two hundred plus employees have carved out a niche for their firm in a highly competitive market. Google simplifies interaction with its users, rather than offering more choices and complexity, as many competitors continue to do. One search on the Google site illustrates just how different Google is from Yahoo! and other competitors. Examine the web sites of several search engines, including Google, Yahoo!, and Alta Vista.

ASSIGNMENT

1. Compare the strategic choices management has made on the Google site (**www.google.com**) that make it stand out from competing sites such as Yahoo! (**www.yahoo.com**) or Alta Vista (**www.altavista.com**).
2. What strategy would you recommend to Google for future growth that is consistent with creating a sustainable competitive advantage?

Chapter Review

SUMMARY

1. Examine the connections between management and e-business planning.
The management process is the ongoing planning, organizing, and controlling of all sorts of activities that personnel throughout the organization are engaged in, including marketing, finance, production and operations, human resources, and so forth. The word *process* suggests that these activities are continuous and never-ending. In a simple sense, then, these activities are the work that people do to keep the enterprise moving toward identified goals with purpose and direction. Organizational structures define the way in which individuals work together—how they solve problems, make decisions, communicate, and share responsibility, authority, and power with one another. Common structures are the bureaucratic, organic, and matrix structures. Operations management involves

the coordination of all the activities related to the production of the products and services that the organization provides to its customers; its focus is on the manufacturing processes, including facilities, capacity, purchasing, inventory, quality control, use of technology, and employees' skills. The objective of operations management is to deliver planned production of products and services within set cost limits. Operations management is continuously seeking ways to reduce costs and improve the quality of the products and services produced. This is accomplished primarily through the study of how work is organized and done so that efficiencies and other improvements can be introduced.

2. **Describe the e-business issues related to leadership, motivation, and corporate culture.**

Businesses that are operating in the fast-changing environment of the Internet need a corporate leadership approach that can motivate employees and support trust and risk taking. The leadership exhibited by a firm's management can have a dramatic influence on whether the firm achieves its goals. In general, e-business activities require a large number of self-motivated individuals who will not flourish in a working atmosphere led by someone with an authoritarian leadership style. Motivation in a business environment refers to the drive that individuals feel to perform their assigned tasks. Research suggests that employees are likely to be more motivated in the work they do when the firm has clearly defined goals and realistic objectives for them to strive for. The term *corporate culture* refers to the general values and behaviors that are considered normal within the firm. Corporate culture sets the tone for ethical behavior, leadership, decision making, risk taking, and the communication behaviors that are generally used within a particular group of employees and across the entire firm.

3. **Explore human resources management, small-business management and entrepreneurial issues, and the role of management consulting in the world of e-business.**

Human resources management is concerned with all of the activities related to acquiring, maintaining, and developing the people who do the work in the firm. Acquiring the employees needed to do the tasks involved in running the firm requires planning for future human resources needs, creating descriptions and analyses of the jobs that will need to be done, finding and hiring employees for these jobs, and integrating the employees into the firm. The Internet has been a boon to small-business and entrepreneurial efforts for tens of thousands of people around the world. The reasons are simple: The traditional barriers to entry that exist for most businesses are far lower for small e-business start-ups. e-Business start-ups do not require large amounts of capital, many employees, and established distribution relationships with suppliers and customers. They can be, have been, and continue to be launched on a shoestring budget, sometimes by one person using a home office; the only critical tool is a computer with access to the Internet. The Internet has also been a boon to the management consulting industry, as the same services that are widely provided for small businesses are also provided on a greater scale to large organizations. Today, e-business management consulting services have attracted a variety of seemingly unrelated companies whose clients are demanding e-business services. Rather than see revenues and possibly clients lost to competitors, a variety of large-scale enterprises have established management consulting divisions or entirely new independent businesses to go after the growing market for e-business management consulting services.

REVIEW QUESTIONS

1. Define the management process.
2. Explain the meaning of each of the components making up the management process.
3. What is an organizational chart and how is it used?
4. Define span of control.
5. What are bureaucratic, organic, and matrix structures?
6. Define operations management.
7. What is meant by corporate culture?
8. What are some special human resources management issues related to e-business planning?
9. What are the advantages and disadvantages of being a small e-business?
10. How can management consulting services help the organization?

DISCUSSION QUESTIONS

1. Discuss the management process, using an example to illustrate your answer.
2. Discuss the importance of using the management process.
3. Why is span of control so important in management planning?
4. Discuss the importance of leadership and motivation in management planning.
5. How can e-business increase productivity?
6. Discuss why outsourcing is a good idea for an e-business.
7. Discuss why opportunities exist for both large and small e-businesses.

Building Skills for Career Success

EXPLORING THE INTERNET

Accenture Corp. is an example of a large-scale management consulting firm specializing in e-business services to clients. Located on the Web at **www .accenture.com**, Accenture is the world's leading provider of management and technology consulting services and solutions, with more than 70,000 people in 46 countries delivering a wide range of specialized capabilities and solutions to clients across all industries. Accenture's web site provides many case study examples to illustrate how the firm has helped its clients with a variety of e-business applications.

ASSIGNMENT

1. Describe one case study example in which Accenture saved its client money.
2. What e-learning applications does Accenture offer?

(continued)

DEVELOPING CRITICAL THINKING SKILLS

Equity and expectancy theories are popular models for gaining insight into motivation. Consider the case of a thirty-year-old executive who, after three years, left a large international consulting firm on the same scale as Accenture. The young executive was earning in excess of $100,000 per year in salary and was making excellent progress along the training and development path set out by the firm. He had learned much about customer relationships and the company's products and selling methods during his time at the firm. While he had been involved with more than thirty projects, he had also gained some specialized expertise that he felt made him very valuable to his clients and his employer.

ASSIGNMENT

1. Using equity and expectancy theories as the basis for your analysis, write a report that would explain the possible motivations for the executive's decision to leave the firm.
2. Given the reasons that you have identified, are there any ways in which the firm can reduce the chances that other executives will follow the same route out of the firm?

BUILDING TEAM SKILLS

Successful organizations are often outstanding because of the leadership of certain key individual managers who have a strong vision about where they want to lead their team. Many of these individuals, like Bill Gates of Microsoft, have written articles and books explaining their passion to those interested in gaining insight to their managerial methods.

ASSIGNMENT

1. Assign each member of your team to search the Internet for material written by a successful e-business executive and prepare a summary report that highlights that executive's vision and reasons for success.
2. Compare the similarities and differences between what each report uncovered and submit a summary analysis.

RESEARCHING DIFFERENT CAREERS

Management consulting firms like Accenture (**www.accenture.com**) are popular choices for students seeking jobs after graduation. These firms generally offer a wide variety of opportunities and provide a track for training and development in specialized fields such as software, systems installations, and customer support. Examine the employment opportunities available at Accenture or some other large management-consulting firm.

ASSIGNMENT

1. Write a brief report describing one job opportunity that you uncovered online.
2. What qualifications are required?
3. Explain why you would or would not be motivated to do the job?

IMPROVING COMMUNICATION SKILLS

The SmartDraw Organization Resource Center (**www.smartdraw.com**) is one of many web sites that provide visitors with opportunities to learn more about communicating organizational structure through the use of charts. The site provides visitors with access to sample software that is useful for illustrating a variety of relationships between people, methods of communication, and workflows.

ASSIGNMENT

1. Describe the basic tools (lines and geometric shapes) that are used in an organizational chart.
2. Create an organizational chart and write a short description to explain what it is communicating.

Exploring Useful Web Sites

These web sites provide information related to the topics discussed in the chapter. You can learn more by visiting them online and examining their current data.

1. Google.com (**www.google.com**), Yahoo! (**www.yahoo.com**), and Alta Vista (**www.altavista.com**) are competing search engine sites.

2. Monster.com (**www.monster.com**) manages half of the online-recruitment market. CareerPath (**www.careerpath.com**) and CareerMosaic (**www.careermosaic.com**) are other major sites.

3. Netslaves (**www.disobey.com/netslaves**) provides a forum where managers can exchange stories about the difficulties of working in a dot-com world.

4. The Warren Shepell Company (**www.warrenshepell.com**) has over 1,000 e-counselors who use email to help more than 3 million employees at 1,300 corporate clients.

5. BigStep (**www.bigstep.com**) provides small businesses with the opportunity to create their own web site for free.

6. Motivated by customers and travel industry vendors who are seeking ways to cut their costs, online operations are being transformed by firms like **www.travelocity.com** and **www.expedia.com**.

7. Accenture Corp. (**www.accenture.com**) is the world's leading provider of management and technology consulting services and solutions.

8. The SmartDraw Organization Resource Center (**www.smartdraw.com**) is one of many web sites that provide visitors with opportunities to learn more about communicating organizational structure through the use of charts.

Financial Planning and Working with Investors

Chapter 11

INSIDE
e-BUSINESS

Nortel Networks Inc.—A Financial Microcosm of the 2000–2001 Crash

At its peak market value of 124 Canadian dollars (C\$124) a share in July 2000, the Brampton, Ontario–based telecommunications equipment manufacturer Nortel Networks Inc. (**www.nortelnetworks .com**) represented 36 percent of the entire Toronto Stock Exchange index of 300 firms. At that time, the firm had achieved spectacular sales growth, with sales reaching nearly C\$45 billion, and had become the top Canadian business organization, with a market capitalization of C\$300 billion. Just as Lucent Technologies (**www.lucent.com**) was a spin-off from AT&T, Nortel emerged from Bell Canada Enterprises as an independent firm to build the fiber-optic and wireless technology infrastructure of the Internet. As telecommunications firms expanded to accommodate the growth in Internet and other telecommunications demand, firms like Nortel quickly moved ahead by providing to customers around the world the computers, cables, and connectors that make up this infrastructure.

From only C\$30 a share in the summer of 1999, Nortel's stock had skyrocketed, reaching new highs daily as the world investment community rushed to put money into all sorts of e-business firms. Like all the firms that were building the Internet infrastructure of the day and for the future, Nortel required massive capital inflows, and investment capital gravitated to the firm as its management presented convincing arguments that the new economy was only getting started and the best was yet to come. Comparisons to the inventions of the telegraph and the automobile a hundred years earlier convinced many investors that e-businesses could deliver increasingly greater returns through growth in revenues that had no end in sight. This optimism eventually created a bubble of stock market overvaluation that was destined to burst at some point. The only real question was when that would happen and whether an individual investor would be able to sell his or her shares before everyone else started selling en masse.

Unfortunately, hindsight is always 20/20. By the time it became clear that sales revenues at Nortel, Cisco Systems, Lucent, and others had reached at least a temporary limit, commitments to major capital expenditures were already done deals. Nortel's acquisitions of other firms were facilitated by the inflated value of Nortel's shares. Nortel management bought firms that had developed new technologies it believed would eventually prove worthwhile to the Nortel product line. Between 1998 and 2001, using Nortel shares as currency, the firm acquired Bay Networks for U.S.\$9 billion, Qtera Corp. for U.S.\$3 billion, Clarify Inc. for U.S.\$2 billion, CoreTek Inc. for U.S.\$1 billion, Xros Inc. for U.S.\$3 billion, Alteon WebSystem Inc. for U.S.\$7 billion, and the Zurich plants of JDS Uniphase Inc. for U.S.\$3 billion. By the summer of 2001, Nortel was obliged to write down the value of those acquisitions on its financial statements by 70 percent. What looked like a quick strategy for acquiring new technologies and growing revenues for the company turned out to be overly optimistic when the industry downturn hit in 2001.

By the winter of 2001, the falloff in sales was clear and a widespread perception of industry overcapacity set in. To help deal with the sudden change in revenues, which had resulted in a record-setting \$19 billion second-quarter loss, Nortel laid off more than 30,000 employees—about a third of its global workforce. With less and less revenue coming in and no immediate turnaround in sight, investors sold Nortel and other Internet-related firms heavily. A year later, the panic selling was over and some sense of how dramatic the fall had been emerged. Nortel shares had fallen to about C\$14 (U.S.\$9), losing more than 88 percent of their value a year earlier and representing

only 8 percent of the Toronto Stock Exchange index. Nortel had lost C$300 billion in market capitalization within a year. Nortel stock continued to fall, trading in the C$6 range before turning up in the autumn of 2001 when appointment of veteran manager Frank Dunn as the new CEO and president was announced. However, the firm's stock value then resumed its fall and reached new lows in 2002, trading in the C$2 range as investors lost patience waiting for the promised turnaround in industry and company fortunes.[1]

Like all e-businesses affected by the sudden freeze in purchasing by customers who could no longer find the financing to continue their expansion into more Internet-related technology, Nortel was hit with heavy investor selling. This was because there was no longer any clear indication of what the company's future revenues and earnings would be. Added to this problem were the announcements of the retirement of Nortel's chief executive officer, John Roth, and chief operating officer, Clarence Chandran, with no clear successors. Given the firm's lack of leadership and direction, investors punished Nortel share value. Rumors about mergers with other technology firms circulated, but in the absence of a new management team and recovering sales, investor confidence remained weak. Undoubtedly, with a new management team in place, if there is a recovery in earnings, share values will once again reflect the firm's technological expertise.

Financial planning is the last of the three major functional areas of the e-business planning process that we need to consider. In this chapter, we will first explore financial planning from the firm's point of view. We'll look at financial tools that are generally useful for illustrating and explaining strategies in the business plan, such as pro forma income and cash flow statements. We will also examine financial matters from the perspective of investors who own shares of publicly traded companies; **venture capital** firms, which help entrepreneurs launch new businesses by providing them with the funding that they need in order to get started; and institutions like banks and insurance companies, which are the major lenders to established businesses.

venture capital
Investment funds provided by firms that help entrepreneurs launch new businesses.

An Overview of Financial Planning and e-Business

financial planning
Determining how each of the marketing and management decisions that have been made during the planning process will be paid for.

budgets
Financial statements that detail the planned expenditures and revenues for some stated period of time.

Functionally speaking, **financial planning** is concerned with determining how each of the marketing and management decisions that have been made during the planning process will be paid for. In a very simple business plan, the work that needs to be done is itemized and the various costs associated with these tasks are totaled up. At the operational level of the firm, local **budgets**, which detail the planned expenditures and revenues for some stated period of time, are prepared. All budgetary information from across the firm is then collected and reorganized to show consolidated information, such as sales or expenses by product line or division of the firm. The business plan arranges these data in whatever way is deemed appropriate to provide information about the firm's expected future course of action; this can include breakeven analysis and the use of charts, graphs, and other displays of financial information. Figure 11.1 shows the sales

FIGURE 11.1 Sales Budget for Hypothetical Technologies Inc and Graphic Display of Sales Data

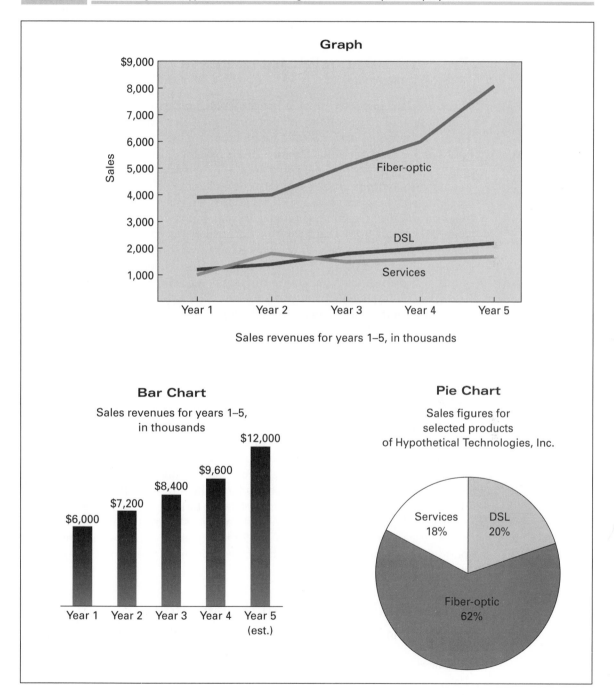

budget and several graphic displays of the data for Hypothetical Technologies Inc, an imaginary firm that we will use to illustrate the form and structure of financial documentation in an e-business plan.

Pro Forma Financial Statements in the e-Business Plan

income statements

Financial statements that list revenues and expenses for a period of time and display the net profit or loss.

balance sheets

Financial statements that list assets, liabilities, and the owner's equity in the firm as of a specific date.

cash flow statements

Financial statements that show the flow of money into and out of the firm.

Business plans generally provide *pro forma* income statements, balance sheets, and statements of cash flows for the coming three to five years. **Income statements** list revenues and expenses for a period of time and display the firm's net profit or loss for that period. **Balance sheets** list assets, liabilities, and the owner's equity in the firm as of a specific date. **Cash flow statements** show the flow of money into and out of the firm. Cash flow statements generally have sections covering *operating activities*, which generate the revenues and expenses that appear on the firm's income statement; *investing activities*, such as large capital purchases or the disposal of items that are no longer needed; and *financing activities*, which involve changes in equity and debt. Investing and financing activities are also reflected in the changes in the firm's balance sheet from year to year. The e-business plan should contain information at a level that is appropriate for the audience it is intended for. Outsiders are not likely to be given the detailed statements used at the operational level of the firm, for instance.

Although a detailed exploration of the financial statements is beyond the scope of this textbook, students are encouraged to prepare them at the level that reflects their degree of familiarity and capability. What is important in the preparation of an e-business plan is to demonstrate an appreciation for the financial implications of the marketing and management decisions you have presented. The financial part of your plan forces you to evaluate the costs and returns of doing what you have proposed and thus provides a reality check on the scale and feasibility of your plan. In the real business world, should formal documentation be required for presentation to, say, potential investors, financial professionals who are familiar with the proper format and terminology would probably be hired. However, they would still need to know the information that you outlined in your e-business plan in order to complete the task.

Figures 11.2 to 11.4 display simplified financial statements that you should be able to use to build the documentation for your plan. If your financial knowledge permits you to produce more sophisticated documentation, then by all means do so.

Understanding Financial Information

A common, and realistic, assumption that is made about new firms is that they will not produce profits or even positive cash flows until the third year of operation or even later. For example, for a long time Internet-based book and CD retailer Amazon.com was spending over $115 million each month to keep the company on track toward the eventual day when it would sell enough merchandise to generate profits for its shareholders. Amazon's operating losses over a

FIGURE 11.2 Consolidated Pro Forma Income Statements for Hypothetical Technologies Inc.

Hypothetical Technologies Inc.
Consolidated Pro Forma Statements of Income
(thousands of U.S. dollars)

	Year 1	Year 2	Year 3	Year 4	Year 5
Revenues	6,000	7,200	8,400	9,600	12,000
Cost of revenues	4,000	4,800	5,600	6,400	8,000
Gross profit	**2,000**	**2,400**	**2,800**	**3,200**	**4,000**
Marketing and administrative expense	750	900	1,050	1,200	1,500
Amortization and depreciation expense	100	120	140	160	200
Research and development expense	55	66	77	88	110
	1,095	**1,314**	**1,533**	**1,752**	**2,190**
Interest expense	10	12	14	16	20
Earnings (loss) before taxes	**1,085**	**1,302**	**1,519**	**1,736**	**2,170**
Income tax provision	**50**	**60**	**70**	**80**	**100**
Net income available to stockholders	**1,035**	**1,242**	**1,449**	**1,656**	**2,070**

period of six years totaled more than $1.2 billion, scaring away some who feared that the firm would never reach the promised profit goals set by visionary founder Steve Bezos.[2] Amazon finally turned a profit in the last quarter of 2001.

Concern can turn to worry, though, if the expected preliminary negative cash flows show no sign of the hoped-for turn toward positive levels after the initial period in which the firm's products are introduced into the marketplace. If a company runs out of funding and there is no infusion of cash from sales, new investors, partners, or some other source, the firm is effectively bankrupt and whatever money, time, and effort has been invested in it is lost. In worst-case scenarios, firms may be forced to sell off entire divisions of their business in order to acquire cash. This is why the statement of cash flows is considered such an important document within the e-business plan. For example, Pets.com was an example of a dot-com start-up that lost control of its finances. Backed by Disney and Amazon, the firm spent $27 million in 1999 on television and other media advertising to generate awareness and sales. The funny advertisements presented by the famous talking dog sock puppet could not create a critical mass of buyers quickly enough to offset the advertising and other operational costs. As a result, for every dollar of pet supplies revenue received, the firm lost five dollars, quickly creating a cash crisis.[3]

FIGURE 11.3 | Consolidated Pro Forma Balance Sheets for Hypothetical Technologies Inc.

Hypothetical Technologies Inc.
Consolidated Pro Forma Balance Sheets
(thousands of U.S. dollars)

	Year 1	Year 2	Year 3	Year 4	Year 5
ASSETS					
Cash	1,625	1,685	2,569	3,666	3,797
Accounts receivable	1,500	1,630	2,282	2,651	3,292
Inventories	750	900	950	1,520	1,701
Other assets	6,450	7,740	8,431	9,134	11,253
Total assets	**10,325**	**11,955**	**14,232**	**16,971**	**20,043**
LIABILITIES					
Accounts payable	1,600	1,920	2,688	4,301	4,670
Long-term debt	500	1,790	2,481	3,184	5,303
Other liabilities	100	120	168	269	538
Total liabilities	**2,200**	**3,830**	**5,337**	**7,754**	**10,511**
SHAREHOLDERS' EQUITY					
Common shares	8,125	8,125	8,125	8,125	8,125
Retained earnings	0	0	770	1,092	1,407
Total shareholders' equity	**8,125**	**8,125**	**8,895**	**9,217**	**9,532**
Total liabilities and shareholders' equity	**10,325**	**11,955**	**14,232**	**16,971**	**20,043**

In 2001, such concerns prompted Amazon.com to modify its planning in order to prove to impatient and critical investors that the company's business would eventually be profitable, despite having operating losses for its first six years. Staffing was reduced to cut expenses, and planned expansion was trimmed to help meet investor expectations and at least halt the negative cash flow that was draining the firm of funds. In June 2001, after the stock prices of Amazon and other technology companies fell, and at a time when ten-year U.S. Treasury bills were yielding about 6 percent, Amazon's convertible bonds due February 2009 had an effective yield of 14 percent. Given Amazon's six years of losses and $1.5 billion of unsecured debt, the bond yield reflected investors' very real concerns and their perception that Amazon could default on its payments.[4] Higher interest rates cost firms more when they must borrow money to operate their businesses, which further exacerbates the difficulty of achieving profitability. Should Amazon

FIGURE 11.4 Consolidated Pro Forma Statements of Cash Flows for Hypothetical Technologies Inc.

Hypothetical Technologies Inc.
Consolidated Pro Forma Statements of Cash Flows
(thousands of U.S. dollars)

	Year 1	Year 2	Year 3	Year 4	Year 5
Cash flows from operating activities					
Net profit (loss) and other cash inflows	6,000	7,200	8,400	9,600	12,000
Net expenditures and other cash outflows	4,865	5,838	6,811	7,784	9,730
Net cash from operating activities	1,135	1,362	1,589	1,816	2,270
Cash flows from investing activities					
Net cash inflows from investing activities	0	0	0	0	0
Net cash outflows from investing activities	500	1,290	691	703	2,119
Net cash from investing activities	−500	−1,290	−691	−703	−2,119
Cash flow from financing activities					
Net cash inflows from financing activities	0	0	0	0	0
Net cash outflows from financing activities	−10	−12	−14	−16	−20
Net cash from financing activities	−10	−12	−14	−16	−20
Net increase (decrease) in cash	625	60	884	1,097	131
Cash at beginning of period	1,000	1,625	1,685	2,569	3,666
Cash at end of period	1,625	1,685	2,569	3,666	3,797

master budget

A compilation of all the budgetary decisions from all levels of the organization.

sales budget

A budget that details the sources of the revenue that the company expects to receive.

need to issue new bonds or other forms of debt, interest costs would be higher, reflecting the riskier financial conditions for lenders.

Budgets become progressively more comprehensive as the budget planning process moves from the operational level of the firm, where departments estimate their funding requirements in anticipation of the work they will be expected to perform, to the divisional level, and ultimately to the corporate level. The firm's **master budget** is a compilation of all the budgetary decisions from all levels of the organization. For example, the **sales budget** details the sources of the revenues the company expects to receive in order to pay its expenses and generate profits. At the operational level, the department responsible for a product line will develop a sales budget that itemizes the revenues expected from each product in the line and perhaps organizes information in several ways, such as according to sales territories and customers. The sales budget helps the department to set performance targets, which we will examine in more detail in Chapter 12.

Besides identifying the sources of the funds that will be needed for planned activities, the financial planning process also attempts to show the broader impact that implementation of the plan will have on the overall financial condition of the firm through pro forma income statements and balance sheets. Without adequate sources of funds and proper financial management, the firm cannot hope to accomplish the goals and objectives stated in its e-business plan. All of these issues are also important to the firm's investors and lenders, who need to consider whether the risk of involvement through equity or debt is worthwhile. The financing activities segment of the pro forma cash flow statement indicates the expected participation of investors and lenders over the planned time period. Failure to receive infusions of cash at planned times will undermine management's ability to succeed with the overall plan.

Developing the Financial Plan to Avoid Failure

People who are preparing a strategic plan for a new business are generally going to be seeking equity from investors, which will allow them to launch the first phase of their business plan. If the first phase turns out satisfactorily for investors, the same participants, or possibly others, are likely to consider a second and often a third round of funding. This was the pattern followed by the hundreds of so-called dot-com or e-business start-ups that were created in the rush to take advantage of the first commercial development phase of the Internet, leading up to the year 2000. Petopia.com and eToys.com, two e-tailing firms created to market well-established brand-name products over the Internet, are good examples of firms that ran out of capital before a sufficient cash flow to carry the firm to its next phase of development could be established. According to research by Softbank Venture Capital Inc., one of the biggest venture capital firms investing in Internet companies, it costs about $15 to $25 million to build a high-profile commercial web site but ten times this amount to set up the warehousing and distribution (fulfillment) system to go along with it.[5]

The high costs of establishing logistical warehousing and distribution systems, excessive competition selling the same products and services, customers who were slow to switch their buying from traditional bricks-and-mortar local retailers to the Internet, high promotional costs to inform potential customers of the firm's existence, poor managerial decision making and the absence of sufficient partnerships or alliances to help establish brand awareness and customer acceptance all contributed to the many early dot-com failures. Failure to meet financial backers' expectations often led to a quick decision on the part of those backers to deny the firm a second wave of investment dollars to continue its drive to achieve profitability. For example, in one month alone, Digital Entertainment Network shut its video streaming site, clothing distributor boo.com closed after spending more than $100 million in only six months of business, and healthshop.com shut its doors completely after failing to meet its investors' expectations.[6]

Sources of Funds

In this section we will examine two prominent sources of funding commonly associated with e-business ventures: venture capital firms and funds from within the organization.

Venture Capital Investors

Venture capital investors perceive a start-up e-business as a high-risk situation and demand compensating terms and conditions for their involvement. In most situations, venture capitalists will not want to take more than a 40 percent stake in a start-up firm in order to give the owner/management team they are backing sufficient entrepreneurial incentive. Also, the thinking is that the less money a firm's management has at stake, the less concerned it will be with the firm's performance and with successfully achieving the goals stated in the business plan.

Venture capital investors are generally not interested in long-term working relationships with start-up firms. Instead, they prefer to support and nurture a management team that they believe can bring the firm to a viable and functioning position in the market, then sell their ownership to others who are interested in a more established investment. They prefer to invest in start-up situations, where the higher risk often goes with a higher payback if the start-up is successful, and then to move on to other firms with good ideas that require capital and perhaps help in creating a network of contacts with potential customers, strategic alliances, suppliers, and so forth. Often, these are the vital resources that boost the chances of success for a start-up management team that has a good idea but lacks sufficient capital and knowledge of networks to make the firm a success.

Venture capital firms will generally place one or more representatives on the board of directors of the firms they have invested in so that they can monitor management's activities more closely and help with decision making. These directors often sit on several boards and look for ways to facilitate business activities, especially among the firms they have funds invested in. Directors will usually receive regular briefings and reports describing in detail how well management is doing at realizing the goals and objectives set forth in the firm's business plan. In essence, the business plan is considered a contractual agreement between venture capital investors and the owner/management team. Both groups want the stated goals and objectives to be achieved as scheduled.

Venture capital firms are major players in the financial gamble to build e-businesses. According to the Corporate Venturing Report, there are more than 200 corporations that make investments in Internet-related start-ups. An estimated $10 billion was invested in 1999, five times the amount invested in 1998. A second-round investment of $10 million in a start-up can easily turn into $100 million if and when the firm goes public through an initial public offering (IPO). For example, Oracle Venture Fund was up some 504 percent in its first year of operation after successful IPOs by both C-bridge Internet Solutions and Red Hat.[7]

The heady early days of aggressive venture capitalism ended with the industry shakeout that began in 2000, when, according to Venturewire Inc, investment in start-ups peaked at more than $90 billion. More than 823 Internet companies went bankrupt between 2000 and 2002, but, according to researchers at Webmergers .com, an estimated 7,000 to 10,000 remain. Furthermore, estimates of $100 billion in venture capital waiting to be deployed suggest that activity will once again become robust when investors who were once burned by losses resume funding new technology and online start-ups.[8]

Conventional Sources of Funds

An e-business venture may be either a completely new business, where no plan has existed previously, or a new addition to a firm's current business plan. In the first case, a complete set of financial plans detailing how the entire enterprise will be expected to perform will be needed in order to explain why investors and lenders should decide to become involved.

In the second situation, however, the firm will need to document how the e-business activities will contribute to existing revenue streams or create new ones and what changes in existing budgets will be required. Planners will need to seek approval for the allocation of internal sources of funding and resources in the current or future master business budget and overall plan. They might argue that the e-business venture is really a new promotional strategy that should replace an existing program or be added to the current promotional effort. For instance, to create a web site, funds that had previously been budgeted for advertising or some other promotional activities might simply be redirected. Senior management might be more easily persuaded of the value of experimenting with a web presence if the first step is a relatively lower-risk and lower-cost project. A cost-benefit analysis might be prepared that justified funding for the construction of a web site dedicated to distributing a variety of types of corporate information to interested publics by showing the short- and longer-term benefits that are expected. Should the venture fail to live up to expectations, advocates can argue, the firm can always return to the current budgetary allocations for promotional expenditures.

Unconventional Sources of Funds

Alternatives to using cash to pay salaries or to acquire other firms in order to expand the business more rapidly have gained a great deal of public attention because of the fantastic gains made by some individuals. In this section we will take a close look at this phenomenon and some of the implications of this financial strategy.

Using Stock Options as a Substitute for Salaries

stock option
The right to purchase a share at a set price, or strike price, between two dates in the future.

One of the funding trends that emerged as new-economy share prices soared was the use of stock options as a substitute for salaries. A **stock option** is the right to purchase a share at a set price, or *strike price*, between two dates in the future. If the price of the shares rises above the strike price, holders of the options can exercise their right to buy the stock at the strike price and then quickly sell it at the higher market price, keeping the difference.

The use of stock options was initially popular as a motivational tool for senior management, but it quickly spread to middle-ranking managers when it was recognized as a means of deferring payment to individuals who otherwise would undoubtedly have demanded higher current salaries for the work they were doing. The expected future value of those stock options drove individual employees to perform better and to be willing to work overtime and weekends, while also allowing the firm to save its limited cash reserves. In many cases, Internet start-ups provided stock options for all employees as a motivational and financial planning tool.

However, stock options are controversial because they allow the firm to avoid charging what would otherwise be tax-deductible salary expenses against current earned income and instead dilute the value of shares owned by regular investors. This occurs because if and when options are exercised, the firm must honor the set purchase price, which is generally well below the market value of the stock. In addition, some executives have made what some regular shareholders consider to be unconscionable gains as part of their executive compensation packages. For

e-Business Insight

Careful—Earnings and Share Values May Not Be What They Seem

According to a survey conducted by the brokerage house Merrill Lynch, thirty-six of the world's biggest technology companies overstated their true 2000 earnings by an average of 25 percent, typically by ignoring the impact of stock option plans. Since these plans would have reduced earnings, the firms' shares may be overpriced because investors are valuing them on the basis of reported earnings. If the fair value of stock option grants had been included in the calculations, 61 percent of the corporate profits would have vanished. The worst offender was Yahoo!, whose $1.3 billion stock option costs would have obliterated its $71 million reported income. Besides failure to report stock option costs, the other common accounting deficiencies include reporting one-time financial gains from the disposal of assets and nonoperating sources of revenue such as pension fund income. Merrill Lynch suggests that that the real earnings of Ericsson AB were 94 percent below what the company reported because of a one-time $25 billion gain in earnings and that Lucent Technologies overstated earnings by 110 percent through the inclusion of $3.6 billion in pension plan income as part of operations. Furthermore, of the earnings reported by the thirty-six surveyed firms, 48 percent were derived from tax breaks on stock options, which will not be available in the following year. Finally, the Merrill Lynch report is also very critical of the earnings reduction strategies used by Nortel Networks and JDS Uniphase, which it claims use creative accounting methods to make their long-term growth rates look better than they really are by immediately writing off costs associated with the acquisitions of other firms. The message to investors is clear enough: Read the details in firms' financial statements and take the banner messages of revenues and earnings with caution until all of the information explaining how these numbers are derived is known.[9]

instance, John Roth, CEO of Nortel Networks, earned $135 million in 2001 as a result of exercising stock options before Nortel shares tumbled in value later that year.[10]

Using Shares as Currency to Grow by Acquisition

Another phenomenon that soared in popularity with the rapid rise in the share values of new-economy businesses was the use of a firm's shares as currency when it acquired other firms. In essence, instead of having to borrow more cash, generate cash through operations, or sell more shares, a firm with high share values could merge with or acquire another firm by exchanging its stock for the other firm's. Often the owners who were surrendering control of their firm were given some portion of the purchase price in cash, but the amount of cash that large firms with high stock prices required if they wanted to grow their businesses through the acquisition of other businesses was reduced by the high value of these firms' shares. For example, in the race to gain technological expertise in the highly specialized optical networking field, the Microelectronics Group of Lucent Technologies acquired Herrmann Technology, Inc., a privately held company based in Dallas, Texas, for approximately $450 million of Lucent stock. Larger firms like Lucent will commonly make this type of acquisition to fill technology or manufacturing capacity gaps in their own operations. On the reverse side of this strategic coin, many small businesses that can be easily integrated into a large firm like Lucent are more than happy to become an operational division and thereby grow at a rate that they would not be likely to enjoy if they remained independent. In exchange, their owners receive shares in the larger corporation, and generally some cash as well.[11] In retrospect, like many other technology acquisitions by large firms, this acquisition might appear to suffer from poor timing, as the industry downturn began soon after.

Evaluating e-Business Risks and Investments

Evaluating whether an e-business activity is worthwhile is typically done using cost-benefit analysis. After comparing the financial and other costs required for undertaking the venture with the financial and other benefits gained, management can better make an effective assessment of the value that the project represents to them.

Perceived Risks and Expected Earnings

From an outside investor's point of view, the decision to purchase equity in a firm or to lend the firm funds is based on the perceived risk level of the investment and the projected returns on invested capital. Many factors might affect these two items, including changes in technology, interest rates, general economic activity, and so forth. Although many (now embarrassed) individuals once argued that the so-called new economy was immune to the ravages of the business cycle that regularly afflicted the traditional industries making up the old economy, the drastic fall in the stock market prices of new-economy leaders like Dell Computer, Oracle, Nortel Networks, Cisco Systems, and all the others during the 2000 industry slowdown clearly put that argument on the junk heap.

What caused these industry giants to gain and then lose fantastic amounts of value in such a relatively short period of time can be explained in simple terms. Values rose because investors believed that the future growth in these firms' revenues would continue to outpace that of firms in the traditional economy, and they were willing to pay for the opportunity to grow their investments faster. Whereas 5 to 10 percent growth in earnings in a year might be considered exceptional for an old-economy business, many of the new-economy firms were growing at annual rates of 40 to 100 percent and more. Investors lost any sense of what normal growth for this sector of the economy was likely to be and so bid up prices to levels that reflected their confidence that revenue growth would make what they were buying today worth so much more in the future that today's purchase price would seem cheap. Unfortunately, for many of these firms, profit growth did not keep pace with revenue growth; often, in fact, profit never materialized. These disappointing trends eventually led to a failure in confidence and the financial collapse of many firms as investors sold their shares.

Needless to say, however, new-economy businesses should be evaluated in the same way and on the same basis as any other business. The primary factor that determines future share value is the firm's **expected earnings**—that is, the difference between its expected revenues and expected expenses. The **price-earnings (P/E) ratio** for any firm is the current price of one share of the firm's stock divided by the earnings per share for the past year. So a P/E of 30 would mean that investors were willing to pay $30 for $1 of current earnings. The expectation, of course, is that the earnings will continue to grow. If the ratio remains the same, then the share value will rise proportionately. If earnings decline, however, the share value will decline proportionately as well.

In order to factor the growth expectations into the analysis of a firm's value, some analysts use the **price-earnings-growth (PEG) ratio**, which is calculated by dividing the P/E ratio by the growth rate. So, if the firm with a share price of $30 and $1 of earnings per share has a projected growth rate of 50 percent, it would have a PEG ratio of 0.6, as illustrated below.

expected earnings
The difference between a firm's expected revenues and expected expenses.

price-earnings (P/E) ratio
The current price of one share of a firm's stock divided by the earnings per share for the past year.

price-earnings-growth (PEG) ratio
A ratio combining growth expectations with the P/E ratio; it is calculated by dividing the P/E ratio by the growth rate.

Price per Share / Earnings per Share = P/E Ratio / Growth Rate = PEG Ratio

$30   / $1   = 30   / 50   = 0.6

Although what constitutes attractive PEG and P/E ratios is a hot topic of debate among investment analysts, as a general rule, a technology firm with a P/E ratio below 30 and a PEG ratio under 1.0 would deserve further investigation to better assess its value as an investment. This is especially true if historically the ratios for the firm have been higher, and thus the company may currently be undervalued.

Historically, the average P/E ratio of the companies making up the Standard & Poor's 500 index has varied from 5.9 in 1944 to 35 in 1999.[12] Before the speculative bubble burst in 2000, many new-economy firms were trading at P/E ratios of 100 or higher, and some firms could not even calculate a P/E ratio, since they had not yet generated any earnings from their revenues. Clearly, the investors who bought these stocks had high growth expectations for the products the firms produced. When that growth failed to reach the expected levels and eventually became unpredictable, investors began to question the value of the shares. Many investors sold at whatever price they could, and the stock markets on which these shares were heavily represented, such as the NASDAQ, tumbled. From its peak at 5,048 on March 3, 2000, the NASDAQ fell 67 percent to 1,619 on April 4, 2001; it later dipped below 1,400 in 2002.[13] Since then, many high tech firms have begun to recover in value, but many others have continued their free-fall—for example, by 2002 Nortel Networks was selling at less than 2 percent of its peak price in 2000—and technology firms in general, as represented by the NASDAQ, were down nearly 80 percent from their peak.

But perhaps another viewpoint should be included here. According to Baruch Lev, professor of accounting and finance at New York University's Stern School of Management and a director of the Project for Research on Intangibles, current accounting methods used to evaluate and measure Internet-related firms are inadequate. He suggests that we need new accounting and finance principles that are better equipped to communicate value in a world of intangibles. We are failing to properly value the most valuable corporate assets, intangibles such as brand, market power, business processes, and research and development; instead, we are focusing on hard assets and current revenues as though online businesses are no different from any other businesses.[14] Critics of current accounting practice also point to the way in which firms measure their earnings. Given that investors in stocks are willing to pay a certain amount of money for every dollar of earnings that a firm generates, these critics say, it is misleading not to distinguish between the different sources of total earnings in company reports. Real performance, they argue, is best reflected by the business's cash flows from operations. Critics suggest that IBM's reported earnings are inflated because they are affected by changes in pension fund accounts, which in turn are linked to the firm's stock market value.[15] At the time of this writing, several financial scandals at major firms, including industry giant WorldCom Inc., suggest the need for closer scrutiny of accounting and financial reporting as well as better governance of the financial institutions involved in auditing business practices.

The Credit Crunch of 2000

The rapid and in some cases fatal financial collapse of Internet-dependent firms in 2000 was a clear illustration of the fact that although the Internet was originally funded by the military and later by educational institutions, it was now very much subject to the same laws of economics as any other industry. The phase of the business cycle in which sales slow and firms are forced to clear excessively large inventories arrived suddenly and provided an unexpected rude awakening for firms like Lucent Technologies, Nortel Networks, Cisco Systems, Celestica, and countless others, like WorldCom Inc., whose fortunes were all interconnected and were heavily tied to the rate at which their customers bought Internet infrastructure technology.

e-Business Insight
eBay Shares Reflect Value

Although most e-business stocks fell dramatically in value during the 2000–2001 downturn, NASDAQ-listed auction-site eBay (**www.ebay.com**) managed to recover quickly to $68 a share and to outperform other well-known Internet players like Amazon and Yahoo!. The reasons can be found in the superior numbers that investors look for when selecting and evaluating shares, such as a 2001 first-quarter profit per share of 11 cents versus the expected 8 cents (a 592 percent increase year-over-year increase), a 79 percent increase in revenues, and the addition of 7 million new users to the 23 million that already were using eBay's services for buying and selling in the fast-growing peer-to-peer market. In the summer of 2001, eBay traded at a P/E ratio of 185 times 2001 earnings and 105 times estimated 2002 earnings, reflecting eBay's long-term growth rate of 50 to 75 percent. The resulting PEG ratio of 3 was virtually unheard of and suggested either overvaluation that would at some point be corrected or in fact the beginning of new revenue growth from expansion of operations.[16] However, as the NASDAQ spiraled downward to below 1,400 in the summer of 2002, eBay traded near $60, reflecting continuing investor confidence in 50 to 60 percent growth rates into 2003.[17]

What caused the sudden slowdown was an old-fashioned *credit crunch*—the inability of buyers to raise funds to purchase more new equipment. This took place because the investors who had made these funds available in the past were becoming more unsure about the ability of some firms to generate enough revenue to pay back loans or to earn sufficient profits from the deployment of these newly acquired technologies. While explaining to shareholders the reasons for the 80 percent drop in the company's stock market value, the CEO of Nortel Networks, John Roth, said that "the lesson we've learned is we need to stay very, very close to the financial component of our customer, as well, because even though the network engineers want to do it and the marketing people have the ambitious plans, if the capital markets are cutting off our customers, we need to be aware of that."[18] What many people had previously seen as an industry without limits to growth because of the productivity improvements its customers derived by transferring more work to the Internet and because of the continuing movement toward convergence of technologies suddenly came down to earth and became an industry like any other—albeit one with greater potential growth than most.

Who Will Survive the Shakeout?

According to veteran financial analyst and former stockbroker Hugh Anderson (**www.unclehughie.com**), the 2000–2001 crash in the stock prices of highly overrated technology firms marked the time when the public finally became aware of just how poor the quality of analysis and advice emanating from major brokerage firms truly was. The reasons for the decline can be attributed mostly to the gradual change in the traditional roles played by analysts and the shift of brokerage firm earnings away from traditional commissions and toward greater reliance on the underwriting and financing of new issues. Rather than investigating and reporting on the firms they were assigned, analysts became trusting reporters of the information they were fed by the management of these same firms. Furthermore, instead of acting as a counterbalance to the brokerage firms' sales teams, they effectively joined in and became promoters of the companies as well.[19]

Bankruptcy or a merger with another vendor can have an impact on a vendor's customers, and the possibility of this should be taken into account during the selection process. According to research by the Gartner Group, only 20 percent of Internet-based providers of software products like CRM will survive to 2004 because of intense competition that will lead to greater consolidation within the industry. The report advised customers to select larger vendors like Siebel Systems (**www.siebel. com**), PeopleSoft (**www.peoplesoft.com**), and Oracle (**www.oracle.com**) to reduce the risk that they might be left without support one day because the vendor's software had been eliminated from the industry through bankruptcy or merger. According to the report, the critical applications that vendors must have in order to have a chance in the market include email, chat, and web-based self-service. Vendors without these lack the potential to remain competitive in the long run.[20]

Conclusions

This chapter examined the importance of finance in the overall planning process, the sources of funding, the role of venture capitalists, stock market valuations of firms, the NASDAQ, and other investment- and finance-related topics. The discussions presented here should help learners grasp the relationship between plans and the funding needed to actually bring them to fruition. Finally, the steps for creating the financial component of the overall e-business plan were presented.

In the following chapter, we will conclude our discussion of the strategic e-business planning process by examining issues related to implementation and control of the plan.

CASE STUDY   RETURN TO INSIDE e-BUSINESS

The experience of Nortel Networks and other e-businesses during the 2000–2001 run-up and crash landing focused attention on several basic points related to the way in which investors evaluate corporations. These involve the stability of the firm's business plan, the basic business models used, and the related major components, including the firm's revenue streams, cash flows from operations, product lines, and management. The saga of Nortel and other such firms will continue to unfold as events under management's control, and those that are not, become evident. You can follow these events on the firm's web site, located at **www.nortelnetworks.com**.

ASSIGNMENT
1. What has happened to Nortel's share value since the summer of 2002?
2. What reasons can you offer, such as new management, changes in customer buying patterns, and so forth, to explain the changes in share values?

Chapter Review

1. **Examine the connections between financial planning and e-business planning.**

Financial planning is concerned with determining how each of the marketing and management decisions that have been made during the planning process will be paid for. In a very simple business plan, the work that needs to be done is itemized and the various costs associated with these tasks are totaled up. At the operational level of the firm, local budgets, which detail the planned expenditures and revenues for some stated period of time, are prepared. All budgetary information from across the firm is then collected and reorganized to show consolidated information, such as sales or expenses by product lines or divisions of the firm. The business plan arranges these data in whatever way is deemed appropriate to provide information about the firm's expected future course of action; this can include breakeven analysis and the use of charts, graphs, and other displays of financial information. Business plans generally provide pro forma income statements, balance sheets, and statements of cash flows for the coming three to five years. A common, and realistic, assumption that is made about new firms is that they will not produce profits or even positive cash flows until the third year of operation or even later. Concern can turn to worry, though, if the expected preliminary negative cash flows show no sign of the hoped-for turn toward positive levels after the initial period in which the firm's products are introduced into the marketplace.

2. **Explore the sources of funds employed by e-businesses.**

Venture capital investors perceive a start-up e-business as a high-risk situation and demand compensating terms and conditions for their involvement. In most situations, venture capitalists will not want to take more than a 40 percent stake in a start-up firm in order to give the owner/management team they are backing sufficient entrepreneurial incentive. Also, the thinking is that the less money a firm's management has at stake, the less concerned it will be with the firm's performance and with successfully achieving the goals stated in the business plan. Venture capital investors are generally not interested in long-term working relationships with start-up firms. Instead, they prefer to support and nurture a management team that they believe can bring the firm to a viable and functioning position in the market, then sell their ownership to others who are interested in a more established investment. One of the funding trends that emerged as new-economy share values soared was the use of stock options as a substitute for salaries. The expected future value of those stock options drove individual employees to perform better and to be willing to work overtime and weekends, while also allowing the firm to save its limited cash reserves. Another phenomenon that soared in popularity was the use of a firm's shares as currency when it acquired other firms. In essence, instead of having to borrow more cash, generate it through operations, or sell more shares, a firm with high share values could merge with or acquire another firm by exchanging its stock for the other firm's.

3. Examine strategies for evaluating e-business risks and investments.

Evaluating whether an e-business activity is worthwhile is typically done using cost-benefit analysis. After comparing the financial and other costs required for undertaking the venture with the financial and other benefits gained, management can better make an effective assessment of the value that the project represents to them. From an outside investor's point of view, the decision to purchase equity in a firm or to lend the firm funds is based on the perceived risk level of the investment and the projected returns on invested capital. Many factors might affect these two items, including changes in technology, interest rates, general economic activity, and so forth. Although many (now embarrassed) individuals once argued that the so-called new economy was immune to the ravages of the business cycle that regularly afflicted the traditional industries making up the old economy, the drastic fall in the stock prices of new-economy industry leaders like Dell Computer, Oracle, Nortel Networks, Cisco Systems, and all the others during the 2000 industry slowdown clearly put that argument on the junk heap. What caused these industry giants to gain and then lose fantastic amounts of value in such a relatively short period of time can be explained in simple terms. Values rose because investors believed that the future growth of these firms' revenues would continue to outpace that of firms in the traditional economy, and they were willing to pay for the opportunity to grow their investments faster.

REVIEW QUESTIONS

1. Explain how budgets are used in the financial planning process.
2. What is venture capital?
3. What does the term *price-earnings ratio* mean?
4. What does the term *price-earnings-growth ratio* mean?
5. How are stock options used to motivate the management of a firm?
6. How should the value of shares be evaluated?

DISCUSSION QUESTIONS

1. Discuss the financial planning process.
2. Why do many e-business ventures fail?
3. Describe the way venture capital investors work with the management of a firm.
4. Discuss the investing strategy followed by a venture capital firm.
5. What are the criticisms of the use of stock options as a substitute for paying salaries?
6. Explain how a firm can grow faster by using its high share value.

Building Skills for Career Success

EXPLORING THE INTERNET

Financial information is widely available on the Internet. Perhaps a good place to explore e-businesses and growth-oriented technology businesses that are focused on the Internet is the NASDAQ web site, located at **www.nasdaq.com**. Here you can look at graphic illustrations of both the NASDAQ stock indexes and individual stocks. In addition, the NASDAQ presents informative articles highlighting technology breakthroughs and provides links to individual firms and other sources.

ASSIGNMENT

1. Summarize the current direction for NASDAQ listed stocks.
2. What reasons does the NASDAQ site give to explain why share values have been moving in this direction?

DEVELOPING CRITICAL THINKING SKILLS

The Internet provides easy access to a variety of financial information about firms whose stock is publicly traded. Management is motivated to publicize positive developments that will contribute directly to revenue growth and tries to counteract any negative information that might be circulating. The firm's web site will generally provide financial statements, prognostications by senior management, press releases highlighting positive financial news, and so forth. Select a well-known firm that you are interested in, such as Microsoft or IBM, and examine its corporate web site for disclosure of current financial information. Then explore news sites like CNET (**www.cnet.com**) or Bloomberg (**www.bloomberg.com**).

ASSIGNMENT

1. What financial information stood out on the corporate web site?
2. What was the view from independent news services?

BUILDING TEAM SKILLS

Developing an e-business plan with partners requires the preparation of estimated future financial statements containing data that everyone can agree with. There is little to be gained, for example, by setting sales estimates well beyond the point that management believes is realistic. After all, any shortfalls that occur are only going to aggravate working relationships at a future date when solutions are needed for the problems caused by the firm's failure to achieve targeted goals. Discuss an e-business idea that your group considers viable, such as establishing an e-commerce site to distribute a specialized product. Estimate the people and resources you will need in order to set up the firm and operate it for the next five years.

ASSIGNMENT

1. Briefly describe the e-business idea.

(continued)

2. Using Figures 11.2, 11.3, and 11.4 as guides, develop your own set of pro forma financial documents.
3. Explain the meaning of your pro forma financial documents.

RESEARCHING DIFFERENT CAREERS

The American Institute of Certified Public Accountants (AICPA) web site (**www.aicpa.org**) provides a variety of information that is useful to accountants. Of particular relevance is information related to business practices over the Internet, such as taxation issues, security for payments, and relationships with suppliers and customers.

ASSIGNMENT

1. Explore the AICPA web site and summarize the content presented.
2. Prepare a report on one item currently considered important to accountants that is presented as an article.

IMPROVING COMMUNICATION SKILLS

Electronic data interchange (EDI) is a precursor of Internet-based communication between large-scale users that is still in use today. In simple terms, EDI uses standardized forms for exchanging information between two computer systems. Typical financial information exchanged using EDI is that found on invoices, order forms, bills, shipping documents, and so forth. Major suppliers use EDI to reduce their order-processing costs and better serve their customers. For example, a major supplier like Procter & Gamble uses EDI to service Wal-Mart stores. Rather than using the network software and hardware protocols available on the Internet, EDI is proprietary. This means that the system used by Wal-Mart and Procter & Gamble may not be compatible with another system used to serve another supplier or vendor. However, the security of the system and other benefits might be superior to those of the alternatives available on the Internet.

ASSIGNMENT

1. Using a search engine, research EDI and prepare a report on the status of its use today.
2. What do you think is the likely long-term future use of EDI?

Exploring Useful Web Sites

These web sites provide information related to the topics discussed in the chapter. You can learn more by visiting them online and examining their current data.

1. Nortel Networks (**www.nortelnetworks.com**) is a leading telecommunication equipment manufacturer that competes with Lucent Technologies (**www.lucent.com**) and other firms to build the fiber-optic and wireless technology infrastructure of the Internet.

2. Hugh Anderson (**www.unclehughie.com**) is a veteran financial analyst and former stockbroker.

3. Siebel Systems (**www.siebel.com**), PeopleSoft (**www.peoplesoft.com**), and Oracle (**www.oracle.com**) are some of the larger vendors of software services.

4. A good place to explore e-businesses and growth-oriented technology businesses that are focused on the Internet is the NASDAQ web site, located at **www.nasdaq.com**. News sites like CNET (**www.cnet.com**) and Bloomberg (**www.bloomberg.com**) provide financial information about firms.

5. The American Institute of Certified Public Accountants (AICPA) web site (**www.aicpa.org**) provides a wide range of financial information that is useful to accountants.

Implementation and Control of the e-Business Plan

Chapter 12

Learning Objectives

1. Examine how the e-business plan is implemented within the firm's organizational structure and integrated into that structure.
2. Describe how management controls the e-business plan by setting performance objectives and standards, measuring and evaluating results, and directing future actions and decisions.

Chapter Outline

Inside e-Business: Cap Gemini Ernst & Young—Helping Clients Implement and Evaluate e-Business Solutions

Implementation of the e-Business Plan

Project Management Scheduling Tools

Problems and Solutions

Control of the e-Business Plan

Setting Performance Objectives and Standards

Measuring and Evaluating Performance Results

Taking Corrective Actions

INSIDE
e-BUSINESS
Cap Gemini Ernst & Young— Helping Clients Implement and Evaluate e-Business Solutions

Cap Gemini Ernst & Young (**www.cgey.com**) is one of the largest management and information technology (IT) consulting firms in the world. The company combines the resources of Gemini Consulting, Cap Gemini IT Services, and (since the acquisition from Ernst & Young LLP), Ernst & Young Consulting Services. The company has a significant presence in the United States, Canada, France, the United Kingdom, Scandinavia, Germany, Austria, Benelux, Spain, Italy, Portugal, Switzerland, Poland, Singapore, Hong Kong, Australia, New Zealand, Japan, India, and Mexico. It offers management consulting services to clients seeking e-business strategic solutions that will provide improvements in production and distribution, reporting, and quality control, and allow the clients to develop an overall competitive advantage in the marketplace. The firm also develops and implements customized software and hardware solutions in partnerships with vendors.

According to a study conducted by Cap Gemini Ernst & Young, 42 percent of North American companies have no idea what the return on their investment in CRM software actually is. The reasons cited include the complexity of costing at the divisional levels, where costs are often transferred from other divisions, and the general weakness in understanding and defining metrics for proper monitoring and evaluation of CRM installations.

The firm advises clients to develop metrics in three companywide areas—marketing, sales, and service— and, more importantly, to do so before considering the acquisition of a CRM installation. Only when this is done can the returns for adopting CRM solutions be readily evaluated in terms of the benefits they are expected to provide, such as reductions in costs, increased efficiencies, improved customer relations, and so forth. Following this approach, Marriott Hotels (**www.marriott.com**) used *marketing metrics* (sales levels before and after implementation of the CRM system), *sales metrics* (the time required to close a sale), and *service metrics* (the cost of servicing an order [a customer] after the sale was completed) to judge its installation a success and provide a basis for control.

Canada Post (**www.canadapost.ca**) selected cost to serve one customer, wait times in the call center, the number of times a customer goes to the web site, and invoice adjustment costs as important criteria for adopting an SAP Inc. (**www.sap.com**) CRM system and as metrics for evaluating its contributions to operations. Setting a target reduction of 50 percent of the annual 48,000 invoice adjustments, the profit-oriented organization expects to cut costs and move customers to more cost effective self-servicing on its web site. Given that the cost of a sales representative visit to a client is about $200 to $300 and the cost of a web site transaction is about 5 cents, the advantages of building revenues through the web site—once the sales staff has established the client relationship— become crystal clear.

Wynne Powell, the president of London Drugs Ltd. (**www.londondrugs.com**), is confident that the western Canadian retail chain will be able to measure the effectiveness of its CRM system solution by comparing the customer satisfaction metrics gathered for the past 22 years with results in the future. And rather than looking for fast returns on its investment in terms of improved profitability, management is confident that the CRM solution will produce noticeable results gradually over the years.[1]

This final chapter of the textbook concludes our discussion of the planning process by looking at how the e-business plan is implemented and then controlled by the firm. We will examine performance measurements that may be used to evaluate how well the firm is achieving its set objectives, as defined in the plan, and the control mechanisms that should guide changes and adjustments in the future.

Implementation of the e-Business Plan

implementation

Carrying out the actual tasks that must be done in order to realize the goals and objectives established in the e-business plan.

Implementation refers to carrying out the actual tasks that must be done in order to realize the goals and objectives established in the e-business plan. Implementation requires coordinated managerial action using all of the organization's resources—informational, financial, material, and human—and the procedural systems that direct how work is done within the firm. The implementation stage of the plan specifies who will perform each task; what special skills, training, supervision, or motivation each person should have; when the work will be scheduled in the firm's overall timetable; the costs associated with the work; how communication between employees will be established; and so forth.

According to research by the Gartner Group, half of all CRM projects fail because management does not properly implement the transition to the new

FIGURE 12.1 Gantt Chart of CRM Software and Computer Installation

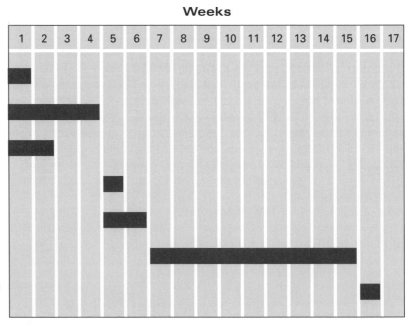

system. Key departments may be left out of the decision-making process, and customer expectations may not be incorporated into the plan. Companies need to take a realistic approach to the complexity of rolling out a system if it is to have a chance of succeeding. They must take into consideration the expectations of users and the difficulties that may ensue from a switch in procedures.[2]

Project Management Scheduling Tools

Scheduling the work that needs to be completed and identifying who will be responsible for each task can be accomplished using a variety of tools, such as Gantt charts and Program Evaluation and Review Technique (PERT) diagrams, as illustrated in Figures 12.1 and 12.2. Gantt charts and PERT diagrams provide project managers with a visual understanding of the sequence of activities and the time required to complete all of the planned activities. Some work may be able to be done simultaneously, as indicated by parallel time lines, while in other cases certain tasks will need to be completed before the next stage in the plan can be started. For instance, installation of computer software and its integration with the firm's back-office system cannot begin until any required new computer hardware has been installed.

FIGURE 12.2 PERT Diagram of CRM Software and Computer Installation

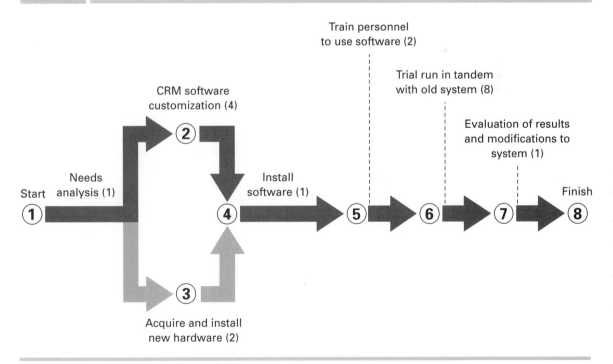

PERT diagrams also provide a clearer understanding of the *critical path* for the project, which is the series of events from start to finish that will take the longest. The critical path not only measures the minimum amount of time required to complete the project but also highlights those activities that can delay the entire project if they are not completed as scheduled. Experienced management consultants can often predict within a reasonable margin of error how long it will take to roll out a new installation for their clients. Often, however, problems can arise that will cause delays and missed expected task completion dates.

Implementation timetables comprise timetables at the corporate, divisional, and operational levels of the firm. Each timetable includes the level of detail appropriate for the managers who are responsible for seeing that the work is carried out successfully. At the operational level, names of individual employees and of others who could replace them if they are not available when the tasks are scheduled might be included to facilitate implementation and reduce the risk of problems caused by a lack of available skilled employees. Furthermore, detailed planning schedules can help management estimate the time and resources required for future work of a similar nature. By comparing the actual results with the detailed original estimates, management can learn how to estimate the complexities of the process and make more accurate assessments of the work to be done. This is especially important for management consulting firms, as they must prepare bids for services they will be expected to deliver to their customers. By examining historical data, management can learn from past errors in judgment and develop more accurate forecasts of the problems that can arise when complex projects are implemented.

Problems and Solutions

According to recent research, as many as two-thirds of software-related projects such as the customization and installation of a CRM system fail to meet their planned delivery dates and budgets. Furthermore, about half of major projects are eventually cancelled as a result of loss of control.[3] These failures to properly plan, implement, and control projects contribute to managers' unwillingness to undertake the risk of major spending projects, especially those whose contributions to profitability or productivity might be questionable. To avoid problems and disappointments as much as possible, a well-thought-out implementation strategy will consider the real time and costs entailed in delivering the project as well as the expected benefits. If customer satisfaction ratings are expected to improve after implementation of a CRM installation, then levels of customer satisfaction should be measured before and after the work is done in order to methodically document the effect of the entire effort.

Problems with the implementation of plans are normal. Planning should be flexible so as to accommodate circumstances that might arise when the time comes to put the plan into action. Since the environmental forces that can influence strategic planning are assumed to be continuously changing, it is to be expected that any plan will require some modification once it is removed from the discussion table and put into practice in the real world. Sometimes environmental changes can be extreme and happen quickly, as was the case with the sudden fall in demand for telecommunications equipment in 2001. Few analysts—experts included—predicted the dramatic halt in new orders from firms like Cisco Systems, Lucent Technologies, and Nortel Networks. As a result of the chain reaction, business plans had to be drastically adjusted at all of these firms and at other firms that were to a greater or lesser degree affected by the sudden fall in technology equipment buying.

Problems also typically arise during implementation of the business plan if the responsibilities for planning and implementation have been separated. Planning is often limited to the corporate and division levels of the firm, with operational-level employees, who generally are the ones who are expected to carry out the assigned tasks, being left out of the planning process. In some instances, higher-level planners might call for some activity that operational staff would quickly dismiss for good reasons. However, the planners do not learn of the difficulties with these activities until problems develop during the implementation of the plan, and information about this reaches them. To avoid delays and budget overspending, planners need to include people at the operational level in the planning process.

Control of the e-Business Plan

control

Management's efforts to monitor, measure, evaluate, and modify the e-business project as needed while it is being implemented in order to ensure the delivery of what is planned.

Control refers to management's efforts to monitor, measure, evaluate, and modify the e-business project as needed while it is being implemented in order to ensure the delivery of what was planned. To accomplish this task, performance objectives and standards for activities must be established. As the plan is implemented, comparisons with performance standards will indicate whether or not the plan is under control. Management will then have to adjust the plan and take corrective action to close any gap between what was planned and the actual events that are unfolding. For example, fraudulent use of credit cards is a growing concern, especially with the growth in Internet-based purchasing. According to research by GartnerG2 of Stamford, Connecticut, $700 million in online sales were lost to credit card fraud in 2001, corresponding to about 1 percent of the $61.8 billion total annual online purchases; online fraud was 19 times as high, dollar for dollar, as fraud resulting from off-line sales. Furthermore, according to Meridian Research, nearly 10 percent of all Internet transactions are suspect, suggesting that costs to banks will cause them to boost charges to merchants unless the problem can be better controlled.[4]

If planning was done well in the first place, adjustments can be expected but radical changes will not be necessary. If radical changes are called for, then a full audit should be done to establish whether the planning process was flawed because of poor research, poor communications, poor information, poor decision making and judgment on the part of management, or some other reason, such as radical changes in the environment that are beyond managers' control. Certainly the rapid collapse of e-business activity in 2001 qualifies as a reason many

e-Business Insight

Internet Allows Fund-Raising Organizations to Control Donations After September 11, 2001

According to AOL Time Warner's not-for-profit online clearinghouse Helping.org (**www.helping .org**), the spectacular surge in online giving after the attacks on the World Trade Center and Washington, D.C., helped fund-raising organizations control the massive amount of data collection necessary to process these gifts. More than half of all donations—amounting to more than $500 million—during the first few days after the attack were made online. By comparison, a 1999 survey by Independent Sector, a Washington-based agency that tracks U.S. philanthropy, reported that less than 1 percent of the $200 billion donated to charities was normally made online prior to September 11, 2001. This change in donor behavior has prompted organizations to look more closely at using the Internet to act as a vehicle for raising funds, maintaining better long-term communication with donors, and controlling the donation collection process. As with profit-oriented businesses, where established brand recognition is important, the agencies that are expected to benefit most from using the Internet are well-established organizations like the American Red Cross and the United Way.[5]

business plans failed to meet managers' and shareholders' expectations. Everyone in the organization should learn from the experience with the goal of returning better prepared to the planning process.

Setting Performance Objectives and Standards

performance objectives
The targeted results of activity, to be achieved through implementation of the e-business plan.

performance standards
More specific points that might be set by the firm or by the industry of which it is a part.

Performance objectives are the targeted results of activity, to be achieved through implementation of the e-business plan, whereas **performance standards** are more specific reference points that might be set by the firm or by the industry of which it is a part. For example, a performance objective for the installation of a CRM system might include improvements in customer service by reducing wait times for placing orders with customer service representatives, whereas a performance standard might be expressed as reducing customer wait time to no more than 2 minutes. According to a recent J. D. Powers study, automobile dealers' web sites are getting better and better at achieving their primary objectives: selling cars online and allowing customers to be more informed and better prepared when they visit dealerships in order to close sales. Sales online increased by 20 to 30 percent from 2000 to 2001, and data indicate that automobile dealers have a higher close ratio when customers are referred to them by manufacturers' web sites. Although independent automobile web site operators like Autobytel (**www.autobytel.com**) and Microsoft's CarPoint (**http://carpoint.msn.com/homepage/ default.asp**) enjoyed early leads in developing online customer relationships and brand recognition, the trend is clearly favoring manufacturers as car customers learn to use the manufacturers' web sites to better understand their considered

metrics
Measurements used to gauge performance and evaluate how well the firm is achieving its set objectives as defined in the e-business plan.

financial metrics
Such things as increases in return on investment (ROI), profitability, sales revenue, profit margins, operating income, earnings per share, cash flow, and market share and reductions in expenses; they are readily measured outcomes and are particularly important to shareholders.

balanced scorecard
An approach to strategic control that calls for also recognizing the contributions to building a competitive advantage in the marketplace that are made by improved efficiency, quality, innovation, and responsiveness to customers.

efficiency metrics
Metrics that focus on the internal operations of the firm, such as the reduction of the time spent entering a customer's order online and other costs associated with the order.

quality metrics
Metrics that measure improvements in the firm's products and services, such as a reduction in the number of complaints the firm receives from unhappy customers.

purchase and even—in growing numbers—to make their purchase online. Furthermore, the study suggests that the Internet is an efficient way to keep in touch with customers and is also a hit with dealers, whose level of satisfaction with manufacturers' web sites continues to increase.[6]

Measuring and Evaluating Performance Results

Performance objectives and performance standards are critical if there is to be any possibility of evaluating performance results and thereby learning from the planning experience. **Metrics** are measurements used to gauge performance and evaluate how well the firm is achieving its set objectives as defined in the e-business plan. For example, research suggests that many retailers have yet to come to grips with the task of designing an online shopping site that is attractive and functional for all global customers. According to a study by Forrester Research, 46 percent of all orders to U.S.-based sites placed by people living outside the United States went unfilled because of process failures. Given that the Forrester study suggests that the average web site gets 30 percent of its traffic and 10 percent of its orders from non-U.S. customers, these results suggest an enormous loss of potential export sales that will continue until web sites better reflect local buyer culture and behavior. Together, these metrics suggest that once this huge gap is filled, profitability will be greatly improved.[7]

Financial metrics—such as increases in return on investment (ROI), profitability, sales revenue, profit margins, operating income, earnings per share, cash flow, and market share and reductions in expenses—are readily measured outcomes and are particularly important to shareholders. A study by the Framingham, Massachusetts, research group IDC (**www.idc.com**) revealed that 80 percent of potential buyers planned to use ROI to evaluate application service provider (ASP) installations. Furthermore, a study of fifty-four ASP installations of CRM, SCM, and other software solutions showed that the five-year ROI was 404 percent. Interestingly, IDC found that more than 56 percent of the firms surveyed reported an ROI greater than 100 percent and that 12 percent experienced an ROI of more than 1000 percent. The average reported initial investment by firms was $399,000 and their average total expenditure for ASP installations reached $4.2 million. However, the average payback period was only 1.33 years.[8]

R. S. Kaplan and D. P. Norton's **balanced scorecard** approach to strategic control calls for also recognizing the contributions to building a competitive advantage in the marketplace that are made by improved efficiency, quality, innovation, and responsiveness to customers.[9] **Efficiency metrics** focus on the internal operations of the firm, such as the reduction of the time spent entering a customer's order online and other costs associated with the order. If orders are entered 20 percent faster, then the same number of service representatives can handle more orders each hour or the company can lower its costs by reducing the number of representatives it employs. **Quality metrics** measure improvements in the firm's products and services, such as the actual download and upload speeds available from an Internet service provider during peak demand periods. A quality metric for service improvements could be the reduction in the number of complaints

innovation metrics
Metrics that measure how quickly the firm can handle the introduction of new products based on changing customer needs.
responsiveness-to-customers metrics
Metrics that measure how well the firm is responding to its customers' needs; these metrics include retention rates and measures of customer loyalty and satisfaction with the firm's services in general, determined by periodic surveys.

the firm receives from unhappy customers. **Innovation metrics** measure how quickly the firm can handle the introduction of new products based on changing customer needs. And finally, **responsiveness-to-customers metrics** measure how well the firm is responding to its customers' needs; these metrics include retention rates and measures of customer loyalty and satisfaction with the firm's services in general, determined by periodic surveys. Metrics like these help define the successes of e-business projects. For example, a recent study showed that less than 1 percent of the more than $1 trillion of government transactions take place over the Internet. IBM put Arizona's vehicle-registration program online and turned the average wait time from 45 minutes to only 3. Furthermore, the cost of registration to the state fell from $6.60 to $1.60, saving the motor bureau about $1.25 million each year. In exchange, IBM earned $1 on each transaction. Clearly, these metrics suggest that more government services will be moving onto the Internet in the future.[10]

Taking Corrective Actions

Performance measurements are needed to allow the firm to know whether or not the implementation of the planned strategies is working as expected. If the gap between planned and actual results is sufficiently wide, then managers should take the necessary corrective action to close the gap, or even consider reexamining the entire planning process if the strategy no longer is realistic or desirable. In this way, progress toward the successful delivery of the plan can be documented and information that may be useful to the development of newly emerging plans can be directed to those who can incorporate these findings into the ongoing planning process, as illustrated in Figure 12.3.

e-Business Insight
Conversion Rate—A Comprehensive Measure of Web Site Performance

According to venture capitalist William Gurley of Benchmark Capital Inc. (**www.benchmark.com**), the most important and comprehensive web site performance metric to look at is the *conversion rate,* or the percentage of visitors to a site that become respondents to offers and activities presented on their screen. If, for example, the conversion rate of visitors to an e-tailing site like Amazon.com were to increase from 2 to 3 percent,

this would translate into an increase in sales revenues of 50 percent. Gurley argues that no other comprehensive metric does as well at measuring the attractiveness or user-friendliness of the interface design, the performance of the site, the convenience of use, the effectiveness of advertising in design and targeting customers, the overall popularity of the site, and the number of visitors who tell others about their satisfaction with the site. According to Gurley, 10 percent or more would be a high conversion rate, while an average might be closer to 3 to 5 percent. Below 2 percent would be considered poor overall performance.[11]

FIGURE 12.3   The Strategic Planning Process

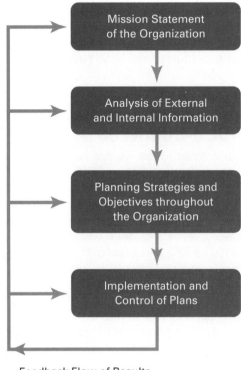

Feedback Flow of Results

After establishing the organization's mission statement, analysis of relevant information leads to the development of strategic plans and their subsequent implementation by the firm. Feedback links assure the continuous incorporation of new information at all steps of the process.

Conclusions

Implementation and controlling activities complete the strategic planning process cycle, as illustrated in Figure 12.3. After creating and implementing their e-business plan for the first time, managers must continually weigh ongoing research and results and then integrate this information into a revised plan for the future. Consider what AOL's first business plan might have looked like as it outlined the strategies that the firm would take to build up a large client base of customers requiring Internet connectivity services.

Today, undoubtedly the plan has evolved to incorporate not only the acquisitions of services and product content from ICQ and Time Warner but also a larger view of the future that reflects new technologies and a growing global market for Internet products and services.

Now that you have completed an examination of the principal concepts of the e-business strategic planning process, you are in a much better position to begin analyzing and reporting on current business strategies. Perhaps you even feel confident enough to begin the process of researching and preparing a plan of your own. Whether the plan involves adding an e-business dimension to an existing business operation or the start-up of an entirely new business, you can feel confident that the critical concepts and procedures have been cov-

ered—the rest is in the details and being right. To help in this regard, the appendices to this book offer a model e-business plan that was actually used to launch a small firm, and also a guide to help you prepare your own plan.

CASE STUDY — RETURN TO INSIDE e-BUSINESS

In sharp contrast to the general perception that any new e-business installation will produce only improved efficiencies and positive outcomes, the results of the attempt to implement a supply-chain management solution at Canada's second largest food retailer, Sobeys Inc. (**www.sobeys.com**), should serve as a warning and indicate how bad things can get even when management is fully behind a project, top-level consultants are engaged, and top-quality software is deployed. After a year of technical difficulties, system crashes that resulted in inventory outages, and repeated failures on the part of SAP Inc.'s (Europe's largest software supplier) technical staff to successfully bring the system online and make it operational, and failing to see any end to

the continuing problems with the system, Sobeys finally scrapped the entire project, writing off more than $90 million in cost to profits.[12]

Although disaster stories on the Sobeys' scale are not common, they underscore the danger of poor planning and implementation of e-business solutions.

ASSIGNMENT

1. What are some things that you have learned from this chapter that might explain why things went so wrong during the implementation of the Sobeys system?
2. How might a consulting firm like Cap Gemini Ernst & Young work with a firm's management to reduce the risks of such a large-scale disaster?

Chapter Review

SUMMARY

1. Examine how the e-business plan is implemented within the firm's organization structure and integrated into that structure.

Implementation refers to carrying out the actual tasks that must be done in order to realize the goals and objectives established in the e-business plan. Implementation requires coordinated managerial action using all of the organization's resources—informational, financial, material, and human—and the procedural systems that direct how work is done within the firm. The implementation stage of the plan specifies who will perform each task; what special skills, training, supervision, or motivation each person should have; when the work will be scheduled in the firm's overall timetable; the costs associated with the work; how communication between employees will be established; and so forth. Problems with the implementation of plans are normal. Planning should be flexible so as to accommodate circumstances that might arise when the time comes to put the plan into action. Since the environmental forces that can influence strategic planning are assumed to be continuously changing, it is to be expected that any plan will require some modification once it is removed from the discussion table and put into practice in the real world.

2. **Describe how management controls the e-business plan by setting performance objectives and standards, measuring and evaluating results, and directing future actions and decisions.**

Control refers to management's efforts to monitor, measure, evaluate, and modify the e-business project as needed while it is being implemented in order to ensure the delivery of what is planned. To accomplish this task, performance objectives and standards for activities must be established. As the plan is implemented, comparisons with performance standards will indicate whether or not the plan is under control. Management will then have to adjust the plan and take corrective action to close any gap between what was planned and the actual events that are unfolding. Performance objectives are the targeted results of activity to be achieved through implementation of the e-business plan, whereas performance standards are more specific reference points that might be set by the firm or by the industry of which it is a part. Performance objectives and performance standards are critical if there is to be any possibility of evaluating performance results and thereby learning from the planning experience. Financial results—such as increases in return on investment, profitability, sales revenue, profit margins, cash flow, and market share and reductions in expenses—are readily measured outcomes. However, R. S. Kaplan and D. P. Norton's balanced scorecard approach to strategic control calls for also recognizing the contribution to building a competitive advantage in the marketplace that are made by improved efficiency, quality, innovation, and responsiveness to customers.

REVIEW QUESTIONS

1. What does implementation of the e-business plan involve?
2. What is a Gantt chart?
3. How is a Gantt chart used in the implementation of the e-business plan?
4. What is a PERT diagram?
5. How is a PERT diagram used in the implementation of the e-business plan?
6. What does control of the e-business plan involve?
7. What is meant by performance objectives and performance standards?
8. What are metrics?

DISCUSSION QUESTIONS

1. What are some of the difficulties associated with implementation of an e-business plan?
2. Explain why implementation of the e-business plan requires organizationwide involvement in order to assure success.
3. Describe the steps in the control process.
4. What might explain a gap between planned performance and actual results?

Building Skills for Career Success

EXPLORING THE INTERNET

The need for radical changes in a firm's existing e-business plans is perhaps most obvious when the core of the firm's current strategy is failing. For instance, after implementing its plan, Napster was sued in the U.S. courts over copyright violations. In many respects, management's ability to control future events quickly evaporated as the courts ordered Napster to modify its e-business plan to comply with international copyright law. Similarly, web sites like Yahoo! that based their strategies on increasing web-advertising revenues have also been faced with the need to radically rethink many of their core assumptions. Examine the web site of a firm that has recently undergone a fundamental revision of its e-business thinking. You can find one by researching one of the many online journals and information gateways, such as CNET (**www.cnet.com**).

ASSIGNMENT
1. Describe the reasons that changes to the e-business plan are needed.
2. How is the firm planning to change its current e-business plan?

DEVELOPING CRITICAL THINKING SKILLS

Some analysts have suggested that where advertising expenditures are concerned, the definition of ROI needs to be expanded beyond simple sales and profits. For instance, Internet advertising might be evaluated as part of an overall integrated media campaign to build brand awareness, identity, and loyalty. To measure these effects properly, changes need to be collected and monitored over a longer period of time using databases of customer information, for which the Internet is an ideal tool, as it provides a two-way channel for communication with customers.

ASSIGNMENT
1. Select an e-commerce web site that you are familiar with, such as Yahoo!, and develop five online survey questions that could be asked of visitors to help measure the changes in the brand equity.
2. As a manager, what other changes would you want to measure over time?

BUILDING TEAM SKILLS

According to a Jupiter Media Metrix (**www.jmm.com**) survey, 36 percent of Internet users would visit a content site more often if it featured a customized layout that allowed the user to select and personalize the content displayed on the screen. Users were particularly interested in customizing financial and news content. Furthermore, according to Datamonitor (**www .datamonitor.com**), global investment in personalization technologies will grow from $500 million in 2001 to $2.1 billion in 2006.[13] Suppose your group were asked to help design a menu that would allow personalization of a web site targeted to students attending your school. Explore a variety of web sites that provide customization of selections such as local news and weather.

ASSIGNMENT
1. Select a web site and identify the web site you have chosen.
2. Create at least three categories of menu choices that would provide personalization and explain why they would make the site more attractive to
   users.

RESEARCHING DIFFERENT CAREERS

A variety of careers are available in the IT industry. Software development
firms like PeopleSoft (**www.peoplesoft.com**), Siebel Systems (**www.siebel.com**),
and SAP (**www.sap.com**) will post positions that they are looking to fill on
their web site, including everything from direct selling of large-scale software
systems to providing customer support online. These different positions require different specialized training, skills, personality, and ambition. This is
especially true where writing customized software code or designing user-
friendly input and output screens is required. Some people might be well
suited for one type of job and not another. In addition to the technical side of
design, the roles played by content experts who prepare the specialized content that appears online and experts who understand how users are likely to
interact with the different screen designs and information flows presented
are also important. Select a firm that you are familiar with and explore the
job opportunities available there. Select one job that you are interested in.

ASSIGNMENT
1. Write a short cover letter addressed to the firm, identifying the position
   that you want to be considered for.
2. Prepare a curriculum vitae that includes details that support your claim to
   be a good candidate for this job.

IMPROVING COMMUNICATION SKILLS

Implementation and control of IT solutions is complex. For example, the
launch of a CRM solution requires understanding and commitment by many
people across all levels of the firm. Gantt charts and PERT diagrams can help
communicate the plan and the set scheduling. Choose an IT project for a
firm and consider the implementation issues involved.

ASSIGNMENT
1. Create a Gantt chart and a PERT diagram to explain the implementation
   of the solution.
2. Write a descriptive letter to one group of employees that explains why the
   firm is adopting the solution and how it will help them in their jobs.

Exploring Useful Web Sites

These web sites provide information related to the topics discussed in the chapter. You can learn more by visiting them online and examining their current data.

1. Cap Gemini Ernst & Young (**www.cgey.com**) is one of the largest management and IT consulting firms in the world.

2. Marriott Hotels (**www.marriott.com**), Canada Post (**www.canadapost.ca**), and London Drugs Ltd. (**www.londondrugs.com**) have all successfully implemented CRM solutions. The experience of Sobeys Inc. (**www.sobeys .com**), Canada's second largest food retailer, should serve as a warning and indicate how bad things can get even when management is fully behind a project, top-level consultants are engaged, and top-quality software is deployed. After a year of technical difficulties, system crashes that resulted in inventory outages, and repeated failures on the part of SAP Inc. (**www.sap.com**), Europe's largest software solution provider, the project was scrapped. Competing software development firms are PeopleSoft (**www.peoplesoft.com**) and Siebel Systems (**www.siebel.com**).

3. IDC (**www.idc.com**), Jupiter Media Metrix (**www.jmm.com**), and Datamonitor (**www.datamonitor.com**) are IT research firms. CNET (**www.cnet .com**) is a research and information gateway for the IT industry.

4. Helping.org (**www.helping.org**) is AOL Time Warner's not-for-profit online clearinghouse.

5. Autobytel (**www.autobytel.com**) and Microsoft's CarPoint (**http://carpoint .msn.com/homepage/default.asp**) are independent automobile web site operators.

6. According to venture capitalist William Gurley of Benchmark Capital Inc. (**www.benchmark.com**), the most important and comprehensive web site performance metric to look at is the conversion rate of visitors to a site into respondents to offers and activities presented on the screen.

U-Swap.com: A Comprehensive Case Study

Appendix A

This appendix presents a comprehensive case study of an actual e-business start-up, using a modified version of the firm's original e-business plan. The case study incorporates all of the vital areas of the business that have been discussed in the textbook. Students can learn a great deal about strategic thinking and practice by exploring a business plan and contemplating the thinking that went into its preparation.

While reading the case study, consider how many conditions may have changed since the plan was created and the best choices for future actions. After reading the case study, write a report that evaluates the firm's strategic thinking at the time the plan was written and recommends a future course of action based on current business conditions. Use references to models and vocabulary from the case and the textbook to back up your statements. Do not simply repeat or summarize the content presented in the case study. The idea behind writing a case study report is to add new information to what is already known. This can be criticism of what was done in the past, a revised set of recommendations for the future, or a combination of the two.

Comprehensive Case Study
and
Model e-Business Plan
adapted from information provided by

Local Student Classifieds

Disclosure

The following is intended for educational purposes only and is meant to complement the content developed in the textbook *e-Business: Strategic Thinking and Practice.* It is designed to provide students with a practical but simplified model of how ideas may be developed into practical business plans. Although inspired by the firm's original business thinking, many content items in this document, particularly financial data, have been modified or excluded in order to both provide learners with an easier-to-understand plan and to respect the confidentiality of the firm and its investors. The author wishes to express gratitude for the kind assistance of Mr. Eduardo Mandri, president and CEO of U-Swap Inc.

This document contains confidential and proprietary information belonging exclusively to U-Swap Inc. It may not be reproduced, transmitted, or shared in any manner or format without the prior written approval of U-Swap Inc. This business plan does not imply an offering of securities.

Table of Contents

Executive Summary

Company Overview

The U-Swap web site, www.U-Swap.com, was launched in September 1999. The company offers an online classified site through which college and university students can buy, sell, or exchange (swap) their articles and services. Students logging on to U-Swap.com are presented with a list of virtual communities identified by individual school names. U-Swap was an instant success, capturing the attention of approximately 10 percent of the student population of its original two campus sites after only one month of operation. The firm has expanded to 31 schools in North America and Europe and has grown to become the leading provider of local student classifieds in Canada.

Available in English, French, and Spanish, U-Swap was custom designed to meet the needs of college and university students. The site features categories that are not found in traditional classifieds, such as textbooks, as well as advanced features such as key word search, comparative shopping, auto-notify agents, and multimedia capabilities. The site now reaches over 10 percent of the total student population on campuses served.

The company was conceived and is run by two McGill University MBA graduates, four university graduates, and a growing network of more than 30 local Campus Representatives and Chapter Affiliates. It has alliances with student portals and other web sites. U-Swap is backed by Internet investment company VC Inc.[1] and is supported by a seasoned board of advisors.

Business Concept

Students represent a very lucrative market. According to Jupiter research, the 16 million American students spend approximately $35 billion each year. Over 85 percent of these cost-conscious individuals buy and sell secondhand goods on a regular basis. Students seek a fast, effective way of completing these transactions with someone in their community. U-Swap meets this need.

U-Swap's strength lies in its local, school-by-school approach. The company's team of Campus Representatives and Chapter Affiliates promotes the local chapters of the site in two ways: with smart, local on-campus advertising and via alliances with clubs and associations. U-Swap's local team ensures that we become an integral part of the community we serve, which results in a highly populated database of local ads. This unique community approach creates significant barriers of entry for new potential competitors and is easily implemented on a global basis.

---

[1] Other investments of VC Inc. include Mamma.com (meta-search engine) and Bam Solutions (online media).

Competitive Advantages of U-Swap

Website tailored to the local community
Highly populated database
Smart, cost-effective on-campus marketing
Team of Representatives and Affiliates
Lower customer acquisition costs
Strong management team and Board of Advisors

Competition

Surprisingly, U-Swap faces very little direct competition at this time. Even competitors such as student portals like College Club.com or Campus Access.com have only a fraction of the database that U-Swap has created, do not have a local, on-campus presence, nor are their web sites tailored to the specific needs of each student community.

Revenue Model

U-Swap has several revenue sources, including service fees from featured classifieds and banner advertising at both a local and a national level. Additional sources of revenue that exist for U-Swap include auction fees, referral sales, and marketing for third parties.

Current and Potential Sources of Revenue

Service Fees (Classifieds)
Auction Fees
Banner Advertising (Local and National)
Referral Sales
Marketing for Third Parties

Financial Overview

U-Swap anticipates revenues of approximately $5 million in four years to be generated from banner advertising, auction and classified fees, e-commerce partnerships, and special service fees, resulting in earnings before taxes of approximately $2 million. The company anticipates breaking even during the second year of the plan.

Company's Ownership

Management has retained a majority of the company's shares. Eduardo Mandri, President and CEO, and Allison L. Dent, Vice-President and COO, hold a majority of management's share of ownership.

The Company

After six months of development, U-Swap launched its online classified web site, u-swap .com, in the form of a beta test at McGill and Concordia Universities in September 1999. The site attracted the attention of approximately 10 percent of the student body, and visitor traffic has been growing exponentially since that time. Today, U-Swap is the leading provider of on-line student classifieds in North America.

U-Swap offers students a forum where they can buy, sell, and exchange virtually anything they want. U-Swap services the French, English, and Spanish communities and is available at 25 of Canada's largest universities. A team of six supports the day-to-day operations of U-Swap, and with auctions under development, U-Swap continues to expand its service offering and revenue sources. The company is now positioned to expand globally and expects to become the premier web site for student classifieds and auctions on an international basis.

The Business Model

U-Swap is based on a P2P community e-business model incorporating several revenue streams and services. Unlike geographically wide-reaching classified sites such as eBay, U-Swap is focused on serving the local student community associated with a single campus. U-Swap has a separate database for each university that is customized on a school-by-school basis. In doing so, U-Swap effectively tailors the system to the needs of each community, thereby providing a superior product for its users and competitive advantage.

U-Swap attracts students to the web site by offering free student classifieds and by using novel cost-effective advertising on campus. As detailed in the marketing section of this report, U-Swap has developed a comprehensive marketing campaign that is implemented and controlled by its team of Campus Representatives and Chapter Affiliates. These local students have in-depth knowledge specific to their campus and help U-Swap tailor the promotional approach needed to succeed.

Alliances with student portals, clubs, and associations further aid U-Swap's acceptance on and off campus. Various student societies promote U-Swap on their private web sites. As a result of these links and advertising, students are made more aware of U-Swap and recognize it as part of their community.

Users are attracted to their campus web site through eye-catching campus posters, campus newspaper advertising, the support of key influencing parties such as student clubs and associations, and by providing a superior product to any alternative choices. As illustrated below, traffic is an essential part of U-Swap's business model as a generator of revenues.

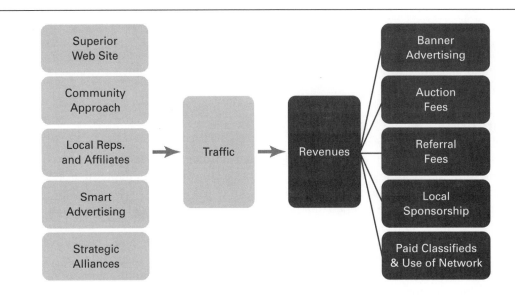

Current and Potential Revenue Streams

Several revenue streams support U-Swap's business model:

a) **Banner Advertising:** Given the targeted nature of the site, advertisers have been eager to purchase banner space on U-Swap. In recent months, U-Swap's banner inventory has been sold at an average cost per thousand impressions (CPM) of $25 (Canadian dollars). Large advertising and media agencies such as Cossette Communications and BBDO have repeatedly purchased U-Swap's banner inventory on behalf of clients such as Visa, General Motors, and Bell Canada.

b) **Auction Fees:** After the introduction of its auction module in January 2001, U-Swap began collecting user fees for successful transactions conducted over the site with a fee structure similar to that of eBay. Fees vary according to the type of item and category sections selected and are expected to yield an average of $3 per item sold.

c) **Local Sponsorships:** U-Swap's local campus approach and product category divisions into sections (i.e., computer hardware and software, sports equipment, etc.) attract the attention of local advertisers that wish to sponsor specific sections of the site. Sponsorships can take the form of banners on the right navigation bar of the web site, direct emails when a user registers or places an ad, coupon pages, or any other type of co-branding activities. While U-Swap's management team sells National Sponsorships, local sponsorships can be pursued by U-Swap's local network of Campus Representatives and Chapter Affiliates, providing an additional local incentive to generate revenues.

d) **Referral Sales:** Students using U-Swap are generally seeking used articles to purchase or specific services like tutoring and language instruction. By offering visitors direct links to vendors who sell the same type of items that are new, U-Swap can generate additional revenue through collaboration with retailers and other online sellers.

e) **Classified Fees:** As a means to increase the exposure and impact of users' advertising, U-Swap provides for the additional purchase of visibility options such as bolded ads, featured ads at the top of the results page, and so forth. Prices range between $3 and $5 depending on the section where the ad is posted and the type of visibility feature selected. U-Swap also earns posting fees from advertisers wishing to reach the student market through either the jobs or apartments for rent sections, where a $20 fee applies to these categories.

In the long run, banner advertising, local sponsorships, and auction fees are expected to remain the principal sources of revenue for the company, followed by classified fees and commissions from sales referred from the site. Please see the Financial Analysis Section of this report for more information regarding revenue mix.

The Web Site

The results of in-depth market research conducted at McGill University in June of 1999 helped define U-Swap's look and service offerings. The figure below provides an overview of the site's main sections (taken from U-Swap's web site).

Sections such as "Textbooks" or "Tutors and Lessons" which are not found on traditional web sites are the backbone of U-Swap. Users appreciate the custom design of the site and have repeatedly praised U-Swap for being a "well developed, clear and easy to use web site."

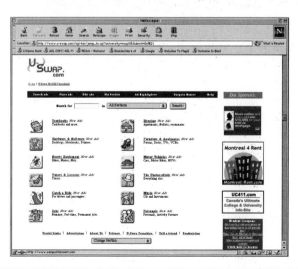

As extremely discriminatory consumers, students seek out sites that incorporate cutting-edge technology and design. U-Swap has successfully done this by incorporating a number of added value features into the web site. These include:

- ▶ **Multimedia Features:** upload photographs, sounds, or video.
- ▶ **Quick Search:** search the entire web site by using keywords.
- ▶ **Auto Notify:** be notified when a new ad matches your criteria.
- ▶ **Shopping List:** select items of interest for later review.

Target Market

University and college students constitute a large and untapped niche market. In United States and Canada, January 2000 enrollment figures were estimated to have reached 16 million and 1.4 million, respectively. The age range for these North American students is between 17 and 26 years of age. They are generally considered to be trendsetters and have a higher than average percentage of disposable income. Additionally, they are characterized as brand-sensitive consumers, tend to purchase higher-priced trendy items, and are heavily influenced by advertising. Jupiter Communications estimates that they constitute a market potential of over $35 billion annually.

Quick Facts About the Student Market
16 Million students in the U.S. alone
90% of students are currently online[1]
60% access the Internet every day[2]
85% buy and sell used items at least 3 or 4 times a year
$35 billion in annual discretionary spending[1]

By offering a service that is needed by these potential consumers, U-Swap has been able to tap into this lucrative niche market

Positioning

To illustrate how U-Swap's positioning strategy has been successful in the student-classified market, we can compare the company to potential competitors using two factors: degree of regional presence and database population (number of ads published). As can be seen from the positioning grid, U-Swap is the only web site that has both a local presence and a large database of ads. Even CollegeClub.com, the largest U.S. student portal with over 40 million dollars of investment, has a much smaller database than U-Swap.

---

[1] Jupiter Communication, 1999.

[2] *USA Today*, August 1999.

Competitors' Grid

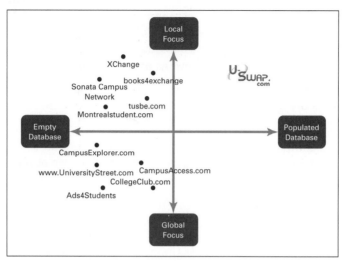

Competitive Analysis

U-Swap faces indirect competition from a variety of old and new forms of classified providers. Local newspapers and campus reviews often contain a classified section that could substitute for the services of U-Swap. Two types of web sites can also be considered indirect competitors: Student portals that sometimes offer classifieds as an extra feature (Campus Access), and local web projects developed by students (University Street). In the online world, however, the only alternative that provides unlimited access, that offers customized, local classifieds, and that hosts a large database of goods for sale is U-Swap.com.

Local Newspapers

Local or campus newspapers present students with an alternative method of buying and selling goods. These indirect competitors are slowly beginning to offer both print classifieds and online classifieds. Fees are charged by word or by line, and range from $10 to $30 per day for a small ad. Placing an ad can be done via phone or fax and generally must be requested at least 24 hours in advance. The categories available are generally not customized to the students' needs.

Student Portals

Student portals are web sites that strive to be the home page of all university students. These sites are generally content-driven and offer member benefits such as free Internet access or free email access. Examples of large student portals that offer classifieds as a subcategory of their site include the following:

- College Club.com
- Campus Access.com

Local Web Projects

Local web projects are small web sites that a student or group of students develop as a school project. Generally these sites are developed on limited budgets and are not promoted outside of their campus. Several of these local initiatives have recently popped up in different cities, but have a very limited user base. Examples of these include:

- Trading Grounds.com
- University Street.com
- Xchange.ca

Although U-Swap's competitors fail to match U-Swap's offering in several ways, for completeness, an in-depth analysis of each, as well as other smaller, less popular sites, is found in Appendix A of this document.

Competitive Advantages

U-Swap possesses many advantages when compared to other potential competitors. As the only site dedicated to serving the exchange (swapping) needs of students, U-Swap has three very hard-to-imitate advantages:

Competitive Advantages of U-Swap
Web site tailored to the local community
Highly populated database
Smart, cost-effective on campus marketing
Team of Representatives and Affiliates
Experienced Management Team and Board of Advisors

The site hosts an extremely large database of concurrent ads, having hosted over 15,000 as of December 2000. This number continues to grow exponentially.

U-Swap also has a strong local presence. Because U-Swap makes it easy for students to exchange goods and services with someone in their community, the company benefits from being accepted as part of the neighborhood.

U-Swap knows how to generate and drive traffic. The company is experienced with attracting students' attention and turning that interest into traffic. U-Swap has proven this ability and will continue to leverage this key factor as the company moves forward.

Furthermore, receiving four prestigious awards has honored U-Swap. The first, an award given by the CATA Alliance (Nortel Networks, The National Post, PriceWaterhouseCoopers, and Jaws Technologies), was awarded to U-Swap's co-founders **for Top Graduate Students in E-Commerce in Canada.** The second award is the **Laureat Octas,** an award given by the Quebec Federation of Technology in recognition of the company's co-founders use of information technology to contribute to student life. The third award is an **Award of Excellence** given by the Canadian Information Productivity Awards for U-Swap's unique use of technology and business approach and recognizing the company as one of **Canada's Top Small Businesses.** Finally, U-Swap was named **Top Young Enterprise.**

At a Glance				
Strengths	**U-Swap.com**	**Newspapers**	**Student Portals**	**Local Web Projects**
1st mover advantage	Yes	No	No	Yes
Local presence	Yes	Yes	No	Yes
Large database	Yes	No	No	No
Customized for students	Yes	No	Yes	No
Advanced features	Yes	No	Yes	No
Strong network	Yes	Yes	Sometimes	No

Marketing Strategy

A large part of U-Swap's success can be attributed to the firm's ability to develop innovative, eye-catching, and cost-effective advertising campaigns that leverage word-of-mouth advertising. U-Swap was careful to identify key hot spots on campus and then develop specific promotional material and events to leverage the local traffic of these areas and attract attention to the site.

Examples of marketing initiatives used by U-Swap include the following:

Offline:

- Handout style flyers
- Bulletin board posters
- Customized U-Swap Post-it notes
- U-Swap car covered with ads
- Direct calls by U-Swap team
- PR with local newspapers

On line:

- Links with key student associations and clubs
- Banner advertising on relevant local sites
- Alliances with portals to replace/become their classified section
- Direct email messages

Management Team and Board of Advisors

The U-Swap.com management team currently consists of the following people:

Eduardo Mandri
CEO/President

Co-founder of U-Swap, Eduardo has a broad range of experience in Finance, Marketing, Consulting, and International Business. As Financial Analyst for Lazard Freres Mexico he worked on the evaluation of large Mexican firms and analyzed business opportunities for foreign companies wishing to establish subsidiaries in Mexico. Two years later he joined Gillette and soon became the youngest Marketing Manager in the organization. Eduardo successfully developed four companies in Mexico, including a medium-sized Metropolitan Courier company, which he successfully sold in 1998. After moving to Montreal, he was a consultant for several projects involving software and Internet companies. Eduardo holds a Bachelor's degree in Business from Mexico's top business school (I.T.A.M) and an MBA from McGill University. Eduardo conceived the idea behind U-Swap and is currently in charge of strategic and financial planning, new technology development, investor relations, and oversees the technical operations of the web site.

Allison L. Dent
COO/Vice President

Allison holds an MBA from McGill University, as well as a Bachelor's degree in Commerce, with a concentration in Finance and a degree in Italian and Spanish from McGill University. Allison possesses a diverse managerial background in the areas of Finance, Strategy, and Information Technology. She began her career as a Finance/Business Consultant with Demers Beaulne and Associates while completing her studies at McGill and later moved to Vancouver to pursue a career in Banking with Bank of Montreal. Not long afterwards she was recruited by one of her corporate clients to become Management/IT Consultant for KnowledgeTech. Allison has also worked with numerous start-up and Internet companies securing financing and developing strategies, and has been a key member in initial stages of three successful web ventures: KnowledgeTech.ca, Bigheart.com, and Webdeveloper.com. Allison is cofounder of U-Swap and oversees all aspects of the business strategy, finance, accounting, legal issues, and media relations as well as marketing.

Thien Ta Trung
Senior Marketing Coordinator—Canada and France

Having worked as a Market Analyst for an International French Company in Paris and Shanghai, Thien has broad experience in the field of marketing. Thien holds a Bachelor's degree in Business with a concentration in Marketing from McGill University. As a management student, Thien earned the James McGill Award two consecutive years, a scholarship reserved for the faculty's top 5 percent. As U-Swap Marketing Coordinator, he is in charge of recruiting and managing the Campus Reps, conducting intelligence reports, developing strategic alliances with students' bodies, and carrying out promotional campaigns.

Board of Advisors

U-Swap's Board of Advisors comprises leading venture capital investment representatives and other highly knowledgeable individuals from the business community able to bring valuable strategic skills to the corporate planning and decision-making level of the company and help open doors to important meetings with potential partners, suppliers, and customers for management at all levels of the firm.

Strategic Development Plan

U-Swap is now prepared to expand globally. U-Swap has begun to penetrate the lucrative U.S. college and university student market by introducing its services at five different schools. In addition, U-Swap launched French and Mexican divisions of the web site in 2000 and anticipates a presence at 330 institutions by the end of September 2001. In total, U-Swap will approach a market of approximately 16.4 million students in four different countries using three different languages. U-Swap anticipates a penetration rate that will yield 1 million unique visitors per month by the year 2003.

Leveraging the success of its current business model, U-Swap has developed detailed divisional- and operational-level plans to manage the anticipated rapid expansion and ensure that it will yield the desired results at the local and corporate level. Each campus site will be treated as a division or strategic business unit (SBU) of the firm and the individual activities that generate revenues will be documented as operational- or functional-level plans. Below is an explanation of the key factors supporting U-Swap's strategic development plan.

Improve Product and Service Offerings

U-Swap will soon begin offering users the option of auctioning their products using Visual Auction software. This new state-of-the-art module offers significant added value for students selling items such as vehicles, sports equipment, and computer equipment, where bidding might bring higher prices and quicker sales of items.

Online classifieds and auctions are quickly becoming the standard for buying and selling products or services at virtual community sites. Furthermore, according to Forrester Research, the consumer-to-consumer auction market is expected to reach $19 billion by 2003.

> **Forrester names online auctions as one of the three emerging e-commerce models, as they are able to create the three critical C's for success on the web: Community, Content, and Commerce.**

Continue Implementing the Chapter Affiliate Program (e-franchising)

The company's successful Chapter Affiliate Program (CAP) will fuel U-Swap's strategic growth. Via this promotional venue, U-Swap will continue to develop and implement novel marketing campaigns as it has successfully done in the past.

Pursuit of More Partnerships

U-Swap intends to continue creating partnerships with key retailers particularly interested in reaching the student market such as consumer electronics vendor Future Shop and Ikea furniture outlets. Each partner would have a smart-banner that dynamically modifies according to users' search requests. U-Swap clients would benefit by having easy access to information on new articles identical to those being offered in the U-Swap classified databases. As mentioned in the Revenue section of this plan, the company would benefit from these alliances through a negotiated shared percentage of all sales generated through the site. Partnerships represent a mutually beneficial relationship for all parties and represent an important source of revenue growth and co-branding opportunities in the future.

Further Develop Network of Alliances

U-Swap's Campus Representatives and Chapter Affiliates operational plans detail how they will continue to work with clubs, student councils, and associations in order to ensure that the U-Swap web site is welcomed on campus. This approach will help create barriers to entry for competitors, smooth entry to new markets by validating our web site, help generate positive word-of-mouth promotion, ensure the right to advertise on campus, lead to the creation of direct links from student council web sites, and increase traffic. In addition, U-Swap will continue to develop alliances with student portals.

Expand the Management Team

U-Swap will continue expanding both its network of Campus Representatives and Chapter Affiliates, as well as its in-house management team. U-Swap already has a training program in place for each of these positions, as well as detailed job descriptions and established operational-level plans with specific objectives to direct activities. The section below provides a brief descriptive outline of team members and the role each plays in the U-Swap management organization structure.

Campus Representatives (CRs) and Chapter Affiliates (CAs)

U-Swap's organization will be built around a local CR or CA at each school campus. These individuals are generally students or groups of students that work with the team of Marketing Coordinators at the corporate level of the firm. Chapter Affiliates have exclusive rights to promote their campus site and share in the revenues generated from banner advertising and local sponsorship. This equity-based approach promotes motivation by local stakeholders. In contrast, Campus Representatives are paid an hourly wage and are responsible for implementing the marketing campaign activities at their campus, such as placing posters, distributing flyers, sending emails to clubs and associations, and so forth. Both parties provide valuable information to the corporate level regarding local market specifics such as competitors, vendors, and upcoming important events.

Campus Coordinators

The Campus Coordinators' key responsibilities include designing and implementing U-Swap's promotional corporate-level strategies, managing the team of Campus Representatives, and supporting the Chapter Affiliates' needs. Each coordinator will be expected to handle responsibilities overseeing operations at approximately ten campus sites.

Webmaster Team

The Webmaster team is responsible for overseeing the functionality of the site, responding to customer inquiries, and customizing the site on a school-by-school basis.

Implementation Schedule

➢ **September 20xx–December 20xx:** Launch site at selected new schools, solidify relationships on campuses, establish new schools via CAP, train new team members, design next marketing campaign, and implement new changes to site. Incorporate paid classifieds at campuses showing high penetration rates.

➢ **January 20xx–March 20xx:** Launch site at selected new schools, solidify relationships, and build local presence via marketing stunts. Develop new site modules and implement Auctions.

➢ **April 20xx–Onwards:** Continue growth via CAP, continue on build on-campus hype, establish next key penetration spots, build alliances and network.

Pro Forma Results and Financial Statements

1. School Presence Rate

By the end of the fourth year of this plan, U-Swap expects to have a presence in 1,098 schools across Canada, the United States, France, and Mexico. It is important to highlight the fact that the United States alone has over 1,500 campuses, leaving U-Swap with substantial opportunity to grow for years to come.

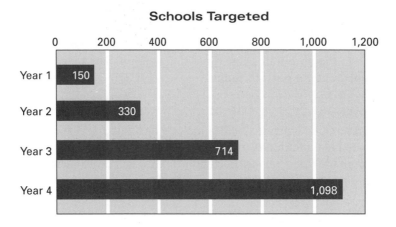

2. Penetration Rate

The penetration rate, which is defined as the proportion of all students at a campus using U-Swap, is expected to increase from 3.1 percent in year 2 to 6.6 percent in year 4. It is important to note that U-Swap has already reached and surpassed a 10 percent penetration rate at most of the schools where it has had a presence for more than four months, making this penetration projection credible and feasible.

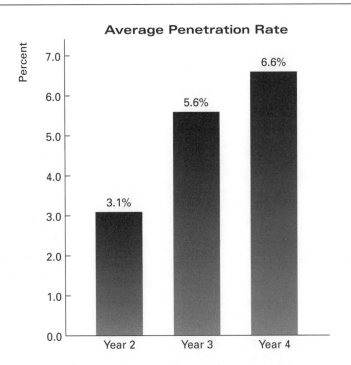

Average Penetration Rate

3. Unique Visitors

U-Swap expects to reach approximately 450,000 unique visitors per month by year 4 of this plan, based on an expected presence in more than 1,000 schools and growth in penetration rates.

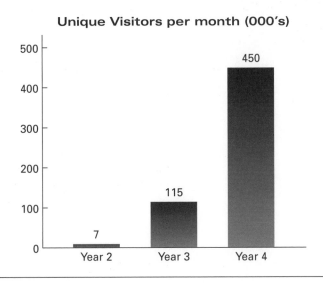

Unique Visitors per month (000's)

4. Distribution of Sales Revenues

Distributions of U-Swap's potential revenue from banner advertising, auction fees, local spon-sorships, and paid classified and referral fees are illustrated in the following graph. These proportions are expected to remain about the same over the life of the plan.

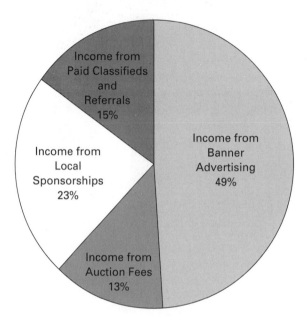

NOTE: Consolidated Pro Forma Statements of Income, Balance Sheets, and Cash Flows would appear here. Students are referred to model statements in Chapter 11.

Appendix A: Competitive Analysis

Competitor	Key Advantages	Key Disadvantages
Village Auction, Inc.	• Dedicated to auctions • Limited success in some U.S. schools • Decent site	• Unappealing site • Unpopulated database • Relatively new • Site often out of order
CollegeClub.com	• Leading portal for college students in the U.S. • Has substantial financial backing (+40 million) • The site has excellent content • Offers many advanced features such as email and voice messaging • Established since 1993 • Large network of students using the site • Offers an auction and classifieds sections	• Their classified and auction sections are not populated and have declined in popularity in past months • Major promotional initiatives limited to United States • Site hasn't been popular in Canada • Only in English • Company founder has recently resigned • Company is said to be in financial difficulties due to burn rate—cash flows
CollegeHQ.com	• U.S. classified site for students that is linked with geek.com and surfer.com • Based in Texas, created by IT/IS students • Site allows users to browse by university	• Site is unpopulated • Has had no promotion • Uses only one global database for all ads, although allows to browse by university • Only in English • Is a secondary business of founders
CampusAccess.com	• Well-developed U.S. and Canadian portal for university students • Smaller version of College Club.com (see above) • Esthetically pleasing and has good content	• Almost nonexistent classified database (has been stagnant for the last 8 months) • Young team with limited number of support staff • Only available in English
www.UniversityStreet.com	• Young, attractive-looking site tailored to university students • Run by two Concordia Commerce students • Strong presence at Concordia University	• Very limited number of users and ads • Very limited marketing • Functionality of site is questionable • Only available in English
Sonata Campus Network	• Portal for specific universities in Canada: U of T and UBC • Very pleasing for users	• Classified database is unpopulated • Fair content • Available at two universities only
tusbe.com	• Large database of books • Focused on exchange of books • Good search engine	• Limited to Toronto area with minimal success • Restricted to offering book exchange forum • Only available in English

Competitor	Key Advantages	Key Disadvantages
XChange	<ul><li>Bilingual site</li><li>Facilitates exchange of textbooks for university and college students</li><li>Fair database books</li><li>Appealing site</li><li>Brand-name sponsorship</li></ul>	<ul><li>Charges users a fee by semester or by year</li><li>Limited to textbooks</li><li>Very limited promotion and access to site</li></ul>
Ads4Students	<ul><li>Ontario-based classified site</li><li>Used good software to build site (same as U-Swap)</li><li>Unique database for each school</li></ul>	<ul><li>Unappealing design and coloring of site</li><li>Time to load site lengthy</li><li>Very new team</li><li>Much is unpopulated</li></ul>
books4exchange	<ul><li>Targeted university students in Canada</li><li>Great name, easy to remember</li><li>Good site functionality</li><li>Large database of books (only at McGill)</li><li>Offers an easy-to-use user interface</li></ul>	<ul><li>Facilitates the exchange of textbooks only</li><li>Is limited by design and name</li><li>Has shown very limited growth</li><li>Lacks infrastructure</li><li>Site not in French</li></ul>

Researching and Preparing an e-Business Plan

Appendix B

This appendix presents a summary of the key steps involved in researching and preparing an e-business plan, and identifies several web sites that can be explored to find additional information. The structured format and guiding questions are designed to help students build a strategic e-business plan for a start-up operation or as an addition to an existing business plan.

Before a business plan is written, research and discussion among team members should focus on answering these questions:

- What is the fundamental purpose and nature of the e-business strategy?
- What are the basic business model and revenue streams going to be?
- What are the industry-level forces at work that are affecting customers, suppliers, and competitors?
- How will the plan create a sustainable competitive advantage for the firm?
- Who are our target customers and what do we know about their behavior, both online and off?
- How much time and money is this plan going to require?
- Who will do the required work, and when?
- How will management implement, monitor, and control efforts to achieve the plan's objectives?

Outline for Writing the e-Business Plan

1. *Cover Page:* The cover page should include the title of the document, the name of the firm, the authors of the report, the date, and any other descriptive information that highlights the intended audience and use of the report.
2. *Introduction:* The introduction should provide a basic description of the firm and the purpose of the report.
3. *Executive Summary:* The executive summary is written last and should contain the highlights of the entire report. Since reports can typically be anywhere from twenty to one hundred or more pages long, executives often read the executive summary to assess whether it is worth their while to read the rest of the report. A good rule of thumb is for the length of the executive summary to be about 10 percent of the total length of the report; so that a twenty-page report might have a two-page summary.
4. *Environmental Analysis:* This section of the report should examine all of the relevant external environmental forces discussed in the first module of the text, including globalization, sociocultural, demographic, economic, competitive, intermediary and supplier, technological, and political and legal forces. Michael Porter's five-forces model, discussed in chapter 6, is particularly useful here. In addition to the external environmental forces that are at work, the report should examine the relevant internal environmental forces, including the firm's management and organizational structure, human resources, informational and knowledge resources, and financial and material resources.
5. *e-Business Model:* A full description of the e-business model and all revenue streams should be presented, along with the rationale for how the plan will create a sustainable competitive advantage.
6. *Marketing:* Here the plan should expand on marketing-related details, such as who the targeted customers are, what we know about their behavior, how the firm plans to modify the current marketing mix of strategies to incorporate any new online activities, and so forth.
7. *Management and Organizational Issues:* This section should provide details such as who will do what specific work, how the organization's communications system will function, and so forth. Documentation and display tools such as Gantt charts and PERT diagrams (discussed in Chapter 12) may be useful here.
8. *Finance:* This section of the plan will probably have three- to five-year financial projections using pro forma income statements, balance sheets, and statements of cash flows, as discussed in Chapter 11. In addition, detailed calculations of breakeven or schedules related to other financial projections along with descriptive interpretations would be presented here.
9. *Conclusion:* A short conclusion, similar in length to the introduction section, should bring the report to a close. It might include suggested action by individuals or a timeline for acting upon the recommendations in the report.

10. *Appendix:* The appendix should contain any supplementary information that would be useful to the reader, such as a sample questionnaire used to gather research data, documents used to prepare the report, and so forth.

Suggested Online Sources of Information for Writing an e-Business Plan

Many suggested outlines for writing a business plan are available on the Internet from consulting firms, government agencies, and financial institutions. Use the information provided by them and any sample plans posted to their sites to learn more about different approaches and styles before preparing your report.

1. U.S. Small Business Administration (**www.sba.gov/starting/indexbusplans.html**)
2. Canada Business Service Centres (**www.cbsc.org/osbw/busplan.html**)
3. American Express (**http://home3.americanexpress.com/smallbusiness/tool/biz_plan/ index.asp?Tools=%2Fsmallbusiness%2Ftool%2Fbiz_plan%2Findex.asp**)
4. Microsoft's bCentral site (**www.bcentral.com/articles/bizplans/101.asp**)
5. Royal Bank of Canada (**www.royalbank.com/business/bigidea/index.html**)
6. Bplans (**www.bplans.com**)
7. Spinoff Centre (**www.spinoffcentre.com/samplebusinessplan.html**)

Endnotes

Chapter 1

1. Based on information available from AOL online press releases. "America Online and Time Warner Announce New Content & Promotional Agreements," February 16, 2000, and "AOL & Time Warner Will Merge to Create World's First Internet-Age Media & Communications Company," January 10, 2000; **http://media.web.aol.com/media/search.cfm**.
2. For more information about e-business definitions, terminology, and strategies see IBM's web site, **www.ibm.com/ebusiness**.
3. Forrester Research, Inc., online glossary; **www.forrester.com**.
4. "U.S. Q4 e-Commerce Sales at $5.3B," *USA Today online*, March 2, 2000; **www.usatoday.com/money/economy/econ0059.htm**.
5. "Small Businesses Buy, but Shy to Sell, Online," May 17, 2000; **http://cyberatlas.internet.com/markets/professional/article/0,1323,5971_365281,00.html**.
6. Robyn Greenspan, "Small Biz Benefits from Internet Tools," March 28, 2002; **http://cyberatlas.internet.com/markets/smallbiz/article/0,,10098_1000171,00.html**.
7. Sue Zeidler, "Napster Lands Deal with MusicNet," *Financial Post*, June 7, 2001, p. C3.
8. "Online Music Sales Will Grow 520% to $6.2 Billion in 2006," Jupiter Media Metrix press release, New York, July 23, 2001; **www.jmm.com/xp/jmm/press/2001/pr_072301.xml**.
9. Special supplement in *Business Week*, February 28, 2000, p. 74.
10. Don Tapscott, "Online Parts Exchange Herald New Era," *Financial Post*, May 5, 2000, p. C7.
11. Spencer E. Ante, Amy Borrus, and Robert D. Hof, "In Search of the Net's Next Big Thing," *Business Week*, March 26, 2001, p. 141.
12. Bill Communications Inc., *Training Magazine*, October 1999; **www.trainingsupersite.com/publications/archive/training/1999/910/910high.htm**.
13. Forrester Research, Inc., "Global eCommerce Approaches Hypergrowth," April 18, 2000; **www.forrester.com/ER/Research/Brief/Excerpt/0,1317,9229,FF.html**.

14. Michael Pastore, "Why the Offline Are Offline," Cyberatlas July 14, 2001; **http://cyberatlas.internet.com/big_picture/demographics/article/0,,5901_784691,00.html#table**.
15. "Industry Projections for 2000 to 2006," Jupiter Media Metrix, June 16, 2002; **http://www.jmm.com/xp/jmm/press/industryProjections.xml**.
16. "Media Metrix Releases Worldwide Internet Measurement Results for Australia, Canada, France, Germany & United Kingdom," press release, May 10, 2000; **www.mediametrix.com/usa/press/releases/20000510a.jsp**.
17. Data available from Nielsen/NetRatings web site; **http://pm.netratings.com/nnpm/owa/NRpublicreports.usagemonthly**.
18. "Media Metrix Releases Worldwide Internet Measurement Results"; "Media Metrix Releases U.S. Top 50 Web and Digital Media Properties for March 2000," press release, April 24, 2000; **www.mediametrix.com/usa/press/releases/20000424.jsp**.

Chapter 2

1. Based on information available from various documentation posted on the IBM e-business web site, located at **www.ibm.com/e-business**, and IBM Global Services article entitled "Fostering Customer Loyalty in the Electronic Marketplace."
2. Thomas L. Friedman, *The Lexus and the Olive Tree: Understanding Globalization*, (New York: Farrar, Straus & Giroux, 2000); Christopher Caldwell, "The Lexus and the Olive Tree (Review)," *Commentary Magazine*, October 1999, located at **www.findarticles.com/cf_0/m1061/3_108/56744998/p1/article.jhtml?term=**.
3. Michael J. Weiss, "Online America," *American Demographics*, March 2001, located online at **www.americandemographics.com/**.
4. "Industry Projections for 2000 to 2006," Jupiter Media Metrix, June 16, 2002; **http://www.jmm.com/xp/jmm/press/industryProjections.xml**.
5. Ibid.
6. Ibid.

Chapter 3

1. Based on information from web sites for Research In Motion, **www.rim.com**; David Olive, "Blackberry Proving Bittersweet Fruit," *Financial Post*, April 14, 2001, p. D1; Spencer E. Ante, Amy Borrus, and Robert D. Hof, " In Search of the Net's Next Big Thing," *Business Week*, March 26, 2001, pp. 140–141; Tyler Hamilton, "BlackBerry Ripens: Canadian Firm's E-mail Device Wins Converts," *Montreal Gazette*, April 18, 2001, p. D4.
2. Peter Burrows, "Technology on Tap," *Business Week*, June 19, 2000, p. 76.
3. John Greenwald, "Busted by Broadband," *Time*, March 26, 2001; **http://www.time.com/time/magazine/article/0,9171,102923,00.html**.
4. Daniel Sordid, "Semiconductor Sales Decline Worst in 15 Years," *Financial Post*, July 3, 2001, p. C8.
5. Jim Middlemiss, "Bet the Farm on Wireless?" *Financial Post*, July 3, 2001, p. E2.
6. Information from Microsoft's web site resources, **www.microsoft.com/net**; Louise Keyhoe, "Much More to .Net Than Meets the Eye," *Financial Post*, March 28, 2001, p. C11.
7. David Akin, "Content a Pretender to Web's Throne," *Financial Post*, February 21, 2001, p. C7.
8. "RealNetworks Announces Plans to Integrate and Distribute the Macromedia Flash 4 Player Technology with RealSystem G2," press release, May 25, 1999; **http://www.realnetworks.com/company/pressroom/pr/99/macromedia.html**.
9. Sean Donahue, "Savings Downstream," Business 2.0, May 15, 2001, **http://www.business2.com/articles/mag/0,1640,14723,FF.html**.
10. Melanie Warner, "Cool Companies 2000," *Fortune*, June 26, 2000, p. 114.
11. Donna Fuscaldo, "IBM Barrels Ahead with e-Sourcing," *Financial Post*, July 24, 2001, p. C7.
12. David Akin, "IBM Ushers In Brave New World with Project Eliza," *Financial Post*, April 27, 2001, pp. C1 and C8.
13. Finbarr O'Reilly, "You Saw the Show, Now Buy the Shirt on Our Web Site," *National Post*, April 23, 2001, p. A1.
14. Ante, Borrus, and Hof, "In Search of the Net's Next Big Thing."

Chapter 4

1. Based on information available from the Zero-Knowledge corporate web site, **www.zeroknowledge.com**.

2. Michael J. Weiss, "Online America," *American Demographics*, March 2001; **www.americandemographics.com**.
3. Associated Press, "Bosses Say They Know Who's Surfing," *Montreal Gazette*, July 16, 2001, p. E2.
4. Paul Lima, "Internet Fights the Fear Factor," *Financial Post*, August 20, 2001, p. E1.
5. Katherine Reynolds Lewis, "Internet Fraud Focus of Probe," *Financial Post*, June 27, 2001, p. C11.
6. Leslie Walker, "Buried Under a Mountain of Spam," *Washington Post*, May 3, 2001, p. E1.
7. "Online Music Sales Will Grow 520% to $6.2 Billion in 2006," Jupiter Media Metrix Press Release, New York, July 23, 2001; **www.jmm.com/xp/jmm/press/2001/pr_072301.xml**.
8. Susan Decker, "Spacey Fights for Web Domain," *Montreal Gazette*, May 7, 2001, p. A13.
9. Jeffrey Birnbaum," The Taxman Cometh," *Business 2.0, August 2000;* **http://www.business2.com/articles/mag/0,1640,6846,FF.html**
10. Based on information available at the TechRocks web site; **www.techrocks.org**.
11. Susan Stellin, "Online Philanthropy: UnitedWay@work," *eCompany Now*, July 2001, pp. 86–87.
12. Amy Harmon, "Whose Net Is It?" *Montreal Gazette*, July 11, 2001, p. C2.
13. David Akin, "Noose Tightens on Right, Net Expert Warns," *Financial Post*, March 27, 2001, p. C9.
14. David Akin, "Ottawa Helps Open e-Commerce Door for Small Business," *Financial Post*, June 28, 2001, p. C9.
15. Nate Hendley, "Of Mice and Women," *Financial Post*, March 19, 2001, p. E8.
16. Austin Macdonald, "Out of Court, Online," *Financial Post*, June 4, 2001, p. E3.

Chapter 5

1. Based on these sources of information: James Harding, "Desperate Napster to Charge Fees," *Financial Post*, February 21, 2001, p. A1; David Akin, "Peer to Peer Seen as the Next Big Wave," *Financial Post*, January 16, 2001, p. C7; James Harding, "Bertelsmann Sees Napster IPO in Future," *Financial Post*, November 6, 2000, p. C11; Paul Schiff Berman, "Danger or Opportunity? Internet's Impact on the Music Business Need Not Be What Some Fear," *Montreal Gazette*, September 18, 2000, p. B3; Spencer E. Ante, "Inside Napster," *Business Week*, August 14, 2000, pp. 113–121; David Akin, "Don't Shoot the MP3 Player," *Financial Post*, May 13, 2000,

p. D11; Don Tapscott, "Napster Secured Page in Internet History," *Financial Post*, May 12, 2000, p. C9; Jon Healy, "Robin Williams Braces for Laughter, Tears, Applause, Heckles . . . by Email," *Financial Post*, April 20, 2000, p. C7; Sue Zeidler, "Napster Lands Deal with MusicNet," *Financial Post*, June 7, 2001, p. C3; Robert Thompson, "Music Industry Out of Tune on Digital Future," *Financial Post*, July 24, 2001, p. C3; **www.napster.com**, **www.mp3.com**, **www.liquidaudio.com**, **www.realaudio.com**.

2. Ibid.

3. Based on information from web sites located at **www.amr.com**, **www.retailexchange.com**, **www.tradeout.com**, and **www.overstock.com**; Carol Pickering, "Web as Surplus e-Store," *Financial Post*, March 5, 2001, p. E1.

4. Based on information from the VerticalNet Inc. web site; **www.vertical.net**.

5. Ken Mark, "Airline Supply Chain System Takes Flight," *Financial Post*, June 18, 2001, p. E11.

6. Stacy Perman, "Automate or Die," *eCompany Now*, July 2001, pp. 60–67.

Chapter 6

1. Based on information available on the Home Depot web site; **www.homedepot.com**.

2. Damien McElroy, "AOL Time Warner Gains Hold in China," *Financial Post*, June 12, 2001, p. C14.

3. Burke Campbell and Murray Conron, "Race to Restructure," *Financial Post*, June 18, 2001, p. E1.

4. Michael E. Porter, "Strategy and the Internet," *Harvard Business Review*, March 2001, pp. 63–78.

Chapter 7

1. Based on information available from the Forrester Research Inc. web site, **http://www.forrester.com/**; Forrester Research Inc. investor information site, **http://www.forrester.com/ER/Investor/PR/0,1309,431, 00.html**; and Forrester Research Inc. press release site, **http://www.forrester.com/ER/Press/ Release/0,1769,684,00.html**; and Tony Schwartz, "If You Work 20 Hours a Day, Your Product Will Be Crap," *Fast Company*, December 2000, p. 324, **http://www .fastcompany.com/online/41/tschwartz .html**.

2. Jeanine Lee Siew Ming, "High-Flying Aptitude," *Montreal Gazette*, June 18, 2001, p. F1.

3. "Kodak Gets Into Digital Films," *Financial Post*, March 5, 2002, p. FP9.

4. Based on information from "NAPM/Forrester Research Announce Results of First Report on eBusiness," press release, January 22, 2001; **http://www.forrester.com/ER/Press/Release/ 0,1769,479,FF.html**.

5. Based on information from the Open Cola Limited corporate web site, **http://www.opencola.com/**; "OpenCola Secures $13M Second Round from Leading VCs," press release, **http://www.opencola .com/press/pressreleases/01-01-17.html**; Mark Frauenfelder, "Nouveau Niche," *The Industry Standard*, October 23, 2000, **http://www.thestandard .com/article/display/0,1151,19498,00.html**; and David Akin, "Canadian Company Invents a New Way to Search the Net," *The National Post*, January 16, 2001, p. A1.

Chapter 8

1. Based on information available on the Media Metrix Inc. home web site, **http://www.mediametrix.com/**; the Jupiter Media Metrix home web site, **http://www .jmm.com/**; the AdRelevance Inc. home web site, **http://www.adrelevance.com/**; "AOL-Time Warner Accounts for One Third of All Time Spent Online," press release, February 27, 2001, **http://us .mediametrix.com/press/releases/20010227.jsp**; the top 50 web sites, **http://us.mediametrix.com/data/ thetop.jsp**; "Jupiter Media Metrix Announces U.S. Top 50 Web and Digital Media Properties for January 2001," press release, February 13, 2001, **http://us .mediametrix.com/press/releases/20010213.jsp**; the Media Central site, **http://us.mediametrix.com/data/ metrixcentral.jsp#n1**; Media Metrix, "Understanding Measurement of the Internet and Digital Media Landscape," online article, **http://us.mediametrix .com/products/us__methodology_long.pdf**; Stacy Lawrence and Mark A. Mowrey, "Investors Scrutinize Media Metrix-Jupiter Merger," *The Industry Standard*, June 27, 2000, **http://www.thestandard .com/article/display/0,1151,16417,00.html**.

2. "Online Polls Are a Cheap and Easy Way to Be Interactive," *Financial Post*, June 12, 2001, p. C8.

3. Michael J. Mandel et al., "Rethinking the Internet," *Business Week*, March 26, 2001, p. 127.

4. Martin Stone, "Survey Shows College Student Shopping Habits," *Newsbytes*, March 6, 2001; **http:// www.newsbytes.com/news/01/162742.html**.

5. Kevin Featherly, "Note to Marketers: Teens Use Web to Buy Offline—Jupiter," *Newsbytes*, September 13, 2000; **http://www.newsbytes.com/news/00/ 155147.html**.

6. I. M. Rosenstock, "The Health Belief Model: Explaining Health Behaviour Through

Expectancies," in *Health Behaviour and Health Education: Theory, Research, and Practice*, ed. K. Glanz, F. M. Lewis, and B. K. Rimer (San Francisco: Jossey-Bass, 1990); W. B. Carter, "Health Behaviour as a Rational Process: Theory of Reasoned Action and Multiattribute Utility Theory," in *Health Behaviour and Health Education: Theory, Research, and Practice*, ed. K. Glanz, F. M. Lewis, and B. K. Rimer (San Francisco: Jossey-Bass, 1990).

7. I. Ajzen and M. Fishbein, *Understanding Attitudes and Predicting Behaviour* (Englewood Cliffs, NJ: Prentice-Hall, 1980); I. Ajzen and T. J. Madden, "Prediction of Goal-Directed Behaviour: Attitudes, Intentions and Perceived Behavioral Control," *Journal of Experimental Social Psychology*, 22 (1986): 453–474.

8. J. Kuhl, "A Theory of Self Regulation: Action vs. State Orientation, Self-discrimination and Some Application," *Applied Psychology: An International Review 41*, no. 2 (1992): 97–129; J. Kuhl, "Volitional Mediators of Cognition-Behaviour Consistency: Self-Regulatory Processes and Action Versus State Orientation," in *Action Control: From Cognition to Behaviour*, ed. J. Kuhl and J. Beckmann (New York: Springer-Verlag, 1985); J. Kuhl and J. Beckmann, "Historical Perspectives in the Study of Action Control," in *Action Control: From Cognition to Behaviour*, ed. J. Kuhl and J. Beckmann (New York: Springer-Verlag, 1985).

9. D. O. Sears, L. Peplau, and S. Taylor, *Social Psychology*, 7th ed. (Englewood Cliffs, NJ: Prentice-Hall, 1991).

10. R. P. Abelson, "Script Processing in Attitude Formation and Decision Making," in *Cognition and Social Behaviour*, ed. J. S. Caroll and J. W. Payne (Hillsdale, NJ: Erlbaum, 1976).

11. L. Festinger, *A Theory of Cognitive Dissonance* (Stanford, CA: Stanford University Press, 1957).

12. D. J. Bem, "Self-Perception: An Alternative Interpretation of Cognitive Dissonance Phenomena," *Psychological Review 74* (1967): 183–200.

13. M. W. Eysenck, *A Handbook of Cognitive Psychology* (London: Lawrence Erlbaum Associates, 1984).

14. I. Ajzen, "From Intentions to Actions: A Theory of Planned Action," in *Action Control: From Cognition to Behaviour*, ed. J. Kuhl and J. Beckman (New York: Springer-Verlag, 1985).

15. Kuhl and Beckmann, "Historical Perspectives in the Study of Action Control."

16. Kuhl, "Volitional Mediators of Cognition-Behaviour Consistency."

17. Kuhl, "A Theory of Self-Regulation."

18. Kuhl, "Volitional Mediators of Cognition-Behaviour Consistency."

Chapter 9

1. Based on information available at the Office Depot Inc. web site; **www.officedepot.com**.

2. Anne Marie Owens, "Mad About Harry," *National Post*, July 10, 2000, p. D1.

3. "Forrester Research Segments B2B Technology Behavior in the Launch of Business Technographics®," press release, January 9, 2001; **http://www.forrester.com/ER/Press/Release/0,1769,474,00.html**.

4. "E-Commerce Numbers Add Up in December," *CyberAtlas*, December 17, 2001; **http://cyberatlas.internet.com/markets/retailing/article/0,,6061_941461,00.html#table**.

5. Eric Hellweg, "A Photo Finish for Digital Imaging," June 26, 2001; **http://www.business2.cSom/articles/web/0,1653,41720,00.html**.

6. Julie Landry, "Ford's Internet Efforts Encounter Roadblocks," December 14, 1999; **http://www.redherring.com/insider/1999/1214/news-ford.html**.

7. Peter Burrows, "Technology on Tap," *Business Week*, June 19, 2000, p. 80.

8. "Online Banking Continues to Disappoint," *CyberAtlas*, September 10, 2001; **http://cyberatlas.internet.com/markets/finance/article/0,,5961_881271,00.html**.

9. Jay Greene, "The Man Behind All Those E-Ads," *Business Week*, June 26, 2000, p. 76.

10. Colleen O'Connor, "Getting Religion," *Business2.0 Magazine*, June 1, 2000; **http://www.business2.com/content/magazine/ebusiness/2000/06/01/12908**.

11. Colleen Valles, "Computer-Makers Are Slow to Embrace Recycling Plans," *Montreal Gazette*, May 23, 2001, p. D3.

12. Patricia Seybold, with Roni T. Marshak and Jeffrey M. Lewis, *The Customer Revolution: How to Thrive When Customers Are in Control*, (New York: Crown Business, 2001).

13. Andy Riga, "Canadians Taking the E-banking Plunge," *Montreal Gazette*, May 23, 2001, p. D1.

14. David Provost, "Up, Up, and Away," *Business2.0 Magazine*, June 1, 2000; **http://www.business2.com/content/magazine/numbers/2000/06/01/10982**.

15. Burrows, "Technology on Tap"; Michael Pastore, "U.S. E-Commerce Spikes in Q4 2001," *CyberAtlas*, February 20, 2002; **http://cyberatlas.internet**

.com/markets/retailing/article/0,,6061_977751,00
.html#table.

16. Dale Buss,"Not So Magical Kingdom," *Business2.0 Magazine*, June 1, 2000; **http://www.business2.com/content/magazine/indepth/2000/06/01/13048**.

17. Andy Riga, "The Global E-library," *Montreal Gazette*, June 20, 2001, p. D1.

18. Donalee Moulton, "e-Tailer Hits the Bricks," *Financial Post*, June 18, 2001, p. E4.

19. Michael J. Mandel et al., "Rethinking the Internet," *Business Week*, March 26, 2001, p. 120.

20. Zhenya Gene Senyak, "Talk Shops," *Business2.0 Magazine*, June 1, 2000; **http://www.business2.com/content/magazine/marketing/2000/06/01/12980**.

21. Will Novosedlik, "Teaming Up for the Wallets of Tech-Savvy Consumers," *Financial Post*, March 22, 2001, p. C9.

22. Kay Parker, "Old-Line Goes Online," *Business2.0 Magazine*, June 1, 2000; **http://www.business2.com/content/magazine/marketing/2000/06/01/12979**.

23. Susan Heinrich, "It Finally Clicks: Web Ads Can Work," *Financial Post*, July 9, 2001, p. C4.

24. Brahm Eiley, "Online Ads Far from Dead," *Financial Post*, June 7, 2001, p. C15.

25. Mandel et al., "Rethinking the Internet."

26. Susan Kuchinskas, "Fair Gamers," *Business2.0 Magazine*, June 1, 2000; **http://www.business2.com/content/magazine/marketing/2000/06/01/12914**.

27. Diana Janssen, "Online Advertising Picks Up Again," Forrester Research Report Press Release, May 2002; **http://www.forrester.com/ER/Research/Report/Summary/0,1338,14576,FF.html**.

28. John Gaffney, "The Online Advertising Comeback," *Business 2.0 Magazine*, June 2002, pp. 118–120.

29. Andy Riga, "Internet Firms Finding New Marketing Tools," *Montreal Gazette*, May 30, 2001, p. D1.

30. Based on data provided online at **http://adres.internet.com/adrates/article/0,1401,,00.html**.

31. Kevin Hogan, "Not the Agents of Change," *Business2.0 Magazine*, June 1, 2000; **http://www.business2.com/content/magazine/indepth/2000/06/01/11008**.

32. Jean Eaglesham, "Junk E-mail Remedy Worries Marketers," *National Post*, April 16, 2001, p. E6.

Chapter 10

1. Based on information from the Google.com web site, **www.google.com**; Andy Riga, "The Search Engine That Could," *Montreal Gazette*, July 4, 2001, p. F1; Michael Porter, "Strategy and the Internet," *Harvard Business Review*, March 2001, pp. 63–78.

2. Michael J. Mandel et al., "Rethinking the Internet," *Business Week*, March 26, 2001, p. 132.

3. Peter Burrows, "The Second Coming of Software," *Business Week*, June 19, 2000, p. 88.

4. Mandel et al., "Rethinking the Internet," p. 120.

5. Werner Antweiller, "The Power of e-Business," *Financial Post*, July 2, 2002, p. FP11.

6. Zhenya Gene Senyak, "Talk Shops," *Business2.0 Magazine*, June 1, 2000; **http://www.business2.com/content/magazine/marketing/2000/06/01/12980**.

7. David Morgan, "Tech Boom Still Driving the Economy," *Financial Post*, July 12, 2000, p. C11.

8. "Context: Extraneous Email Reported" *eCompany Now*, July 2001, p. 42.

9. Peter Burrows, "Technology on Tap," *Business Week*, June 19, 2000, p. 82.

10. Steve Bennett, "Wings and a Prayer," *Business2.0 Magazine*, June 1, 2000; **http://www.business2.com/content/magazine/indepth/2000/06/01/13040**.

11. Arthur Ciancutti and Thomas Steding, "Trust Fund," *Business2.0 Magazine*, June 1, 2000; **http://www.business2.com/content/magazine/ebusiness/2000/06/01/12910**.

12. Based on information at Oracle Corporation's corporate information web site; **http://www.oracle.com/corporate/**.

13. Shawn Tully, "The Party's Over," *Fortune*, June 26, 2000, p. 156.

14. Kyle Foster, "Gates Still Richest Man," *Montreal Gazette*, June 22, 2001, p. D1.

15. Rod McQueen, "If It Makes You Feel Better, Call Nortel Deal a 'Recall,'" *Financial Post*, June 6, 2001, p. C9.

16. Michael Petrou, "Striking a Nerve," *Financial Post*, July 8, 2000, p. D7.

17. Sheila McGovern, "Forget E-mail; Let's Do Lunch," *Montreal Gazette*, March 19, 2001, p. F1.

18. Nate Hendley, "A Shrink's Couch on Your Desk: Online Counselling," *Financial Post*, March 5, 2001, p. E4.

19. James Underwood, "Should You Watch Them on the Web," *CIO Magazine*, May 15, 2000; **http://www.cio.com/archive/051500_face.html**.

20. Ilan Greenberg, "The PC Crowd," *Red Herring Magazine*, May 18, 2000; **http://www.redherring.com/mag/issue51/rd.html**.

21. Michael Schrage, "You're Nuts if You're Not Certifiable," *Fortune*, June 26, 2000, p. 338.

22. "Plus Ca Change: Job Boards Search for Work," *Business2.0 Magazine*, June 1, 2001; **http://www.business2.com/content/magazine/filter/2000/06/01/12973**.

23. Petrou, "Striking a Nerve."
24. Michelle Conlin and Kathy Moore, "Dr. Goodnight's Company Town," *Business Week*, June 19, 2000, p. 192.
25. Morgan, "Tech Boom Still Driving the Economy."
26. Sandra Dillich, "Training or Learning," *Computing Canada*, June 23, 2000, p. 25.
27. Susan Stellin, "Online Courses Effective, Cheaper," *Financial Post*, May 11, 2001, p. C2.
28. Sandra Mingail, "Sift Gold from the Software Pile: How to Choose a Package," *Financial Post*, March 5, 2001, p. E4.
29. Susan Stellin, "Online Courses Effective, Cheaper," *Financial Post*, May 11, 2001, p. C2.
30. Robyn Greenspan, "Small Biz Benefits from Internet Tools," March 28, 2002; **http://cyberatlas.internet.com/markets/smallbiz/article/0,,10098_1000171,00.htm**).
31. Alan Joch, "E-Business Without the E-Cost," *Fortune's Small Business Online Magazine*, July 16, 1999; **http://www.fsb.com/fortunesb/articles/0,2227,320,00.html**.
32. Carlye Adler et al., "The FSB 25," *Fortune's Small Business Online Magazine*, February 8, 2000; **http://fortunesb.com/articles/0,2227,565,00.html**.
33. Kim Hanson, "Angels May Be a Startup's Best Bet in Tough Times," *Financial Post*, March 22, 2001, p. C9.
34. American Society of Travel Agents web site, **www.astanet.com**.
35. Tyler Maroney, "An Air Battle Comes to the Web," *Fortune*, June 26, 2000, p. 315.
36. Michael Newman, "The Gideon Bible," *eCompany Now*, July 2001, p. 72.
37. Jill Vardy, "Boards Build Credibility," *Financial Post*, June 22, 2001, p. C6.
38. Based on information available on the firm's web site, **www.accenture.com**.

Chapter 11

1. Wayne Lilley, "Widowed and Orphaned," *National Post Business Magazine*, July 2001, pp. 55–60; "FP500 Canada's Largest Corporations: And the Winner Is. . .," National Post Business Magazine, June 2001, p. 96; Donnald MacDonald, "Nortel Investors in Nightmare," *Montreal Gazette*, June 16, 2001, p. C1; Mary Lamey, "We Overpaid for Firm: Nortel," *Montreal Gazette*, June 16, 2001, p. C1; information available on the Nortel web site, **www.nortelnetworks.com**.
2. David Akin, "Amazon.com Plummets on Talk of Cash Crunch," *Financial Post*, June 24, 2000, pp. C1, C2.

3. Susanne Koudsi, "Why Is This Sock Puppet Still Smiling?" *Fortune*, June 26, 2000, p. 54.
4. Larry MacDonald, "Time for Tech Bonds," *Montreal Gazette*, June 13, 2001, p. D3.
5. Michael J. Mandel et al., "Rethinking the Internet," *Business Week*, March 26, 2001, p. 120.
6. Kim Girard and Sean Donahue, "Crash and Learn: A Field Manual for Ebusiness Survival," *Business2.0 Magazine*, June 11, 2000; **http://www.business2.com/content/magazine/indepth/2000/06/28/13700**.
7. Brenon Daly, "Venture Forth," *Business2.0 Magazine*, June 1, 2000; **http://www.business2.com/content/magazine/investing/2000/06/01/12932**.
8. Staff writers, "Numbers: A Bright Future for Technology Startups," *Business2.0 Magazine*, June 2002, pp. 32–33.
9. Steve Maich, "Tech Profits Overstated," *Financial Post*, June 20, 2001, p. D1.
10. Rod McQueen, "If It Makes You Feel Better, Call Nortel Deal a 'Recall,'" *Financial Post*, June 6, 2001, p. C9.
11. Based on "Lucent Technologies Acquires Herrmann Technology, a Leading Supplier of Optical Devices for Next-Generation DWDM Networks," Lucent Technologies press release, June 19, 2000; **http://www.lucent.com/press/0600/000619.coa.html**.
12. Paul Kedrosky, "The Meaning of Cheap," *Financial Post*, March 17, 2001, p. D11.
13. NASDAQ web site statistics; **www.nasdaqnews.com**.
14. Jim Griffin, "Rethinking Internet Valuation," *Business2.0 Magazine*, June 1, 2000; **http://www.business2.com/content/magazine/vision/2000/06/01/10989**.
15. Bethany McLean, "Hocus-Pocus: How IBM Grew 27% a Year," *Fortune*, June 26, 2000, pp. 165–168.
16. Robert Farzad, "Ebay's Price Leaves No Room for Error," *Financial Post*, June 28, 2001, p. D3.
17. Based on estimates calculated by Zacks Investment Research and presented on MSN.com. July 5, 2002.
18. Andy Riga, "Lowdown a Shock: Roth, Nortel Chief Takes Heat from Investors at Annual Meeting," *Montreal Gazette*, April 27, 2001, pp. C1, C3.
19. Hugh Anderson, "Research Credibility Hits Bottom," *Financial Post*, February 21, 2001, p. D4.
20. Jennifer Brown, "E-based CRM Vendors in for Fight," *Computing Canada*, August 24, 2001, p. 1.

Chapter 12

1. Geoffrey Downey, "CRM: What's It Worth?," *eBusiness Journal*, July 2001, pp. 14–15.

2. Shane Shick, "Why CRM Projects Fail," *eBusiness Journal*, October 2001, p. 16.

3. Michael MacMillan, "Enterprise Computing—Hidden Problems," *Computing Canada*, June 15, 2001, p. 21.

4. "Plus Ca Change: Fraud Fund," *Business2.0 Magazine*, June 1, 2000, **http://www.business2 .com/content/magazine/filter/2000/06/01/12973?page =5**; and *CNN.com, "Survey: Online Fraud Tops Off-line,"* March 4, 2002, **http://www.cnn.com/2002/TECH/ internet/03/04/fraud.online.survey/**.

5. Charles Gillis, "Terrorist Attacks Prompt Surge of Online Giving," *National Post*, September 27, 2001, p. A7.

6. Thomas Watson, "Automakers Hit Back in Online Battle," *Financial Post*, June 25, 2001, p. C3.

7. Mohanbir Sawhney and Sumant Mandal, "Go Global," *Business2.0 Magazine,* May 1, 2000; **http://www.business2.com/content/magazine/ indepth/2000/05/01/11057**.

8. Based on "PeopleSoft eCenter Measures Up to the Test of ROI," PeopleSoft article, November 2001; **http://www.peoplesoft.com/corp/en/ent_strat/ articles/ecenter_roi.asp**.

9. R. S. Kaplan and D. P. Norton, "The Balanced Scorecard—Measures That Drive Performance," *Harvard Business Review*, January–February 1992, pp. 71–79.

10. Jeffrey H. Birnbaum, "Death to Bureaucrats, Good News for the Rest of Us," *Fortune*, June 26, 2000, pp. 241–242.

11. J. William Gurley, "The Most Powerful Internet Metric of All," CNET News.com, February 21, 2000; **http://news.cnet.com/news/0-1270-210-3287257-1 .html**.

12. Hollie Shaw, "Sobeys to Put $49 M Software Charge Behind It," *Financial Post*, June 28, 2001, p. C6; "Software Snafu Hurts Sobeys," *Montreal Gazette*, January 26, 2001, p. C1.

13. Michael Pastore, "Consumers Turn Backs on Bells and Whistles," *CyberAtlas*, September 11, 2001; available online at **http://cyberatlas.internet .com/big_picture/applications/article/ 0,,1301_881121,00.html**.

Glossary/Index

Key terms, which appear in **boldface**, *are followed by their definitions.*